MYSTERIES OF THE PAST

MYSTERIES OF THE PAST

BY

LIONEL CASSON

ROBERT CLAIBORNE

BRIAN FAGAN

WALTER KARP

EDITOR
JOSEPH J. THORNDIKE, JR.

PUBLISHED BY AMERICAN HERITAGE PUBLISHING CO., INC., NEW YORK
BOOK TRADE DISTRIBUTION BY CHARLES SCRIBNER'S SONS

Library of Congress Cataloguing in Publication on Pg. 314

ISBN 0-8281-0410-7

CONTENTS

On a mountain top in Turkey, the stone head of Antiochus I, who ruled in the first century B.C., gazes out upon his long-forgotten kingdom of Commagene.

INTRODUCTION

When the first Spanish explorers landed on the shores of the Caribbean they heard tales of El Dorado, a native king clad all in gold, who lived in a palace sheathed in golden plates and commanded an army that fought in golden armor. In search of this fabulous ruler and fabulous land the Spaniards, and after them the English, the Scots, the Germans, the Danes, and the Swedes, all plunged into the jungles and deserts of the New World. They seized what gold they could find—the accumulated treasure of centuries—but they never found El Dorado, and at last they learned the reason. There had indeed been a Gilded King, the ruler of a tribe in the Colombian highlands on the shores of Lake Guatavita. On a certain day each year he was stripped naked, smeared with balsam gum, dusted with gold, and rowed out on the lake, where he plunged into the water and thus symbolically cleansed his people of sin. Just twelve years before Columbus landed in the New World, El Dorado had been overthrown by enemies, and the golden rite was ended forever.

It was a great mystery while it lasted. It furthered the exploration of the New World, led to the downfall of native American empires, and lured four generations of adventurers to hardship, despair, and often death. But in the end, the dream of limitless gold went the way of so many other contemporary myths—myths of maritime monsters, of boiling seas below the equator, of the hole at the bottom of the earth.

It is easy to laugh at mysteries long since dispelled. It is easy to say, in relief or regret, that there are no mysteries anymore. But anyone who cherishes the belief that we are less gullible than our ancestors should not read the bestseller lists or turn on the television set. If he does, he will find that cities in the Andes were built by gods from outer space, that Noah's Ark has been found on Mount Ararat, and that travelers are avoiding the Bermuda Triangle as if it were the thirteenth floor, or a black cat, or the underside of a ladder. The famous Bigfoot, which began as a tongue-in-cheek newspaper feature, now engages the attention of the National Geographic Society, Smithsonian Institution, and the United States Forest Service. He is cousin perhaps to the Abominable Snowman, who was tramping the high Himalayas a few years back. He is, according to one school of thought, a surviving representative of Neanderthal man, thought to have been extinct these thirty-five thousand years.

Then there is the Loch Ness monster. The search for Nessie is a major international undertaking, financed by *The New York Times*, the National Geographic Society, and the British government. It supports a lively industry in books, records, hats, jeans, T-shirts, and "monster burgers." The solution of the Loch Ness mystery might not be as great a catastrophe as the bankruptcy of Rolls-Royce or the loss of the Concorde's landing rights, but it would be one more body blow to the United Kingdom's balance of international payments.

If nothing else, the lively interest in these matters offers proof of the enduring public appetite for mysteries. From the time when men saw a wood nymph in every tree to the time when they looked for a UFO on every clear night, mysteries have held their grip on human imagination. The mysteries of earlier days were generally tied to religion, whereas mysteries of today may, like astrology, be in some sense a substitute for religion. Either way, they satisfy some deep human need to believe.

At least it may be said for the fans of Bigfoot and Nessie that they have not lost all touch with reality. It is possible that a monster, or a tribe of monsters, does inhabit Loch Ness, and it is barely conceivable that some real creature may lurk behind the shape of Bigfoot. But no need for proof seems to constrain those writers who address themselves to mysteries in the history of human life and civilization.

The current market for these mysteries of the past was opened up some 27 years ago with the publication of *Worlds in Collision* by Dr. Immanuel Velikovsky. It was Velikovsky's thesis, argued with a virtuoso marshalling of ancient history and myth, that a giant comet came so close to the earth some 3,500 years ago, and again some 700 years later, as to cause all kinds of natural catastrophes. Eventually, according to Velikovsky, the comet settled down in orbit as the planet Venus but not before it had produced such phenomena as Noah's Flood, the parting of the Red

Sea for the Israelites, the sun's standing still for Joshua, and the disappearance of the "lost continent" of Atlantis.

The reaction of the scientific establishment was distinctly cool. As the Harvard astronomer Harlow Shapley put it, "If Dr. Velikovsky is right, the rest of us are crazy." But the put-down of Velikovsky did not stem the flood of speculation. Some of the most sensational theories have come from the writings of the mystic, Edgar Cayce, who received his revelations while in a trance.

One of Cayce's predictions was that Atlantis would rise again from the floor of the ocean in 1968, somewhere in the Caribbean. Eager followers began scanning the shallow waters of the Great Bahama Bank and, sure enough, in 1968 two of them sighted some great blocks of stone under sixteen feet of water off the island of Bimini. To true believers these are the risen buildings of the fair continent described by Plato as having disappeared nine thousand years before his time. But oceanographers do not think so. The fact is that natural rock formations look misleadingly man-made, as witness the strange formations off the northern coast of Ireland. True believers of another era called them "The Giants' Causeway."

The biggest jackpot in the field of ancient mysteries has been hit by a Swiss writer named Erich von Däniken. In *Chariots of the Gods* von Däniken advances the notion that in the remote past, some thirty to fifty thousand years ago, the earth was visited by beings from another star system. Von Däniken finds the image of these ancient "sky gods" in prehistoric art, such as a figure from a Tassili cave in Africa who looks rather like a modern astronaut, and a carved figure on a Maya stele who might be riding in an Apollo spaceship. He even knows where the visitors landed and took off—on the strange linear earth markings made by the Nazca Indians on a plateau in the Andes (see pages 32–33)—although why a sophisticated spaceship should require "landing strips" is not entirely clear. Most imaginatively of all, he suggests that the heavenly visitors interbred with the primitive earth dwellers of the time to produce Homo sapiens. This is indeed a neat explanation of the sudden leap forward in human evolution which occurred at about that period, and which is explored in more sober fashion in our Chapter 4.

It is, of course, possible that visitors from a more advanced civilization did bring to our planet the knowledge of mathematics and physics that went into the building of the pyramids and Stonehenge (see Chapter 2), and even that they had sufficient control over their own genes to interbreed with humans. It is possible that in the dim past some island mass existed in the Atlantic or the Pacific or the Caribbean and later sank in a geologic cataclysm. It is possible that a civilization—or many civilizations—existed on earth before the last ice age and disappeared without a trace.

In the infinity of chance all things are possible. But as of now no scrap of evidence has been found to indicate that any of these particular things are true.

It seems a pity that popular writers have wasted so much time and imagination on these false mysteries. For the human record is filled with real mysteries that challenge the best minds among archaeologists, anthropologists, linguists, climatologists, and historians. It is with these real and significant mysteries that this book deals. To explore them, we have enlisted the talents and knowledge of four principal authors. Lionel Casson, who wrote six of the twelve chapters, is a Professor of Classics at New York University and an authority, in particular, on the trade of the ancient world. Robert Claiborne is a science journalist, the author of books on human evolution, climate, and other topics. Brian Fagan is Distinguished Professor of Anthropology at the University of California at Santa Barbara, author of *The Rape of the Nile,* and the forthcoming *The Elusive Treasure: The Story of Early Archaeologists in America.* Walter Karp is a former contributing editor of *Horizon* magazine and author of *Indispensable Enemies.* Two other writers, Ormonde deKay Jr. and Richard Cravens, contributed the short pieces which follow each chapter and which deal with lesser but still legitimate mysteries. It is hoped that with these talented guides the reader will be better able to judge the merits of the latest speculations about megalith builders, jungle ruins, early transatlantic voyagers, and the like.

—Joseph J. Thorndike, Jr.

One day in 120 B.C. a half-drowned sailor was brought to the court of King Ptolemy VII of Egypt at Alexandria. After being nursed back to health and taught Greek, he gave out the story that he was an Indian, sole survivor of his crew, and offered to prove it by showing anyone whom the king picked the way back to his home. Since Eudoxus of Cyzicus, a well-known explorer, happened to be in town, the choice fell upon him, and under government auspices, he twice sailed to India and back.

Eudoxus' voyages, historically speaking, were epoch-making, for they represent the first ocean crossings on record. But they hardly qualify as great feats of navigation. From perhaps as early as the third millennium B.C., Indian and Arab seamen had been plying the waters between the western shores of India and the Persian Gulf. By at least the first millennium B.C. they were making their way from India to the east coast of Africa or the mouth of the Red Sea, carrying precious cargoes of Chinese silks, Far Eastern spices, and other luxury goods. The traffic was extremely lucrative, and they had no intention of letting any others in on it. And so they managed for centuries to keep to themselves a trade secret, the behavior of the monsoon winds. These, with splendid convenience, blow from the northeast during October to May and then shift to precisely the opposite quarter for the summer; sailing vessels were thus ensured a fair wind for both legs of the journey.

Eudoxus' Indian must have told him about the monsoons. So, assured of an easy voyage, traveling a route that generations of anonymous skippers had gone over before, and knowing precisely what he would find at the other end, Eudoxus was hardly in the position of a Columbus or Magellan. Only during the homeward leg of the second voyage did a bit of excitement develop when he was carried farther south than he expected and ended up on the coast of Africa below Cape Guardafui. Here, too, things continued their even course: he made friends with the natives in the best explorer tradition by giving them strange delicacies (bread, wine, and dried figs did the trick) and picked up a few words of their tongue. It

was after he got back that he ran into trouble. Both times he landed with an invaluable cargo of spices and perfumes and gems, only to see Ptolemy's customs agents confiscate all of it. In a way they posed for him the same problem as the closing of the Suez Canal did recently for Mediterranean shippers. His solution anticipated theirs: he readied an expedition to sail all around Africa from west to east and thus bypass Egypt. He fitted it out to the nines, even taking aboard a number of dancing girls; whether for the harems of Indian rajahs or to help while away the long hours at sea, we cannot be sure. He shoved off from Gadir (Cadiz) in the south of Spain, but when he had got as far as the Atlantic coast of Morocco, a mutiny forced him to return. Undiscouraged, he equipped a second expedition just as carefully, set sail, and vanished without a trace.

Eudoxus never considered going to India by a westward route across the Atlantic. He and his fellow skippers knew it was theoretically possible but, unaware of the existence of the Americas, reckoned it too long a voyage: "If the immensity of the Atlantic Ocean did not prevent us," wrote Eratosthenes, the great Greek geographer of the third century B.C., "we could sail from Spain to India." There are not even any instances of involuntary crossings of the Atlantic, of sailors blown willy-nilly back or forth—although a few scholars have tried their hardest to find some. The Greek guidebook writer Pausanias, who lived in the second century A.D., reports that he met a ship captain named Euphemus who told him how his vessel had been carried right through the Strait of Gibraltar and across the open sea to the "Islands of the Satyrs," where he met natives who were wild, had red skins (or hair, the Greek word may be translated either way), had tails like horses', only a little shorter, and who without a word made a grab for the women aboard; to get rid of them they had to leave behind a slave girl whom these creatures "violated not only in the usual way but over her whole body as well." Pausanias perhaps can be excused for not recognizing a sailor's yarn, but not the modern commentators who gravely suggest that Euphemus may have been swept all the way to the West Indies, where, according to the reports of the first Spanish visitors, the natives were red-skinned, wore detachable horses' tails, and behaved abominably.

Euphemus' is but the earliest of a series of wild tales

OVERLEAF *(pages 8–9): Early Norse vessels, loaded with people and animals, are carved on rocks at Tanum, Sweden. Their high prows and sterns prefigure the design of the Viking ships more than 1000 years later. Incised areas have been chalked to bring out the design.*
PAOLO KOCH. PHOTO RESEARCHERS

that the Atlantic has spawned, tales whose tellers convinced themselves, and far too many others, were sober truth. One of the very wildest was taken as gospel by the whole intellectual world of the seventeenth century. In 1641 Antonio de Montezinos, a Portuguese Jew, made a voyage to South America and reported that, while journeying near Quito in Ecuador, he met up with a native who, to his astonishment, was Jewish. What is more, the man took him on an arduous week-long trip through the hinterland to a remote spot where an entire community of Jews was living: Antonio actually heard them recite in Hebrew the traditional prayer, "Hear, O Israel." Returning to Europe, he reported his find to Menasseh ben Israel, the most eminent Jewish scholar of the day and an author who had wide readership among non-Jews; no less an artist than Rembrandt was illustrator for one of his books. Menasseh published the spectacular news in a slim volume called *The Hope of Israel,* which, written originally in Spanish, was swiftly translated into Latin, Hebrew, and English; the English version went into three editions within two years. The notion that the Lost Tribes of Israel had crossed the ocean to America had struck others as much as a century earlier, but Menasseh was the one who brought it to public attention, who launched it on its extended career.

Before long Antonio's tale of Israelites who had wandered to America was escalated into a theory which put them among the founders of New World civilization, a theory that reached its heyday in the nineteenth century. Britain's Lord Kingsborough, for example, went through the family fortune and landed in debtors' prison no less than three times (he died there the last time) in order to publish de luxe, superbly illustrated volumes proving that the Mexican Indians were descendants of the Lost Tribes. The Mormon sacred writings speak of two waves of Israelite migrants, an early one of "Jaredites" who found their way across the Atlantic during the confused times after the toppling of the Tower of Babel and a later one made up of the followers of a certain Lehi who shook the dust of Jerusalem about 600 B.C., shortly before the rest of the city was led off into the Babylonian captivity.

How the émigrés negotiated the thousands of miles of open water bothered no one since the Bible had a built-in explanation. The Lost Tribes had presumably gotten themselves lost sometime after 721

B.C., the year that King Sargon II of Assyria conquered the northern part of Palestine and deported all who lived there, resettling them in the upper reaches of the Tigris and Euphrates. At least two centuries before this, Solomon had "made a navy of ships in Ezion-geber . . . on the shore of the Red Sea" which he manned with Phoenician "shipmen that had knowledge of the sea" and which "came to Ophir." If the ships of the day could make it to Ophir which, as we shall see in Chapter 7, supposedly involved a round trip of three years, obviously they could take an Atlantic crossing in stride.

The Bible pointedly mentions that Solomon used Phoenician crews. The Phoenicians were for a long while the mariners par excellence of the ancient world. They even boasted considerable oceanic expertise: not only did they sail to Ophir, but according to a tale reported by Herodotus, about 600 B.C. a fleet of Phoenician galleys successfully circumnavigated the continent of Africa.

With such impeccable nautical references, it was inevitable that the Phoenicians sooner or later would qualify as early transatlantic voyagers. One of their champions, writing in 1822, claimed that he knew of a manuscript—it was no longer available for consultation, of course—drawn up by a Phoenician named Wotan who told how he saw the Tower of Babel being built and how he came to the New World when forced out of his home by the Israelites. Another, writing a few decades later, "proved" that the Maya were descended from the inhabitants of Tyre who transferred to America when their city was besieged and taken by Alexander the Great. And, some years ago, Cyrus Gordon, a recognized authority on Semitic languages and an impassioned believer in pre-Columbian voyages to America, announced in the *New York Times* his discovery of proof positive that a group of Phoenicians had landed in Brazil. His information came from someone who had bought a scrapbook for a few pennies at a benefit sale and found in it a letter, written in 1874 by the head of Rio de Janeiro's museum, which included a copy of a transcription of a stone inscribed in Phoenician characters. The inscription conveniently supplied all the details one could possibly desire: the exact identity of the party that had erected the stone (a commercial venture from Sidon), the date (19th year of Hiram, or 534 B.C.), the point of departure (Ezion-geber, just like Solomon's expeditions to Ophir). Gordon's pub-

In 1969 Thor Heyerdahl, the Norwegian scientist-adventurer, set out to prove that the ancient Egyptians could have crossed the Atlantic in reed boats such as those depicted in their bas-reliefs (opposite, above). To build a vessel in Egypt, he brought Indians from Lake Titicaca in Peru, where similar reed boats are in use today (opposite, below). An earlier vessel, the Ra, had sunk in the Atlantic, but the Ra II proved seaworthy. Though it wallowed deep in the sea as the reeds became water-logged, constantly drenching the crew (above), it made its landfall at Barbados after 57 days.

lication of this document was by no means the first. The original transcription had mysteriously materialized as an enclosure in a letter addressed to the head of the prestigious Instituto Historico e Geographico Brasileiro, had been discussed, had been published, and eventually dismissed as spurious; one guess is that it had been forged for the delectation of Emperor Pedro II of Brazil, who was both an accomplished Semitist and a devoted patron of the Instituto. The new copy, Gordon was convinced, was the real thing. The inscribed stone itself, naturally, had gone the way of Wotan's manuscript.

Around the beginning of the eighteenth century the drums started to beat loud and strong for the ancient Egyptians. Napoleon's Nile campaign had opened the country up. The Western world, awed at the sudden revelation of what had been achieved there in the days of the pharaohs, was ready and eager to accept ancient Egypt as the fountainhead of all civilization. So, when European visitors to Mexico returned with glowing tales of the tremendous monuments reared by the people who had lived there long ago, monuments that were sometimes pyramidal in shape or decorated with hieroglyphic carving, everything seemed to fall into place: migrants from the Nile must somehow have had a hand in shaping what happened in the New World.

But the Egyptians, unlike the Phoenicians, posed a nautical problem. They designed their sailing vessels primarily for use on their great river, reed rafts for small craft, very lightly constructed planked boats for the larger. The reed rafts have gained a reputation for seaworthiness that they absolutely do not deserve,

thanks to the derring-do of Thor Heyerdahl, his compulsion for crossing open water in primitive style and his skill at publicizing the feat. His voyage in the reed raft he named *Ra,* he tells us, was triggered by an article he happened to read on the many points of similarity between the cultures of Peru and ancient Egypt, including what he considered a striking fact, that the Peruvians used reed craft on their Lake Titicaca just as the Egyptians had on the Nile. Since, in his view, "men of antiquity were . . . dynamic, imaginative, inquisitive, courageous, clever . . . stronger than men of push-button times," they would have had no trouble crossing oceans in such craft, and there we have the explanation of all those cultural parallels. To clinch the matter, Heyerdahl — no puny push-button type he — showed the world how it was done. To be sure, the Egyptians had planked boats, but there was no sense crossing the ocean in one of those because everybody, Heyerdahl included, was well aware that until the arrival of Columbus, the Americas knew only rafts, dugouts, and the like.

We do not know how dynamic, imaginative, inquisitive, courageous, clever, and strong Egyptian sailors were, but they had enough common sense to keep their reed craft out of open water. There they used their planked boats. But these, while adequate for plying along the Levantine coast to Lebanon or down the Red Sea to Somalia, were clearly not for steady transatlantic work between the mouth of the Nile and the shores of Mexico. How, then, was this accomplished? One favored solution has been to make sober fact out of Plato's allegorical tale about an imaginary continent called Atlantis.

The countless words that have been written about lost Atlantis all go back to a handful of pages in the Dialogues, the *Timaeus* and the *Critias,* particularly the latter. Plato, who was as much poet as philosopher, has Critias relate a myth, one that Critias explains he heard when but ten years old and at third hand: it was told him by his ninety-year-old grandfather, who had gotten it from his father, who in turn had gotten it from Solon. According to Solon, when he was traveling in Egypt, he met certain priests who claimed to have records which showed that nine thousand years earlier Athens was the strongest and best-governed state of all, that there existed in that remote age an island called Atlantis located outside the Pillars of Hercules (the Strait of Gibraltar) and bigger than North Africa and western Asia com-

CONTINUED ON PAGE 16

EARLY OCEAN CROSSINGS

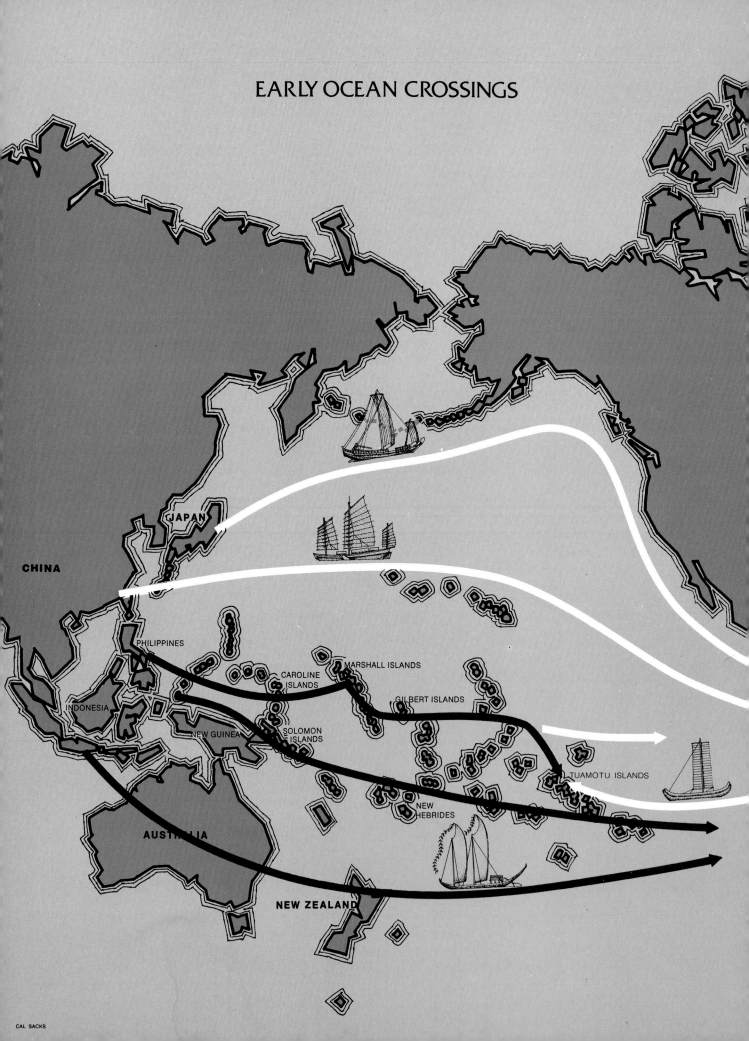

CHINA

JAPAN

PHILIPPINES

INDONESIA

NEW GUINEA

SOLOMON
ISLANDS

CAROLINE
ISLANDS

MARSHALL ISLANDS

GILBERT ISLANDS

NEW
HEBRIDES

TUAMOTU ISLANDS

AUSTRALIA

NEW ZEALAND

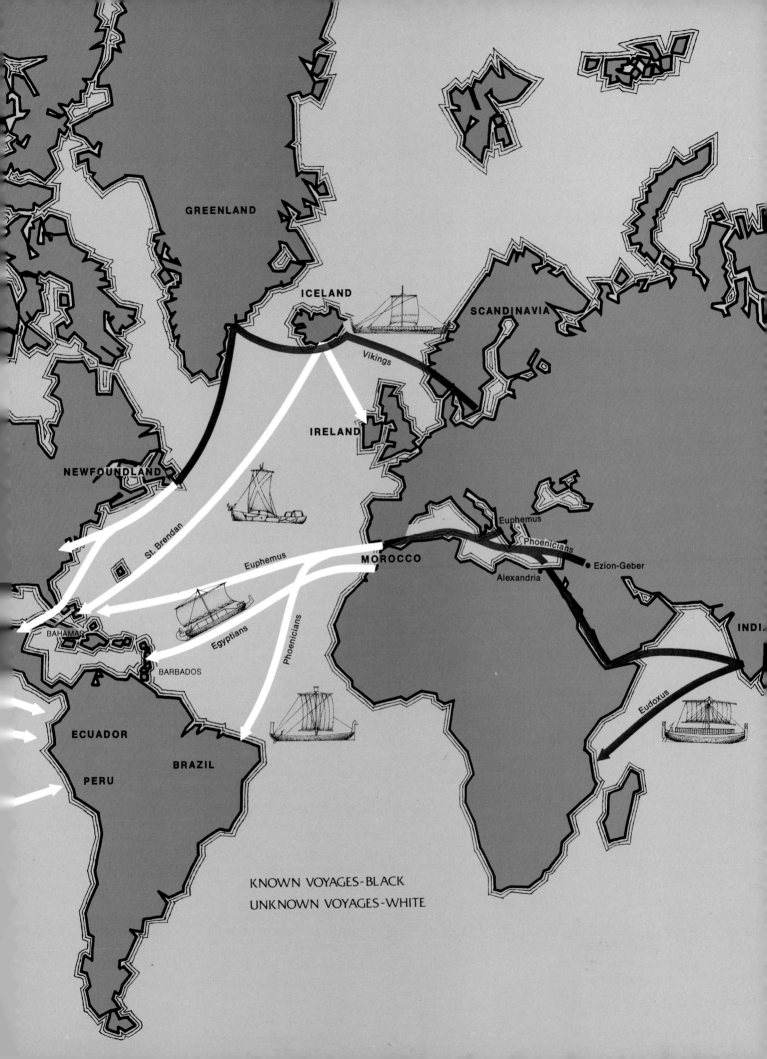

GREENLAND

ICELAND

SCANDINAVIA

Vikings

IRELAND

NEWFOUNDLAND

St. Brendan

Euphemus

MOROCCO

Euphemus

Phoenicians

Ezion-Geber

Alexandria

INDI.

BAHAMAS

Egyptians

Phoenicians

BARBADOS

Eudoxus

ECUADOR

BRAZIL

PERU

KNOWN VOYAGES-BLACK

UNKNOWN VOYAGES-WHITE

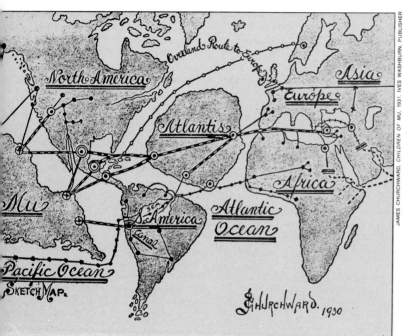

JAMES CHURCHWARD, *CHILDREN OF MU*, 1931. IVES WASHBURN, PUBLISHER

ROBERT STACY-JUDD, *ATLANTIS, MOTHER OF EMPIRES*, 1932. DEVORSE AND CO.

CONTINUED FROM PAGE 13

bined, that its king tried to enslave Greece and Egypt, that Athens fought on alone after all others had deserted, and that one day earthquakes and floods swallowed up Atlantis and the Athenian army with it. Plato's ancient readers never once thought of trying to locate Atlantis, any more than we would of locating Utopia or Shangri-la. The search began some two millennia after he wrote—and has never stopped. Savants like Montaigne and Voltaire seriously debated the island's existence, a learned Swede of the seventeenth century wrote no less than three volumes to demonstrate it was in Scandinavia, and the stream of books which prove to the authors' utter satisfaction precisely where it must have been still burbles along. Two were published in 1969. Both connect Atlantis with the Aegean island of Thera, half of which (see Chapter 3) disappeared into the sea in the wake of a volcanic explosion now dated about 1600 B.C. One, more cautious, merely takes Thera as the inspiration for the tale; the other boldly identifies it as the lost Atlantis. Plato, of course, talks not of a pocket-size island but an enormous land mass, not in the Aegean but in the Atlantic, and destroyed a dim 9,000 years earlier; but all this leaves the authors undaunted—undauntability, however, seems to be one of the strong points of most writers on Atlantis.

The new continent solved everything. With its vast bulk filling most of the ocean, ancient voyagers no longer had to traverse thousands of miles of open water to go from the Old World to the New; all they had to do was get over a negligible stretch on either side, and thereafter they did most of their traveling on foot and, what is more, across a land that happened to be a veritable paradise.

Atlantis proved so convenient that it opened up other heady possibilities besides an Egyptian migration to America. A school of thought arose that reversed the traffic, that sent Mayas scuttling eastward across this paradise to bring pyramids to the valley of the Nile. The most dazzling idea, and the one that probably came to command the greatest number of adherents, was that Atlantis itself deserves the credit for being the fountainhead of civilization. The lost continent, some asserted, had supported a superlatively gifted people who, long before the disastrous total drowning, thought up things like pyramids and hieroglyphs, and, migrating eastward and westward, were the common source for both Egyptian and Mayan civilizations. Even professional academics, presumably sober seekers of fact, succumbed to Atlantis' allure. A. W. Brøgger, noted Norwegian archaeologist and director of the museum at Oslo during the thirties, connected it with Bronze Age seafaring of the second millennium B.C. The mariners of the time, he was convinced, were so able and daring that they not only made their way along most of the coastline of western Europe but actually got to America, and their discovery of the new continent was the nugget of truth behind Plato's tale.

Another voyager seen dimly through the mists of the North Atlantic is Saint Brendan. According to Irish legend, he set sail in the sixth century A.D. with fourteen monks from the monastery of Clonfert in Galway. Their boat was "a very light little vessel, ribbed and sided with wood, but covered with oak-tanned ox-hides and caulked with ox-tallow"—what is now called a curragh. After forty days at sea, they landed on an island where they found a great castle and a table laid for them with bread and fish. During the next eight years Brendan sailed from one magical island to another, met such notables as Judas Iscariot and Pontius Pilate, and witnessed many marvels but, so far as our records show, left no material trace of his presence on American shores. Their next stop was not so successful; when they built a fire to cook their food they discovered that their landing place was the back of a very angry whale.

One ghost which long haunted the Atlantic will do so no more. The Aztec god Quetzalcoatl was described by early friars in Mexico as blond-haired and fair-skinned. As a result, he was hailed as an early arrival from the Old World and identified with Saint Thomas the Apostle, Saint Brendan, an errant Norseman, even someone from Atlantis traveling about to spread Atlantean sweetness and light. A recent study based on a scrupulous examination of New World materials, including illustrations, has been able to demonstrate that contrary to legend, Quetzalcoatl was dark-visaged and black-bearded, in other words, a purely local figure.

Users of the Atlantean land route, Lost Tribes of Israel, Phoenician businessmen or refugees—these are the best the ancient world can offer for the honor of having been the first to cross the Atlantic. We have to move down the centuries to the early Middle Ages to arrive at a serious candidate—the Vikings. For the longest while their claim was based only on the sagas, their epic tales starring Eric the Red, his son Leif, Olaf Tryggvesson, and other mighty mariners and brandishers of the battle-axe. In the last few decades it has triumphantly received the confirmation of archaeological discovery.

© NATIONAL GEOGRAPHIC SOCIETY

All the Vikings, whether Danes, Swedes, or Norwegians, were expert seamen; but the Norwegians, living in a land whose coast was lined with excellent harbors and faced the open water, were the most skilled and daring. For their voyages they developed the robust, graceful galleys that we know so well from three Viking tombs, uncovered between 1867 and 1903, in which the illustrious deceased had been laid to rest in their boats. In such ships Viking seafarers had by A.D. 800 made their way to the Faroe Islands north of Scotland, and within a century thereafter established themselves firmly in Iceland. And around 900 a certain Gunbjørn, en route from Norway to Iceland, was blown far past his destination to catch sight of the coast of Greenland.

But a landing on Greenland had to wait almost a hundred years, until Eric the Red appeared on the scene. Eric was a Norwegian settled in Iceland who, having been banished from there for three years for committing murder, decided to spend the time looking for the land Gunbjørn had seen so long ago. With a boatload of family and some kindred spirits, he left in 982 and managed to get to the southwest coast of Greenland, the less formidable part, where he set up camp and spent the three winters of his exile. He then went back to Iceland, collected recruits for a colony on Greenland, as he dubbed the new country,

17

and sailed off with a fleet of 25 ships filled with men and their families and animals. The journey was so hard that, of the 25, only 14 came through, but it was enough to found a permanent settlement near what is today called Julianehab. Danish archaeologists excavating the site have found Eric's very house, a typical Viking "long house" whose great hall, which served as kitchen and bedroom as well as living room, was 49 feet long and 15 wide and whose walls were of solid earth 10 feet thick.

Eric's more famous son Leif started as a missionary: he left Greenland for Norway, became a Christian there, and then was sent home to convert the members of his father's colony. But his heart was not in it, particularly since his father took a dim view of the project. By about 1000 he gave up proselytizing for exploring. Some years earlier Gunbjørn's experience had been repeated: this time a boat going from Ireland to Greenland had been carried clean past it to unknown shores—the captain reported three sightings of land, twice of a well-wooded coast and once of a rocky ice-bound island. Leif bought the boat and with a party of thirty-five set out to investigate. They came upon the rocky island easily enough, then a wooded area, and two days later an island with abundant grass. On the mainland opposite they hit upon a most surprising find—vines with grapes; they were sure of it, because one of the company was from Germany, where vines were an everyday sight. This was so impressive that Leif called the place "Wineland," or Vinland, to give it the form we commonly use. They decided to spend the winter in this pleasant land where there were no frosts, where the grass stayed green almost all year round, where day and night were of far more equal duration than in Greenland or Iceland. In the spring they sailed home. Sometime later Leif's brother Thorwald came back, found Leif's abandoned huts, and spent two years looking about until, in a scuffle with a great number of natives in skin boats, he was killed by an arrow. In the following years, yet two more expeditions reached the new land and spent some time there before returning home.

The events related above, we must keep in mind,

18

are not told in archival documents or even contemporary chronicles but in poems chanted by Icelandic bards centuries after having taken place. How much, then, is history and how much poetic imagination?

The consensus has always been that the sagas have a core of solid fact, that Vikings actually did get to the New World and establish some sort of settlement there. But the matter was recently put beyond all doubt when a Danish archaeological team, conducting excavations from 1961 to 1968 at l'Anse aux Meadows on the northernmost tip of Newfoundland, unearthed the remains of houses and boat sheds, a bronze ring-headed pin, and other material, all of it unquestionably Norse and datable to about 1000. No one, however, will go so far as to suggest that these are the actual remains of Leif's expedition, that northern Newfoundland is Vinland. The site of this fabled land that was green almost all year round, had abundant forests, had rivers teeming with salmon, was inhabited by natives using skin boats, and, above all, grew grapes in profusion, has provoked nearly as much argument and theorizing as the lost Atlantis.

The conservative-minded prefer to place it as near as possible to Greenland, in Baffin Island or the vicinity. For long the grapes were an obstacle, but that has changed: an account, only recently unearthed, written by an English naval surgeon who made several voyages to Newfoundland in the sixteenth century records that he saw there "wild grapes incredible"; if they were there in his day, they would certainly have been there in Leif's, when, as the historians of climate argue, warmer weather prevailed over the northern Atlantic (see Chapter 10). Even warmer weather would hardly have produced abundant forests and a soil that was green all year round, but stumbling blocks of this sort can always be dismissed as bardic embroidery or the like.

The less conservative have offered locations along the east coast as far south as Virginia. Many submit in evidence a round tower at Newport, Rhode Island, which, they stoutly assert, shows unmistakable marks of Viking workmanship. Others equally stoutly assert, and with more reason, that it shows unmistakable marks of colonial workmanship, and nothing at all

19

earlier. Then there is the notorious Kensington Stone, which a few use to argue for Viking penetration as far as the Midwest. During the last century a stone turned up with a perfectly preserved inscription in Runic letters, the standard Viking script, on a farm near Kensington, Minnesota. The owner handed it over to the local bank to put on display, and when it was handed back to him as a forgery, dumped it on his backyard, where he used it for a step. Along comes a certain Hjalmar R. Holand, who is interested in it, is given it, and then spends the next fifty years passionately defending its authenticity. In addition to the stone, Holand had other Viking artifacts to offer: four axes, a battle-axe, some swords, and three rather light halberds. Unfortunately, none of the artifacts had been found in situ, and the halberds turned out to be not halberds at all but tobacco cutters made last century by the Rogers Iron Company of Springfield, Ohio, for the American Tobacco Company to advertise their Battle Axe Plug Tobacco. Until some less suspicious inscriptions or some real halberds are found or some other conclusive form of evidence, we must admit that we do not know where Leif's Vinland was. But that he, or some of his contemporaries, crossed the Atlantic is now certain.

We have thus far awarded the honors for the Indian Ocean and the Atlantic. How about the honors for the Pacific?

Like the Atlantic, it has inspired its fair share of fanciful tales of crossings that preceded Columbus': Buddhist monks who sailed off toward the east in the fifth century A.D.; Koreans escaping from Chinese tyranny; survivors of a fleet which Kublai Khan had sent out against Japan and which was almost totally destroyed in a storm; survivors from an expedition dispatched down the Persian Gulf by Alexander the Great; and, inevitably, the Lost Tribes. One school has taken a leaf from the book of Atlantis and conjured up a lost continent in the Pacific, Lemuria or Mu. It once stretched, we are assured, from Easter Island to the Ladrones off Panama, and its inhabitants, whose record for creativity was right up to the mark set by the Atlanteans, triumphantly carried Mu's gifts to civilization westward to China and India and eastward to America.

By the nineteenth century the problem of New World civilization began to interest anthropologists and archaeologists as well as freewheeling amateur

ED RANNEY

theorizers. Today, after more than a century of patient excavating and collecting and observing and study, some more or less convincing conclusions have been formulated. The American Indians are physically protomongoloid; they must, therefore, have come from Asia. They arrived in a series of waves almost certainly by way of Alaska; the migrations took place around 15,000 to 28,000 years ago (new evidence may very well set the date further back), toward the end of a glacial period when so much water had been frozen into ice that the sea level was low enough to leave an isthmus between Asia and America across what is now Bering Strait. Over the centuries they filtered south, reaching as far as Patagonia. Starting as primitive stone age hunters and fishers, they gradually climbed the standard rungs in the ladder of civilization: they learned pottery making, farming, metallurgy, building on a large scale, writing.

But, as more and more data were amassed and sifted, curious apparent coincidences began to crop up: certain Mayan art motifs strangely resembled certain Chinese motifs; certain pots found in Mexico looked strangely like some found in China; certain architectural elements found in Yucatan looked strangely like some found in Cambodia, and so on.

All this brought great joy to the hearts of those anthropologists and archaeologists who belonged to the "diffusionist" school of thought. Diffusionists are convinced that invention is so precious and rare an act that it usually occurs only once. Thus, as they see it, the plow, the wheel, the sail, the art of writing, etc.,

CONTINUED ON PAGE 24

20

Remarkable parallels are found in the religious art of American and Asian cultures. Directly above is a sculpture of Quetzalcoatl, the Mayan "lord of life," that dates from about the fourteenth century. He is being consumed by a serpent, whose form he will take in his next incarnation. At right above is a statue of the Mucalinda Buddha, dating from the twelfth century in Cambodia. He is seated on the coils of a great snake, whose protecting hood rises over the Buddha's head.

At right, the giant stone head comes from the Olmec culture that flourished in Mexico some 3,000 years ago. Its Negroid features have excited speculation about the possibility of early contact between Africa and America.

22

Another striking similarity is found in the gestures of these two deities, one Chinese of the fifth century A.D. and the other Mayan of the seventh or eighth century. Directly above, the Buddhist holy man Maitreya raises his left hand, palm outward, in the "Wu-Wei" gesture, signifying "Fear not," while his right (now missing) was lowered, with palm forward in the "Shih-Yuan" gesture meaning "The wish is granted." The Mayan corn god at right above makes the same gestures with opposite hands but with similar meanings. In these parallel hand positions some scholars see evidence of transpacific contact. Others view them as universal gestures which might naturally be made by people of any culture and depicted by their artists.

Controversy hangs over the Mayan sculpture on the opposite page, which adorned a stele at Copan. Some scholars say it is obviously an elephant, comparable to the elephant at Sanci, India, on this page. But there were never elephants in the New World and the last mammoths of any kind had long been extinct when this was carved.

ELIOT ELISOFON, TIME-LIFE PICTURE AGENCY

CONTINUED FROM PAGE 20

got to the peoples who have them by having diffused, through trade, travel, war, cultural exchange, or what have you, from the place of first invention. So they hailed these resemblances as proof that artistic influences had diffused from Asia to America—whence it followed that there must have been crossings of the Pacific centuries, perhaps millennia, before Magellan. They pointed to motifs on Chinese bronzes of the Shang or Chou period and similar motifs in the so-called Taijín style of Mexico; to Chinese pottery of the Han period and similar pottery found in Guatemala; to the lotus motif as treated in Buddhist art and its very similar treatment in sculptures of Yucatan; to the way figures are represented sitting or "diving" in Hindu-Buddhist art and the very similar way they appear on sculptures from the Mayan centers of Palenque or Chichén Itzá. Such likenesses, they insist, must reflect some early impact of the Asian Old World upon the New.

Some went further and claimed that artistic influence was just the icing on the cultural cake the Old World fed to the New. Robert Heine-Geldern, an Austrian prehistorian of the diffusionist persuasion, claimed that there had been a "vast maritime expansion" of the peoples of coastal China toward the east, with hardy Chinese mariners shuttling between China and America from as early as 700 B.C. By 200 B.C. he brings sailors from India into the picture, has the Chinese drop out about A.D. 200, and has Indians, along with others from neighboring lands, carry on so that transpacific voyaging "was never really interrupted until the 9th, or perhaps, the 10th century A.D. Why it finally ended, we do not know." By the time it did, he concludes, the New World had learned from Far Eastern visitors how to work metal, reckon time, write, build monumental complexes—and a host of other sophisticated skills. So impressive were Heine-Geldern's scholarly credentials, so wide his erudition, so vast his output, that his ideas were listened to with grave attention.

The trouble with the diffusionists' case, whether for modest and limited contacts or Heine-Geldern's grand scenario, is that it has as little hard evidence to support it as the theories of the freewheeling amateurs. The stylistic parallels exist—but the dates just cannot be made to coincide. A Chinese bronze of the Shang period, which ended about 1000 B.C., has an amazing resemblance to a pot found near the mouth of the Amazon—but the pot dates A.D. 1200 at the

Therefore, these scholars conclude, the sculptors must have had knowledge of the beasts from transoceanic voyagers. But other scholars say the sculpture is the head of a macaw, with the beak unnaturally lengthened. They compare it to other carved macaws on Mayan temples, such as the one shown in the picture above it.

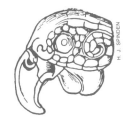

very earliest. Motifs found in China during the Chou period do indeed resemble some from the Taijín-style monuments uncovered near Veracruz, but the Chou period ended about 200 B.C. and the Taijín parallels date A.D. 300 or 400. A temple at Tikal in Guatemala looks very much like one in Cambodia, but this time the New World side of parallel is too early; it was built in the fifth century A.D. and the other a good five centuries later. Some very ancient pottery found in Ecuador, which has been dated 3000 B.C., seemed for a while to make a chronological fit with Japanese pottery of the same period. Recently, however, doubts have been raised about the age of the material from Ecuador; 1000 B.C., it has been suggested, would be more in line.

Moreover, no Chinese or Indian object — or any object at all from the Old World — has been found in the New in archaeological levels that date to pre-Columbian times. If Chinese or Indian traders did come regularly, they somehow left no tangible trace whatsoever of their presence. Nor did they pass on to the people they traded with any of their very useful discoveries such as the wheeled vehicle, the working of iron, the domestication of cows or pigs or horses, the planting of wheat (the New World fed on corn). Last but not least, there is the matter of Chinese seamanship. The Chinese for a very long while preferred to let others do their ocean hauling. In the first and second centuries A.D., for example, so far as we can tell, Chinese silk went to India either overland or in Indian boats, and continued from there in Indian, Greek, or Arab bottoms. After that, most of the Indian Ocean traffic was in the hands of Arabs. The first securely dated Chinese voyage to another continent did not take place until the fifteenth century A.D.

If one is still convinced that the similarities are too many and too close to be explained away as coincidences, that there is enough smoke to suspect some fire, in no way could it have been a gigantic conflagration of annual trading fleets such as Heine-Geldern envisages. Perhaps there was a series of tiny flames lighted by random, involuntary visitors. The winds and currents of the North Pacific trend eastward. Any craft caught helpless in their embrace can easily be carried clean across the ocean; in fact, there are records to show that, for example, between 1775 and 1875 about twenty Japanese junks were blown, against their will, to the west coast of America and deposited at various points between Alaska and Mex-

ico. If Japanese vessels in the last century, why not Chinese or Indian or Malaysian during all the long centuries that preceded the arrival of Columbus? There must have been a certain number that ended a storm-tossed journey on this side of the Pacific. Perhaps a few of the hardier spirits among their crews risked the long sail back home, but most must have chosen to live on where they landed. Eventually they either died out or became wholly absorbed, leaving behind only tantalizing, indirect reminiscences of their presence such as art motifs, pottery shapes, and the like.

What about the South Pacific? If the North Pacific had the winds and currents to bring people willy-nilly across to America, the South Pacific had the mariners to do it of their own free will. The South Pacific is a world of multitudinous far-flung fragments of land; the name "Polynesia" derives from Greek elements that mean "many islands." By the time Europeans arrived on the scene, most islands, including those separated by great stretches of open water, had already been populated by the Polynesians.

The standard craft of these skilled seamen was a canoe balanced by an outrigger and driven by a rig that enabled it to travel to a certain extent against the wind. For transporting large groups, they used double canoes made up of two hulls yoked by booms and with a platform spanning the space in between, an embryonic version of the catamarans that are the latest wrinkle in yacht design today. These ran large enough to accommodate as many as two hundred and fifty persons. Piloting such unsophisticated vessels fearlessly and with consummate ability, the Polynesians managed to reach almost every bit of land in the South Pacific. Their original home seems to have been southeastern Asia. From there they filtered through Micronesia or Melanesia and, at no very remote age, perhaps the fifth century A.D., made their debut in western Polynesia. The period of their most active colonization very likely was as late as the twelfth to fourteenth centuries. The voyages involved were recalled in many a Polynesian legend recounting how heroic navigators arrived at various distant destinations by following certain stars.

Anthropologists and historians, impressed by such tales and noting the presence of Polynesians on Hawaii and Easter Island and other isolated spots, came to the conclusion that the Polynesian skipper, by using every primitive means of navigation avail-

able—not only stars but observation of wind and wave direction, of the flight of migratory birds, of the distinctive clouds that hang above islands—could sail for weeks over trackless ocean to make a landfall on a tiny target. They credited him, in effect, with being able to set and hold a course as accurately as Europeans equipped with compass, log, and a knowledge of celestial navigation. And in the process they credited the Polynesians with a notable attainment—that of being the first people to have intentionally made their way over, if not all of the Pacific, at least a good part of it.

A few decades ago, as will happen, the pendulum swung the other way. In 1963 Andrew Sharp published his *Ancient Voyagers in Polynesia* in which he took a hard-eyed look at all the available evidence and concluded that the Polynesians conducted regular two-way traffic at the most over 300 miles of open water and usually only 100 to 200, in other words, voyages of but a day or two (their fast-stepping canoes easily covered 100 miles in twenty-four hours in good weather, and skippers waited for good weather before venturing out of sight of land). This in itself is achievement enough to place the Polynesians high on the honor roll of maritime races. But, Sharp claimed, no regular traffic between points farther apart is recorded, for it was beyond their powers. Stars are of scant help on north-south courses and of no help on any course during the day or cloudy nights; wind and wave direction can change in an instant; and no skipper dares count on steady sightings of distinctive birds or cloud formations. Polynesians certainly did reach and populate the shores of Hawaii and Easter Island and other remote spots, but the founding fathers did not navigate their way there—they were brought by chance, with ladies luckily present to be pressed into service as founding mothers. Polynesian legend is full of stories of canoes blown by storm to far places, and many instances were noted by the Europeans who lived among the islanders before traditional ways had changed. Inevitably, each year a certain number of fishermen or travelers en route to nearby destinations were caught by sudden worsen-

26

Petroglyphs of bird-men (crouching humans wearing masks with round eyes and long beaks) cover a stone cliff, below, on Easter Island. Each September when migratory birds arrived at their nesting place on the offshore rock, swimmers raced out to find and bring back an unbroken egg. The similarity of these glyphs to the figures on a pottery bead from Ecuador (opposite) suggests some connection between the two cultures.

ing of the weather and carried out to sea. Most went to their death, but a lucky few would end up on some strange island and settle down to a new life there.

The pendulum, however, had swung too far. Sharp had performed an important and necessary service in demonstrating that the Polynesians, though as fine a race of seamen as the world has ever seen, were no workers of miracles. But he ended up giving them less credit than they deserve. In recent years investigations carried out by David Lewis have readjusted the balance. Lewis took a number of voyages over open water lasting as long as a week or more and covering on one occasion nearly five hundred miles, with the navigation totally entrusted to Polynesian skippers who had had lifelong training in the age-old methods. Some of the voyages were in native craft, some in his own boat with the charts, compass, and other modern paraphernalia locked up. He watched attentively as his pilots during the nights steered by certain selected stars, following first one and, when it set, another; they knew the sky so well that, when it

was cloudy, a momentary glimpse of a single star was enough to reassure them they were on course. During the day they steered by the sun, and when there was none, by the direction of the swells caused by the trade winds. When they neared their destination—and their estimate of the vessel's progress was uncannily accurate—they would begin to watch for changes in the swells caused by the presence of land, for changes in the speed, color, and massing of the clouds, for the first sight of those birds that daily fly out to sea to feed in the morning and return home at night. What is more, Lewis discovered that these navigators had developed a special sense that told them, wherever they were, even when storms had blown them far off course, in which direction home lay. He was convinced that the skipper of the storm-tossed canoe that had first been blown upon the shores of Hawaii could have found his way back.

And this brings us to the crucial question. We know that Polynesians were blown as far as Easter Island, a thousand miles to the east of any other land

Stylistic resemblances are found in the bronze work of China and stoneware of pre-Columbian Peru. The vessel below is a sacrificial jar from the Shang dynasty of China (1523-1027 B.C.) in the form of a tiger devouring (or some say, protecting) a man. The mortar on the opposite page, carved in the form of a puma, comes from the Chavin culture of the Andes (800-300 B.C.).

inhabited by them, where they created the society which honored its dead chieftains with the giant statues that are the hallmark of the place. Could they not have been blown two thousand miles farther, all the way to the coast of South America and, with their remarkable spécial sense, made their way back? This question, a matter of debate for the learned in obscure professional journals and books, in 1947 was suddenly made twice as complex and thrust into the limelight by Thor Heyerdahl.

The Polynesians, Heyerdahl reminded everyone, were not the only gifted sailors in the area. The dwellers along the west coast of South America were their peers; they were able to cover great distances with their favored type of craft, a seagoing raft made of light balsa logs. Even more significant, the winds and currents between South America and Polynesia in the warmer latitudes are prevailingly easterly: a Polynesian would have to buck both to get to South America, whereas a Peruvian needed merely to raise sail and coast. To clinch the argument, Heyerdahl made his celebrated grand gesture: he built a balsa sailing raft, the famed *Kon-Tiki*, shoved off from Callao in Peru, and 101 days and 4,300 miles later fetched up on one of the islands in the Tuamoto group. Having launched *Kon-Tiki* so successfully, Heyerdahl then launched his pet theory, that the Polynesian islands were first settled by South Americans who had been carried there by wind and current, as he had.

As things turned out, it was a lot easier to keep *Kon-Tiki* afloat than the theory. Heyerdahl marshaled what seemed to be an impressive list of proofs. By the time his opponents had finished taking potshots at them, not one was left standing. The coup de grâce was delivered by Eric de Bisschop, even wiser than Heyerdahl in the ways of seagoing rafts, when he undertook to demonstrate that a raft could just as well do the voyage in the opposite direction.

To cross vast expanses of open water in little boats seems to have been de Bisschop's greatest joy in life, and he added extra zest by refusing to learn how to swim. He cut his teeth on small Chinese junks, sailing all the way from Australia to Hawaii on one that was no more than twelve tons, with a single overworked assistant for crew. In 1937, hitting his stride, he sailed a 37-foot double canoe from Hawaii to Australia, through the Torres Strait, across the Indian Ocean,

around the Cape of Good Hope, up the Atlantic to the Strait of Gibraltar, and into the Mediterranean as far as Cannes; it took him fourteen months in all. In 1956, exasperated by all the publicity *Kon-Tiki* and her skipper had been getting, de Bisschop decided, though he was by now sixty-five years old and suffering from emphysema, to demonstrate that, despite Heyerdahl's talk of winds and currents permitting a raft to voyage only east to west, one could also do it from west to east. He first pointed out, in arched-eyebrow surprise, that Heyerdahl had much to learn about sailing his own *Kon-Tiki*. Heyerdahl had fixed *Kon-Tiki*'s daggerboards—planks thrust vertically between the logs down into the water to serve as a sort of centerboard—permanently in place. But, de Bisschop explained, naval historians have known all along that these were movable; by ingeniously raising and lowering them, the raftsmen were able to sail their primitive craft against the wind and were not totally at its mercy. De Bisschop's answer to *Kon-Tiki* was *Tahiti-Nui*, a raft of bamboo logs fitted, it goes without saying, with adjustable daggerboards. In November of 1956 he left from Tahiti, holding a course due south into lower latitudes where he knew he had a chance to pick up westerlies. When he reached the vicinity of 33°, he headed for South America and, sometimes swiftly, sometimes painfully slowly, made his easting, until by May he was near Juan Fernandez Island, no more than five hundred miles from Valparaiso, his intended destination. Here he ran into a series of vicious storms, the raft became too battered to be trusted, and he reluctantly abandoned it and allowed a Chilean warship to carry him and his crew to safety. A year later he had readied *Tahiti-Nui II* and on April 13, 1958, sailed from Callao to repeat Heyerdahl's feat. But the sea is a dangerous gaming partner, and de Bisschop had gambled once too often: four months after departure he and his crew ended up on a reef off Rakahanga in the Northern Cooks. His companions did their best to save him, but he was dead by the time they got him on the beach. It was the way he had always wanted to go—and he had made his point: with ordinary luck a seagoing raft could get from Polynesia to South America and back.

But that was all that he or Heyerdahl had proved: that a raft could make it. And the others who have crossed the oceans in reed boats or skin curraghs or dugouts simply remade the same point, one which students of the sea have been perfectly aware of all along, that sailors have always been able to cover amazing distances in small and flimsy craft. What needs proof is that some actually did cover the distance between the South Pacific islands and South America, one way or the other. And that proof no amount of nautical derring-do can furnish.

At this point we return to the diffusionists. The proof exists, say they. It is supplied by certain animals, artifacts, above all, plants that are found in the New World but must have arrived there from the Old or vice versa. How, they argue, if not by man's agency, did the New World's sweet potato get to Polynesia or its corn to India or its peanuts to China? Or the Old World's bottle gourds and coconut palms to the New? How, unless by man's doing, did the cotton strains arise that require a combining of Old and New World strains? Up until two decades ago the diffusionists rode the tide of opinion; with these and other arguments they seemed destined to overwhelm all doubts.

But the doubters managed to hold the line. In 1968 a conference took place at Santa Fe on the topic "Man Across the Sea." At one point in the proceedings a speaker was able to declare, "Those who used to believe that there is botanical evidence of significant pre-Columbian contacts between the Americas and the rest of the world can carry on in their belief; those who doubted it may remain disbelieving. Agnosticism has not yet been put to flight by revelation." As the conference proceeded, it was clear that he could have stated it more strongly. Recent critical studies had knocked the props from under proofs that had once seemed impregnable. Peanuts early in the game had been quietly dropped from consideration for lack of proper evidence. Corn was put on the "very-doubtful" list. Gourds and coconuts, the botanists now insist, could very well have drifted across the ocean without any human aid. The combining of cotton strains is better explained by natural

means at a very early date when climate and continental outlines could have been much different. Even the sweet potato, for long the sturdiest of them all, finally succumbed to enemy fire. The sweet potato is native to America and is called in Peruvian tongues *kumar;* it is found in Polynesia, and the general Polynesian word for it is *kumara.* The conclusion seemed obvious that some far-wandering Polynesians had brought it back from South America, name and all; in the post-*Kon-Tiki* era, this was expanded to include the possibility of far-drifting South Americans bringing it to Polynesia. But linguists now argue that, despite the apparent similarity, *kumar* and *kumara* have nothing to do with each other; the botanists argue that, just like bottle gourds, the sweet potato could have made it on its own across the sea; other specialists argue that the transfer could well have been post-Columbian; and all agree that the history of the sweet potato is just too doubtful to serve as proof positive of pre-Columbian transpacific voyages.

And so it has gone with the rest of the evidence offered. The diffusionists brought up certain fishhooks made of shell in the South American fashion that are in use among the Polynesians—their opponents argued that these could have crossed the ocean embedded in fish that got away. The diffusionists brought up the New World chicken, which is derived from Oriental, not European, species and which in many places has a non-Spanish name; their opponents argued that these names, often marked by the element *kuk,* could very well be onomatopoeic, and that Dutch pirates from Bali could as easily have brought chickens to South America as pre-Columbian Orientals.

When all sides had had their say at the 1968 conference, the balance had tipped perceptibly in favor of the doubters. They had succeeded in making the true believers uncomfortably aware that any crossings before Columbus, whether of storm-tossed Japanese fishermen, drifting Peruvian rafters, wind-riding Polynesian sailors, at best had had only a microscopic effect on the botany, agriculture, art, society, etc., of either the New World or the Old compared with what happened with such lightning speed right after Columbus. In other words, if there had been such crossings, from the point of view of history, they were hardly worth the fuss made about them. The honor of conquering the Pacific stays with Magellan.

ARE THESE "LANDING STRIPS OF THE GODS"?

GEORGE GERSTER, RAPHO/PHOTO RESEARCHERS

If you were to fly south from Lima along the coast of Peru, the Pacific would stretch away on your right, while on your left the Andes would present a wall of rock that opened out now and then in valleys. From May through November the space between the mountains and the sea would be blanketed in fog, but during the rest of the year a ribbon of dark-gray desert would unroll beneath you: a bleak prospect of plains and low hills, with occasional patches of irrigated greenery around the valley entrances. Spectacular at first, the view would become monotonous until, nearing the Palpa Valley, you would suddenly spy strange markings on the Nazca Plain below — markings which stretch for over thirty miles along this arid tableland, in a variety of shapes and sizes: lines, broad and narrow, running straight and abruptly stopping; other lines intersecting to form rectangles, triangles, and trapezoids; still others outlining a bird (above, right), a monkey, a spider, a whale, a lizard, a flower. These stylized images are, you would perceive, hundreds of feet long, while the straight lines extend in various directions for thousands of feet.

How were these gigantic "graffiti" made? Simply by removing the top layer of stones and pebbles, dark from prolonged contact with the air, to expose the lighter soil beneath. This plateau was the homeland of the Nazca Indians, a pre-Inca people remembered for their exquisite ceramics and textiles. It is believed that the markings were made at some time between 100 B.C. and A.D. 700; and the fact that, fragile though they are, they remain intact, shows just how rainless, if frequently fogbound, is this region.

But why were the markings put there, and what do they mean?

Perhaps because they look like nothing in particular from ground level, few people seem to have given them much thought until they revealed themselves at last to aviators flying over them. Yet even then no serious inquiry into their meaning was undertaken before June 22, 1941 — the Southern Hemisphere's winter solstice — when Dr. Paul Kosok, a visiting American professor of history, was startled to see the setting sun touch the horizon just above the end of a straight line at the base of which he was standing. It occurred to him that the lines must make up an immense network of astronomical calculations. Later, in Lima, he communicated his theory to Dr. Maria Reiche, a German-born mathematician and astronomer; she became its most ardent proponent, tirelessly charting and measuring the lines and comparing them to the positions of stars and planets throughout the year. And after Kosok died in 1959 she continued, in the face of mounting skepticism, to propagate his theory.

Unfortunately for the theory, however, computer tests run in the early 1970s indicated that the skeptics were right: actual correspondences between the lines and celestial bodies turned out to be about as frequent as would have been the case had the matter been left to chance. But if the lines remained mysterious, the pictures did not: most scholars agreed they had been drawn in the open, and on a large scale, to be seen by sky-dwelling gods.

Inevitably, the best-selling author Erich von Däniken has his own theory about the Nazca markings. Reconnoitering extraterrestrial astronauts, he suggests, landed there briefly and took off again, leaving tracks in the soil; to induce them to return, the Nazcans deepened these lines and drew new ones, and when this lure failed added "sacrificial symbols" of animals, birds, and insects. By this account markings like those shown at left are — as, indeed, they appear to be — landing strips. But while few scientists would deny the charm of von Däniken's story, fewer still lend it credence, and the straight lines in the Nazca desert remain today one of the unsolved riddles of the planet.

WHO RAISED THE MEGALITHS?

After Jacob dreamed his dream of a ladder that ascended to the heavens, he "took the stone that he had put for his pillows, and set it up for a pillar, and poured oil upon the top of it."

When Joshua was in Jordan, he was commanded to "take . . . hence out of the midst of Jordan . . . twelve stones. . . . And those twelve stones, which they took out of Jordan, did Joshua pitch in Gilgal [as] a memorial unto the children of Israel for ever."

To set up a stone or stones as a sacred memento is something that seems to come naturally to people; examples abound from almost all ages in almost all quarters of the globe. No one, however, went in for it as enthusiastically or strenuously as the early inhabitants of western Europe—of France, Spain, Portugal, and the British Isles—where the monuments are of such size that we have coined the word *megalith*, from the Greek meaning "big stone," to describe them.

Some megaliths are tall big stones set in the ground like pillars; we call these menhirs, a name suggested by the French savant Legrand d'Aussy, who even during the hectic years of the French Revolution found the time to study and lecture on France's megaliths. *Menhir* is from the Breton meaning "long stone," and Breton is a Celtic dialect; Legrand d'Aussy was taken not only by the sound but by the idea of using a term from a descendant of France's ancient language.

What Jacob erected, then, we would call a menhir. His stood in impressive isolation. But menhirs also occur in clusters, either in circular patterns—what the French call cromlechs, from the Breton for "curved stone"—or in rows called alignments. Joshua's memorial was either a cromlech or an alignment.

Though the peoples of western Europe erected their fair share of menhirs and clusters of menhirs, both are outnumbered by yet another kind of megalithic monument, a tomb in the form of a chamber made out of big stones, what the French, again adopting a Breton word that appealed to Legrand d'Aussy, call a dolmen. The chamber may be oblong, square, round, or polygonal; it may have subsidiary rooms leading off the sides, it may have a long corridor lead-

ing to it; it may be just a modest box measuring a few feet or a veritable gallery nearly a hundred feet long. Whatever the shape or size, the one feature all dolmens have in common is that they are built, either in whole or in part, of rough-quarried massive slabs put together like a house of cards. The smallest and simplest dolmens have two slabs set on end to form sides and a third laid across for a roof. Big dolmens will have two dozen or more slabs for the sides and a line of huge capstones for the roof. In most cases the dolmen, after being completed, was buried under a mound, either round or oblong, which held it together and protected it. Today, many happen to be freestanding, and during the nineteenth century a great argument raged, one side claiming that this is the way they always were, the other that the mounds had been swept away by man or nature.

Whether menhirs or dolmens, megaliths, no doubt about it, deserve their name. A dolmen near Antequera in southern Spain has a capstone that measures some 28 feet by 20, is over three feet thick, and weighs 100 tons. The celebrated Bagneux dolmen, on the outskirts of Saumur in western France, one of the biggest in existence if not the biggest, is made up of 13 mammoth slabs that form a chamber 61 feet long, 20 feet wide, and 10 feet high. The nine slabs of the sides and back are all over a foot thick, and the biggest of them measures 20 feet square; the four capstones are all two feet thick, and the biggest is a Brobdingnagian chunk 22½ feet by 25 that weighs 86 tons. A British admiral, curious as to how heavy the colossal slab actually was, worked out the figure and estimated that 3,000 men would have been needed to handle the piece. The largest menhir still standing, the Kerloaz menhir in Finistère in the westernmost part of Brittany, is 40 feet overall, a quarter of which is sunk in the ground. The king of them all may be the menhir called Er Grah near Locmariaquer in southern Brittany—over 75 feet long, only seven feet shorter than the obelisk that is in front of St. Peter's at Rome. We have to say "may," for it now lies on the ground in four pieces, and there is some argument as to whether or not the pieces actually go together. Not only individual menhirs but the clusters of them as well run to impressive size. The cromlechs, the stone circles, range from wee rings, like the cromlech of Beaulieu in the Department of Indre-et-Loire in west-central France that is but 13 feet in diameter, to England's Avebury, a vast

OVERLEAF (*pages 34-35*): *Some of the megaliths in the great circle of Stonehenge frame the rising sun on midsummer morning. Superimposed on the photograph is a diagram of Stonehenge today, showing in solid white megaliths now standing as well as those that have fallen.*
GEORG GERSTER, RAPHO/PHOTO RESEARCHERS

expanse with a diameter of over 1,200 feet.

Menhirs, cromlechs, dolmens—these Breton-derived terms gained currency because they appealed to the French savants of the eighteenth century who, observing so many megalithic monuments in their country, were convinced that these were the work of their Celtic forebears. When the nineteenth century brought into being scientific archaeology, and observations were made on a wider scale and in less haphazard ways, it quickly became apparent that the big stones were by no means the exclusive possession of France. There are plenty of them there, all right—recent figures list 4,350 dolmens, and 2,070 menhirs, 30 cromlechs, 110 alignments—but they are hardly less common in southern Sweden, Denmark, northern Germany, Holland, the British Isles, Spain, Portugal. The density record actually goes to Denmark: the group of islands between the mainland and Sweden has no less than 3,500 megalithic monuments.

Then, by the middle of the century, it became equally apparent that western Europe had no monopoly on megalithic monuments either. They began turning up in Minorca, Malta, Sardinia, Bulgaria, the Caucasus. In Africa, examples were found in Ethiopia, the Sudan, and around Dakar, and a whole belt of them stretching along the Mediterranean coast, with a particularly heavy concentration in Algeria. They turned up in Palestine, Iran, Pakistan, Tibet, central and southern India—in India in numbers second only to western Europe. They turned up in Japan, Indochina, Sumatra, even the remote interior of Borneo. One of the many puzzling aspects of the megaliths is why they are *not* found in certain areas. Why in Minorca but not Majorca? Why in the Caucasus to the north of Asia Minor and in Palestine to the south but not in Asia Minor itself? Why in Japan but not in China? Such questions have only been put recently, now that we are aware of the ubiquitousness of megalithic monuments. The prime question was—and still is—who built them?

Men of the Middle Ages had no doubts: these huge constructions were the work of supernatural beings. The names they gave them in many cases are still in use: the Giant's Chamber, Devil's Den, Gargantua's Bed, and the like. In subsequent, more rational centuries people tried to fit them into history, but they were limited by the amount of history they knew. The Archbishop of Uppsala, for example, writing in 1555, thought they were the work of Goths. The next century saw the rise of a theory that, thanks to its romantic and gory appeal, swiftly gained hordes of passionately committed adherents. The monuments, according to this theory, were built by the Celts and specifically for use by their famous priests, the druids. It was known from bits of information dropped by Caesar and other ancient writers that the druids formed an extraordinarily powerful body among the Celts and that their worship included human sacrifice. The Celtists, conjuring up visions of flinthearted, knife-wielding priests, took the dolmens to be altars suitable for these primitive rites: the roof slabs were big flat tables on which the hapless victims were laid out, and the side slabs provided height enough for the congregation to get an unobstructed view of the bloody proceedings.

As late as the second half of the nineteenth century, when sober ideas were being promulgated that squared with the ever-growing body of archaeological information, people were still deep in romantic theories about druids. In 1840 near Niort in west-central France a dolmen was uncovered whose contents included a skull that had been trepanned; thirty-five years later M. A. Babert de Juillé, a judge at Niort who doubled as curator of the prehistoric section in the local museum, devoted an article to it which explained that it must have belonged to a druid who had undergone the operation in order to have "freer and easier access to inspirations from on high"; he then went on to argue that such a custom surely had some connection with the tonsure of Christian clerics. (Even today, every Midsummer Eve, a bevy of contemporary "druids," dressed in what they conceive to be proper Celtic clerical garb, solemnly gather at Stonehenge and pass the night parading and chanting "Hark, oh Spirit, and hear us now concerning this our sacred vow" and similar sentiments while a squad of policemen keeps order and television crews record the proceedings.)

All along there were some voices that refused to indulge in romance, though they were not often listened to. Legrand d'Aussy, the man responsible for our using the terms *menhir* and *dolmen*, back in 1795 had no doubt that dolmens were tombs, and from the presence of stone axes in them, he concluded that they must be thousands of years old. Prosper Mérimée, who served as Inspector of Historic Monuments in France from 1834 to 1853, found time not only to write the novel *Carmen* but to carry out his

CONTINUED ON PAGE 40

Two fallen stones, looking like giants' couches (below, left), lie among the long lines of standing menhirs at Carnac in Brittany. The 50-ton megalith directly below is one of 80 that were dragged 24 miles overland and erected in a circle at Stonehenge.

PAUL CAPONIGRO

A stone slab, resting upon two uprights, forms a dolmen at Pentre-Ifan in Wales. Such arrangements, found all over western Europe, were often the doors or sides of burial mounds. Many were originally buried in mounds of earth but now stand free as gaunt monuments to their builders.

CONTINUED FROM PAGE 37

duties in exemplary style: he surveyed the megaliths in person, did all he could to stop road and bridge builders from cannibalizing them for stone, and presented incontrovertible arguments against the theories of the Celtists. Then, in 1865, a Swiss archaeologist, Baron de Bonstetten, published his *Essai sur les dolmens,* which demonstrated the distribution of the monuments all over the world. This changed the rules of the game. Even the most committed Celt-fancier was not quite ready to assert that druids had operated from Portugal to Japan. But if Celts had not built them, who had?

The Baron and others, not aware, as we are today, of how much megaliths vary in date from place to place, had a ready answer: they were all put up by a far-wandering race of megalith builders who made their way from north to south leaving behind a spoor of these massive monuments. In 1872 an English architect, James Fergusson, in a book he called *Rude Stone Monuments in All Countries: Their Age and Uses,* suggested that these megalith builders had arisen in India in pre-Roman times and had carried their practice to north Africa and then Europe, the whole movement taking place just before and during the early days of Christianity.

About the same time a Danish scholar, Conrad Engelhardt, published an article in which he not only reviewed the worldwide spread of megalithic monuments but made some cogent observations about their date. In Scandinavia, Great Britain, Ireland, and northern France, he pointed out, the dolmens never contain any metal and so must belong to the Stone Age; in Portugal, Spain, southern France, and north Africa they often have objects of bronze. Farther east they even have objects of iron, and, indeed, in India were still being built! For, by this time, megalithic tombs were being excavated in increasingly careful fashion, their contents inventoried and studied; the results made it perfectly clear to serious scholars like Engelhardt that theories of druid altars were a lot of nonsense. The majority of the dolmens contained bones, and usually not of one or two bodies but of a great many; in other words, they were tombs, and very likely collective tombs, used for burials over an extended period. Furthermore, theories like Fergusson's, which brought the monuments down to historical times, were out of the question too, at least so far as western Europe was concerned. The grave goods found in the tombs there consisted of flint arrow-

PAUL CAPONIGRO

CONTINUED ON PAGE 43

Sites of megalithic monuments ring the coasts of western Europe and the Mediterranean. Those marked on the map below are only a tiny fraction of the total: over 900 in the British Isles alone. Small drawings mark monuments of special interest: Stonehenge, a dolmen at Sonderholm in Denmark, a "porthole tomb" in Cornwall, a tholos tomb at Los Millares in Portugal, a temple in Malta.

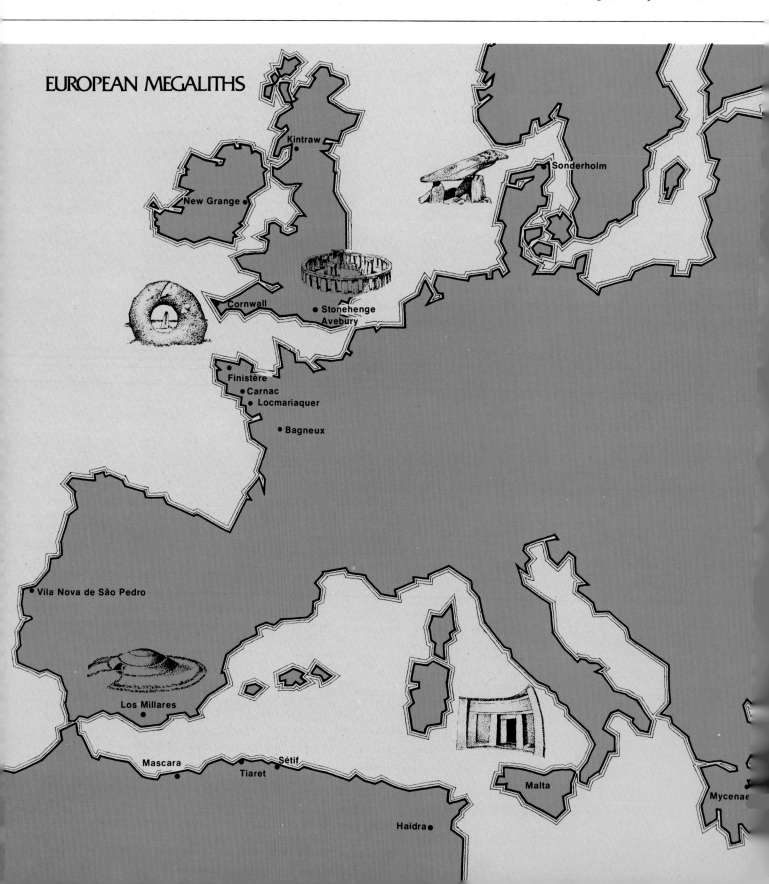

EUROPEAN MEGALITHS

Kintraw

Sonderholm

New Grange

Cornwall

Stonehenge
Avebury

Finistère
Carnac
Locmariaquer

Bagneux

Vila Nova de São Pedro

Los Millares

Mascara
Sétif
Tiaret

Malta

Mycenae

Haïdra

Megalithic monuments are also found in Japan, Korea, Sumatra, Borneo, and especially in India, where they cluster as thickly as in western Europe. The Asian menhirs and dolmens closely resemble the European in their shape and construction, and in their use as tombs, but they are generally smaller and more recent, dating from as late as the seventh century A.D.

heads and knives, tools and ornaments of stone and bone, beads of amber or rock crystal or callais (an imperfect form of turquoise), ornaments of shell—in short, the same sorts of objects excavated in the various neolithic sites in the general areas where the tombs stood. Occasionally bronze objects turned up, and imitations in stone of bronze objects. On the basis of all this, the scholarly consensus was that Europe's megaliths dated to the third and second millennia B.C., that is, they had been built by people who, whether in Spain, France, the British Isles, or Scandinavia, had not gone beyond a neolithic level of civilization, though no doubt, as the bronze finds showed, they had some contact with the more advanced peoples around the Mediterranean.

But what of the megaliths outside of Europe? When Engelhardt wrote he was struck, as we are today, by the family resemblance all megaliths have, whether on one side of the globe or the other. India has menhirs, alignments, and cromlechs that look just like those in Britain and France. The dolmens of Europe and Asia are similar not only in ground plan and mode of construction but even in details. One European type, for example, instead of a doorway has a hole cut in one side, rather resembling a porthole — and the same kind of porthole dolmens are found in India. What is puzzling is not so much the geograpical separation—that could be explained—but the chronological: only lately have we come to realize how great is the gap in dates. Europe's dolmens with portholes go back to the third and second millennia B.C. while India's belong well within the Iron Age, not earlier than the eighth century B.C. and some as late as the second A.D. The thick belt of megalithic tombs across north Africa belongs to the centuries just before and after the birth of Christ, the Japanese examples date from the second B.C. to the seventh A.D., and the megaliths discovered not long ago in the remote areas of Borneo are even younger, A.D. 800 to 1000. Only those in Malta and Palestine fit chronologically with their European counterparts.

Our awareness of this problem, however, is a recent development. To be sure, Engelhardt had noted that iron objects turn up in Indian dolmens, but he and his contemporaries had no idea how late in the Iron Age some of them dated. In any event, soon after he wrote, A. de Mortillet, an indefatigable student of France's megaliths, launched the theory that the monuments all over the world were not the

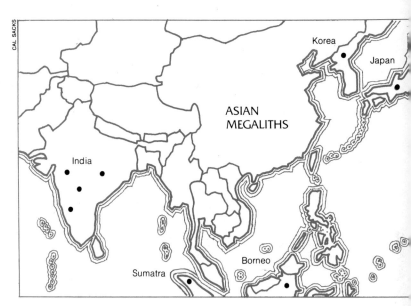

work of one race but of peoples of various races and cultures, all of whom had somehow been infected with the idea of building such monuments; it was this that had spread rather than the builders themselves. Then came the news of Heinrich Schliemann's dramatic discoveries at Mycenae, his uncovering of the giant beehive tombs there. Although these were of carefully dressed stone and not rough slabs, they seemed to belong in a general way to the dolmen family. And they appeared to have a particular affinity with certain chamber tombs along the Mediterranean coast of Spain. So the theory arose that people sailing from the Aegean area had landed on the Spanish coast, had planted the megalithic idea there, and thence it had traveled by land and sea, including the Atlantic, around to France, Britain, and so on.

But that took care only of Europe. What of the rest of the world? At this point the diffusionists move to the center of the stage. Diffusionists, as we mentioned earlier, are convinced that invention, whether of the humble hoe or the fine art of writing, is so precious and rare an act that it usually occurs only once. Obviously megaliths ought to be no exception. In 1912 the noted British prehistorian T. Eric Peet published his *Rough Stone Monuments and Their Builders,* in which he gave his carefully pondered conclusion that the megaliths everywhere were probably built by one race in an immense migration or series of migrations. Peet, however, was honest enough to admit he had no idea where it all started.

Staunch diffusionist though he was, Peet did not hold a candle to Grafton Elliot Smith. Smith spent a lifetime trying to convince everybody that the arts of civilization were created by a master race living in ancient Egypt who, traveling far and wide, passed them on to the rest of the world. Inevitably megaliths were included on the long list of what we owe these ubiquitous geniuses. As a matter of fact, megaliths figured high on the list, for he called his heroes' culture "heliolithic," from the Greek words for "sun" and "stone"; they were, above all else, worshipers of the sun and builders of megaliths. His disciple William Perry, in a book he published in 1923 titled *The Children of the Sun,* told how Egyptian trading missionaries sallied forth to seek precious metals and minerals and to proselytize on behalf of their native sun worship. This wild idea had one serious result: it triggered in soberer minds an interesting line of thought—were perhaps prehistoric missionaries the answer to the problem? After all, Christian missionaries, merely by going about preaching the word, were able to cause Christian houses of worship to rise in all quarters of the world; could not a people who had the custom of putting away their dead collectively in tombs of massive stones have gone about the world spreading the gospel of megalithic burial? V. Gordon Childe, the brilliant and persuasive prehistorian whose views reigned almost supreme during the middle of this century and who was a committed diffusionist, talked inspiredly of the erection of these tombs in honor of "megalithic saints." The very paths

the missionaries may have taken were worked out by following the geographical distribution of tombs of the same general type. Missionaries who preached burial in tombs with porthole entrances probably made their way from southern France overland to northern Germany and on to Sweden, since these are the places where such tombs are prevailingly found. Another group preaching a different style may have gone from the Mediterranean along the Pyrenees to Brittany, England, Ireland. A third may have sailed along the coasts of Spain and Portugal and then gone on to Ireland, Scotland, Denmark, Sweden.

But missionaries were not the only seed Perry planted that flourished. His Egyptians, you will remember, in addition to proselytizers were seekers of metals and minerals, in other words, prospectors. Indeed, he had earlier written a book on *The Relationships between the Geographical Distribution of Megalithic Monuments and Ancient Mines.* Once Perry had pointed it out, prehistorians were struck by the coincidence: megaliths *do* seem to be concentrated in places rich in metals, in Andalusia, Cornwall, Brittany, and the like. As a result, the conviction grew that prospectors as well as missionaries were among the propagators of the megaliths. The trouble is, precisely in regions where you would expect to find metal objects in the tombs there are none, and so the proponents of the idea have to squirm uneasily with talk of a "sociological tabu" or "customary usage."

Theorizers about missionaries or prospectors at least limited themselves to central and western

The classic image of the druid, with flowing robes and long white beard (below, left), was created by Aylett Sammes in 1676. One legend had it that Stonehenge was erected for an ancient Danish king (below, center); another that the stones were magically transported from Ireland by Merlin, the sorcerer of King Arthur's court. The view below right is from a 1740 book, Stonehenge, a Temple Restor'd to the British Druids.

Europe, where the tombs, chronologically and culturally, could reasonably be put together into a more or less homogeneous group. Robert Heine-Geldern, the Austrian prehistorian, whose imagination was as vigorous as Perry's or Smith's, let it soar all over the world. He conjured up two waves of megalithic influence, one earlier and one later, that flooded out from the heartland in the Mediterranean and washed up monuments as far as the shores of southeast Asia and the Pacific. The two waves were to let him get around the awkward disparity in dates. And his conviction was so strong and authoritative that his ideas held sway among scholars who concentrated on the Far East as Childe's did among those interested in Europe.

By the 1950s, however, archaeologists had a new means of checking the chronological foundation of such theories. Willard Libby, the Nobel Prize chemist, had shown that, as soon as a plant or animal dies, its content of carbon 14, a radioactive isotope, begins to drop at a fixed rate; thus, by measuring the amount of carbon 14 in any organic material, such as the bones, charcoal, wood, etc., that turns up in megaliths, one can determine within a certain margin of error its approximate age. Sir Mortimer Wheeler was excavating in India and revealing how late were the megaliths there. People were taking cognizance of the fact that in other places they were even later. All this made it abundantly clear that facile theories of waves of megalithic culture or emigrations of prospectors or, as Glyn Daniel, a ranking prehistorian tartly put it, of "traveling undertakers persuading the natives to adopt a new style of tomb," were not going to solve the mysteries of the megaliths. Authors of the most recent studies, such as Daniel, have accepted the inevitable and separated the European monuments from the others. Daniel, dating them roughly 2500 to 1000 B.C., was convinced that the original idea arose in the Aegean, where we find collective burials going back to the third millennium B.C., and he opts for Minoans as the carriers of the idea. Either as traders, perhaps in search of metals (among other things), or simply as adventurers looking for new homes, in any case, people of strong religious conviction, they sailed westward and settled in the middle and western Mediterranean. They brought there the idea of collective burial in tombs either cut into the living rock or built up of rough masonry. The natives, simple neolithic farmers and herders, adopted the practice but translated the tombs into megalithic architecture, that is, used the same type and shape but switched to big stones as their building material. Other scholars have introduced variations, but the theme has remained the same: the inspiration for the building of megalithic tombs and monuments came from the more highly developed peoples of the eastern Mediterranean.

These were cogent ideas thought up by men who had long pondered the problem—but the last few years have blown them all sky-high. As more and more radiocarbon dates accumulated, it became increasingly evident that the megaliths were a good

BOTH PGS CIRCLES AND STANDING STONES 1975. BY HADINGHAM. COURTESY WALKER & CO

deal older than anyone had imagined. Daniel, for example, had assigned dates of 2500 B.C. to 2000 B.C. to the early specimens; radiocarbon tests showed that any number of tombs in Brittany went back to 3000 B.C. and even earlier. It was still possible to make the theory of an eastern Mediterranean influence fit—but just barely, since the Aegean tombs, which theoretically had started it all, could not be pushed any further back. Then, in the 1950's, someone figured out a way of running a check on radiocarbon dates. California boasts certain trees—bristlecone pines—that are thousands of years old; the exact age can be figured by counting the annual tree rings. If one ran a radiocarbon test on the wood from any given ring, theoretically the two dates should coincide. The trouble is, they did not; the radiocarbon test consistently yielded a date younger than the actual age of the tree. And the farther back in time one went, the wider the discrepancy; an object that had a radiocarbon date of, say, 2000 B.C. probably was actually 500 years older, one of 3000 B.C. probably 700 to 800 years older. It had given the prehistorians pause when radiocarbon tests put the graves in Brittany back to the fourth

millennium B.C.; now they had to adjust to the fact that these very likely go even further back, to the fifth. One of the few points on which there had been general consensus was that certain tombs in southern Spain and Portugal were the earliest of their type and that the type had been carried from there first to Brittany and thence to Ireland; now it looks as if it was the other way round.

Thus, the whole movement that scholars have so carefully worked out must either be scrapped or thrown into reverse: if the idea of burying the dead in monumental tombs had been spread, by traders or prospectors or missionaries or undertakers or others, the spreaders were the primitive peoples of western Europe and the receivers were in the Aegean world. If Smith or Perry were still alive, they would have to face the horrifying thought that their Egyptian master race had gotten the idea of building pyramids from illiterate barbarians of the north.

Back in the 1860's some of the first serious writers who tried to unravel the puzzle of the megaliths had suggested that the influence indeed did go from north to south; are we, then, back to square one? Well, not quite yet. What has happened, rather, is that the diffusionists are abandoning the field in headlong retreat. Stuart Piggott, one of the most distinguished prehistorians, now holds that megaliths, having arisen independently in historical times, in India and Japan and elsewhere, could very well have developed the same way in prehistoric times. Another prehistorian, Colin Renfrew, is more specific: he plumps for independent invention in at least four places, Denmark, southern Britain, Brittany, Iberia, arguing in ways that, but ten years or so ago, would have brought upon him thundering salvos from diffusionist guns.

If we are still in the dark about who thought up the idea of megaliths, whether one people or many, and how it spread—if it did spread—what about a second crucial question: what was their purpose?

To answer this, let us first turn to the dolmens, putting aside the menhirs and clusters of menhirs for a moment. To the great chagrin of the druid-minded, the presence of bones in so many of the dolmens made it clear that these were tombs. But were they all tombs? And just what kind of tombs were they?

As noted earlier, dolmens were hardly ever used for just one or two bodies. They were for multiple

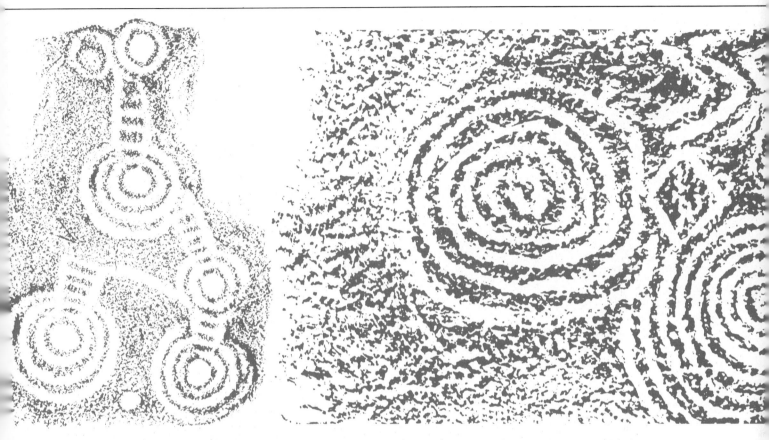

burials, the number at times running into the hundreds. One tomb near Carcassonne in southern France turned out to contain the bones of 300 bodies of all ages and both sexes. Another at Aveyron held 203 bodies—185 adults and 18 children. The bones are invariably in pieces and in utter disorder, to such an extent that excavators time and again remark upon the fact. One tomb in Denmark was so stuffed, it gave the impression of having been filled to the brim with the capstone off and then closed like an overloaded suitcase. Sometimes one or two skeletons are found intact amid a welter of scattered bones, and this has led to the theory that the tombs were intended for chieftains, whose bodies were carefully laid to rest amid others, tossed in helter-skelter, or retainers, wives, concubines, and servants, who were slaughtered to accompany the deceased to the next world. Others think that the tombs were really ossuaries, that the bodies were kept elsewhere until the flesh had disappeared, and then the bones were casually pitched in. But most believe that we are dealing with collective graves kept in operation over very long periods, constantly being opened to receive more

bodies, the ones already there being trampled upon and shoved aside every time a new corpse was brought in.

But is it right to call them all tombs, whether chieftains', collective, or otherwise? In at least one-third of the dolmens that have been discovered and searched, no bones at all were found. Of these, most contained grave goods, but many were just plain empty. For this, the excavators have a ready explanation: the tombs had been robbed. Now, there is no question that over the centuries many a dolmen has been robbed. However, though some robbers may have been antiquarian-minded enough to make off with the flints and other stone tools they came across, why in the world would they take the trouble to cart off load upon load of old bones, down to the very last tooth? Moreover, of two neighboring dolmens, one will have its share of bones and grave goods, but the other will have not a thing in it. And what happened in the tombs that have grave goods but no bones? One suggestion is that the nature of the soil destroyed the bones, but that does not sound very convincing. Another is that all the old bones were

The walls of a megalithic temple, larger and more elaborate than the tombs of western Europe, rise on the seacoast of Malta. The temple was never used for burials, but contained altars for worship.

C. M. DIXON

cleaned out, presumably to make room for new, but then, for some reason, no new bones were ever put in. The fact is, some dolmens, including, as it happens, the most impressive, such as the great one at Bagneux, apparently never held bodies at all. What is more, Bagneux and others like it were not covered by a mound, as was the usual practice among the dolmen builders, but were left in the open. Were they perhaps tomb-shaped temples for some worship connected with the dead? If so, what kind of worship? The prehistorian Fernand Niel has been particularly impressed by the way the bones are almost always in fragments, often tiny fragments; in a recent book he mutters darkly about cannibalism being part of the rites, claiming that, much as we do not like to face the idea, all the signs point to it. In any event, he con-

cludes morosely, the users of megalithic tombs that have been studied do not seem to have honored so much as insulted their dead.

Niel also discusses how dolmens are oriented. They do not face just any way. A definite effort was made to align them north-south or east-west, and in the latter case, often toward the point at which the sun rose on the days of the equinoxes and solstices. And the builders seem to have searched out locations which were on a level high enough to command a view of the horizon in the desired direction. This is why, Niel thinks, they were willing to haul the massive stones they needed miles and miles: proper orientation took priority over availability of building material. At this point we have reached the subject that has fueled the hottest argument of all the many

48

about the megaliths — their possible connection with the heavenly bodies. To discuss it, we must leave dolmens and turn to the menhirs and their clusters, including the most celebrated megalithic monument of them all, Stonehenge.

Stonehenge is a complicated cromlech of mammoth stones visible from miles away as one travels over Salisbury Plain in southern England. Dolmens impress only by their massiveness: their house-of-cards construction is the simplest possible, and in any event, they were, with few exceptions, totally hidden under mounds. Stonehenge was made to be seen, and its stones, as big as any dolmen's, were not just rough-quarried; some were carefully squared and smoothed and fitted together with precisely cut joints. It is a veritable piece of architecture, the earliest in northern Europe, the neolithic equivalent, in its way, of a Roman arch.

Geoffrey of Monmouth, England's twelfth-century historian, thought that Merlin's magic had wafted Stonehenge's colossal members from Ireland and erected them. When James I visited the site in 1620, he promptly gave orders to his renowned architect Inigo Jones to draw up a plan of it; Jones concluded it must have been the work of Romans, for only they, so far as he or his contemporaries knew, had the expertise to create such a structure. By the next century the credit had been transferred to the Celts. A committed Celt-fancier, William Stukeley, in 1740 published a book called *Stonehenge, a Temple Restor'd to the British Druids* which attracted readers for over a century and set the ball rolling so briskly that, as we have seen, it is still going.

Indeed, few hard facts about Stonehenge were available until very recently, when a proper archaeological excavation was started in 1950 and went on for over a decade. The site, it turns out, had not been built all at once. There were three phases, extending over many centuries, and it was only the last that was responsible for the imposing ruins we see today. The first Stonehenge — Stonehenge I, as the archaeologists call it — was merely a big circle, about a hundred yards in diameter, marked out by a ditch and low earthen embankment, with a gap at the northeast for an entrance. Remains of postholes about the center make it almost certain that a round wooden building had stood there. In addition, just within the embankment was a circle of 56 holes, good-sized

LA VALLETTA. MUSÉE NATIONALE – SCALA

This terra-cotta statuette called the Sleeping Lady, only four and a half inches long, was found in a Maltese tomb.

holes, two yards wide and one deep; a British antiquarian, John Aubrey, had first spotted them back in the seventeenth century, so they have been dubbed the Aubrey Holes. Sites consisting of a circular area with a round building in its middle are common enough in southern England; no doubt they served as centers for some sort of religious observances. They come in various sizes, the smallest a mere 10 yards in diameter, the largest as much as 550. The earliest Stonehenge is but one more of the same type, and of middling size. What marks it out from all the others is an unhewn 16-foot menhir, the so-called Heel Stone, outside the circle, about 100 yards from the entrance gap in the embankment.

Some centuries later this simple circle-cum-roundhouse was made rather more complicated, and we come to Stonehenge II. Two rings of menhirs were added, an inner one about 40 feet in diameter and an outer one about 80, surrounding the middle portion of the original circle but not exactly concentric with it, set about three feet off-center. The stone of the menhirs, distinctively blue in color, is not local; in 1923 geologists determined that it was mostly dolerite and some rhyolite, which could only have come from quarries in southern Wales, one hundred fifty miles away as the crow flies. Stonehenge II also saw the building of a causeway leading off to the northeast. The old entrance gap in the embankment

49

did not quite coincide with it, so the gap was adjusted to conform. The Heel Stone was left where it was, which meant sitting a little off to the side of the center line of the causeway. Probably the four stones called the Station Stones may date from Stonehenge II or, more likely, Stonehenge III; we will have much to say about them in a moment. They form a big rectangle, 245 feet by 105, and their diagonals cross right at the center of the new blue-stone rings.

In its third and last phase Stonehenge was totally transformed. The rings of blue menhirs were removed to make way for the two monumental features so prominent today, the horseshoe of five trilithons — freestanding doorways, as it were, each consisting of a pair of jambs topped by a lintel — and the thirty 15-foot piers capped by a continuous lintel that form a 108-foot ring surrounding the whole. The trilithons and ring were made of the local sandstone, huge blocks that had been carefully dressed and joined with dovetails and mortises and tenons. Even more remarkable, the uprights taper toward the top, occasionally being convexly curved — the same sort of subtle touch used in the columns of Greek temples to counteract the distorting effects of perspective. The menhirs set up in Stonehenge II were not exactly puny, but the size of these new elements is astounding. Some of the individual stones weigh better than 50 tons. The largest trilithon towers 22½ feet high, and its lintel is 16 feet long and four feet thick. As a last step, the two sets of bluestones were restored. So, in its final phase, Stonehenge consisted of the following:

- a big stone, the so-called Altar Stone, marking the center of the circle, which in Stonehenge III remained the same as in Stonehenge II
- a horseshoe, 40 feet in diameter, of bluestones six to eight feet high, embracing the center, with its open end oriented toward the northeast, toward the causeway
- a horseshoe of five massive tilithons embracing the bluestone horseshoe and oriented in the same way
- a circle, 80 feet in diameter, of bluestones eight to 10 feet high, enclosing the trilithons
- a circle, 108 feet in diameter, of 30 piers surmounted by a continuous lintel, embracing the whole
- the four Station Stones mentioned above.
Naturally the question is: who built it and when?

Until but a few years ago there was complete consensus in the scholarly world: the locals of Britain, primitive neolithic farmers as they were, might have done the actual labor, but they could not possibly have designed it, or been responsible for the advanced technique it displays; they must have had help from elsewhere. In the vicinity of Stonehenge are numerous burials with grave goods so rich that the bones laid to rest there can only have been of chieftains. Often the grave goods include goldwork and curious faience beads, and scholars made a convincing case that these bear a distinct resemblance to goldwork and beads found in the fabulous graves Schliemann had uncovered at Mycenae. It all seemed to hang together: the luxury of the British tombs indicated that the local chieftains had the wherewithal to indulge in exotic imports, and the presence of the goldwork and the beads pointed to Mycenae as at least one source of supply; could not Stonehenge's architectural sophistication, its advanced building methods, have come from there? Who knows — perhaps a Mycenean architect had been called in to supervise the work! The case appeared to be clinched when, in 1953, one of the excavators spotted on an upright of the outside ring a carving of what looked like a dagger of a well-known Mycenaean type.

The Mycenean connection solved the question of date as well as inspiration. Since the great age of Mycenae falls, in round numbers, between 1600 and 1300 B.C., and since the style of dagger on the carving apparently went out of fashion about 1500, Stonehenge was placed about that time. In 1959 the first radiocarbon date for it became available: 1720 B.C. This was rather earlier than people expected, but still well within the range, because one had to allow a margin for error of three hundred years either way.

In discussing the theory of an eastern origin for the dolmens, we saw that it had a flourishing life of over half a century before it was cut down by the recent revolution in dating. The Mycenean connection has been, as it were, nipped in the bud. The new date proposed for the great building period at Stonehenge is 2100 to 1900 B.C. — a time, in other words, when the Mycenaeans themselves were just primitive neolithic farmers. Suddenly the demonstration that British goldwork and beads have links with Mycenae does not seem quite so convincing; suddenly the dagger carved on one of Stonehenge's piers no longer looks quite so Mycenaean (anyway, even if it

Around the village of Carnac in Brittany stand long rows of menhirs—more than 3,000 in all—stretching for two miles across the countryside. One theory is that they served as a sort of megalithic graph paper on which the movements of the sun, moon, and stars could be plotted.

FRENCH GOVERNMENT TOURIST OFFICE

does, it could have been carved there long after the pier had been put up). There is no getting around it: the creators of Stonehenge, not only of its first phase (now dated as far back as 2600 B.C.) but also of the spectacular last phase, must have been the local inhabitants of Salisbury Plain. They must have had not only the social organization to supply the labor needed for quarrying, hauling, and erecting the mighty stones but the imagination to design the structure and the technology to dress and assemble its members. And, if we hearken to certain voices that have recently been raised, on top of all this they may have had a mathematical and astronomical expertise far, far greater than anyone has ever dreamed of granting to a relatively primitive people. This brings us finally to a critical issue, the one raised by the unmistakable way in which dolmens were oriented toward heavenly bodies: were menhirs and cromlechs so oriented? If so, did they have an astronomical purpose?

Jacob's menhir and Joshua's cromlech (or alignment), we are distinctly told, were set up as sacred objects, to be revered or worshiped. Few of us have doubted that all menhirs and cromlechs were erected for more or less the same reasons. What we are in the dark about is the nature of the religion that inspired the reverence or worship. It so happens that, in western Europe at least, many Stone Age monuments bear carvings, and a common motif among these is a stylized picture of the sun. It is not at all hard to imagine the neolithic inhabitants of the area as sun worshipers; after all, the cult has had its appeal for peoples as varied as the ancient Egyptians and the American Indians.

For years we have been aware of a key feature of Stonehenge that demonstrates beyond doubt its intimate connection, at least in its latter phases, with the sun. If at dawn on June 21, the day of the summer solstice, you look from the Altar Stone at the middle

CONTINUED ON PAGE 54

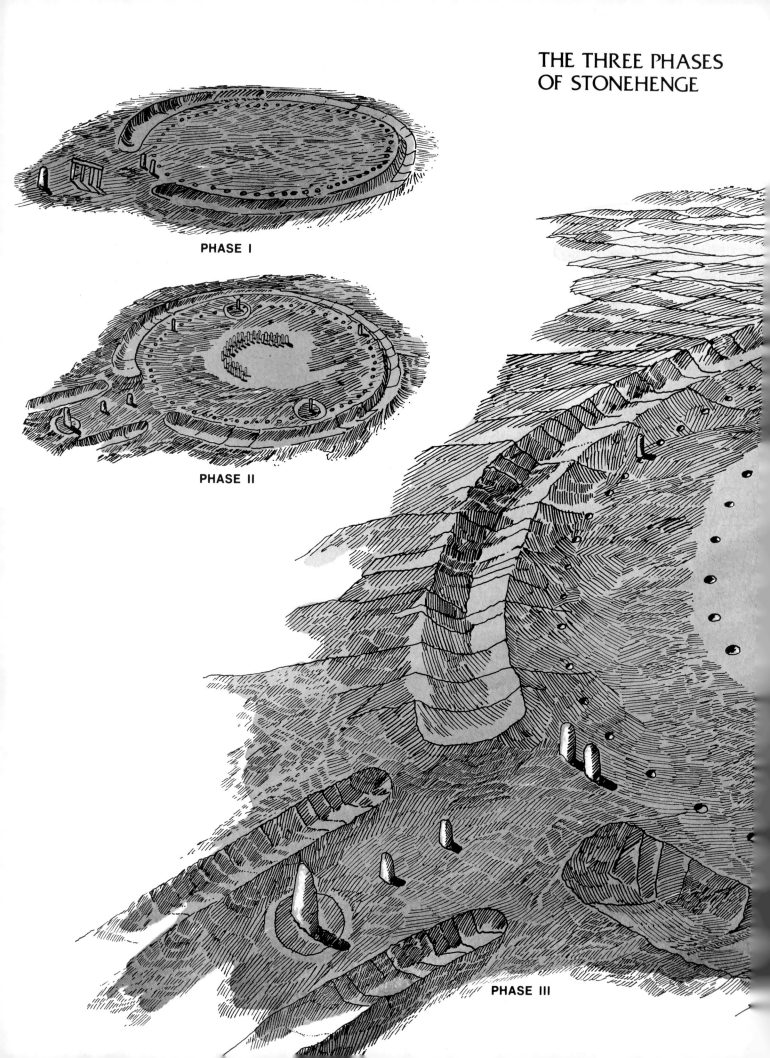

THE THREE PHASES OF STONEHENGE

PHASE I

PHASE II

PHASE III

Stonehenge has existed as a megalithic site on Salisbury Plain since about 2600 B.C. In its first phase it consisted of two concentric embankments with a ditch between them. Within the embankments were dug the 56 Aubrey Holes. The 16-foot Heel Stone, and possibly other standing stones, were put in place. In the center of the circle there was probably a wooden structure. In phase two the builders erected at the center of the enclosure two concentric incomplete rings of bluish menhirs. Dating from this period or later are the four Station Stones, which supposedly served as astronomical sightlines. In its third phase the builders erected the huge megaliths we see today: a horseshoe of five freestanding trilithons and, surrounding it, a complete circle of 30 piers, capped by a continuous lintel of horizontal stones. The arrangements of bluestones were removed but later put back in among the larger stones. In the center probably stood an altar stone. The work was completed about 1400 B.C.

VICTOR LAZARRO

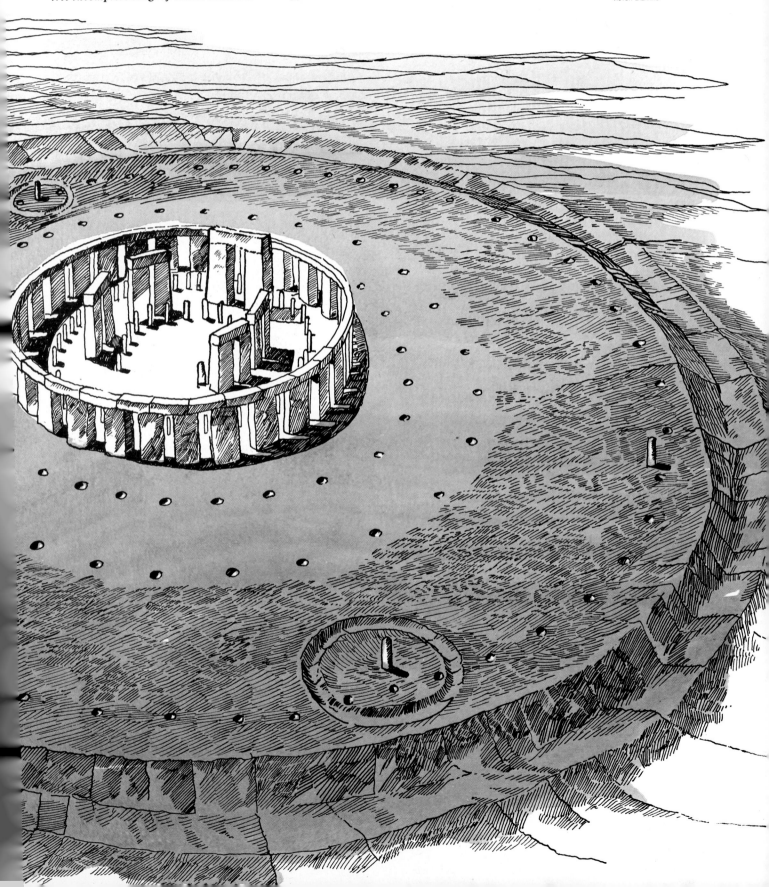

CONTINUED FROM PAGE 51

of the monument along a line that passes through the center of the opening in the horseshoes, then on through the center of the entrance gap in the embankment and down the causeway—in other words, along the main axis of the whole structure—your gaze will be directed almost to the point on the horizon where the sun will rise. At the time Stonehenge was built, the main axis was aligned right on the exact spot, but because the earth wobbles a bit in its rotation, the sun now rises a bit to the east of where it did when Stonehenge was new. (It does not and never did rise over the Heel Stone, as is so often asserted, but west of it, and in the second millennium B.C. even farther west than today.)

In 1963 Gerald Hawkins, an astronomer on the faculty of Boston University, whose interest was sparked during a visit to Stonehenge on June 21, the day of the summer solstice, dropped a bombshell. Stonehenge, he claimed in an article published that year, was a true astronomical observatory. The next year a second article argued that part of the structure was a "neolithic-style computer." And the following year he wrapped everything together in a book confidently titled *Stonehenge Decoded*. In Hawkins' view Stonehenge was far from being just an ornate temple dedicated to sun worship where priests could hold their ceremonies, including the welcoming of the midsummer sunrise, in properly imposing surroundings. Not just the main axis of the structure but practically every stone in the place provided sightlines to notable heavenly events, the moon's as well as the sun's: the point where the sun set, in addition to where it rose, on June 21; where it rose and set on December 21; the points where the moon rose on both those dates—two points each, the most northerly and the most southerly, since the moon is so much more variable in its motions than the sun. What is more, there was a device that enabled Stonehenge's priests to maintain the records and do the calculations necessary to predict eclipses, despite the fact that they had no system of numerical notation, much less a system of writing. The clue lay in the mysterious Aubrey Holes. These amounted to a kind of ancient computer; they had been dug to hold tallies that, by being moved about the various holes, enabled neolithic priests to do what later ages did with writing and numbers. There were 56 holes since a 56-year lunar cycle was involved.

Hawkins pointedly referred to his own use of a

modern computer not only to determine the precise position of the heavenly bodies in relation to Salisbury Plain around 1500 B.C.—for he took this as the date of erection—but for the calculation of all possible alignments. For many people the mere mention of the magic word "computer" was enough to hail Hawkins as the solver of Stonehenge's enigma; when archaeologists were reluctant to join in the applause, they were dismissed as old-fashioned die-hards, too wrapped up in the Stone Age to appreciate the wonders of the age of electronics. But the die-hards stubbornly stuck to certain cogent objections: Hawkins had derived his alignments from a multitude of stones and holes, even restored and assumed stones and holes, that came indiscriminately from all three of Stonehenge's phases; he had derived the data he fed into the computer from ordinary published plans that simply were not accurate enough for his purposes; he had based key sightlines—those that he claimed gave the point of sunrise on December 21 and one of the points of moonrise on that day—on holes that the archaeologists assured him were not man-made; others of his sightlines just did not point to the heavenly events he said they did; and the famous Aubrey Holes, far from holding tallies for centuries, looked to the archaeologists as if they had been filled up right after being dug.

But then one of the highest possible authorities, Fred Hoyle, the renowned British astronomer, came forth to deliver his seal of approval. Hawkins was indeed right, wrote Hoyle, Stonehenge *was* an astronomical observatory for all the complicated functions that he claims, not excepting the prediction of eclipses. The only trouble is, he was totally wrong on how eclipses were predicted. It could not possibly have been done the way he says. The Aubrey Holes were not for tallies. They represented the ecliptic (i.e., the path of the sun through the stars), and by moving about stones that represented the sun, the moon, and the nodes of the moon's orbit (i.e., where it crossed the ecliptic) in complicated ways, the priests of Stonehenge could have predicted practically any eclipse that had occurred.

The most controversial claim the astronomers were making for Stonehenge, one which, if substantiated, would without question qualify the structure as a veritable astronomical observatory and its users as veritable astronomers, was that it was intended for predicting eclipses. To do this one needs to record

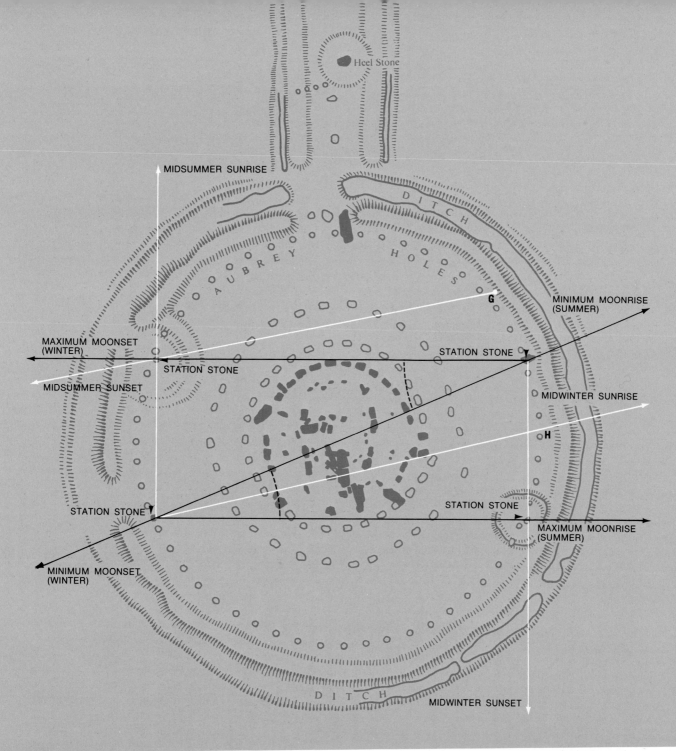

Heel Stone

MIDSUMMER SUNRISE

MINIMUM MOONRISE
(SUMMER)

G

MAXIMUM MOONSET
(WINTER)

STATION STONE

STATION STONE

MIDSUMMER SUNSET

MIDWINTER SUNRISE

H

STATION STONE

MIDWINTER SUNRISE

STATION STONE

MAXIMUM MOONRISE
(SUMMER)

MINIMUM MOONSET
(WINTER)

MIDWINTER SUNSET

CAL SACKS

observations of heavenly events and the intervals between them over long periods, periods that may
exceed the lifetime of any individual. The Babylon-
ians and other ancient peoples had learned to make
such predictions, but they all had at their disposal a
system of numerical notation as well as of writing.

At the heart of Hawkins' and Hoyle's claim lie the
56 Aubrey Holes. These belong to Stonehenge's earliest phase, so the astronomical knowledge being argued for would go back to at least the middle of the
third millennium B.C. Both men assumed that the
holes were used for holding tallies or markers. The
archaeologists argue that this cannot possibly have
been the case, if, as they believe, the holes were filled

up soon after they had been dug; besides, what was
found in them was mostly cremated bones, so if they
were used for anything it must have been burials.
Hawkins says that the 56 holes were part of a "computer" based on a 56-year lunar cycle. Hoyle says that
prehistoric men could not possibly have worked out
Hawkins' system and that the holes are a "protrac-
tor." Other astronomers say that Hawkins' 56-year
cycle is an invalid concept and that Hoyle's hypothesis does not at all require the number 56. Besides, as
Richard Atkinson, who has written the standard
handbook on Stonehenge, acutely remarks, Hoyle
has shown how *we* might use Stonehenge for predicting eclipses, but could neolithic Britons have done it?

The total lack of agreement among the experts hardly inspires confidence: if Stonehenge was so manifestly a structure designed for predicting eclipses, there should be at least some meeting of minds on how it was done. In 1857, in order to settle whether cuneiform had really been deciphered, the Royal Asiatic Society challenged scholars to submit translations of a newly discovered inscription; four did so, the results were found so alike that there could no longer be room for doubt, and the issue was declared settled. When the astronomers who have been studying Stonehenge come up with at least convergent ideas, then we may be readier to believe that its priests knew how to predict eclipses.

its original position, one is fallen flat, and two have disappeared.) Newham and Hawkins point out that the short sides of the rectangle are parallel with Stonehenge's main axis. So, when one looks along them to the northeast, one sights, just as along the axis, upon the point of midsummer sunrise. If one looks along them in the opposite direction, toward the southwest, one sights upon the point of midwinter sunset. And the line of the long sides marks, in the southeast direction, the southernmost point at which the full moon rises at midsummer, and, in the northwest direction, the northernmost point at which it sets at midwinter. Both men were struck by the same idea as to why Salisbury Plain was chosen for

MICHAEL CRAIG, *THE ATLAS OF EARLY MAN* BY JACQUETTA HAWKES—DORLING KINDERSLEY, LTD.

Happily, some of Hawkins' findings do converge with those of another student of Stonehenge—although he was unaware of it. Stonehenge offered sightlines, Hawkins argues, not only for the midsummer sunrise but other movements of the sun and, more significant, of the moon. It happens that the same ideas had been put forth by a retired British engineer, C. A. Newham, in a little book, privately printed, called *The Enigma of Stonehenge.* Both Newham and Hawkins independently came upon an interesting feature of the so-called Station Stones, that group of four marking a big rectangle whose diagonals cross at the exact center of the monument and whose purpose has hitherto been a mystery. (One still stands in

the site; at its latitude the lines of midsummer sunrise and moonrise cross at right angles and so a rectangular disposition of observation points is possible.

The claim that Stonehenge was so sophisticated an astronomical observatory that its priests could foretell eclipses has been greeted, as we have seen, by much shaking of heads. On the other hand, many are convinced by Newham's findings, confirmed by Hawkins', that Stonehenge had an astronomical dimension going well beyond a mere orientation toward the midsummer sunrise. It was a temple whose worship somehow involved celebrating notable risings and settings of both sun and moon throughout the year. In order to conduct this worship, its priests had developed the skill to identify these events with considerable accuracy.

If, then, this unique megalithic monument had a number of specific astronomical functions, indeed was set on a site deliberately chosen for such functions, what of its humbler relatives, the cromlechs and alignments, even the lone menhirs? Were they objects of veneration and no more? Or were they too astronomically useful? Here we come to a bombshell dropped by a Scot professor of engineering that makes Hawkins' seem like a firecracker. In a steady stream of articles bulked out by two books, Alexander Thom has tried to demonstrate that the menhirs and cromlechs of Britain and Brittany, in addi-

One's first reaction on hearing statements like this is to dismiss them as the brainstorms of a crackpot. But Alexander Thom is no crackpot. He has a formidable command of astronomy and mathematics, and he has spent years patiently surveying, with the very highest standards of accuracy, practically every menhir and cromlech that stands in Britain and many of those in Brittany as well.

Thom omits Stonehenge, for there the observations depend upon very short sightlines, from the Altar Stone down the causeway, from one corner to another of the rectangle formed by the Station Stones. At the sites that he concentrates on, he assumes that the priests operated in a different way,

tion to whatever religious purposes they served, were instruments for determining certain risings and settings not only of the sun and moon but of first-magnitude stars. Indeed, so astronomically accomplished were the neolithic priests that they had a knowledge of the moon's motions that was not to be improved upon for three thousand years. The computations we work out algebraically or geometrically they did with the help of certain distinctive fan-shaped alignments of stones that have been found; these were, so to speak, a megalithic style of graph paper. There is no question that they were able to predict eclipses; it was for this that they acquired so detailed a knowledge of the moon's behavior.

which, by offering far longer sightlines, produced a much higher degree of accuracy. He assumes the use of a distinctive feature on the horizon—a peak, a notch, a slope—to mark the point where a heavenly body rose or set. He did not get this idea out of the blue; it is a procedure not at all uncommon in illiterate societies. The Hopi Indians, for example, who lived in settled farming communities, had a whole agricultural calendar based on the sun's risings over irregularities on the southern skyline. They appointed a special religious official, the "sun watcher," whose job was to make the daily observations and who, keeping a tally on a notched stick, apprised the populace of the imminence of important dates. Very much

The bristlecone pine of the American West, oldest of living things, has revolutionized the technique of dating ancient objects. From its rings dendrochronologists created an 8,000-year yardstick against which to check the accuracy of radiocarbon dating. The new dating overturned the theory that the megalithic monuments of western Europe had been copied from Mycenaean tombs or Egyptian pyramids; they are older than either.

the same system was in vogue in certain backward Russian villages until a few generations ago. However, merely marking when heavenly bodies arise over a horizon point, while adequate for a calendar, is too rough and ready for astronomical purposes. This is where the megaliths come in. To gain a properly precise sightline, two points are needed, a backsight and a foresight, just as on a rifle. The menhirs, as Thom sees it, were the backsights, the horizon features the foresights. A menhir would be so placed as to enable a viewer to sight along one of its faces to, say, a slope, ideally 10 to 20 miles away, which marked the exact point of the rising or setting of some first magnitude star, or of the sun or moon at significant times such as the solstices or equinoxes. Some sites were for solar observations, some for stellar, some for lunar, some for a combination. All

sites were chosen to allow split-second accuracy in making the observation, for, among other considerations, only thus could the precise length of the year be determined, and only with the determination of the precise length of the year could eclipses be predicted.

When Thom had completed surveying the monuments of Britain, he transferred his attention to France, and it was while working with the welter of megaliths around Carnac that he generated his most controversial idea. Carnac boasts one of the most impressive and puzzling of all megalithic monuments, a series of vast alignments, like an army of stone soldiers in extended order of march. Ten to 13 columns of menhirs, comprising 3,000 units in all, stretch over the countryside for almost two miles. Not far away, near Locmariaquer, lie the four pieces of Er Grah. According to Thom, this giant 75-foot stone was a man-made substitute for a feature on the horizon; it served as the foresight for lunar observations from a variety of backsights in the area. The army of stones was, as at certain other sites, a neolithic substitute for graph paper.

Even if we grant only Thom's minimal claims, we must face up to the fact that the inhabitants of northern Europe at the time these megaliths were put up, toward the end of the third millennium B.C. and the beginning of the second, possessed a truly remarkable skill in mathematics and astronomy.

And not only in mathematics and astronomy but, to get to a second bombshell Thom has dropped, in geometry and surveying as well. Many cromlechs are circular; the laying out of these required no more than a certain adeptness and a lot of care. But many others are elliptical and egg-shaped, and the two shapes are repeated in site upon site in different sizes. How was it done? Only, says Thom, by the use of geometry. For example, the egg shape comes out easily and regularly if one starts with a pair of 3-4-5 triangles set back to back—in other words, there is every likelihood that the cromlech builders knew this supremely useful geometrical figure, the same that the ancient Egyptians used for surveying their fields, what we call a Pythagorean triangle. Very likely they knew, at least approximately, the value of π. Most striking of all, Thom, with a bulging file of exact measurements to support him, has made a strong case for believing that the megalithic builders, including those of Brittany as well as Britain, all used a fixed unit of measurement, what he calls the "megalithic yard," 2.72 feet (.829 meters) long. His surveys, he asserts, reveal that the designers of cromlechs and alignments strove, as far as possible, to make all the dimensions—diameters, radii, sides of triangles, intervals, etc.—multiples of the megalithic yard.

As a matter of fact, new archaeological excavations are making more apparent than ever that the neolithic peoples of western Europe were adept in the whole general area of civil engineering as well as in geometry and surveying. Stonehenge is only one example of their ability to plot and erect a monument of imposing size. Recently, Silbury Hill, not far from Avebury in Wiltshire, has been thoroughly investigated. Dating around 2750 B.C., it is the biggest man-made mound of antiquity, rising to a height of 130 feet and spreading at its base over well nigh five and a half acres. It turns out that it was put up in successive stages, like a layer cake, and the planning was so accurate that the midpoint of the topmost layer, 130 feet above the midpoint of the bottommost, and countless years of work later, overlies it almost exactly. In Belgium a flint mine of about 4300 B.C. has been discovered which had to go through nearly 30 feet of unstable gravel and sand to reach the desired flint-bearing beds, where it fanned out into a web of galleries.

Once we have recognized what these people were capable of in other fields of endeavor, it becomes easier to grant them commensurate credit in astronomy, as Thom would have us do. We must bear in mind that his case rests not on demonstrable proof but only on a high order of probability. As one stands by a given menhir and looks about the horizon, there are, considering all the astronomical events that the ancient priests theoretically were interested in, no less than 60 possible sightlines, 60 possible notches or other horizon features which that menhir can point to. Thus, at any given site, we must ask ourselves, as one expert who reviewed Thom's book put it, "are the notch-phenomena sufficiently striking to persuade us to accept their significance even after allowing for the fact that there are some sixty 'candidate' notches per site?" His own conclusion was that, out of 40 sites Thom argued for, only 14 were "impressive."

It is a pity that no single site, no matter how high the probability of its astronomical use, is able to fur-

nish the proof that clinches beyond the possibility of doubt. At one, archaeological remains in the vicinity turn out to be of the wrong date, at another one would expect archaeological remains but there are none, and so on. A fundamental uncertainty bedevils even Thom's grandiose conception of Er Grah as a mighty man-made foresight: it now lies in four pieces, and some say it toppled while being erected and so was never used, while others think the pieces do not even go together.

Thus, one kind of doubt or another beclouds the various individual instances. It is the massive sum total of Thom's findings that tips the balance in his favor, and the scales seem to incline farther that way the farther he pushes his surveys. A growing number of scholars are ready to concede his minimum point, that the megalithic monuments of Britain and Brittany were not just sacred objects often oriented for mystic religious reasons toward heavenly bodies but, over and above all that, were astronomical instruments providing sightlines for the very accurate determination of significant events in the movements of the sun and moon.

However, he has not achieved the same measure of support for his more daring conclusion, that the creators of the megaliths boasted the astonomical expertise, the accuracy of observation, the capacity for computation, and the organization for maintaining extended records with no system of numeration or writing that enabled them to use these monuments for predicting eclipses. Not only archaeologists but fellow astronomers are skeptical. They point to the important consideration of weather. Were the skies so consistently clear in those days, particularly along the horizon, where clouds or haze are so very common, as to allow a succession of observations of split-second acccuracy such as Thom's assumptions require? One particular process that he attributes to the priests would require lunar observations for three successive nights, and bad weather on any one night would delay for years the chance of redoing it. And what of the natural features? A thick mantle of forest covered much of Britain and Brittany at one time, and tall trees could very well have made a difference in the notches and slopes that now seem so useful as astronomical foresights; was the landscape so denuded of trees as has been argued? Indeed, Thom's assiduous scenting out of astronomical significance in so many apparently random stones has re-

The stone ring on the facing page is a curious variation in megalithic architecture. The chiseled hole probably served as the entrance to a "porthole tomb." The ring and the menhir behind it stand on the Penwith Peninsula in Cornwall.

minded one commentator of a story told about the great student of ancient astronomy, Otto Neugebauer: he once found calendrical significance in the teeth of his pocket comb.

Newham and Hawkins demonstrated that Stonehenge was set up to take lunar sights as well as solar. Now Thom has shown that Stonehenge was not at all unique, that there were places for taking such sights all over Scotland, England, and Brittany. And strange to say, his scrupulously scientific researches seem to be bringing us right back to the darlings of the eighteenth-century romantics—the druids.

As we know from over a century of archaeological research, the population of western Europe during the second millennium B.C. and earlier was a neolithic folk who lived in small village communities and kept themselves alive by means of the simplest form of agriculture. Most of them inevitably spent their days in the farmer's humble round. But among them there must have been a small select class of priests trained in the technique of watching how the sun and moon inexorably advanced toward certain fixed points on the horizon so that they could announce to the populace that at such and such a moment the sun would start its annual sinking in the heavens or its annual rising or the like, and thereby set in motion whatever ceremony traditionally celebrated these events. Thousands of years later, when Caesar was carrying out his conquest of the Celtic tribes of Gaul, he heard about just such a class of priests, the druids. Here is what he reports about them:

It is believed that their discipline was developed in Britain and from there was carried into Gaul, and today, those who wish to go into the subject more deeply generally go there to study . . . It is said that they learn by heart a vast number of verses. Thus, some spend twenty years in the discipline. They consider it a crime to entrust these matters to writing, even though they use the Greek alphabet for almost all other purposes . . . They conduct much discussion of the heavenly bodies and their motions, of the size of the universe and the Earth.

Could not these priests Caesar was told about be the heirs of a discipline that went back thousands of years? It seems to fit together so well: the center of study was Britain; there was great importance given to "the heavenly bodies and their motions"; and the tradition was maintained of learning everything by

heart. It is precisely in Britain where we find the menhirs and cromlechs that Thom has identified as observatories, and the users, since they knew neither numbers nor writing, had to depend upon memory.

A little knowledge is a dangerous thing. It makes mysteries more mysterious.

A decade ago there were reasonable hypotheses to explain the megaliths. Menhirs and cromlechs were objects of veneration, as described in the Bible, objects whose simplicity bespoke a remote primitive origin. Dolmens, those chambers of primitive construction that served as collective tombs, reflected a type created in the eastern Mediterranean which spread throughout the backward neolithic communities of the West, thanks to the activities of traders, settlers, missionaries, prospectors, adventurers. That astounding megalithic monument, Stonehenge, owed its design and construction to help from some advanced civilization, most probably Aegean.

All this now goes into archaeology's rubbish heap of abandoned theories. The menhirs and cromlechs of western Europe no doubt were objects of veneration, connected with a religion that centered on the heavenly bodies. But, we have now learned, they were also instruments, surprisingly effective despite their clumsy form, for determining critical moments in the motions of the sun and the moon. The people of western Europe started putting up their massive dolmens and digging their deep flint mines long before the Near East or Mediterranean embarked on projects of such magnitude. Though living in simple neolithic farming communities, they had developed the social organization and strength that permitted them to carry out public works on a veritably gigantic scale, works requiring the labor of hundreds over years and years. Without writing or a system of numerical notation, they had achieved an outstanding skill in surveying and geometry.

Yet, whereas the peoples of the Near East and Aegean marched on to achieve an advanced civilization, those of western Europe, having reached the remarkable stage that they did, marked time there, continued to live at their simple level, and only went the rest of the way much much later under guidance from their southern neighbors.

How did they manage to get as far as they did? Why did they stop? We have done nothing more than exchange new mysteries for old.

WHO KILLED THIS MAN 2,000 YEARS AGO?

On May 8, 1950, a young archaeology professor at Aarhus University in Denmark was delivering a lecture when he was summoned to the telephone. Some men cutting peat, the caller told him, had found a body: would he like to see it? Within minutes the professor, Dr. Peter Wilhelm Glob, was on his way with several students to Tollund Fen, a peat bog about thirty-five miles west of Aarhus. There, seven feet down in a cut, a human foot and shoulder protruded from the wall of peat. When more peat was removed, a bowed head came in view. And as dusk fell, a dark-brown man took shape, curled up on his side as if sleeping, and naked except for a leather cap and belt.

So little decayed was this corpse (see opposite page), so well preserved by iron-bearing acids in the peat and by its total insulation from air, that its discoverers had concluded it was that of someone recently murdered, and alerted the police. But Glob knew that a hundred or more bodies, stained brown by the peat, had turned up within the previous two centuries in the bogs of Denmark, northwest Germany, and the Netherlands; he therefore guessed that the man had lived and died during northern Europe's Iron Age, around the beginning of the Christian era. And, indeed, microscopic examination of pollen in the surrounding peat dated his burial to about two thousand years ago.

Tollund man's head and face (above) were uncannily lifelike in appearance: his eyes were shut, and though his brow was furrowed, his expression was serene. This impression of tranquillity was shattered, however, when, on removing a lump of peat from beside the head, the excavators found, around the neck, a noose of twisted leather thongs pulled chokingly tight. "After this discovery," Glob later wrote, "the wrinkled forehead and set mouth seemed to take on a look of affliction."

Clearly, this man had been hanged or strangled, then dumped in the bog. But by whom, and why? Before an attempt could be made to answer these questions, the body had to be carefully repacked in the same peat, crated, and shipped off to the National Museum in Copenhagen for study and further preservation; that done, Glob and other Danish archaeologists launched a concerted inquest into the mystery.

Had Tollund man been executed for some crime? Glob thought not because, unlike some other "bog bodies," this bore no signs of violence other than the marks of the noose. The Nordic peoples, until they turned Christian many centuries later, associated hanging less with punishment than with offerings to their gods. For the same reason it likewise seemed improbable that the man had been the victim of foul play. From the start, then, the signs pointed to his having met his end in a pagan ritual, as a human sacrifice to appease the gods and help assure their favor toward those who survived him.

The man's nakedness presented no problem: he had presumably worn trousers and a tunic of linen or some other fiber-based fabric, gathered in at the waist by his belt, which had quickly disintegrated. Nor did the absence of material objects about him imply a mean or squalid death; for, as the ancient Celts reasoned, why would a person entrusted to the keeping of a god or goddess want or need possessions? The absence of heavy branches weighing him down or stakes arranged so as to pin him in place made it plain that his slayers had no fear of his possessing an evil spirit that might return to haunt them. Then there was the question of his place in the community. As chance would have it, his hands were decom-posed, but the well-preserved palms of other men buried in the same or similar circumstances very often proved to be smooth, the palms not of hardworking peasants but of members of a privileged leisure class.

Was Tollund man a priest, then? If so, in the service of what god or goddess? No one can say for certain, but the investigation did finally turn to the question of the deity to whom he was sacrificed. Here, two clues shed light. The first was the finely worked leather noose, reminiscent of the neck ring appearing in representations of the Earth Mother, Nerthus, as her only adornment. The second was the dead man's last meal, eaten twelve to twenty-four hours prior to his sacrifice, the remains of which were still in his digestive tract. "It consisted," Glob has written, "of . . . just those grains and flower seeds which were to be made to germinate, grow and ripen by the goddess's journey through the spring landscape." Since it contained no trace of summer or autumn fruits, Tollund man must have been killed in late winter or early spring, the right season, obviously, for propitiating the divine being who could grant or withhold the gift of fertility—and survival.

And so, on what was more likely than not a raw, chilly day, Tollund man may have given up his life, perhaps even willingly, for his fellows' sakes, and succumbed to the clammy embrace of the Earth Mother. She, in return, kept him largely intact for twenty centuries, and may even now be watching over his preserved head, on display in a museum six miles from the spot where it first came to light.

On the island of Crete in the third and second millennia before Christ there lived a people of uncommon grace and elegance. The archaeological remains reveal that their leaders dwelt in open, sprawling palaces with mazelike complexes of rooms. Pictures decorating the walls portray the men with tight metal belts about their midriffs to emphasize their slimness and the women in stiff corselets which pinched their waists and pressed their bare breasts forward and upward. Scenes of festivals show that among the important events in the program was one in which young men and young women leaped over the backs of bulls.

The Greeks of later ages knew of these people, but only dimly, as a mythical race. Legends told that the first king of Crete was a son of Zeus called Minos and that his grandson, also named Minos, became so powerful that his sway extended to far-off Athens: each year the city had to send seven youths and seven maids to his court at Knossos, where they were thrust into the Labyrinth as food for the Minotaur, "Minos' bull," a creature with human body but the head of a bull. This went on until Athens' legendary hero Theseus slew the monster. Perhaps the Labyrinth is a mythical reflection of the Cretan palaces with their maze of rooms, and the Minotaur of the part played by bulls in Cretan religion.

At about the same time, across the water from Crete on the peninsula of Greece, there lived the earliest ancestors of the Greeks. The archaeological remains reveal that they were a warlike people: they dwelt in strongholds on rocky hilltops surrounded by massive walls of stone, and their leaders went into battle resplendent in bronze armor and riding in chariots. They were strong on the sea as well as the land, strong enough, eventually, to sail to Crete and conquer the island. Finally, they in their turn were destroyed, and so completely that, to their descendants, the Greeks of later times, they became as mythical a race as the Cretans—though far more important. For, as we now realize, the warrior-kings who owned the grim castles archaeologists have unearthed at Mycenae, Pylos, Tiryns, and elsewhere,

◄OVERLEAF (pages 64-65): Two stone lionesses stand guard above the main gate to the citadel of Mycenae. From these massive walls warriors went forth to occupy the Minoan palaces of Crete and later to fight the Trojan war. Superimposed in white are letters from the Mycenaeans' Linear B script. HASSIA, PARIS

were the prototypes of Homer's heroes, of Agamemnon, Nestor, Achilles, and the rest of the cast of characters of the great epic of Troy.

Where did these peoples come from, one of them the creators of a unique and beautiful civilization, the other the inspirers of literary figures whose names still stir our imagination? What brought each of them in turn to an untimely and violent end?

Until about a century ago we did not know that either of these peoples even existed. Greek history started with what Herodotus and Thucydides told about; the distant past of the Greeks went no further back than, say, the eighth century B.C., just before they emerge in the light of history, already settled in the cities whose names have become household words—Athens, Sparta, Corinth, and so on. To be sure, the Greek poets, notably Homer, sang of ancient heroes and the interminable war they waged against Troy, but all that, we assumed, was legend. Then, in the 1870s, Heinrich Schliemann began his celebrated excavations, and in a trice the world became aware that what these poets had sung of was to be taken very seriously indeed, that the vague "heroic age" in which Homer's characters lived had been a flourishing period of Greek history. Schliemann had first run across its remains at Mycenae, the city where Homer's Agamemnon, commander in chief of the Greek forces at Troy, was reputed to have held sway; and so he named its people the "Mycenaeans." We have learned since that the civilization he uncovered included many more centers than just Mycenae, but the name has stuck, though some writers, to avoid ambiguity, have switched to "Achaeans," Homer's name for the Greeks. Achaeans or Mycenaeans, both mean nothing more or less than "Bronze Age Greeks," the Bronze Age being roughly 3000 to 1200 B.C.

In 1901 archaeological history repeated itself: Sir Arthur Evans, digging at Knossos near the northern coast of Crete, came upon the imposing remains described at the opening of the chapter. It was clear that the people he had discovered were not Greek. He could not read their writing, so he had no idea what they called themselves; he dubbed them Minoans, after the famous Minos of Greek legend, and the name has stuck.

Since the days of Schliemann and Evans, excavation has gone on steadily, and the finds have been

studied from all possible angles. As a result, we have been able to form some idea of the way of life of both peoples and the vicissitudes they passed through.

The Minoans were the first to reach maturity. Their civilization got under way about 2800 B.C., but for some eight hundred years they lived a humble, undistinguished existence. About midway during this period appear the first signs of a rise in their fortunes: rich jewelry turns up in excavations, and there are indications of contact with Egypt across the water. Then, with inexplicable suddenness, the Minoans take a giant step out of their simple village communities into sophisticated urban complexes. At various centers, including Knossos, palaces begin to rise. By 1700 these have reached a peak of development, have become monumental two-story buildings surrounding a vast central court, the ground floor accommodating workrooms and storerooms and chapels and living quarters, and the upper, reception and dining halls. Walls were plastered and decorated with paintings, and the facilities included the nearest thing to modern plumbing the ancient world was ever to produce. What banquets took place were served on dishware of superb quality. These edifices were palaces pure and simple, elegant places to house the ruling figure and his operations of government, with no thought given to defense. They were the likes of Versailles, not London Tower.

The men who put up these imposing structures did not gain the wealth to do it by the sword, for nowhere do we find pictures of fighters and fighting, which are practically the artistic stock-in-trade of Crete's neighbors in the Near East. There are no warriors' trappings in the tombs, and fortifications are conspicuously absent throughout the island. Apparently the Minoans feared no foreign enemies and were so peaceable by nature they did not even fight with each other. Their money must have come from overseas trade; archaeologists have uncovered their pottery in Egypt, the Near East, and Aegean Islands, and Greece, enough of it to prove steady contact with all these places. They were remarkable not only in their unwarlike way of life but in their art; with its use of spiraling, swirling shapes, its interest in the beauty of movement, and its predilection for nature's forms, it is totally unlike any other before or since. The paintings on the palace walls show us their love of stately processions, of hunting wild animals, of dancing and acrobatics and the great spectacle of bull-leaping.

The Minoans spoke a tongue all their own, which has resisted all efforts to decipher it. Since they were in steady touch with the Near East and Egypt, they surely knew about both cuneiform and hieroglyphic writing; yet, for several centuries, they were content to remain illiterate. Eventually they gave in, but instead of borrowing one or the other system, as in so much else they went their own way, devising a series of pictographs which, about 1700 or 1600 B.C., they transformed into a set of linear signs. Several hundred clay tablets in this script have been found in the ruins of their palaces about the island, but all we are able to read are the signs that stand for numbers and fractions. There are so many of these, it is clear that the tablets are official government records or the like and not literature. This Minoan system of writing is called by scholars, for lack of any better name, Linear A.

The Mycenaeans—that is, the Bronze Age Greeks —also passed through centuries of humble village life. The remains show that they lived in little houses huddled together and that few people could afford to spare anything of value for grave goods. They remained isolated from all foreign contacts except with Crete. They imported some Minoan pottery, and their own potters liked to copy Minoan shapes for the local ware.

Then, about 1600 B.C., there is a change, as sudden and spectacular as the one Crete had gone through. In the town of Mycenae excavators have uncovered a circle of graves dating from this time which are a world apart from anything earlier. The burials were marked with slabs decorated with incised scenes of men fighting and hunting from chariots, and swords and daggers are prominent among the grave goods. The grave goods in general are of superb quality, the work of skilled craftsmen, and a veritable profusion of the objects are of gold. No question about it, very important persons had been buried there, kings who were honored above all others, who commanded the maximum in wealth and services, and who were particularly proud of their ability with weapons. This extraordinary circle of graves is found only at Mycenae; it must have contained the bodies of founding fathers or the like because it was reverentially maintained during the whole of the city's existence. Around 1500 B.C. another style of burial comes into favor which was even more expensive since it involved a monumental tomb built up of carefully hewn stone

As the lion was the emblem of warlike Mycenae, so the bull was the symbolic animal of Minoan civilization. This head is one surviving fragment of a large painted relief at the palace of Knossos. As the embodiment of male potency, the bull probably figured in fertility rites.

blocks to resemble a gargantuan beehive, the whole being buried under a mound. The biggest one, popularly called the Treasury of Atreus, although it is a tomb and not a treasury and no one knows who was buried in it, was erected in the fourteenth century B.C. at Mycenae: it is 48 feet in diameter, 43 to the tip of the dome, and the doorway is topped by a lintel made of a single stone that weighs perhaps 100 tons. Greece had seen nothing like these structures before; indeed the ancient world was not to see a bigger round building until the Roman emperor Hadrian put up the Pantheon fifteen hundred years later. These tombs were for the ruling dynasties (far more modest affairs took care of the nobility), being reopened whenever a member died. About 1400 B.C., the lords of the land expanded their architectural interest to include equally imposing residences for their life on earth: at Mycenae, Tiryns, Pylos, and other centers, archaeologists have uncovered the remains of great palaces, all dating to this time. These, however, are not at all like the Minoan, not pleasant and open, but massive, frowning structures cased in ponderous walls, a combination of palace and fortress. It is easy to see how the kings who ruled from such palaces and were buried in the mighty round tombs could become the prototypes for the heroes of Homer's epics.

Though the town of Mycenae was probably the richest center of the Bronze Age Greeks, others like Pylos, Tiryns, Athens, and Thebes were not far behind. Each seems to have been capital of a petty kingdom rather than lord of its neighbors, although, to judge by the nature of the palaces and other fortifications, it may not have been for lack of trying. The wealth for all the large-scale building came, as had the Minoans', from overseas trade. Archaeologists have traced the trail of Mycenaean pottery even farther, not only from Crete but from Sicily and southern Italy in the west to Asia Minor, the Levant, and Egypt in the east. The Mycenaeans, it would appear, had taken over Minoan trade and expanded it; with their taste for war, they probably added the profits of piracy and raiding to their legitimate gains.

The Minoans had made their great leap into a rich and complex way of life three centuries before the Mycenaeans, and the latter were aware of its attractions even during their humble days; when they, too, became rich and powerful, they took from Crete as prodigally as young America did from Europe. The Minoan way of painting inspired their art, Minoan palaces gave them their taste for architecture on the grand scale, Mycenaean ladies dressed *à la minoenne*, Mycenaean scribes used a system of writing adapted from the Minoan, the system scholars call Linear B. Since Linear B tablets—that is, tablets written in the early form of Greek that the Myceneans spoke—have been found in the palace of Knossos after 1450 B.C., amid signs of burning and pillage, we can only conclude that the Bronze Age Greeks, having taken over the Minoans' trade, art, dress, and script, topped it all off by taking over their land, or at least a part of it.

Then, about 1300 B.C., Mycenaean Greece itself came upon hard times. By the end of the century or shortly after, its cities, fortresses and all, were in ruins, its art had degenerated, the technique of writing had been forgotten, impoverishment was widespread—in a word, the brilliant age had come to an ignominious end.

From roughly 2000 to 1200 B.C., then, two peoples in succession dominated the Aegean and eastern Mediterranean, the Minoans and the Mycenaeans. To trace their history, all we have to go on are the archaeological finds; the tablets of the Minoans, as mentioned above, have not yet been deciphered, and those of the Mycenaeans are but haphazard, brief, and bald palace records. And though the finds are rich, pottery and grave goods and ruins of buildings and the like can only tell us that a people was prosperous or poor, was isolated or in touch with others, had lived undisturbed or had suffered destruction, not why it was rich or poor, why it went in for foreign contacts, what was the nature of these contacts, why it suffered destruction. We can guess that the Minoans must have been a skilled seafaring people to have gained through overseas trade the surplus wealth that enabled them to build their fine palaces. We can guess that the Mycenaeans must have been equally skilled as seafarers—perhaps the art of the sea was another of the many they learned from the Minoans. And, since they had a taste for fighting that the Minoans lacked, they very likely were seafighters as well; their warlike accomplishments, as we know, included landing on Crete and seizing territory there. But how did they get to Greece in the first place? Or the Minoans to Crete? When? Who was there when they arrived and what happened to them?

The athletic feats of bull-leapers (see pages 76-77) in-
spired Minoan artists. The ivory carving at left repre-
sents a jumper in midair; the bronze at right shows a
jumper landing on the bull's back.

I n March, 1970, a three-day conference was held
in England at which specialists in Greek archaeology
and language from all over Europe and America were
brought together to present their views on "Bronze
Age Migrations in the Aegean." From the outset it
was clear that the participants were almost exclusively interested in a very particular migration: the one
that had brought the Greek people – that is, the first
people who spoke the Greek language – into Greece.
Sometime toward the end of the meeting, one
member was moved to take the floor and announce
gloomily that "since in the few days of this archaeo-
logico-linguistic colloquium we have heard the
Greeks being brought into Greece from every direction save the south and in every post-mesolithic millennium B.C. except the first, one conclusion emerges

with tremendous clarity: neither archaeology nor
linguistics can tell us anything for certain about the
movements of people." He might have added that
that was not going to affect in the slightest the intention of archaeologists and linguists to keep on trying.

Now, Greek is one of the Indo-European languages, so who the Greeks were and whence they
came is bound up with the larger question of the
Indo-Europeans, itself big enough to merit a chapter
all its own (Chapter 11). What concerns us here is not
from where and when the group of Indo-Europeans
who were eventually to become the Greeks set off on
their wanderings but rather the end of their trail:
from where did they enter the Greek peninsula and
when was it? Their entry might have been quick and
violent, an invasion, or slow and gradual, an infiltra-

tion. Either way, we can only look to the excavators for help, and this raises a knotty point: is it possible to establish a connection between archaeological remains and language? If people speaking a certain language enter and settle down in an area, will this necessarily be reflected in the archaeological record? What if they prefer to use the kind of dishware they find in their new homeland instead of continuing to use their own, or decide that the way the natives bury their dead or build their houses is better than their own? Conversely, does a change in the archaeological record necessarily reflect the arrival of a new people speaking another language? Is it not possible that a settled population, sparked by trade or travel or what have you, will of their own accord change their dishware or burial methods or house design?

Two generations ago archaeologists never doubted that the connection existed. And in the case of the Greeks, they found it in a kind of pottery called Minyan ware. Back in 1873 Schliemann, while digging at Orchomenus in central Greece, uncovered a good deal of pottery that was mostly grey with a distinctive soapy texture; he christened it "Minyan" in honor of Minyas, who, according to Greek legend, ruled Orchomenus and its people, the Minyans. By the end of the 1920s a lot of Minyan ware had been found, all consistently dating just after the beginning of the second millennium B.C. and later. Suddenly things seemed to fall into place: Minyan ware must be the pottery the Greeks used; so these arrived in the Greek peninsula just about 1900 B.C., probably from the north.

This view held the field right up to a decade or so ago. Then Minyan ware, or what seemed to be it, began to turn up in quantity in Asia Minor dating several centuries earlier. Forthwith a new theory: the people who would eventually become the Greeks did not enter the peninsula from the north. In the course of their wanderings from the Indo-European heartland, they came at some point to Asia Minor, where they settled down, leaving the telltale remains of their presence, Minyan ware. Then from Asia Minor they made their way by sea to Greece, where we again pick up the spoor of their Minyan ware. This theory just about had time to get enshrined in the new edition of the authoritative *Cambridge Ancient History* when not only it but the whole convenient linking-up of Greeks with Minyan ware came under deadly fire. Early forms of Minyan ware, say today's

HERAKLION MUSEUM, CRETE

This faïence figurine, with a snake in each hand, is probably the Minoan earth goddess.

experts, can be detected right in Greece itself, in excavation levels dating about 2500 to 2300 B.C. And let us have no more talk of its connection with the arrival of the Greeks. It marks only a local technological achievement: whoever were living in central Greece learned to make a new kind of pottery.

So much for the theory that brought the Greeks on the scene around 1900 B.C. As a matter of fact, aside from Minyan ware, there had been little else to support such a date. It is marked by no significant break in the archaeological record, no level showing indications of widespread destruction that one could tie up with the arrival of invaders. A much better case could be made for a period several centuries earlier, 2200 or 2100 B.C. A number of Bronze Age sites in the neighborhood of Argos—Tiryns, Lerna, Assine,

71

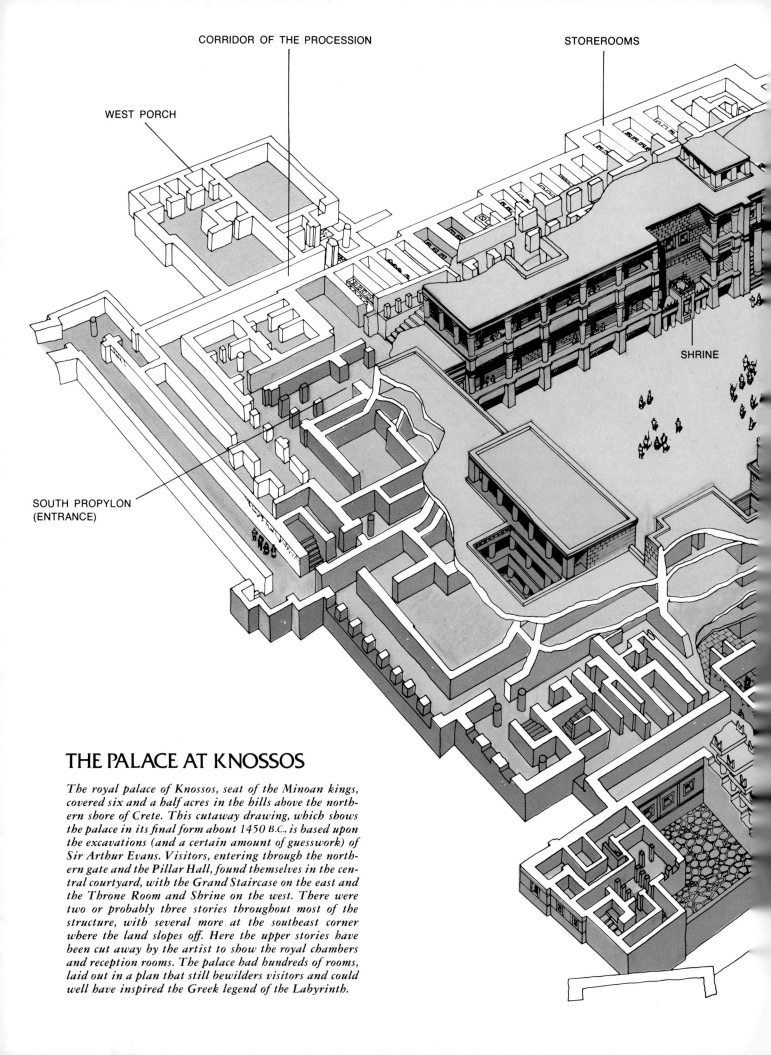

CORRIDOR OF THE PROCESSION

STOREROOMS

WEST PORCH

SHRINE

SOUTH PROPYLON
(ENTRANCE)

THE PALACE AT KNOSSOS

*The royal palace of Knossos, seat of the Minoan kings,
covered six and a half acres in the hills above the northern shore of Crete. This cutaway drawing, which shows
the palace in its final form about 1450 B.C., is based upon
the excavations (and a certain amount of guesswork) of
Sir Arthur Evans. Visitors, entering through the northern gate and the Pillar Hall, found themselves in the central courtyard, with the Grand Staircase on the east and
the Throne Room and Shrine on the west. There were
two or probably three stories throughout most of the
structure, with several more at the southeast corner
where the land slopes off. Here the upper stories have
been cut away by the artist to show the royal chambers
and reception rooms. The palace had hundreds of rooms,
laid out in a plan that still bewilders visitors and could
well have inspired the Greek legend of the Labyrinth.*

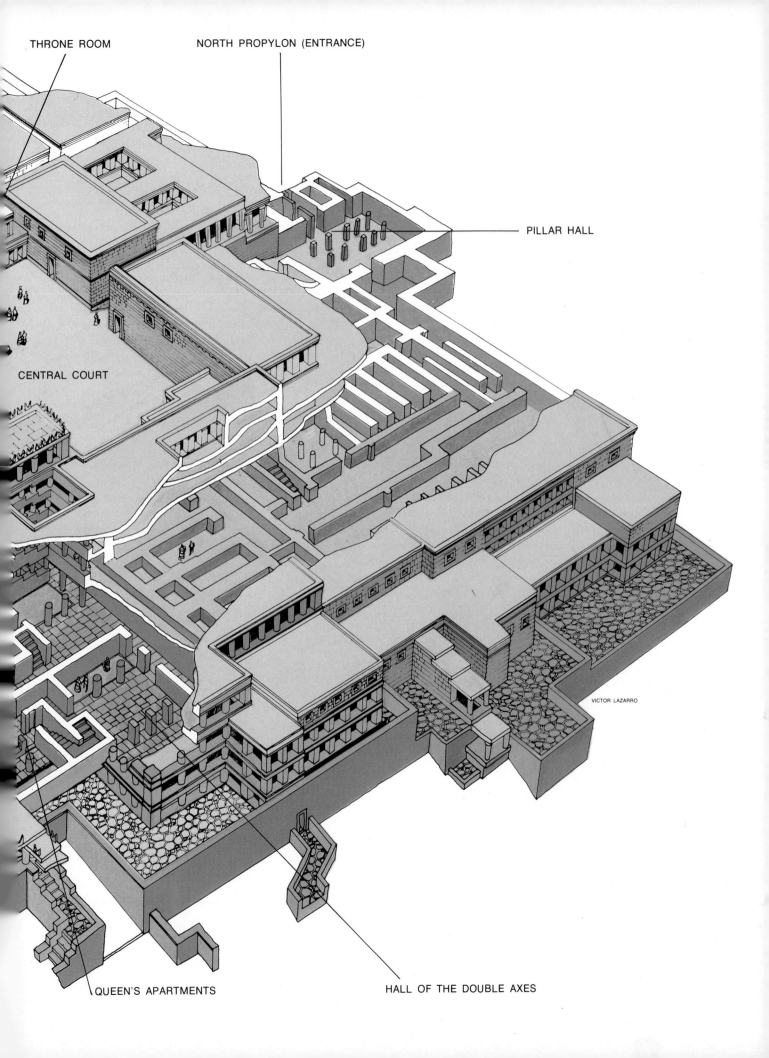

THRONE ROOM

NORTH PROPYLON (ENTRANCE)

PILLAR HALL

CENTRAL COURT

VICTOR LAZARRO

QUEEN'S APARTMENTS

HALL OF THE DOUBLE AXES

This alabaster throne (opposite) in the palace at Knossos was last occupied by a Minoan ruler about 1450 B.C. (The mural, with a guardian griffin, has been much restored.) At left below is a bathroom with stone tub. The palace had a system of running water, drains, and even, in the queen's quarters, a flushing toilet—amenities not known anywhere else until a thousand years later.

to name the clearest examples—all show a level of destruction dating about this time, followed by levels in which there are noticeable innovations—different kinds of pottery, different style of burial, imports from abroad. It all seems to add up to the arrival of strangers on the scene. The cautious leave it at that, but bolder spirits identify the newcomers as Greeks.

Archaeology, like so many phases of human endeavor, has its fashions, and invasion at the moment is somewhat *démodé*. Even those who call these newcomers Greeks do not think of them as flooding into the peninsula like Hunnish hordes but only as the first of a steady stream of migrants who, over the years, settled down and carved a place for themselves amid whatever peoples were already living there. Another very recent school of thought takes a still harder line and recognizes neither hordes nor migrants, not in 2200 or 1900 or any other time. Whatever destruction appears in the archaeological record, they say, is not enough to justify raising the cry of the invaders; a burned palace can be the work of a careless cook as well as a ruthless enemy. As they read it, there are no significant signs of interruption from the

earliest traces of settled communities in Greece, about 6000 B.C., right down to the end of the Mycenaean civilization, around 1200. They can point to Crete as an historical parallel. There—and no one contests the fact—the remains reveal an unbroken continuity. Around 3000 B.C. we find indications of something new, but not invaders, just a minor influx of peoples from Asia Minor say some, from the Levant say others. No large-scale arrival of non-Minoans can be identified on the island until the Mycenaeans, shortly after 1450 B.C., marched in and took over Knossos.

Now, since no one knows what the Minoans spoke, language can play no part in unraveling their history. But it very much plays a part when it comes to the Greeks. If one argues that the population of Greece never changed, then the people who arrived in 6000 B.C. must have been remote but direct ancestors of the people we find there in the Bronze Age talking Greek. At this point the linguistic experts step forward to enter a demurrer: they are unhappy about the idea; it does not fit in well with the total solution of the Indo-European question to have the future speakers of Greek in the peninsula that early.

To balance those who deny us invaders of any sort, there is a small group who offers us invaders far more picturesque than mere users of Minyan ware. Remember that the Mycenaeans' great leap forward was marked by the appearance of an upper crust of warriors who went in for fighting and hunting from horse-drawn chariots and who were buried in elaborate circular tombs under big mounds, "tumuli" to use the technical term. On the lower Volga steppes of south Russia archaeologists have identified a people, the so-called Kurgans, who go as far back as the fifth millennium B.C. They were a pastoral folk with a love of horses, a taste for fighting, and the habit of burying their dead under tumuli. According to their most enthusiastic proponent, Professor Marija Gimbutas, the Kurgans somehow learned to be as adept with ships on the seas as with horses on land, they became the "Vikings of the fourth millennium B.C." By land and sea they flooded from their Russian homeland all over the Balkans and eastern Mediterranean as far as Italy, entering the Greek peninsula about 2300 B.C. Others who share her views are more cautious and have the Kurgans embark on their wanderings much later, about the middle of the third millennium B.C., and hold within limits the extent of their operations.

74

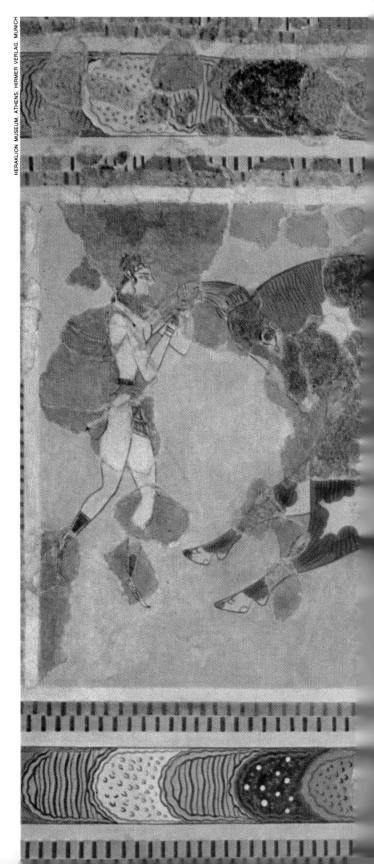

But all are convinced that these are the founding fathers of the Mycenaeans. Some would have it that they came in two distinct waves: the earlier arrivals during the third millennium B.C., were the first people who spoke Greek in the peninsula; the later newcomers, just before 1600, set themselves up as masters of their brethren who had come before them and had created the small but powerful and wealthy states which interred them in such magnificence.

However, the scholarly world as a whole is not exactly ready to swap Minyan-ware folk for Kurgans. As one reviewer has remarked tartly, "Kurgans in south Russia are very well, and so is a Kurgan sphere spreading into parts of eastern Europe as described by Professor Gimbutas . . . nor are third millennium and later movements out of Russia in dispute; but it is plain misleading to label burials under round heaps of earth, of whatever kind, and however distant, as some writers do, 'Kurgans,' and therefore to link them with south Russia."

So one has one's choice. Bring the Greeks in as early as the seventh millennium B.C. to remain in undisturbed occupation of the peninsula for millennia. Or bring them in during the second half of the third millennium B.C., either as a slowly infiltrating group probably by land from the north or as a fast-moving pack of Kurgans by land and sea, with a later wave of particularly pugnacious hard-riding members to explain the Mycenaean warrior class that appears around 1600. Unquestionably, future writers will add still other options.

Turning to Crete, we discover that we have hardly any options. Three-quarters of a century of excavation and study have not unlocked the secrets of this gifted people who spoke a language all their own, worshiped gods all their own, developed an art and architecture and style of writing all their own. Those who bring the ancestors of the Greeks to Greece around 6000 B.C. have suggested that the ancestors of the Minoans moved into Crete from Asia Minor at about the same time, and even argue that that mysterious language of theirs was, like Greek, some form of Indo-European. Few, however, are convinced, least of all the linguists. We simply have no idea who the Minoans were or what triggered the development of their very special civilization.

Having emerged from the darkness that envelopes and obscures the birth of the Minoans

This mural of two young boxers was buried for more than 3,000 years after the explosion of the volcano of Thera. Unearthed and reconstructed from fragments, it shows each of the boys wearing a single boxing glove, the first such gloves known. The current excavation of the ancient city, lying under as much as 200 feet of volcanic ash, has proven that Thera was a cultural satellite of Minoan Crete.

and Mycenaeans, we plunge into the equally murky circumstances that surround their death.

The Minoans' end came first. By 1450 B.C. there were unmistakable signs of destruction all over the island, and shortly after 1400 the civilization that had glowed so brightly diminishes into the dim flicker of low-level village existence.

About seventy-five miles or so north of Crete is Thera, a small island distinguished by a vigorous volcano which has had a strenuous career over the centuries. Just about the time that Minoan civilization was approaching its end, it erupted more violently than even Krakatoa during the notorious explosion of 1883. The whole center of the island disappeared into the sea; a blanket of ash, in places almost a hundred feet thick, covered what was left, totally burying an entire town; and ash was blown all the way to Crete, as we can tell from test cores bored into the sea floor roundabout. For some archaeologists Thera offers the perfect solution to the mystery of the Cretans' demise: they were killed by ash that smothered animals and vegetation and by eruption-induced quakes that toppled and burned buildings. As usual, there are others to argue that there is little or no connection. These are the positions taken by professionals who have studied the finds and have at least some respect for the laws of evidence and logic. Less inhibited souls have seized upon the eruption to explain the legend of the lost Atlantis. The story of a sunken continent, they hold, was inspired by the chunk of Thera that was swallowed up by the waters; or, more generally, by the presumed destruction of Minoan civilization after the big blow. Others find in the explosion of Thera an explanation for the story in Exodus of the parting of the Red Sea that drowned Pharaoh's army. It was inspired, they propose, by the tsunami, the post-explosion tidal wave, which presumably reached all the way to Egypt.

There is no question that Crete was hit and hit hard about 1450 B.C. Palaces and towns all over the island were destroyed, and thereafter many of the towns and all the palaces save Knossos were abandoned. This was thoroughly refurbished and reinhabited—but not by Minoans, by Mycenaeans. We find not only their typical warrior-style burials but, to clinch the identification, tablets written in Linear B, that is to say, Greek. Then, shortly after 1400 B.C., Knossos was struck again, this time fatally.

Where does Thera come in? Either everywhere or

The modern island of Santorini is the remnant of ancient Thera. The explosion of its volcano in 1600 B.C. left a deep harbor where the cone-shaped mountain had been. Some scholars believe that hot ashes and a tidal wave from the explosion destroyed the Minoan centers on Crete 70 miles away, but the dates do not match. Others identify Thera with the "lost continent" of Atlantis.

HAROLD E. EDGERTON

nowhere, depending on how one dates the sequence of events. Archaeology has revealed that the Minoan town on the island was a thriving community whose houses were decorated with splendid frescoes. Sometime before the great eruption, the volcano must have begun to act up menacingly enough to scare people away from their homes, for the excavators have found no bodies in the ruins of the town, not even any valuables. Things then must have quieted down so that clean-up squads could be sent in—we have found the stone hammers they used for knocking down weakened walls—but not for long. Then came the big blow that sent half the island to kingdom come, buried the town, and spewed ash as far as Crete.

The latest style of pottery found under the ash dates about 1500 B.C., so that presumably fixes the time of the disaster. The palaces in Crete, however, to judge from the style of pottery just under their destruction levels, were hit about 1450. Some people solve this discrepancy in half a century by arguing that the big blow really took place later than 1500, that there are distinct archaeological indications of a considerable lapse of time between the moment people fled the town and the great explosion. That is why there is such a gap between the latest pottery in the town and the latest in the palaces just before their destruction: for quite a while the Therans must have been drinking, cooking, and eating somewhere else, not in their houses. The argument, of course, hinges on the evidence for the interval between eruptions, and as so often happens, this is controversial. On the

house ruins there seems to be, here and there, a thin layer of dirt overlain by volcanic ash; the dirt, it is claimed, is the result of weathering, and weathering needs time to take place. Not at all, runs the counter-argument, the dirt is merely debris of some sort, perhaps the crumbling of parts of the mud-brick out of which the houses were made, and cannot be taken as proof of weathering.

Others try to plaster over the difference in date. One way is to tinker with the dates of the pottery, bringing the pottery from Thera down to 1470 and that from Crete up to the same date. Another way is to attribute the destruction on Crete not to the eruption itself but to its after-effects, notably the tsunami, which, it so happens, needs not follow hard upon an eruption but may be caused by a geological collapse years, even decades, later. However, some of the affected palaces are hundreds of feet above sea level—one as much as 1,235—and that seems too high for any tsunami, no matter how big, to get to. And even palaces near the shore show no signs of damage by water, only by burning.

On the opposite side of the fence are those who insist on the difference in date and draw the inevitable inference: the eruption at Thera, no matter how attractive it appears as an explanation of the destruction on Crete, had nothing to do with it. To bolster their case, they point to the palace of Kato Zakro in eastern Crete, destroyed by raging fire and abandoned; there fragments of volcanic glass, which geologists are certain came from Thera, seem to have turned up *under* the destruction level, and that would

MARBURG ART REFERENCE BUREAU

mean the palace's end came *after* the big blow. They can also bolster their case with the latest radiocarbon dating. Radiocarbon tests were made on material from Thera, and the results seemed to agree well enough with the dates based on the pottery. But we have recently come to realize—we treated this matter in more detail in Chapter 2—that the radiocarbon method consistently underestimates, that its figures must be revised upward. The new radiocarbon date proposed for the eruption on Thera is about 1600 B.C.— which would eliminate any possible connection with the destruction on Crete. If, then, the disaster that hit the island was not nature's doing, it can only have been man's. We know that Mycenaeans are shortly afterward installed at Knossos; either they or some

other invaders must have been the culprits.

What happened next is too obscure even to supply fuel for argument. The Mycenaeans at Knosssos could have stayed there only until a decade or so after 1400, because at that time the palace suffered total destruction. This, unquestionably, was the work of men, but which men, whether other Mycenaeans, invaders from elsewhere, or revolting Minoans trying to drive out their oppressors is anybody's guess. Whoever delivered the blow, it was enough to reduce Crete to a humble existence and remove it from the mainstream of history for centuries.

So much for the last days of the Minoans. Now it is the turn of the Mycenaeans. Here we have other than just archaeological clues to follow. There are the Linear B tablets, which have been found at Pylos and Mycenae and a few other Mycenaean centers, as well as at Knossos; there are references—hardly crystal clear but more eloquent than mute stones and pottery—in Hittite and Egyptian writings; and there are the Greek legends, notably Homer's tale of the Trojan War. Unfortunately, instead of clearing the skies, the wider range of information just brings in more clouds by widening the range of possible answers. What ended the great Greek Bronze Age civilization that around 1400 B.C. seemed to dominate the whole of the eastern Mediterranean? Take your choice: Greek invaders, non-Greek invaders, civil war, economic collapse, drought.

We mentioned earlier the change in attitude of today's archaeologists, the dim view they take of conjuring up invasions to explain the vicissitudes of prehistoric peoples. Perhaps their predecessors did rather overdo it, greeting every appearance of a new style of pottery, a new style of burial, a new type of weapon or ornament as the mark of new, hostile faces on the scene—although, in the light of the later history of the Mediterranean or most other parts of the world, you can hardly blame them. In any case, they were certainly convinced that Mycenaean civilization fell before the fire and sword of ruthless invaders.

A century of excavation has revealed that, between roughly 1250 and 1150 B.C., all the great Mycenaean centers were burned and pillaged and eventually totally destroyed. In some, life revived on a very reduced scale, but many died completely. In the Peloponnesus, for example, of 150-odd Mycenaean sites, only 14 continued to show signs of habitation. Clearly, the population of Greece was drastically thinned. Among the survivors, great tombs, palaces, opulent riches, and the like, were things of the past; in levels of 1150 B.C. and later, archaeologists have found only small huddled houses, poor and badly decorated pottery, scant evidence of foreign contact, and no traces of wealth whatsoever.

The civilization did not fall in a day but over the course of almost a century. Around 1250 B.C., at Mycenae, houses outside the city wall were badly hit; at Tiryns, part of the citadel; and the area around Argos was devastated. Between 1250 and 1200 the western Peloponnesus took the beating: at Pylos the palace and town were wiped out, and all of Messenia suffered disastrously. Toward the end of the century came the turn of the east again: this time Mycenae and Tiryns were burned and sacked, as were settlements near Athens, in Boeotia, in Phocis, in Achaea—it was the grand finale of the era of the mighty palace-fortresses.

The archaeological jigsaw puzzle of this age includes one small piece off in Cyprus that can be fitted in very neatly. Excavation at the site of Enkomi there shows, as on the mainland, widespread destruction about 1250 B.C. But this was followed by extensive rebuilding in 1220 or so, and the architecture and pottery reveals it to have been the work of Mycenaeans. They must have been refugees who fled their war-torn land to make themselves new homes overseas.

As we indicated earlier, the generation of archaeologists who dug the Mycenaean sites had no doubts about the cause of the destruction they were laying bare—invaders. But invaders from where? A second wave of Greeks, the Dorians, was one of the suggestions first put forth. The Dorians, during the subsequent historical age of Greece, were a large and important segment of the population; they included, for example, the redoubtable Spartans. Herodotus and Thucydides report a well-established tradition that the Dorians were the latest arrivals on the scene, that they broke into the peninsula from the north and gradually fought their way through the Greeks already settled in it until they ended up dominating most of it. Why could it not have been they, tough and lean barbarians pitted against Mycenaeans softened from years of opulent living, who were the destroyers? This solution, offered almost a century ago, still appeals to many scholars.

But the Dorians are by no means the only candidates. The thirteenth century B.C. was a most troubled age, one in which all sorts of marauding bands, even menacing conglomerations of them, were on the move.

We know this thanks largely to two oft-cited Egyptian inscriptions. The first, erected by Pharaoh Merneptah in 1220 B.C., tells of an unsuccessful attempt to invade Egypt from the west by an army of Libyans who were aided and abetted by certain "northerners from all lands" or, as they are called elsewhere, "peoples of the sea." Thirty years later Egypt faced an even worse threat, as we learn from an account that was inscribed on the side of a temple by Ramses III:

*The foreign countries made a conspiracy in their islands.
... No land could stand before their arms. ... A camp was
set up in one place in Amor [northern Syria]. They
desolated its people, and its land was like that which has
never come into being. They were coming forward toward
Egypt, while the flame was prepared before them. Their
confederates were the Peleset, Tjeker, Shekelesh, Denyen,
and Weshesh. .... The northern countries which were
in their islands were quivering in their bodies.*

The enemy apparently attacked from Palestine both
by land and sea, but Egypt's defenders managed to
send them reeling back. A huge picture illustrates the
battle, and we can see that the Egyptians faced not
just a band of casual raiders but a migrating horde,
for the fighting men are accompanied by oxcarts
loaded down with their families and goods. The
inscription happens to mention that, before descending upon Egypt, the juggernaut had already flattened
the Hittites. The Hittites had been one of the great
powers of the age, maintaining an empire centered
on Asia Minor; now, like the Mycenaeans, they were
no more. Excavation has revealed that their capital
was burned and sacked.

Who made up this murderous mob? Of the peoples listed, the only one we can identify with cer-

*This sleeping lion cub, designed perhaps as a gold pen-
dant, was fashioned on the island of Crete, which had no
lions. In the Mycenaean art of the mainland the lions are
full-grown, fierce, and often larger than life-size (see following pages).*

82

tainty are the Peleset: they are the Philistines, who,
after the defeat at Egypt's border, retreated no farther than southern Palestine and settled there to play
their famed role in the drama of Saul and David. The
Shekelesh may be the Siculi, a people we later find
inhabiting the island of Sicily. The Denyen may just
possibly be the Danaoi, a name used of certain
Greeks. The Weshesh and Tjeker are anybody's
guess.

The Shekelesh, as it happens, were also among the
"northerners from all lands" who had joined with the
Libyans in their attempt on Egypt in the days of Merneptah. This attack, too, was a large-scale invasion of
miscellaneous marauders. The "northerners" included half a dozen races besides the Shekelesh; the
names, in their Egyptian guise which, among other
quirks, cavalierly dispenses with vowels, has given
rise to heated scholarly wrangling. Are the *trs*, usually
vocalized as "Tursha," Etruscans? The *lk*, vocalized as
"Lukka," Lycians? The *srdn*, vocalized as "Sherden,"
Sardinians? Most important, does *ikws*, vocalized as
"Akawasha" or Akaiwasha" or "Ekwesh," represent
an Egyptian's attempt at writing "Achawoi," the
Bronze   Age   Greeks'   name   for   themselves,
"Achaeans," as we anglicize it? Most scholars think so
—which would mean that Bronze Age Greeks were
joining up with the various bands that were on the
prowl toward the end of the thirteenth century B.C.

There are other signs that point in the same direction. We learn from cuneiform documents excavated
from the ruins of the Hittites' capital that the large-
scale movement that delivered the coup de grâce to
them had been preceded by chronic attacks on their
coasts from hit-and-run raiders, among whom was a
particularly annoying bunch, the *Ahhiyawa,* as Hittite
scribes write the name. Ever since the documents in
which it appears were first published, scholars have
been unable to resist the temptation to identify these
Ahhiyawa too with the Achawoi, the Achaeans.

At this point we turn from prosaic archival records
to epic poetry: does not Homer report on Greek
fighting and looting and destroying along the coasts
of Asia Minor? The Trojan War, when you come
down to it, was a concerted raid by a combined force
of Greeks from all the well-known centers of the
Mycenaean world—men of Mycenae led by Agamemnon, men of Pylos led by Nestor, men of Tiryns,
the Minyans of Orchomenus, and so on—upon a rich
and powerful city on the northwest coast of Asia

"I have gazed upon the face of Agamemnon," wrote Schliemann when he found this gold mask in the grave circle at Mycenae. It is indeed the image of a royal personage, buried with him according to Mycenaean custom, but it is 300 years older than Agamemnon, who supposedly led Greek forces against Troy around 1200 B.C.

A lion hunt is depicted in inlays of silver and gold on this ceremonial bronze dagger, found at Mycenae. Four spear-carrying soldiers and an archer meet the charge of the huge beast. The figure-eight shields and tight waist-bands show Minoan influence but the fine inlaid work was a Mycenaean speciality.

Minor. Greek tradition places the war around 1200
B.C., and archaeologists have found at Troy a man-
made destruction level that more or less squares with
this date.

The "peoples of the sea"—that is, the various rest-
less peoples whose movements created such turmoil
in the latter half of the thirteenth century B.C.—
might very well have cut a swath of desolation
through Mycenaean Greece on their way to do the
same to Asia Minor and the Levant. Yet, if they had,
what are Greeks doing fighting at the side of their
enemies in the attack on Egypt in 1220? A possible
answer is that the victors took them along either as
unwilling conscripts or, more likely, eager volun-
teers. This would also explain their appearance in the
Hittite records: Greeks had joined up with the large-
scale movement eastward that ended by wiping out
the Hittites and all but breaking into Egypt.

The expedition against Troy, however, is harder to
explain. The archaeological record shows, beyond a
shadow of doubt, that by 1200 B.C. Mycenaean
Greece had been largely laid waste. Is it conceivable
that precisely at that time the population would be
sending out a numerous well-equipped force to go
adventuring off the coast of Asia Minor? One way
out of the impasse is to assume, as some do, that the
story, though it may have a kernel of fact, is largely
fantasy; Homer, after all, was an epic poet, not a historian. This view, however, makes the archaeologists
uneasy; they point to the many instances in which
their findings have brilliantly confirmed Homer's
words: the riches of Mycenae, the powerful defenses
of Troy (though not its riches), the ultimate destruction of Troy. Another, less drastic way out is to assume that the Greeks in attacking Troy were just
doing more of what is reflected in the Hittite documents, carrying on marauding expeditions. Perhaps
together with some of the "peoples of the sea,"
perhaps under their auspices, Homer, with the li-
cense of a poet, exaggerated the size and make-up of
their forces and discreetly omitted mention of any
authority-wielding allies.

A wave of non-Greeks, then, some or all of those
whom the Egyptians lumped together as "peoples of
the sea" or "northerners from all lands," is a second
candidate, as well qualified as the Dorians, for the
role of destroyers of Bronze Age Greece. Their ir-
ruption into the land would have sent all in their path
running for their lives. Some, as we have seen, found

new homes overseas, in Cyprus and perhaps elsewhere. Others did not have to go so far: archaeologists think they detect signs of refugees settled
around Athens, which somehow was bypassed by the
destruction. And, if the Akaiwasha or Ahhiyawa are
Achaeans, then still others must have followed the
maxim to join whom you cannot lick. The invaders
did not linger long enough to leave any archaeological trace of their presence; having done their
damage, they continued on their way to Asia Minor
and Egypt. Behind them they left a vacuum into
which, some time later, there poured the last wave of
Greeks, the Dorians.

The theory of invaders, Greek or non-Greek, held
the field until just recently, when it ran into the current fashion of explaining prehistory in terms of internal developments as against influences, pressures,
attackers, or what have you, from outside. The anti-
invasion contingents point to the total absence in the
archaeological record of any signs of newcomers.
They emphasize that there is nothing in the Hittite or
Egyptian documents to connect the "peoples of the
sea" with a movement against Greece. They argue
that the long-drawn-out course the destruction took,
extending over a century, does not fit the actions of
hostile bands, who presumably would have moved far
more quickly. And they bring into the picture certain
well-known Greek legends that they think have a
bearing. The story of Agamemnon, for example:
while he was off leading the armies at Troy, his wife
Clytemnestra and her lover Aegisthus seized the government of the city, and when Agamemnon came
home, assassinated him; his son Orestes, on growing
to manhood, paid the usurpers back in their own
coin. Or the story of Odysseus, who, on his return to
Ithaca, had to take up arms against the suitors, that is,
competitors for the crown. Put it all together, say
they, and it adds up to not invasion but civil strife.

This, of course, raises yet another question: why
an outbreak of such strife all over the land after so
many centuries of urban peace? Some offer an answer couched in economic terms: the Mycenaeans'
prosperity was based on their commerce; the well-at-
tested widespread movements, such as those of the
"peoples of the sea," must have disrupted this commerce; the result was unemployment, want, and, ultimately, violence on the part of the have-nots, a
Bronze Age revolt of the masses. Those Greeks we
find fighting with the "peoples of the sea" were the

This is a view of the inside of the dome of the so-called "Treasury of Atreus" at Mycenae, looking straight up from the center of the floor. The circular layers of stone converge at a point 43 feet above the base, making this the greatest dome before the Roman Pantheon. The building was actually used as a tomb.

bolder spirits who left dim prospects at home to seek a better fortune elsewhere.

A variation on this theme has been promulgated by a scholar with a particularly adventurous imagination, Rhys Carpenter. As he sees it, what ended Mycenaean civilization was civil strife, all right, but not triggered by a falling off of trade or any such purely economic consideration. The culprit was nature: melting of the polar ice cap caused a worldwide climatic change, and the wind patterns of the Mediterranean shifted, bringing a deadly drought to the area. One effect was to send the "peoples of the sea" on their wanderings; they were primarily after food, not booty. In Greece it drove starving Mycenaeans off on the same search—hence the depopulation that the archaeologists have noted. Eventually things got so bad that the rank and file, driven by hunger, took the law in their own hands and stormed the palace-fortresses of their betters. The Black Horse of the Apocalypse did the damage, not the Red.

A bold and dramatic plot—but the critics are cool. They point out that the evidence for melting of the ice cap at the end of the thirteenth century B.C. is, to say the least, controversial. They bring up the case of Athens: the archaeological record shows no destruction, and there are even indications, as we noted

above, that refugees settled there; was the drought so discriminating that it bypassed Athens and other regions? And why was the destruction so uneven chronologically and geographically? Did it take longer for the people of Pylos to go mad with hunger? It so happens that, when the palace at Pylos was burned, the administrative records of the year, written in the Linear B script on soft clay tablets, were baked hard by the fire and so preserved, and they give no sign whatsoever that anything was wrong with the agriculture of the realm. Certain sites reveal the taking of defensive measures that included the strengthening of walls and the securing of the water supply; these imply something on the order of large-scale attack, not civil disobedience.

Dought, however, fits in so well with civil unrest that writers who favor this rather than invasion have tried to salvage some of Carpenter's theory. They trim it down from a worldwide climatic change to a modest localized drought, enough to cause the shortages that would make people resort to violence. One ingenious suggestion uses drought to turn the theory of invaders on its head: the drought, it is argued, released enough civil violence to unseat the ruling class not only in the various centers of Greece but in the Hittite world and elsewhere. This created a power vacuum, and into it poured the miscellany of invaders the Hittite and Egyptian documents talk about. In other words, the downfall of the Mycenaeans was not caused by invasion—the invasion was caused by the downfall!

For almost two centuries after the close of the Bronze Age, the Greeks lived a poor and isolated existence. Finally, about 1000 B.C., they began to emerge from obscurity, and within two or three more centuries were moving rapidly into the forefront of history. By that time the glittering age of the Mycenaeans, with its great lords who were elevated far above the rank and file, who lived in opulent splendor, who were mighty warriors and hunters, had been transformed into nothing more than a dim memory perpetuated in Homer's verses.

When the Greeks joined forces to confront the Persians at Thermopylae in 480 B.C., the city of Mycenae could send only eighty soldiers. It had had a great fall, and all the world's archaeologists and all the world's linguists have different ways of putting the pieces together.

88

This arched corridor of massive stones is the entrance to the citadel of Tiryns, a neighboring city in the early Greek culture to which the general name Mycenaean has been attached. Tiryns was the home of Perseus, who became its king, in Greek legend, after cutting off the head of the Gorgon Medusa.

WHO CAN READ THE PHAISTOS DISK?

It is a small, curious artifact—a disk slightly more than six inches in diameter and covered with symbols on both faces. As a glance at the photograph opposite reveals, some images are easily recognizable: a fish, a warrior's head, a bare-breasted woman, and a bird. Others are not so familiar, such as dot-filled circles and triangles and the wide-angled, sideways "V." Altogether, 45 different symbols have been employed in making 241 separate impressions, and these are clustered in groups of two or more into 61 compartments—30 on one disk face, 31 on the other. The compartments are aligned along a spiral that coils into the heart of the disk, so that the owners must have turned it round and round in their hands as they "read" it.

But were they reading—and if so, what? That question has posed one of the most intractable puzzles to archaeologists and linguists since the disk first saw the modern light of day on the island of Crete in 1908. The discoverer was an Italian archaeologist, Luigi Pernier, who was digging at a magnificent Minoan city-palace called· Phaistos. The newly rediscovered Minoan civilization was already yielding up rich vestiges of palaces, labyrinthine passageways, and golden treasure hordes. Excavators also had retrieved thousands of red clay tablets inscribed with the two—equally incomprehensible—scripts of the Minoans, which had been labeled Linear A and Linear B.

Even amidst this archaeological bounty, the Phaistos disk was something special. For one thing, it had been ceramically fired to preserve it, unlike the thousands of tablets that had been baked—and only accidentally preserved—by the destructive fires that had ravaged the palaces. Some scholars argued that it might not be Cretan at all—but no one could point to a likelier place of origin because nothing like the disk had been unearthed anywhere else either. There

was also controversy about whether it should be read from the outer edge inward, or vice versa.

The vast libraries of Crete, containing the multitude of Linear A and Linear B tablets and the Phaistos disk, kept their secrets through decades of brain-wrenching research. Then, in 1953, an amateur British philologist, Michael Ventris, accomplished the stunning feat of deciphering Linear B characters. As thousands of theretofore unreadable Minoan records began to be translated, scholars turned again to the Phaistos disk. Efforts to decipher it followed a pattern: an arbitrary value, or meaning, was assigned to one or more characters, and then a translation was developed, based on frequencies of occurrence and comparison with the syntax and vocabularies of Linear B. The results were often ingenious—and altogether different.

For example, three symbols found together were the serpent's tail, the eagle (bird) and the circle with seven dots. Professor Cyrus Gordon of Brandeis University offered—then later rejected—an interpretation of the three as: "The predatory bird flies over the threshing floor in the town." Two German philologists read the same three as "from the sacrificial drink." A partial translation of the disk by American philologist Benjamin Schwartz rendered it as a sort of road map for pilgrims, describing temples and sacred places of Crete.

In each case, the problem was the same. The philologist might be correct or he might be totally wrong. Without some form of external verification, such as the Rosetta Stone which unlocked the meaning of Egyptian hieroglyphics, attempts to decipher the Phaistos disk remained no more than elegant exercises in linguistic logic.

In 1971, however, a gifted amateur in the Ventris tradition, Leon Pomerance of New York, offered a bold new theory about the disk. Searching for external clues, Pomerance noted that many preliterate societies depicted the cosmos as a circle. He further observed that some figures on the disk resembled images on an ancient Egyptian ceiling from Dendera that was known to be an astronomical chart.

Pomerance decided to test his hunch that the disk symbols were not script at all, but pictorial representations of star clusters. He charted the varying arrangements of three symbols—the serpent's tail, the eagle and the dotted circle—as they appeared on the disk. Then, New York's Hayden Planetarium reconstructed and projected overhead the night-time skies as they had appeared over Crete four thousand years earlier, when the disk was made. And the progressive juxtaposition of constellations known as Serpens Cauda (serpent's tail) and Aquila (eagle) and the Pleiades (circle with seven dots) appeared on the planetarium ceiling in the exact arrangement as they were shown on the disk.

A conclave of experts meeting on Crete has given cautious endorsement to Pomerance's theory: that part of the Phaistos disk was a star chart to be used as a farmer's almanac. When certain constellations appeared in the sky as shown on the chart, it was time to plant or to reap certain crops. Still, Pomerance acknowledges that his researches account for only six of the disk's sixty-one compartments. Plant-like symbols, he suggests, may link to other star clusters as a guide to proper periods for collecting herbs, and other symbols might be celestial guides to navigation. If Pomerance proves correct, whoever ultimately reads the Phaistos disk in its entirety is likely to discover that an ancient scholar created one of the most concise and useful almanacs ever fashioned.

WHAT CAUSED THE SUDDEN RISE OF MODERN MAN?

Between 45,000 and 40,000 years ago something extraordinary happened in the development of mankind. Deposits from that period contain the first skeletal remains of people physically indistinguishable from ourselves; apart from the changes wrought by time, the bones could be found in any modern cemetery or medical school. In itself, this is not very remarkable. What is extraordinary is that these people, within a relatively short time — less than 10,000 years — made themselves not merely the dominant type of human being but the *only* type. The previous human population, commonly if loosely called the Neanderthals, simply disappeared.

Where did the modern men come from? Somehow, somewhere, they must have evolved out of some Neanderthaloid population. And they must have possessed, by genetic chance, some characteristics that gave them an evolutionary advantage over all other living members of the human race. But what could those characteristics have been that enabled them to triumph so rapidly and so completely? This is the mystery that lies at the very beginning of the history of Homo sapiens.

The uniqueness of the sudden appearance of one human type — and the disappearance of another — can be better grasped if we briefly survey some earlier stages in human evolution, and the far slower pace at which they occurred. The first creatures that can be called even approximately manlike turn up in the fossil record of some four to five million years ago. These were the Australopithecines, who for several million years roamed the grasslands and savannas of eastern Africa, from Ethiopia to the South African veldt. In many ways the Australopithecines were apelike; no larger than a modern chimpanzee, with apish, prognathous (protruding) jaws, heavy ridges over the eyes, and small brains. However, they also walked habitually on their hind legs, and their feet could no longer grip objects, as do apes' feet.

Their life-stlye was also something more than apish. Though they must have relied predominantly on plant foods — fruits, shoots, and roots — they also seem to have regularly hunted small game, as no ape

◀ *OVERLEAF (pages 92-93): Archers attack a herd of deer that includes two fawns in this redrawing of a scene painted on a rock wall at Castellon, Spain, between 8000 and 5000 B.C. Superimposed are the stone tip of a spear or arrow and barbed harpoons of bone or antler.*

does (chimps do kill and eat small animals, but very infrequently). They doubtless used a variety of natural objects as tools, as chimps frequently do, but also modified or shaped natural objects to make them more efficient tools, as chimps seldom do. In particular, they hammered pebbles into crude cutting or chopping tools — something no chimp has ever been seen to do. If they were something less than man, they were also something more than apes.

The Australopithecines remained on the scene for at least four million years, during which time they evolved into several distinct species. One of these, dating perhaps from as early as three million years ago, was a relatively large-brained type that some prehistorians call Homo habilis, the "skillful man." How skillful Homo habilis actually was is still less than clear. Certainly he made tools and hunted larger game, but so, it seems, did other Australopithecines of that time. And given the sparse and scattered traces left by this stage in human evolution, it is seldom possible to be sure which tools or animal bones are to be matched with which human skeletal remains. Judged simply on the basis of brain size, however, it seems pretty certain that habilis was the most intelligent animal of the time — though doubtless he was below the level of a modern moron.

Habilis endured for several million years, by which time he had evolved into the still larger-brained Homo erectus. The name, like many zoological terms, is somewhat confusing: erectus stood little, if at all, more erect than habilis, or even the earlier Australopithecines. But the title of Homo ("man") seems beyond cavil. Erectus tools were somewhat better made than those of earlier "men," and moreover continued to improve, though very gradually. Appearing perhaps a million and a half years ago, erectus had, by seven hundred fifty thousand years ago or earlier, spread from Africa into Europe in the north and as far as Java and China in the east. In the process he evolved a key human invention: the use of fire. Initially, fire probably served merely for warmth, but gradually it came to be used to barbecue game and for such simple technologies as hardening the points of wooden spears.

As a hunter, erectus was skillful enough to kill such formidable beasts as elephant and rhinoceros — enterprises which must have involved a degree of planning, cooperation, and communication among members of a hunting band. From this, no less than

from his capacity to use fire — not least to keep the fire burning — one must conclude that erectus possessed the rudiments of foresight: a capacity to cope with future contingencies as well as present necessities. This ability to deal with absent objects and situations is what linguistic specialists call displacement — a trait which they consider a prime hallmark of a true language. It seems very probable, therefore, that erectus must have evolved the rudiments of humanity's most distinctive achievement: a system of noises which served as symbols of absent objects and events, and thereby enabled him, as it does us, to deal with things even when they are not present.

With erectus, the pace of human evolution speeded up somewhat. He held the stage for less than a million years, and during that time evolved very noticeably, with a larger brain and a more sophisticated technology. By perhaps one hundred thousand years ago, in fact, he had become the human type often called Neanderthal, the immediate predecessor of modern man. Technically, the term refers only to the inhabitants of Europe, North Africa, and western Asia, with contemporary human populations elsewhere classed as Neanderthaloid. However, all these people — with a few significant exceptions we shall discuss later — resembled one another sufficiently, in both physique and technological skills, to make Neanderthal a convenient and not grossly inaccurate name.

Without for the moment examining the Neanderthals in detail, we can say that they were biologically successful. They inhabited a whole range of environments, from forest to grassland and from tropical Africa to Europe in the early stage of the last glaciation — the latter a habitat which must have been as demanding as Labrador or western Alaska today. They survived successfully for some 60,000 years — and then, almost overnight, vanished. The earliest remains of modern man date from no earlier than 42,000 years ago; the latest Neanderthal remains, from no later than 35,000. In a mere seven millennia modern man moved to center stage and Neanderthal vanished into the wings.

In seeking to unravel the mystery of why this remarkable event occurred, we must first try and reconstruct *what* occurred. We begin with our cast of characters: Neanderthal, who ruled the earth for some 60,000 years, and modern man, who has ruled

it for the last 40,000 — and may, for all we know, rule it for a million, if he does not ruin it first.

Physically, the Neanderthals were almost completely modern. Most of them were stocky and big-boned, but no more so than many people today, and of course stood fully erect. This fact may come as a surprise to those who have seen Neanderthals depicted as stooped, hulking figures, as much apes as men. The misconception is based on some spectacular blunders by the distinguished French paleontologist, Marcellin Boule, who around the turn of the century made the first detailed reconstruction of a Neanderthal skeleton. From his reconstruction Boule deduced that Neanderthal was "brutish" and "clumsy" with apelike, partly prehensile feet, a shambling, bent-kneed gait, and a mind of "a pure vegetative or bestial kind." A careful re-examination of the same skeleton some fifty years later revealed that Boule had been wrong on almost every count. His "prehensile" feet had been produced by wrongly positioning the skeleton's big toes; the "shambling walk" derived from an equally inaccurate reconstruction of the knee joint. The owner of this particular skeleton must, indeed, have stooped markedly — but only because of a bad case of spinal arthritis.

It seems clear that Boule, expert or not, must have been quite as much influenced by his own preconceptions as by the actual bones in front of him. Like other prehistorians of his day, he was searching for the "missing link" between ape and man. Neanderthal, the leading candidate for that role, must therefore have been very apelike. Moreover, the turn of the century was also a time when many living primitives were seen as something less than human (and therefore, of course, the destined wards of the superior Europeans). One alleged expert even claimed that the Negro "rarely stands quite upright," and possessed a partly prehensile foot — statements which make clear that the man either never saw a Negro or possessed a monumental capacity for seeing what he wanted to see. In this kind of atmosphere, the Neanderthals, more primitive than any living people, must have been seen as even less human.

We now know that only in their skulls did the Neanderthals differ anatomically from ourselves. Their brains, indeed, were at least as large as our own. But the brain, and the skull that contained it, were differently shaped — bulging at the back, and with a low, sloping forehead in front. The eyebrow ridges were

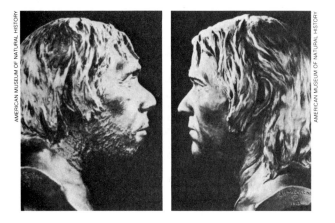

AMERICAN MUSEUM OF NATURAL HISTORY

AMERICAN MUSEUM OF NATURAL HISTORY

© DORLING KINDERSLEY LTD. LONDON

heavy, the jaws massive and prognathous, with a rounded, backward-sloping chin—not exactly what we call a "weak" chin, but certainly a receding one, quite different from the typical, right-angled modern chin. Except for its modern brain capacity, the Neanderthal skull stood about midway between that of Homo erectus and our own.

Just how "human"—in our terms—did the Neanderthal face look? Answering this question involves trying to reconstruct the soft tissues that overlay the skull—and this is a less-than-exact science, with considerable margin for error either way. Thicken the lips a little to push the mouth farther forward, broaden and flatten the nose slightly, and Neanderthal will look distinctly apelike—especially if given plenty of hair on neck and shoulders. Thin the lips, sharpen the nose, and remove the hair, and he is "a man and a brother." Some prehistorians claim that the average Neanderthal, bathed, shaved, and dressed in modern clothes, would attract no attention on a bus—to which another prehistorian has retorted that personally *he'd* get off the bus.

When all is said and done, however, human is as human does. And when we look at the archaeological record of what the Neanderthals did—the implements they fabricated, the ways in which they lived (so far as these can be reconstructed)—they seem remarkably human. In some ways.

To begin with, the animal bones unearthed around their encampments testify that they were skillful hunters. Hunting for food, not sport, they took whatever game was available, but favored the larger species, which gave them the highest return of food per hunter-hour: deer, wild cattle, antelope, gazelle, and zebra, depending on local availability. On occasion

they took more formidable game: the cave bear, bigger than a modern grizzly, the woolly rhinoceros, and even the elephant and mammoth, the latter towering more than twelve feet, better than double the height of its hunters. These daunting creatures may have been met face to face (or face to trunk) but were more likely trapped in pitfalls or maneuvered into swamps, where, immobilized, they could be safely dispatched.

For hunting as well as self-defense, the Neanderthals doubtless possessed spears of fire-hardened wood, as had Homo erectus before them. They probably also fabricated more sophisticated "compound" spears, with keen stone points lashed to wooden shafts. Certainly the points are there in the earth, and if they were not spear points—as their shape and size suggest—it is hard to imagine what else they might have been.

One can, however, make too much of the Neanderthals as mighty hunters. Studies of contemporary hunting peoples show that plant foods invariably make up more than half their diet (unless, as in the Arctic, these are unavailable); there is no reason to think the Neanderthals were any different. They must have gathered tender shoots such as fern or wild asparagus in spring, berries in summer, nuts and seeds in fall, and starchy roots in any season. Small game was probably felled with rocks or with throwing-clubs comparable to the modern boomerang.

How plant foods were prepared—if they were not consumed raw—we cannot know, since all traces of them have vanished. Game was probably barbecued over the family fire, though findings at some Neanderthal sites suggest more sophisticated culinary techniques—apparent "griddles" of flat stones on which a fire could be set, allowed to burn down, and then swept off, so that a venison or mammoth steak could be fried in its own fat and juices. The Neanderthals knew how to make knives and other cutting tools by striking sharp flakes off pieces of flint or other hard rock. Meat, and no doubt other things, was cut with flint knives—sometimes, it appears from scratches found on Neanderthal incisors, by biting into a piece of meat held in one hand and sawing off the bitten chunk with a sharp blade.

These stone knives and most other Neanderthal tools were made by the "flake" method, which in both sophistication and efficiency was a marked improvement over the earlier "core" technique. The lat-

96

Members of a cave-dwelling family attend to their chores. While a man wearing a necklace of animal teeth chips blades for tools from a chunk of flint or obsidian, a woman, presumably his mate, roasts meat. The children help. At the cave mouth skins draped over poles keep rain and wind out of the sleeping quarters.

ter, known since erectus times, involved nothing more intricate than hammering at a lump of flint or other fine-grained rock until it reached the desired shape. In the immediate pre-Neanderthal period, core tools were often carefully and symmetrically fashioned, but the process itself was no more complicated than whittling—a piecemeal but steady progression toward a desired shape. A single "core" of stone would yield only a single tool.

The flake technique probably began simply as a by-product of core technology, when some clever erectus realized that a thin, sharp flake struck off the core could itself be used as a tool. Neanderthal toolmakers, however, learned to prepare the rock in such a way that a whole series of flakes could be obtained from a single core. This was both more sophisticated and more economical: whereas the original core technique would yield no more than about eight inches of cutting edge from a pound of rock, the Neanderthals could get at least forty inches of edge from the same quantity of raw material.

With their stone tools the Neanderthals undoubtedly made other tools of wood, though none has survived. The varied Neanderthal tool kit—whose full extent we can only guess at—was used not merely to kill and butcher game but also to dig up and chop plant foods, and to prepare animal pelts. Neanderthal flake "scrapers," examined under the microscope, show marks of wear indicating that they were indeed used to scrape flesh and fat from hides—the first step in preserving them. Presumably this was preparatory to some primitive tanning technique, perhaps employing animal brains, human urine, or simply smoke —all used by contemporary primitives. There can be little doubt that some of the hides were used as clothing—sometimes, no doubt, merely slit to make a sort of poncho, but sometimes, probably, laced together with rawhide, sinew, or plant roots, thereby producing a warmer, more airtight garment. Stone punches found at some Neanderthal sites suggest this, and in any case it is hard to imagine how, without reasonably airtight clothing, the Neanderthals could have survived in the subglacial regions where some of them lived.

Other hides must have been used for shelter— thrown over a framework of branches to make a crude wigwam, and the sides weighted down with stones or heavy bones. In some places the floor of the hut was dug out well below ground level, providing

further insulation. Though Neanderthal is often thought of as a "cave man," this was true only in the relatively few areas where natural caves existed; in other cold regions, it was build a hut or freeze. Even some cave floors bear traces of huts built *within* the cave for further warmth; in others, the cave mouth may have been closed off with hide "drapes." With these manifold technologies, the Neanderthals survived and apparently flourished in such demanding environments as subglacial Europe, the Russian steppe, the African rainforest, and even parts of central Asia. Simply from a practical standpoint, then, the Neanderthals were successful. But they were more than practical; they possessed considerable imagination and what we would call sensibility. They —or some of them—seem to have been the first people in the world to bury their dead. Moreover, they placed in the graves tools and joints of meat strongly suggesting a belief in an afterlife where the deceased would need food and equipment. One burial, in a cave in eastern Iraq, contained pollen from eight different flowers, including wild relatives of the grape hyacinth, bachelor's-button, and hollyhock. Since the flowers could not have grown in the cave, nor been carried there by animals, it seems likely that the corpse had been strewn with wildflowers gathered on the nearby hillside.

Yet other findings testify to the dawning of ritual and magic. In the Swiss Alps, a Neanderthal cave contains a cache of cave-bear skulls in a sort of box made of natural stone slabs, with other skulls set in niches along the walls. (Bear cults have been described among many recent primitive peoples, from Siberia to the American Arctic.) A dig in Lebanon revealed the dismembered bones of a deer which had been placed on a bed of stones and sprinkled with powdered red ochre—the color of blood. What these Neanderthals were doing we will never know, but there can be little doubt that they were engaged in some sort of magic. Still another variety of sensibility is shown by pencil-shaped bits of mineral pigment, which seem to have been rubbed repeatedly against some soft surface—an animal hide or, more likely, the hide of the hunter himself, or his wife.

From everything they did, in short, the Neanderthals must be classed as human. They possessed a technology sophisticated and diverse enough to let them survive in a variety of habitats, buried their dead with some sort of ritual, engaged in magical

Twenty-seven thousand years have passed since unknown artists painted this piebald horse and another,
partly visible at lower left, in a cave at Pech Merle,
France. The handprints around the animals are thought
to represent the hunter's magical hold over his prey.

rites, and probably adorned their persons with paint.

Yet quite as significant as the things the Neanderthals did are the things they did not do. Though they utilized the meat and hides of four-footed beasts—plus a variety of vegetable foods—they seldom dined on fish or fowl. The contrast with modern man shows up clearly at two caves on the southern coast of South Africa. Both contain materials of Neanderthal date, as well as later deposits that must have been left by modern man. Both levels contain animal bones, including those of the seal and the (flightless) penguin, along with mollusk shells. But bones of fish and flying birds are far fewer in the Neanderthal deposits, suggesting—as the excavator himself notes—that "active fishing and fowling may have been beyond [their] technological capabilities."

Finally, though the Neanderthals may have adorned themselves with paint, they knew nothing of jewelry—beads, bracelets, and the like. The "flower burial" mentioned above suggests that they were not insensitive to the aesthetic qualities of natural objects—yet they made no aesthetic objects of their own. In other words, the whole spiritual and technical province of art, found in some form among virtually all modern peoples, was for them nonexistent.

Surveying the Neanderthal cultures more comprehensively, over the 60,000 years or so they endured, perhaps their outstanding trait is their conservatism. Neanderthal technology, ingenious though it was, consisted primarily of mere improvements on inventions made long before. Though they manufactured flake tools more efficiently and systematically, they were not the first to make such tools. Though their huts were probably warmer than those of their predecessors, those earlier men had been building shelters of some sort for over 100,000 years, as has been shown, for example, in recent diggings on the French Riviera. The only cultural "breakthrough" in Neanderthal times is in the area of magic and ritual—undoubtedly an important exception, but also an isolated one. Though they inhabited the earth for much longer than modern man has been on the scene, their cultures do not seem to have changed in any major way during all that time. Successful they were, but notably innovative they were not.

Where modern men originated, and precisely when, we do not know. Some anthropologists believe that they evolved out of earlier Neanderthaloid populations in several different parts of

Two processions of horses, deer, and bulls (examples of the now extinct aurochs) come together above the entrance to the Great Hall of France's famous Lascaux Cave. Stone Age painters depicted their fellow humans only rarely and rather sketchily, but showed great respect for animals in their careful renderings of them.

the world (see Chapter 7). The prevailing opinion is that the evolution occurred in only one place. In any case, western Europe seems ruled out, despite the fact that the term Cro-Magnon, from a cave in southwestern France where many remains have been found, is often applied to all early humans of the modern type. The fact is that the time gap between Neanderthal and modern remains in that area seems too short for one population to have evolved physically into the other.

On present evidence, the most promising area is the Near East. In the 1930's a number of skulls were dug up near Mount Carmel, Palestine (now Israel), at a site called Mugharet es-Skuhl (Cave of the Kids). None was truly Neanderthal, though some were almost so. Others were more modern, while one—the famous "Skuhl V" skull—was almost modern: smallish brow ridges, higher forehead, rather pointed chin, and less prognathous jaws. The Skuhl site is believed to date from between 40,000 and 50,000 years ago, or right at the end of the Neanderthal period. The skulls may, indeed, have represented crosses between Neanderthals and modern types—but if so, where were the latter? More likely, the Skuhl bones are those of a transitional population,

modern in some respects but not all. By all the laws of evolution, such a population must have existed somewhere, some time, and the Skuhl bones are still its only plausible remains.

Wherever and whenever they originated, modern human beings soon proved markedly different from their predecessors. In looks, to be sure, they probably did not differ radically from the Neanderthals, but their acts amounted to what can fairly be called a cultural revolution. Prehistorians, whatever their personal theories on the rise of modern man, have no disagreements on this. Thus, Robert J. Braidwood of the University of Chicago declares that the late Stone Age cultures "differ markedly from the older traditions ... in that they persisted for much shorter spans of time" and also showed much more regional variety, with five or six regional sequences in France alone. Grahame Clark, the distinguished British pre-

101

The pregnant mare at left is part of a complex mural in a chamber at La Pileta in southern Spain. The fact that Stone Age artists frequently portrayed female animals pregnant attests to their concern for the survival of the creatures on which they depended for food.

Carved from a piece of reindeer antler, this bison licking its flank shows the carver's sophistication in solving a problem in perspective.

historian, is equally definite. The new cultures, he says, were "more dynamic . . . they changed comparatively rapidly and . . . displayed a notable facility for devising artifacts [tools] for specialized functions." All of which can be summed up by saying that modern men were far more innovative than their Neanderthal precedessors. Even disregarding the last 10,000 years, in which the pace of invention has speeded up from a walk to a trot and eventually a headlong gallop, modern men and women, in a mere 30,000 years, produced far more inventions than the Neanderthals had done in twice that long — more, indeed, than the entire human line had produced during its millions of years on earth.

One of their most distinctive inventions was the blade technique of tool-making. The Neanderthals, as we have seen, knew how to strike sharp flakes off a core of flint or obsidian — and a blade is no more than a long, narrow flake. But it was modern man who discovered how to mass-produce them. This was done by preparing a flat top on a core of flint or obsidian and then striking a series of blows around the edge with a stone hammer or a bone punch. Similar blades have been produced by such researchers as Don Crabtree of the University of Colorado: the toolmaker works around the edge of the core in an inward spiral, at each stroke producing another blade until the core becomes too small to handle. The blades have straight and extremely sharp edges — when Crabtree demonstrates the technique, he cautions his audience not to handle the blades lest they cut themselves. More to the point, perhaps, is that whereas the flake technique yielded perhaps forty inches of cutting edge per pound of stone, the blade technique yields between ten and forty *feet*.

Occasionally the blades were used "as is"; more often they were retouched, with delicate pressure from a bone point, into a variety of tools far too numerous even to list. In one small area — the Dordogne region of France — one finds "backed blades," with one dull edge like a modern knife blade; chisel-like "burins," used for cutting and carving wood and bone; "tanged points," with one end narrowed for insertion into a spear or dart shaft; notched blades for rounding the shafts, like a modern spokeshave; narrow-pointed drills or awls, and scrapers of half a dozen patterns. Perhaps the most striking Dordogne tools were those of the so-called Solutrean culture (about twenty thousand years ago), though not all of

these were made of blades. The Solutrean "laurel-leaf" and "willow-leaf" points, shaped as their names suggest, were painstakingly chipped and retouched into thin and beautifully symmetrical forms; some may have been inserted into handles to serve as daggers or short swords, others served as spear points.

Nor did the inventors limit themselves to stone and (presumably) wood tools. As the stone burins suggest, they also fabricated bone, antler, and ivory into useful forms. A bit of bone pointed at one end and deeply notched at the other would serve to tip a spear shaft; a bone rod with a hook carved at one end would be used as a spearthrower or "atlatl," enabling the hunter to fling his weapon harder and farther than with his unaided arm. (One prehistorian has compared the throwing ability of a man with a spear-thrower to that of a baseball pitcher with arms hanging below his knees.) Other pieces of bone were made into harpoon heads, with hooked barbs cut on one side (later, on both). The most sophisticated of these, dating from perhaps twelve thousand years ago, includes a ridge close to the base, suggesting that a cord was tied to the harpoon head (the ridge would prevent its slipping off). When the barbed head was plunged into the hunted animal, the cord would then serve to haul it in — suggesting that the device was used to spear salmon or other large, freshwater fish (the harpoons have been found only at inland sites).

Other inventions imply additional technologies. By 30,000 years ago or earlier, people were making bone needles — at first merely rounded bone slivers, but later with actual eyes. Evidently, clothing was no longer being laced but was cut, fitted, and sewn together, to make snug Eskimo-type garments that would have been welcome in an ice-age winter. It

103

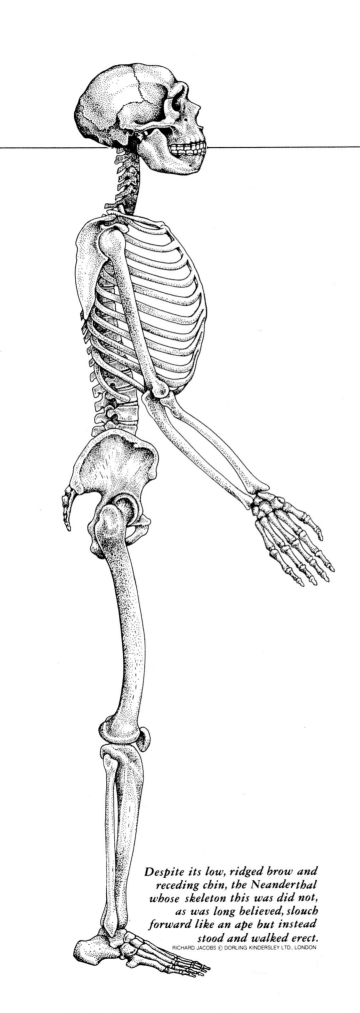

Despite its low, ridged brow and receding chin, the Neanderthal whose skeleton this was did not, as was long believed, slouch forward like an ape but instead stood and walked erect.

must have been garments of this sort, combined with improved versions of the Neanderthal's excavated "pit house," that enabled modern man to colonize the New World by way of the Bering land bridge some 20,000 or 30,000 years ago.

There is no direct evidence when the bow itself was invented. Nonetheless, by some 15,000 years ago or earlier, one finds small points clearly intended to tip very lightweight projectiles—so light that even an atlatl could hardly have given them much striking power. The likelihood that these points were arrowheads is strengthened by a picture on the walls of a Spanish cave dating from a few thousand years later, which shows bows and arrows being used to hunt deer (see pages 92–93). With the atlatl, man had learned to apply the principle of a lever to propel a projectile; with the bow, he had employed what was in effect a spring (the bowshaft) to the same end.

Another key invention, that of boats or rafts, must be inferred from indirect but conclusive evidence: the colonization of Australia some 30,000 years ago. Neanderthal and even erectus skulls have been found as far east as Java, but there is no reason to think that these earlier men traveled by water: during any glacial episode, the shallow straits which separate Java from Sumatra and Sumatra from the Asian mainland would have been dry land. East of Java, however, the gaps between islands were too deep and too wide for swimming. The water craft by which early modern man reached New Guinea and Australia may originally have been devised for fishing, but evidently soon became a means whereby entire families could be transported to new lands.

The cave painting mentioned earlier, no less than the invention of personal jewelry, symbolizes the expansion of human consciousness into an entirely new region: art. As we have seen, the Neanderthals seem to have been sensitive to the aesthetic appeal of flowers and perhaps other natural objects, but their aestheticism was essentially a spectator sport. Modern men became active participants. By 30,000 years ago or so, they were scratching crude sketches of horse and mammoth on bits of stone or bone; in another five or ten thousand years they were drawing on cave walls with bits of charcoal or mineral pigment; and by 15,000 years ago had progressed to vigorous, vibrant paintings of the animals that surrounded them, and on whose meat they depended

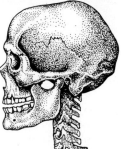

for subsistence: the horses and wild cattle of Lascaux, the charging bison of Altamira in northern Spain, and mammoth, reindeer, elk, ibex, wolf, and lion in endless procession along the walls of a score of caverns.

Prehistorians have vigorously debated the "meaning" of these cave paintings. The traditional theory is that they were a kind of hunting magic, designed to ensure plentiful game and a successful chase. Proponents of this theory point out that the paintings are almost invariably of animals (very few human figures occur before about twelve thousand years ago), and are located in deep and sometimes almost inaccessible areas—places that no one would seek out for everyday purposes. Many of the paintings, indeed, must have been made under the most difficult conditions—not least, the absence of natural light. (This problem, it appears, was overcome by yet another invention, the lamp—a hollowed-out stone, presumably containing rendered animal fat and a wick of fiber, hair, or moss.) The French expert André Leroi-Gourhan has argued that the very arrangement of the paintings, with different animals assigned to different cave areas, was based on some occult principle.

A less dogmatic view is taken by two British prehistorians, Peter Ucko and Andrée Rosenfeld. They also cite studies of modern primitives such as the Australian aborigines which indicate that paintings are made for all sorts of reasons: to work magic, to record some noteworthy event, or simply because the artist felt like painting—art for art's sake, in fact. Some cave drawings, they note, are distinctly erotic (indeed, apart from their sensitive draftsmanship, they are indistinguishable from drawings found in such modern caverns as public washrooms); these, say the two experts, may well have been drawn for no other reason than—eroticism. In art as in other human endeavors, there seems no reason to think the cave artists had motives less diverse than our own.

Be all that as it may, art was almost from the earliest times an important part of the life of modern men. Careful examination indicates that in fact they did not limit their paintings to the deep caverns but also decorated more accessible, residential areas—where, however, the paintings, more exposed to the elements, have largely deteriorated. They modeled animals and human figures in stone and clay, carved them in bone and ivory on their atlatls and other tools. In a mere twenty-five thousand years, they not only invented the basic concept of art but the actual

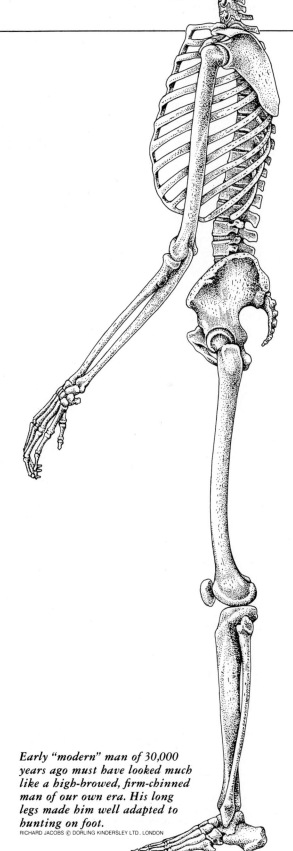

Early "modern" man of 30,000 years ago must have looked much like a high-browed, firm-chinned man of our own era. His long legs made him well adapted to hunting on foot.

RICHARD JACOBS © DORLING KINDERSLEY LTD., LONDON

CELEBONOVIC, GENEVA

techniques of engraving, drawing, painting, modeling, carving in both low and high relief, and sculpture.

Nor was their art only visual. A cave in the foothills of the Pyrenees has yielded no less than eight pieces of hollow bone with fingerholes cut into them —prehistoric "penny whistles" some eighteen thousand years old which are the direct ancestors of the medieval recorder and (at a somewhat greater remove) the modern flute. A few thousand years later, a painter in another French cave depicted a man playing what may have been a musical bow—ancestor of the harp and lute. Another very likely early musical invention is the drum—at first probably no more than a hollow log beaten with a heavy stick or bone, but later perhaps skin-covered like a modern drum.

Perhaps the most enigmatic of all modern man's early inventions is suggested by bones bearing long rows of scratches. Microscopic examination reveals that the scratches were made by stone points of slightly different shapes—and therefore, presumably, at different times. Alexander Marshack, a science writer who has done research in the area, believes that at least some of these bones were calendars with which the makers kept track of the phases of the moon. Not all prehistorians accept this theory, but whatever the makers of these prehistoric tally sticks were doing, they must have been keeping records of something—the moon's nightly changes, the number of animals killed in successive hunts, or even the score of a game whose rules have vanished with its players. In so doing, they were foreshadowing a later and even more revolutionary invention: writing.

The enormous environmental changes which confronted the human race in many regions as the glaciers receded (see Chapter 10) by no means checked the flood of invention; if anything, they swelled it. Europe alone saw the fabrication of fishhooks, specialized fishing spears, nets, and traps to exploit the resources of lake, river, and ocean. The dog was domesticated, though where this first happened is not known. By about 10,000 years ago, human society was on the verge of another cultural revolution, based on the invention of agriculture and stock raising. Within a mere 7,000 years thereafter, mankind would invent pottery, weaving, the plow, the wheel, monumental architecture, and writing. No less striking, as an index of humanity's innovative capabilities, is how many of these inventions were made independently or semi-independently by several different peoples. Pottery was invented independently at least three times—in eastern Asia (probably Japan), western Asia, and Mexico—whereas writing was invented independently in the Old and New Worlds, and reinvented—using altogether different sets of characters—half a dozen times in the former.

It seems clear, then, that modern man—and modern woman too—was above all an innovator, an inventor, a tinkerer who devised new ways of doing things, new techniques of art, often for no other reason than that they *were* new. Far more than the Neanderthals or any earlier people, they were somehow driven to reshape both their environment and their own technologies, sometimes for practical ends, sometimes to fulfill spiritual needs, deep or transitory. And it seems virtually certain that it was this capacity for innovation that produced their spectacularly sudden success. It would, at the very least, have made them much more efficient hunters and food gatherers, thereby swelling their numbers to the point that they could, at best, have absorbed the sparse Neanderthal populations and, at worst, have simply exterminated them as irksome competitors.

But to say that modern men succeeded because they were innovative really says very little; the deeper and far more important question is: why? Some 40,000 to 50,000 years ago, some sort of revolution occurred in the human mind, if we can in any way judge from the products of that mind before and after. What sort of revolution was it? It is here that we get into one of the most difficult and controversial areas of prehistory—the origins of language and the speech of early man.

Theories on the origins of language are many. There is the "Boo hoo" theory, which sees language as beginning with noises made under strong emotion; the "Woof woof" theory, in which it began as imitations of animal noises; the "Look out!" theory of language as a warning system; and the "Yo heave ho" theory of language as a way of organizing group activities. All are at least mildly plausible—and all are totally unprovable. The earliest, most primitive human languages, it has become clear, originated so long ago—up to a million years—as to be undiscoverable by any technique short of a time machine. Indeed, until quite recently many scientific bodies maintained a sort of taboo on even discussing the ori-

CELEBONOVIC, GENEVA

gins of language, feeling that—like perpetual motion—it was simply a waste of time.

Recently, however, a number of scientists—notably, Philip Lieberman of Brown University—have cracked that taboo. They have done so by focusing, not on the evolution of language as such but rather on that of the apparatus that produces it—the vocal tract with which human beings generate the variegated noises that, when suitably combined, say something.

Experiments over the past twenty years have demonstrated that "linguistic capability" of a sort is not limited to our own species. Chimpanzees in particular have been taught to use symbols to represent objects and events, to combine the symbols into meaningful sequences equivalent to sentences, and even to create new sequences that they have never seen before. But the symbols in question are invariably visual, not auditory: bits of plastic of different shapes and colors, or hand signs adapted from the human languages of the deaf. No chimp has ever learned to talk. An important reason, it appears, is that their vocal tracts are not designed for the purposes of human language.

The human vocal tract, like that of other land vertebrates, consists basically of two parts: the larynx or voice box, which contains the vocal cords, and the supra-laryngeal tract, which combines the pharynx—the part of the windpipe just above the larynx—with the oral and nasal cavities. The larynx may have originated simply as a valve for keeping foreign substances out of the lungs, a function it still serves (when the valve fails to close properly, we say that something has "gone down the wrong way"). In man and many other animals, however, it has taken on another function: making communicative noises. When its vocal cords are forced together and air is forced between them, they begin vibrating, producing sounds of various frequencies. The precise frequency will depend both on the individual and on the situation. Shorter or lighter vocal cords, like shorter or lighter musical strings, will produce higher frequencies, as will tenser vocal cords (when we become excited—i.e., generally tense—the pitch of our voices tends to rise). Yet another variable is how vigorously the air is being pushed through the cords; a vigorous push, as in a shriek of fright, will produce a higher-pitched sound. In addition to the basic or "fundamental" frequency, the larynx's sound output also includes harmonics—higher frequencies with a particular mathematical relationship to the fundamental.

In man and some other animals, the fundamental-cum-harmonics signal emitted by the larynx can be modified by changing the shape of the supra-laryngeal tract—e.g., by opening or closing the mouth, raising or lowering the tongue, routing the signal through the nasal passages. The effect is to mute certain harmonics, while allowing others to sound with almost undiminished energy. And it is—to oversimplify somewhat—the particular pattern of unmuted frequencies (called formant frequencies) that enables us to distinguish one speech sound from another, even when the fundamental frequency differs markedly. Thus a singer can sing the vowel AH on any one of two dozen or more different tones (frequencies), yet we still recognize it as that vowel and no other.

For a number of reasons, Lieberman has focused primarily on the role of vowels in human speech. He points out that since a given sound signal is modulated into one of several vowels by changing the shape of the supra-laryngeal tract, then the more flexible and manipulable that tract, the more different vowels can be produced. And it is in this respect that the human vocal tract is unique. In all other mammals, including our closest relatives, the great apes, the larynx lies high in the throat, making the pharynx very short. In effect, the pharynx and oral cavity together constitute a single, slightly curved tube, whose caliber can be manipulated by lifting and lowering the tongue, opening or closing the mouth, and (in a few species such as the chimpanzee) by rounding and protruding the lips.

The human vocal tract, by contrast, is constructed on what Lieberman calls the two-tube model. The larynx lies deep in the throat, making the pharynx almost as long as the oral cavity, with which it forms a right angle. And—here is the key point—*each tube can be manipulated independently.* The pharynx can be constricted by drawing the tongue backward, while the oral cavity remains open, as in the vowel AH. Alternatively, the pharynx can be left open while the oral cavity is narrowed by raising the tongue, as in the vowel EE. Finally, both the oral cavity and the pharynx can be left open, but still separated into two tubes by a constriction between the raised back of the tongue and the back of the palate, as in the vowel OO. Various intermediate degrees of closing the

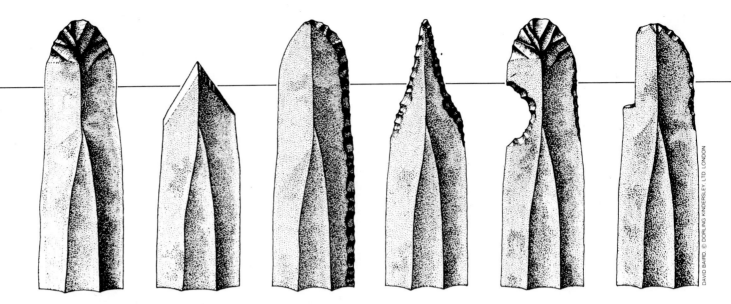

Early man lived in other
Ukraine, where wood wa
moths' bones to hold do
houses. The conical, mud
Mesopotamia (front) and

two-tube vocal tract by
respect it is *less* efficien
makes it more likely tha
jects will be lodged the
will be quickly dislodged
likely than Neanderthal
cident. Given this eviden
of the two-tube tract, it n
compensating advantage -
is better communication.

The evolution of the
connected with another a
difference between Nean
the reduction in size of
have reduced the chewing
— and hence the amount
extracted from a given
prehistorians have suggest
changes may have been an
the vocal-tract changes.
modern pharynx is longer
thals, but is also bent at a r
be if the two are to be m
(by the back and upper sur
tively). As a result, the m
longer overall, is actually s
dimension. Anatomically,
achieved by a similar short
which would necessarily m
massive, prognathous Near

If the Neanderthal voca
perfect instrument whose
needed piecing out with g
evolution of the modern v
have provided a powerful
offset its anatomic disa
however, the improvement
count for the extraordinary
cultural innovation cited ear
chology that language is t
human thought: we think in
other kinds of images (e.g.,
tion of this is that when we a
variably "hear" a series of wo
follows the progression of o
is above all with words, whi
objects and events in the w
can think about these things
are present — a number of oth

pharynx, oral cavity, or both, plus (in some cases) rounding and protruding the lips, produce the dozen or two other vowels found in human languages.

However, Lieberman believes, the three vowels just mentioned are not simply three of many possible vowels: rather, they possess special properties which other vowels do not. He notes, for example, that though languages vary greatly in their "vocabulary" of vowels, nearly all include these three — and all include at least one of the three. An important reason for this, he contends, is that all three are unusually stable — that is, they remain intelligible despite much individual variation and even sloppiness in enuncia- tion. In one experiment, a series of short words con- taining 10 different vowel sounds was recorded by 10 different individuals. The words were then "shuffled" and played back to a panel of 70 listeners for iden- tification. Words containing EE (e.g., "heed," "beat") were correctly identified 99.9 per cent of the time, with words containing AH and OO doing almost as well. By contrast, the vowel in "head" and "bed" was correctly identified only 90 per cent of the time, so that "bed" might sometimes be heard as "bad" or "bid." For this reason Lieberman describes EE, AH, and OO as "the optimum sounds for human com- munication," in that of all the vowels they are the least ambiguous.

EE and (to a lesser extent) OO are important in another way: they enable us to estimate the size of the speaker's vocal tract. This process, called "scal- ing," is essential for identifying particular sounds, since the pattern of frequencies characteristic of a given sound will vary with the size of the vocal tract producing it. Scaling can be achieved by listening to the individual speak for a few seconds. But it can be accomplished much more quickly by hearing

EE or, less certainly, by hearing OO.

But what has all this to do with the problem of Neanderthal and modern man? Simply this: the Neanderthals seem to have had primitive vocal tracts, so shaped that they could not produce the full range of sounds on which we rely for communication.

If one has a reasonably complete fossil (or other) skull, one can make a cast of plaster or plastic which will show the shape and approximate size of the vocal tract. Detailed measurements of such a cast fed into a properly programmed computer will then reveal the range of sounds that the tract in question could produce. This computer "modeling" has been done with casts from several varieties of humans and other primates, both modern and extinct; the modern re- constructions serve to check the accuracy of the tech- nique. That is, if the computer model of a modern primate's vocal tract tells us that it can only produce certain sounds, and if we then find that in fact it only does produce these sounds, we can be reasonably sure that models based on fossil skulls will tell us ac- curately what sounds their owners could and could not have made, even though their voices have been silent for a hundred thousand years.

Chimpanzees, for example, have the primitive, one-tube vocal tract. According to the computer, this should be able to produce the vowels in "bit," "but," and "put" — but not the key vowels in AH, EE, and OO ("bah," "beat," "boot"). In fact, chimps have never been heard to produce any of these three vowels. Much the same is true of the newborn human infant, whose vocal tract resembles that of the chimp in both shape and phonetic limitations. It is only at about three months that growth begins reshaping the tract toward a fully human form — with a corre-

sponding expansi
Computer stud
dicate that its cap
of a chimp. It c
"bet," "bat," "but,
of "bit," but—ev
that of "bought."
of the three mos
OO. Other comp
derthal vocabular
been somewhat li

From the stand
number of differe
important. Hawaii
makes do with or
consonants—and
manage with only
Neanderthals coul
sounds—but these
special vowels (wh
EE and OO). For
Neanderthal spee
than that of mode
mation ambiguous
inefficiency would
marked in dealing
of a stranger) and
familiar voice un
could not be ident
the dark, or outsi
therefore, that Ne
under these specia

there—Binford finds an "enormous," even "drastic" increase in the bones of a single species, wild cattle, evidently slaughtered by the dozens and even hundreds, in preference to other species.

Significantly, Binford notes, the same type of specialized hunting centering on a single species of large herd animal is found in later, unquestionably modern sites in Europe (the best-studied region). There, 80 to 90 per cent of the bones are typically from one species—in western Europe, usually reindeer (occasionally horse); in eastern Europe, generally mammoth.

Wild cattle must have been relatively fearsome quarry as compared with deer, gazelle, or even horse. These animals survived in eastern Europe until a few centuries ago, and from contemporary descriptions Binford characterizes them as "fierce, temperamental and extremely agile," with the largest bulls standing as much as six and a half feet at the shoulder. (European wild cattle are thought to have contributed to the ancestry of the Spanish fighting bull.) Binford sees the preference of some Near Eastern late Neanderthal populations for tackling these very formidable beasts as deriving from the creatures' migratory habits. Great herds of them, she believes, must have regularly moved from their winter pastures along the coastal plain to summer pastures in the mountains—a view that is consistent with what we know of the ecology of the region between forty and fifty thousand years ago. And hunting communities located in the narrow valleys connecting plains and mountains could—if their techniques were sufficiently sophisticated—have ambushed the moving herds and killed them in quantity. (It is worth noting that the specialized hunting of a single migratory species, i.e., one that can be killed during only a small portion of the year, implies another new technology: food preservation. A community which obtained the bulk of its meat during a few weeks of intensive hunting in spring and fall must obviously have evolved some way of preserving the meat—by drying, or smoking—for consumption during the months when the herds were elsewhere.)

The new, specialized hunting techniques, Binford believes, must have involved, among other things, cooperation among relatively large groups of hunters—much larger than the small "extended family" groups in which most Neanderthal populations are thought to have lived. Thus she sees the shift in hunting methods as involving the "linking up of formerly self-sufficient small bands" into groups capable of dealing with large numbers of wild cattle—perhaps by organizing a stampede into a ravine or box canyon, as later hunting peoples unquestionably did.

Binford therefore sees the mere presence of large migratory herds as setting up a "selective pressure for larger numbers of humans to aggregate." And—though she does not say so—it could well have set up a similar selective pressure for better communications. The aggregation of large numbers of people implies an ability to communicate easily with relative strangers—which, as we saw earlier, may have been rather poor among the typical Neanderthals. Rapid—and unambiguous—communication would have been even more essential in organizing the minute-to-minute, even second-to-second, shifts in tactics needed to deal with a herd of "fierce, temperamental and extremely agile" animals.

Though Binford has not made the point, the late Neanderthals of these sites, e.g., Skuhl, *were anatomically capable of such communication.* Though in some respects their skulls were "transitional," their vocal tracts seem to have been fully modern. If they indeed needed more efficient communications to engage in specialized hunting, they possessed the vocal apparatus for it.

Admittedly, this line of reasoning is not, by itself, very strong. Binford herself notes that her deductions about hunting techniques are based on findings at a very small number of sites, and can only be confirmed by many more diggings in the eastern Mediterranean. We cannot even be certain that earlier Neanderthals, despite their primitive vocal tracts, could not have engaged in the new type of hunting—merely that, on present evidence, none did.

Similar reservations apply, in measure, to the other lines of reasoning already cited. Reconstructions of the Neanderthal vocal tract, and Lieberman's conclusions about its phonetic limitations, seem pretty firmly founded—but his further conclusions on its communicative inefficiency are merely deductions, albeit very plausible ones. Likewise, the connection between the presumed inefficient Neanderthal language and inefficient Neanderthal thought is unproved and probably unprovable—at least until we know a great deal more about thinking processes than we now do. All we can say at present is that inef-

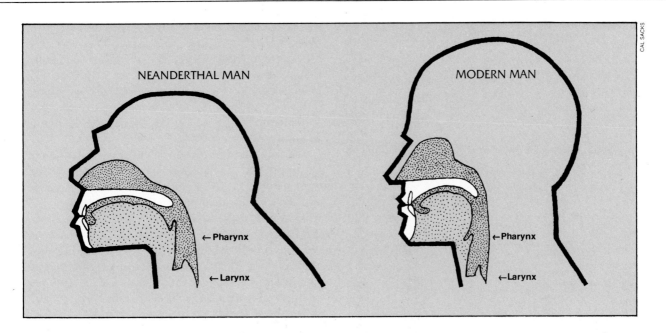

NEANDERTHAL MAN   MODERN MAN

← Pharynx

← Larynx

← Pharynx

← Larynx

CAL SACKS

ficient thinking is certainly consistent with the static, noninnovative character of the Neanderthal cultures.

What we can say about all these facts and theories, be they certain, probable, or merely plausible, is that *they fit together*. Greater efficiency in communication would explain the otherwise disadvantageous changes in skull and vocal tract between Neanderthal and modern man. It would—or could—explain the sharp increase in innovation. It would, finally, have facilitated, if it did not actually make possible, the new hunting methods that Binford has postulated.

Moreover, these converging lines of reasoning are essentially independent in that they are based on quite different sets of facts. The increase in innovation is based on the actual material remains left by the Neanderthals and their successors, and while the archaeological record for both groups is admittedly incomplete, it is hard to believe that further diggings would much reduce the contrast between the two. Lieberman's conclusions about Neanderthal vocal communication are based on the anatomy of Neanderthal skulls and on the science of phonetics. Binford's hunting theory, finally, is based on quite different archaeological remains: the proportions of animal bones found at sites in a particular type of location. Any of these theoretical pillars may be insecurely based—but the fact that they converge at the top surely makes for a firmer structure than their individual shakiness might suggest.

This explanation of the sudden rise of modern man—that the "new breed" possessed more efficient speech and thinking processes than the old—also helps explain equally the sudden disappearance of Neanderthals. For however one explains this disappearance, it implies that in contrast with modern man they were seriously inferior in numbers, technology, or (probably) both.

The possible fates of the Neanderthals can be summed up as absorption, exclusion, or extermination, or some combination of these. That is, they may have interbred with their successors to the point where they disappeared as an identifiable group; they may have been pushed by their more successful competitors into steadily less hospitable environments until they died off; or they may have been actively exterminated as troublesome competitors.

There are precedents in later human history for all these possibilities. The native Hawaiians, for example, have so interbred with later and more numerous immigrants to the islands that they have almost vanished as a distinct group. The South African Bushmen, though they still exist, apparently occupy a far smaller and less attractive part of Africa than they did ten thousand years ago, having been pushed out by the expansion of Negro populations from the north and, later, white ones from the south. Finally, the Tasmanian aborigines were wiped out during the nineteenth century by European settlers.

113

One need not choose among these possibilities to realize that all of them imply that modern man must have possessed powerful numerical and/or technological advantages over his predecessors. If the Neanderthals were absorbed through interbreeding, it must have been by a much larger population of the modern type. If they were more or less peacefully pushed out of existence, this too argues for superiority in numbers—as the bushmen were pushed into their semidesert habitat by the far more numerous Negroes and whites. Finally, extermination implies either numerical or technological superiority. In warfare as in pugilism, the rule is that "a good big man will, generally, beat a good little man," and if modern populations beat the Neanderthals, they must have been bigger, better at warfare, or both.

Looking at the question more closely, we find that we need not even choose between numerical and technological superiority, since the former implies the latter. If modern men indeed greatly outnumbered the Neanderthals, this can only have occurred because the moderns possessed superior survival skills—presumably including the new hunting techniques already mentioned—that would have enabled them to extract much more food from a given area. (The more food, the more children reach adulthood.) Yet the Neanderthals, despite what must have been

several thousand years of contact with modern man, never managed to acquire those skills. Was it because they were technologically conservative, wedded to their own ways of doing things, as some modern primitives are? Or did the new skills and technologies perhaps involve communicative and intellectual capabilities which the Neanderthals simply did not possess?

We may never be certain of the answer. All we can be sure of is that modern humanity in some way had what it took; the Neanderthals did not. We can be equally certain that, whatever modern men and women had, they were from the beginning innovators, inventors, manipulators of their environment, their societies and their own minds, seeking new ways of doing things, new experiences, new horizons. The tide of human innovation has waxed and waned at different times and places, yet has everywhere shown its power; there is almost certainly no human culture today that much resembles those of 30,000 years ago. Even the bushmen or the aborigines of central Australia, though clinging to what seem ancient ways of life, have evolved sophisticated skills enabling them to survive in habitats where most other peoples—including most Europeans—would perish of hunger or thirst. The Neanderthals, during twice 30,000 years, refined their survival skills hardly at all—and whatever the ultimate reason, that seems to be why they perished from the earth.

If it was the capacity to innovate which "made" modern men, it may—ironically—be that same capacity which will unmake them. Almost throughout history, but especially during the last century or two, humanity has adopted new technologies, constructed new styles of social organization, with little or no thought for the ultimate, or even immediate, consequences of these innovations. We design new machinery that can consign hundreds of thousands to chronic unemployment; introduce new medical technologies without inquiring how the expanding populations these create are to live; cast new substances into our air and water that may, for all anyone knows, eventually poison us or our descendants. Modern man innovated and kept innovating, thereby becoming a spectacular biological success—by far the most numerous large animal on earth today. But that very success has generated a need for new—and more considered—types of innovation if we are to escape the fate of the Neanderthals.

Though they look fresh, these footprints in the mud of a French cave are more than 10,000 years old. What the young people who left them were up to—play, an initiation rite, or just walking around—is anybody's guess.

WHERE DID THE ETRUSCANS COME FROM?

In theory we should know a lot more about those shadowy people, the Etruscans. They lived, after all, not so very long ago, in the millennium just before Christ. From their homeland of Etruria in west-central Italy they were, moreover, in regular contact with other Mediterranean peoples: the Greek colonists of southern Italy and Sicily, their sometime enemies; the transplanted Phoenicians of Carthage in North Africa, their allies; and, finally, an aggressive people on their southern flank, the Romans. Their contributions to Roman civilization — in art, architecture, and city planning, in military organization and tactics, in dress, manners, and customs, in technology and, especially, religion — are many and well documented. And although the Romans, after subjugating them, blotted out most visible signs of their existence, the Etruscans left behind, in underground cemeteries loaded with paintings, statues, and other artifacts, a rich and curiously appealing record of their vibrant civilization.

Yet they remain an enigma because, unlike other vanished peoples, they do not speak to us through their writings. At about the time of Christ, Livy wrote that only a few generations earlier, Roman youths had studied Etruscan literature. But apart from thousands of brief funerary inscriptions and a few scattered texts none of this literature has survived. The inscriptions and texts are in characters from a Greek alphabet, so we can pronounce them. Making sense of them, however, is another matter: Etruscan is not an Indo-European language, and since no other known language is close enough to Etruscan to allow for useful comparisons, our knowledge of it is scant.

But if we cannot look directly into the minds and hearts of the Etruscans, we can still learn much about them from the artworks and household objects they stored in their subterranean necropolises for the use of their dead. Sculptures like the one on the opposite page show women and men as equals, keenly enjoying their physical, earthly existence. They loved sports and spectacles, music (notably of the flute) and dancing, hunting and gaming, and reveled in the pleasures of eating and drinking. And sex. In the fourth century B.C. a Greek historian wrote that "It is not shameful to the Etruscans to be seen not only preparing 'to do the thing,' but also performing it." When friends and relatives have feasted together, he went on, "the slaves bring to them . . . first prostitutes, by and by pretty young boys, then even the women married to those who took part in the festivities. They all engage in making love. . . ."

Since the Greeks frequently warred against the Etruscans their remarks about them were not always free of bias, and the Romans, later, were even less reliable, being at pains to blacken the reputation of these vanquished neighbors from whom they had learned so much.

The real mystery is where the Etruscans came from. It was the near-unanimous belief of ancient historians that they had migrated from Lydia in Asia Minor. After a long famine in the country, according to Herodotus, the king sent half his subjects to sea "in search of a livelihood elsewhere. They . . . finally reached Umbria in the north of Italy, where they settled and still live to this day. Here they changed their names from Lydians to Tyrrhenians, after the king's son Tyrrhenus, who was their leader." (The Greeks called the Etruscans Tyrrhenoi and the Romans Tusci, names perpetuated, respectively, in those of the Tyrrhenian Sea and the province of Tuscany.)

But another Greek historian, Dionysius of Halicarnassus, who lived in the first century B.C., held a different belief: that the Etruscans had not migrated to Italy but were indigenous to Italy. And certain scholars of the eighteenth century came up with yet another theory: that the Etruscans had come south over the Alps from central Europe. Modern archaeology has uncovered the remains of an iron-using people, predecessors of the Etruscans on the latters' turf, who did come into Italy from the north around 1000 B.C. They have been labled Villanovans, after Villanova, a surburb of Bologna.

Today, most scholars lean to a modern version of the ancient tradition, holding that the Etruscans sailed to Italy from Asia Minor or the eastern Aegean and displaced the Villanovans. But a growing number of dissenters disagree. There is, they point out, no evidence of a sharp break between the Villanovan and Etruscan cultures that such a massive incursion would have produced. And the Etruscans could easily have acquired their eastern ways — as the Greek colonists south of them certainly did — through their commerce with Eastern peoples.

Did the enigmatic, pleasure-loving Etruscans come from the east or the north; did they simply arise in their native Italy? The final answer, no doubt, belongs to the Etruscans, and the possibility remains, faint but tantalizing, that it may yet, one day come to light.

WHO WERE THE MOUND BUILDERS?

When the American colonists of the eastern seaboard crossed the Alleghenies they made a puzzling discovery. Scattered across the Ohio River flood plain were strange earthen mounds—some of them small hummocks but some of them elaborate man-made hills. Long embankments, evidently built as fortifications, hugged the bluffs overlooking the river. Some of these earthworks were so big that it would have taken hundreds of workers to build them.

Even the earliest settlers, before the American Revolution, wondered at these earthworks. Who could have built them? Surely not the Indians they found in the country. The Indians were simple forest people who left little mark on the land they occupied.

In the course of clearing the land the settlers plowed under many of the smaller mounds, but they dug into some of them. Usually they found human skeletons, sometimes buried alone, sometimes in small groups, often enclosed in wood-sided chambers. Sometimes the skeletons were surrounded by artifacts—clay vessels, wooden masks, statuettes of stone or clay, and soapstone pipes carved to represent birds and frogs. Ornaments, in the form of serpents or of bird claws, or in geometric designs, were cut out of copper or of mica, which shone like silver and was often mistaken for it. There were constant rumors that gold and pearls had been found in the mounds too, and, although these proved false, they were enough to attract a small army of treasure hunters. No one got rich, but in the course of their digging, the treasure seekers turned up enough artifacts to convince skeptics that a people of fairly advanced culture had once occupied the land.

In a few cases the mounds were treated as monuments worth preserving. The Ohio Company, a speculative venture organized in 1786 to sell and develop land, built its new township of Marietta around a complex of ancient earthworks. The townspeople enclosed them in a park, felling the trees and setting the area aside as a public grazing ground. In a moment of curiosity one of the promoters, the Reverend Manasseh Cutler, sat down and counted the number of growth rings in one of the trees felled during his visit. Finding that there were 463 rings, he concluded that the mounds had been built before A.D. 1300. Cutler had anticipated the science of dendrochronology, or tree-ring dating, by at least a century.

From promoters like Cutler, from government officials, from cartographers who used the mounds in surveys, reports of the discoveries soon reached the east. There, in the cities and colleges, men of learning were mystified. In their own part of the country they had seen no evidence of an advanced Indian society. Besides, it had suited them to believe that the Indians were merely creatures of the woods, as transitory as the birds and with no more established right to the land. To have believed otherwise would have called into question the moral right of the white men to seize and develop the land in the name of civilization.

Who, then, had built the mounds? A whole generation of scholars and armchair travelers began speculating about a "vanished race" of people who had occupied the land before the Indians and left only the mounds to mark their passing. To explain the extinct civilization, the scholars drew upon what knowledge they had of the ancient world—mainly of Egypt, Greece, and Rome—and upon their reading of the Scriptures. In doing so they revived many of the same fanciful notions conjured up by an earlier generation of savants to explain the very existence of Indians in the New World. One such theory proposed that the mounds had been built by descendants of the eight survivors of Noah's flood. Another, advanced in the sixteenth century by the Spanish writer Pedro Sarmiento de Gamboa, held that the ancestors of the Indians had come from Atlantis before that legendary continent sank beneath the ocean. Now the Atlantis theory was quietly readjusted and migrants from Atlantis became specifically the builders of a vanished civilization in the middle west. Alternatively, the seventeenth-century Dutch theologian Joannes Lumnius had argued that the Indians were descended from one or more of the ten Hebrew tribes exiled by King Shalmaneser of Assyria, as explained in II Kings 17:6. A refinement of the Ten Lost Tribes hypothesis turned one of these tribes into the mound builders.

To these new versions of earlier speculations, the nineteenth-century savants added theories based upon what they deemed to be more scholarly study. Some combed classical writings, including especially Homer's epics, for references to burial mounds and

earthworks. The Greek hero Achilles had been buried under a huge earthen mound, and so had Hector, the Trojan warrior. Did this not suggest a connection between ancient Greece and trans-Appalachian America? Others pondered the reports of Spanish explorers describing the elaborate civilizations they had found in Central America. Could the mounds have been built by Maya or Toltec people who had moved northwards into the Mississippi and Ohio valleys? What all these theorists agreed upon was that the mounds had been built by "a superior race, or more probably a people of foreign and higher civilization" who had occupied America long before the North American Indians.

The romantic speculations of the scholars were seized upon with glee by popular authors who wrote of the closing chapters of a mighty empire of mound builders destroyed by ruthless invaders. Josiah Priest made a fortune with his epic *American Antiquities and Discoveries in the West*, published in 1833. Over twenty thousand copies were sold in two and a half years by door-to-door salespeople. The public loved the epic of the white mound dwellers of "great intelligence," who "perished among the yells of their enemies." There were sieges and heroic battles, massacres and great ceremonials, always the hint of a glorious and mysterious past. Cornelius Mathews' *Behemoth*, released in 1839, was an entertaining historical nonsense epic aimed at the popular market. A huge, elephantlike creature appeared among the mound dwellers, ravaged their settlements, defeated entire armies, and massacred thousands. The great hero Bokulla finally destroyed Behemoth by starvation and restored peace to a grateful nation.

The myth of the mound builders was given its loftiest expression by the New England poet William Cullen Bryant. During a visit to Illinois mounds in 1832 he felt the spirit of thousands of dead warriors beneath his feet:

And are they here—
The dead of other days—and did the dust
Of these fair solitudes once stir with life
And burn with passion? Let the mighty mounds
That overlook the rivers, or that rise
In the dim forest crowded with old oaks,
Answer, A race, that long has passed away,
Built them;—a disciplined and populous race
Heaped, with long toil, the earth, while yet the Greek

Was hewing the Pentelicus to forms
of symmetry, and rearing on its rock
The glittering Parthenon. . . .
Then enter the villains:
The red men came—
The roaming hunter tribes, warlike and fierce,
And the mound-builders vanished from the earth. . . .

What these scholars and poets and assorted thinkers of eastern America could not accept was the simple idea that the mounds had been built by the ancestors of the very Indians whom the white settlers had been displacing.

Yet there were plenty of intellectual Americans who were not taken in by the popular legend. One of these was Thomas Jefferson, who included a love of archaeology among his manifold interests. As early as 1781, in reponse to a French questionnaire he had received during his term as governor of Virginia, he wrote a lengthy essay explaining the "laws and money, products vegetable and mineral," and other matters of interest in his native state. In addition to describing the living "aborigines," he wanted to explain their origins. Since neither whites nor Indians could shed much light on that matter he turned to some mounds near the Rivanna River not far from Monticello—some of the few that existed east of the Appalachians and north of the Carolinas.

The Jefferson dig, a series of trial trenches and a larger cutting, was one of the first American excavations undertaken to obtain answers to specific questions. The mound he chose was about 40 feet across and 12 feet deep. He found that it contained "collections of human bones, at different depths, from six inches to three feet below the surface." The bones had been "heaped in promiscuous confusion." There were at least three layers of human remains, so carefully laid out that Jefferson concluded his mound was a regular burial place in which as many as a thousand bodies had been deposited. He also discovered that his mound was "of considerable notoriety among the Indians." Only some 30 years before a party of Indians had been observed worshiping at the tumulus. Almost certainly, their ancestors had built it.

With this brilliant insight Jefferson had casually solved the mystery of the mound builders. But it took another half century for the scientific community to provide the supporting evidence. Meanwhile

Beaten-copper raven or crow
WERNER FORMAN

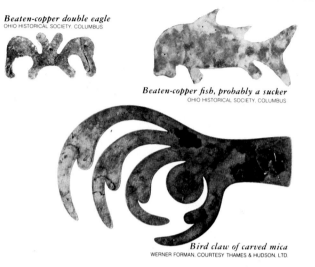

Beaten-copper double eagle
OHIO HISTORICAL SOCIETY, COLUMBUS

Beaten-copper fish, probably a sucker
OHIO HISTORICAL SOCIETY, COLUMBUS

Bird claw of carved mica
WERNER FORMAN, COURTESY THAMES & HUDSON, LTD.

the reports of rich finds in the Ohio mounds led to many more excavations and new speculation.

Early nineteenth-century excavations were little more than treasure hunts with pickax and shovel, even dynamite. The objective was fine artifacts and art objects, preferably as spectacular as those being dug up in Italy, Greece, and Egypt. "I think there can be little doubt that the opening of the North American tumuli will reward the labourers with valuable spoils," wrote the naturalist Benjamin Smith Barton in 1799.

The treasure hunting and wholesale destruction led inevitably to more serious inquiry, by people concerned by the rapidly vanishing archaeological record. Caleb Atwater, the postmaster of Circleville, Ohio, developed a passionate interest in mounds. Between 1815 and 1820 this worthy official compiled a detailed report on Ohio mounds, a research project that was spurred by the callous liquidation of so many. He traveled widely in the state, measured and surveyed dozens of earthworks, and followed up any isolated discoveries that came to his ears. Atwater poured scorn on the "degraded" life of the living Indians, who could never have built the mounds. He ruined his sober observations by speculating that the earthworks had been constructed by an extinct population of mound builders "as numerous as that which once animated the borders of the Nile." He was merely reflecting the Biblical obsessions and colonial attitudes of the time.

The next step towards debunking the old myth came in the mid-nineteenth century, when the American Ethnological Society commissioned two Ohio

men, Ephraim George Squier, a journalist, and E. H. Davis, a physician, to make a survey of ancient mounds. Their report, published by the newly founded Smithsonian Institution in 1848, is a classic account of the earthworks of the middle west that is still consulted today. Squier and Davis surveyed hundreds of sites, producing beautifully executed plans. Some of these serve as the only record of sites that were destroyed in later decades. The two men excavated over two hundred mounds, surveyed many earthworks and enclosures, and assembled a huge collection of artifacts from their digs. They tried to assemble a body of well-authenticated data to replace the wild speculations of the day. But they reached the same conclusions as many of their contemporaries. The great earthworks were part of a system of defense erected by the mound builders to protect themselves against invaders from the northeast. And again the Indians were the unspoken usurpers. "They," wrote Squier scornfully, "were hunters averse to labor, and not known to have constructed any works approaching in skillfulness of design or in magnitude these under notice."

For all its prejudices, the Squier and Davis monograph was a turning point in mound studies. The impressive corpus of information within its covers. was a starting point for all future inquiries. Many were the analogies that could now be drawn between Indian artifacts and those found in the Squier excavations. No one seriously interested in the problem could afford to ignore the results of two hundred excavations, however casual. The work of the two Ohio men was the foundation for later research projects supported by the Smithsonian Institution, the new Peabody Museum at Harvard University, and, most important of all, the U.S. Bureau of Ethnology.

Not until the 1880s was the myth of the mound builders fully laid to rest. In that decade, Professor Cyrus Thomas carried out for the Bureau of Ethnology a thorough survey of more than two thousand sites. For the first time it was possible to appreciate the extent of the mound builders' culture. Mounds and other earthworks were densely distributed along the Ohio and Mississippi valleys, in Tennessee and the Gulf states. They were found in western New York State, along the southern shores of the Great Lakes, in southern Wisconsin, and as far west as Nebraska, the Missouri Valley, and Arkansas. Most of the mounds were conical in shape and relatively

This splendidly stylized serpent, carved from mica, was probably worn during Hopewell serpent-cult rituals. The skilled Hopewell craftsmen, the finest metalworkers in North America before the arrival of the white man, worked in both mica and copper, as the copper artifacts at left demonstrate.

OVERLEAF: *The Great Serpent Mound, built by the Adena Indians, coils for almost a quarter of a mile along a ridge in southern Ohio. Its jaws at right clasp an oval mound thought to represent an egg or possibly a frog. The serpent was not a burial place but a religious monument, perhaps meant to be viewed by the sky gods.*
TONY LINCK. SHOSTAL

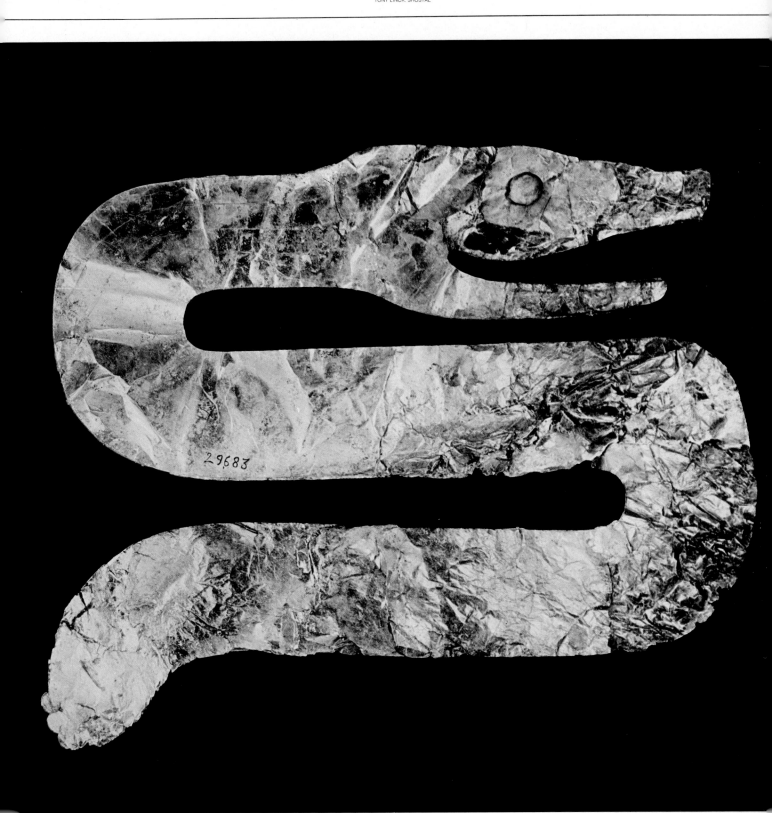

small, but some were enormous. The Grave Creek Mound in West Virginia was over sixty feet high, while many Mississippi Valley mounds were even larger. At some sites these rectangular, flat-topped mounds, reaching a height of over a hundred feet, were grouped around open plazas. Particularly impressive complexes were built at Moundville in Alabama and at Cahokia on the Mississippi, now part of East St. Louis but at one time the greatest Indian center in the country.

In his survey of the sites Cyrus Thomas not only dug many sites but collected four thousand specimens. In addition he combed files and library shelves for Indian traditions and early explorer's accounts of the people living in mound country at the time of European settlement. When he was through there was no basis for doubting that the living Indians were descendants of the same race as the people who built the mounds.

The eighty years since Cyrus Thomas completed his report have seen a revolution in archaeological methods, new dating techniques, and elaborate classification schemes developed to put the thousands of American mound sites in some sort of chronological relationship with each other. We now know that most of the mounds and earthworks were built within the last three thousand years. North American Indians were building mounds while the Olmec and later the Maya were rising to prominence in Mexico. They were still building them at the threshold of recent historical times. But, by the time the first white settlers crossed the Alleghenies, no trace of the mound builders remained but their silent earthworks.

The history of the mound builders, as we can now reconstruct it, begins soon after the beginning of agriculture in what is now the eastern United States. Until then the Indians of the area had lived by hunting game and by gathering wild foods. But around three thousand years ago they began making clay vessels, an innovation that accompanied the appearance of agriculture in many parts of North America. The pottery, which is found in their habitation sites, was made with a distinctive gritty temper and often decorated with fabric or cord impressions.

Some villages that were occupied about this time were of considerable size. One of them, called the Baumer site, lies on a prehistoric natural levee of the Ohio River in southern Illinois, an area rich in vege-

This red cedar mask with shell inlays for the eyes and mouth was probably worn by a shaman during the Deer Ceremony, a ritual dance to promote good hunting.
AMERICAN MUSEUM OF NATURAL HISTORY

table foods, fish, land mammals and mollusks. The settlement covered more than ten acres and was made up of houses about sixteen feet square.

No one knows whether the inhabitants were actually farmers. They used pottery and dug substantial storage pits for conserving winter food. But the impact of agriculture on the economy, if it was practiced at all, was minimal. The "Baumer" people were skilled hunters with stone-tipped arrows. They gathered a variety of vegetable foods and caught fish in the rivers. So diverse were the food resources of their environment that they may have had little need to supplement their diet by farming.

Nevertheless, the use of local strains of corn, beans, and squash after 1550 B.C. gave people the surplus of food and time needed to engage in some communal activities. About 1000 B.C. the first signs of mound building appear in the middle west. Some villages began to bury their dead under low earth mounds, a new custom that spread throughout the middle west within a few centuries. Although the exact place of origin for mound building is unknown, the more elaborate early examples are centered in the Ohio Valley, within one hundred fifty miles of Chillicothe. Some of the earthworks are simply narrow ridges that enclose large tracts of land. Their significance is unknown. Burial mounds are sometimes found within the enclosures, while other mounds are found in groups by themselves.

This earliest of mound-building cultures is called "Adena," after an Ohio site of that name. It emerged about 1000 B.C. and lasted until about A.D. 200. The Adena people lived in small, scattered villages and built round houses, using wattles or withes for the walls and thatch for the roofs. Whether they sowed crops or simply harvested the grains that grew wild around their villages is a matter of doubt.

By studying the distribution of similar artifacts in different burial mounds, anthropologists can deduce a good deal about the social structure of Adena villages. For instance, masks of a particular design, found only in certain mounds, may be taken to indicate that the individuals buried there honored the same ancestors. Thus it seems likely that in the Adena culture, as in living cultures that have been studied, families were linked by ties of kinship — what anthropologists call lineages. By descent from a common ancestor the lineages of one village might be further linked with lineages of another village in larger relationships, or clans. The leaders of such clans and lineages would probably have enjoyed a special social and economic status in Adena society.

The ties of clan and lineage may also have enabled the Adena people to maintain links not only with neighboring villages but also with much more distant communities. And these distant kin connections may have served as important catalysts for long-distance trade and for the spread of culture. The influence of Adena burial customs, religious practices, and artistic traditions can be detected over a wide area, perhaps as far afield as Chesapeake Bay and New York State.

Adena religious customs reveal a preoccupation with death. On many occasions the scattered Adena villages must have joined together in the work of building large communal burial mounds and conducting elaborate funeral ceremonies. We may picture them assembling with hundreds of baskets, in which they brought earth to build the mound, layer upon layer. Sometimes a single corpse, evidently that of an important person, was buried in a large mound. At other times a group of bodies, perhaps those of clan leaders or members of a single family, were buried together. Most often the burial mounds were built over a period of years, as layers of bodies were added, until the summit was reached. Some corpses

were cremated and the ashes interred in a clay-lined pit. Others were smeared with red ochre before burial. Usually the bodies were unadorned but occasionally stone ornaments or engraved slabs were placed in the graves.

After a thousand years Adena culture waned, and the religious and burial customs of the first mound builders gradually went out of fashion. The Adena traditions were replaced with new and highly distinctive religious cults that first made their appearance in Illinois and then spread eastward into Ohio. This "Hopewell" culture, named after an Illinois mound group, eventually expanded widely over a huge portion of the eastern United States, stretching from the Mississippi River to Florida.

Like the Adena, Hopewell society was based on economic patterns that had been established for centuries. The Hopewell people probably cultivated corn and other crops, but hunting and gathering were still of critical importance in their economy. At the Skovill site in the Illinois Valley, for example, so many acorns and other nuts grew within range of the village that a combination of wild products with wild turkeys, squirrels, and deer provided enough food year round for several hundred people. The inhabitants collected shellfish and went fishing if they felt like a change of diet. In spring and fall they left their permanent base camp for a while and hunted migrating waterfowl at the Illinois River. Perhaps the Illinois Valley settlements were exceptionally favored, but they certainly reveal what a broadly based economic tradition the native Americans enjoyed.

Hopewell settlements are still somewhat of a mystery, for most archaeologists have concentrated on their mounds and earthworks. Many people lived in rectangular or oval-shaped houses with domed and thatched roofs; one example found under the Seip mound near Chillicothe, Ohio, was about 25 feet long and 18 feet wide. The villages were permanent settlements. But we know little of their political and social organization. Perhaps, like the Adena people, different communities were linked by clan and lineage ties that reached beyond the confines of a single village or group of villages. The Hopewell seems to have been a society without social class, but clan or lineage leaders enjoyed a special prestige that is reflected in the great wealth of their burials. We do not know how precedence between various lineages was established. Conceivably they competed with one another in according the most lavish burials possible to their leaders, thereby gaining prestige and higher status from a form of conspicuous consumption that created an insatiable demand for luxury objects and funeral treasures. A preoccupation with death and status seems to have been at the heart of the Hopewell religion, as it was of the Adena.

Hopewell burial customs were similar to Adena customs but on a larger scale. The builders of Crook's Mound in Louisiana began by raising an earthen platform in which 168 bodies were buried; then 214 more were placed on top of the platform before the mound was completed above the burials. On some mounds baskets of soil were piled 40 feet high.

Important individuals were buried with lavish arrays of ceremonial vessels and other valuable objects. Since the fashions in these grave goods changed rapidly through the centuries of Hopewell burials, they provide the archaeologists with markers on a time chart of Hopewell life. The vessels bear finely modeled ducks and birds of prey, often combined with geometric, grooved, and zigzag designs. Some pots have symmetrical ears that serve as handles. Figurines modeled in clay represent both men and women with braided, knotted hair styles and woven robes; sometimes a female figure is seated, with a baby at her breast.

The Hopewell artisans worked in copper, mica, obsidian, soapstone, and wood as well as clay. Although the culture's heartland is relatively small, the ceremonial artifacts and raw materials used to make them came from an enormous area of North America. Hopewell craftsmen mined the surface copper ore of the Lake Superior region. From the copper, which they heated and hammered into thin sheets, they made head and breast ornaments, often bearing elaborate repoussé animal motifs, as well as flat axes, spearheads, beads, amulets, and other trinkets. Sheets of mica were cut into striking lustrous silhouettes of bird talons, human figures, and abstract designs. For some time the Hopewell craftsmen obtained obsidian for knives and arrowheads from the Yellowstone area of Wyoming. Other rocks came from Montana and North Dakota, as well as from sources in Illinois and Ohio. Conch shells and other marine ornaments were traded from the distant Gulf Coast. Soapstone was especially prized because from it Hopewell craftsmen carved pipe bowls in the

form of beavers, frogs, birds, bears, and humans. These distinctive pipes rank among the finest of American Indian achievements.

The array of raw materials and finished products buried with Hopewell leaders can only have been assembled by sophisticated and well-organized trading relationships. Many archaeologists believe that the various cult products — copper ornaments, pipe bowls, and so on — were made by small groups of specialized craftsmen working at certain locations, perhaps at the sources of the raw materials. The products of these craftsmen were then dispersed all over the Hopewell area through trade networks that moved commodities, grain and other foodstuffs, as well as cult objects, over hundreds, even thousands, of miles. The result was the concentration of luxury goods in the hands of people who enjoyed high prestige and special status in Hopewell society. Few of the finest Hopewell pieces show signs of wear, presumably because they were soon buried with their owners.

The pervasive influence of Hopewell culture, with its elaborate burial ceremonies, is surprising when one realizes that there were few Hopewell settlements of any size. Hopewell culture was centered in a well-defined heartland in Ohio and Illinois, but its cultural and religious influences were felt far outside that region. The Hopewell sphere extended from the Alleghenies to the western borders of the Mississippi Valley, north to the Great Lakes, south to Florida and the Gulf states. But the Hopewell should not be

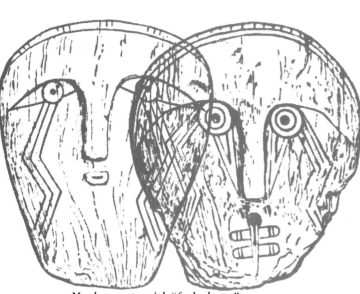

Mask gorgets with "forked eyes"

The shell gorgets on these pages bear motifs of Mississippian art, including "forked eyes" that may denote tears, lightning, or facial painting. Some archaeologists connect them with a "Southern Death Cult," which arose in the wake of DeSoto's devastating 1539 expedition.

thought of as a monolithic culture, rather as a loosely knit group of societies that prided themselves on a rigid conformity to certain religious and artistic conventions. This conformity is reflected in a remarkable uniformity of art objects, funerary rites, and burial customs throughout the Hopewell sphere.

Hopewell trading networks, based as they probably were on scores of individual trading partnerships, made more people aware of the wider world around them, gave them a wider perspective than that of immediate family and kin. The trade may have depended on thousands of individual bonds of friendship between people in different communities. These friendships probably involved the regular exchange of luxury goods, in situations where the gifts could not be refused, and were a form of cement for formal, almost political, if not religious, relationships.

The complicated overlay of ritual and artistic tradition that forms the most distinctive feature of the Hopewell is so exotic and polished that many Hopewell art objects seem at first glance to be almost alien to a simple agricultural society. But closer examination reveals the strong links both between the ancient and modern Indian art motifs and between cult objects and the normal, everyday domestic artifacts of the Hopewell. Hopewell ceremonial-artistic traditions were as distinctively American Indian as those of the ancient Egyptians were char-

Ceremonial figure or shaman

acteristically Egyptian in inspiration and tradition.

The Hopewell people enjoyed a remarkable efflorescence of artistic and religious creativity from about 200 B.C. until A.D. 550. It is difficult to explain this sudden acceleration of cultural development. Some people believe that the grafting of corn cultivation onto the basic Adena subsistence pattern may have had a dramatic effect on population growth. As agricultural productivity increased, so did more ambitious trading activity and wider political connections than had ever existed before. But, whatever the causes of Hopewell prosperity, after seven hundred years the trading networks broke down and Hopewell influence on any wide scale declined sharply.

Regional variations on the Hopewell theme continued to flourish, not least among them the so-called "Effigy Mound" culture centered on the upper Mississippi Valley. The Indians of that area built mounds in the form of animals — panthers, lizards, deer, bears — as well as birds. Most of the mounds contain several burials, often at critical joints in the figure — at the heart, hip, or knee. No one can explain the effigy mounds, which can best be seen from the air. Were they representations of clan symbols? Did burial at a certain point on the mound have a special significance? Although the effigy mounds of Minnesota and Wisconsin certainly owe their ultimate religious inspiration to the Hopewell, we simply do not know what they meant.

The Great Serpent Mound, near Chillicothe, Ohio, must rank as the most extraordinary Indian monument of all. This huge earthwork uncoils along an Ohio ridge for 1,254 feet. The jaws of the serpent are open, clasping a low conical mound in the shape

Sacred fire symbol

Sacrificial rite figure

Ceremonial figure or shaman

of an egg. The body of the snake twines along the hilltop, its tail tightly coiled in a spiral. The serpent mound was nearly destroyed in the late nineteenth century but, fortunately, Harvard University was able to purchase the earthwork before the farmer who owned it could plow it under. It is now an Ohio state park. The Serpent Mound is not a burial mound, nor does it appear to have any connection with the effigy mounds of the upper Mississippi Valley. Most archaeologists believe that the serpent may have had a special mound-builder symbolism. Few share the belief of a well-known nineteenth-century Baptist minister, who argued that the great serpent was built by the Creator himself to commemorate the site of the Fall. In that interpretation, the serpent is about to swallow the forbidden fruit, represented by the small mound between the jaws. In support of his claim, the minister cited Job 26:13: "His hand hath formed the crooked serpent."

The decline of the Hopewell culture is still imperfectly understood, but it is possible that a rapid and dramatic population explosion may have strained the limits of the economic system, causing competition between different trading networks and rupturing long-established economic and political relationships. We know that by A.D. 600, the cultural primacy in North America had passed from the Hopewell area to the lower Mississippi Valley. The fertile flood plain between St. Louis and New Orleans nurtured the greatest of all North American Indian states, that named by archaeologists the "Mississippian." For at least eight centuries from A.D. 600, this remarkable society dominated the Mississippi Valley and in-

fluenced a vast area of central and eastern North America as well. Yet most traces of the Mississippian people had vanished by the time white colonists settled in their homeland in the eighteenth and nineteenth centuries.

The scale and flamboyance of Mississippian society dwarfed anything known before in North America. Its enormous ceremonial centers, brilliant artistic traditions, and elaborate cosmology seem at least partially alien to the earlier cultures of the mound builders. The truncated pyramids and huge plazas of Cahokia and other Mississippian ceremonial centers have an almost Mexican air. Simple burial mounds went out of fashion. A new religious symbolism was abroad, reflecting a fascination with human sacrifice, sun, and fire, all characteristically Mexican ritual concerns. These seemingly foreign elements were superimposed on an indigenous North American society.

A thousand years ago a visitor to the Mississippi Valley at harvest time would have found a shimmering plain of ripening corn. We can imagine him walking through village after village, following a series of small paths. On the way he meets dozens of people, some carrying baskets of wild produce, others with the morning's catch hanging from a stick. The pounding of grain pestles echoes from the villages as the women prepare the evening meal. Occasionally, a group of traders passes by, with bundles of pottery or obsidian knives. After a while the visitor's route brings him to a wider pathway trodden flat by thousands of feet. Soon the great pyramids and mounds of the Cahokia ceremonial center come into clear view, towering above the villages and corn fields. The largest mound covers sixteen acres and

131

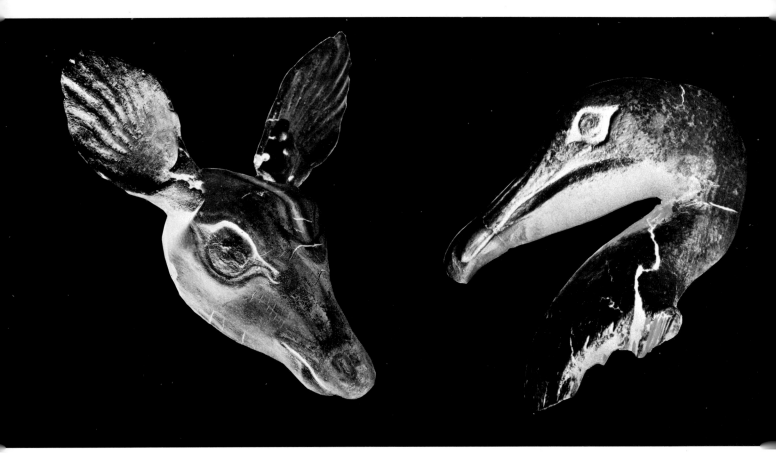

the temple on its summit is over one hundred feet high. As the sun goes down, the great earthworks cast long shadows over the countryside and the smoke from thousands of evening fires forms a light pall over the sunset.

The social structure of Mississippian society was reflected in the layout of Cahokia. At one end of a central plaza stood the great temple, a symbol of the religious and political hierarchy which governed every aspect of Cahokian life. Around it rose other mounds, some of them the foundation for warehouses, administrative buildings, and the homes of nobles. Stretching out from the city were the villages of the farmers who raised the surplus food to support the nobles and contributed the labor to build the great mounds.

Annual ceremonies marked the times of planting and harvest. It was then that the finest products of the Mississippian craftspeople were displayed in the market. Copper, shell, stone, pottery, and wood were used in a remarkable range of ritual objects. Copper

sheets were embossed with human portraits, shell disks with complex religious images that included birds, spiders, and the sun. Jars were modeled in the form of human heads, often with painted faces or signs of tattooing. Some of the faces are weeping, a hint that Mississippian cosmology may have linked tears with rain. Conch shells were adorned with distinctive fork-eyed and weeping-eye motifs, a form of abstract symbolism that is a major theme in Mississipian art.

There is a restrictive convention about Mississippian artistry that is striking even to the casual observer. A select and carefully controlled range of motifs was favored, associated with pottery, conch shells, copper, and masks in various materials. These include sunbursts, a human hand depicted with an eye in the palm, various stylized human facial expressions. These symbolisms have some analogies in recent Indian cosmologies, but are thought to be derived in part from Mexican cults, with their preoccupation with the sun, rain, and gods of fire.

132

Exquisitely carved wooden figures of a deer and a pelican (opposite), dating from A.D. 800 to 1400, figured in rituals of the Key Marco culture of Florida. Later, pottery vessels like the effigy pot at right may have been used in Southern Death Cult ceremonies.

What god or gods the Mississippians worshipped we do not know. Many of the carved human figures are thought to depict shaman priests who played a prominent part in the cult, perhaps at times assuming the role of the living god in spectacular sacrifices and public ceremonies. Certain small, long-nosed masks are called god masks, though some experts think they represent the *pochteca*, Mexican itinerant traders who are thought to have introduced many new elements into Mississippian society.

The Mississippian seems strangely alien after the long centuries of Adena and Hopewell efflorescence in North America. The same basic economy of subsistence agriculture, hunting, and gathering still continued as it had done for centuries. But now society had branched off in new directions, creating a hierarchical superstructure with values that seem rigid and ostentatious. The vast ceremonial centers, pyramids, and great plazas recall Mexican religious patterns with their insistence on public display. The critical religious and secular decisions of state were now centralized under the control of a religious elite, just as they were among the Maya and other Mexican states. Many archaeologists believe that the Mississippians acquired these alien beliefs from Mexico, through trading contacts with the great empires to the south. Perhaps some Mexican priests actually settled in the Mississippi Valley. We do not know whether they did or not, but by the time white men got their first look at Mississippian culture, it represented a fusion of Mexican and native North American cosmologies, architectural styles, and social usages.

Hernando de Soto and his conquistadors were the first Europeans to observe a native North American culture. When they crossed the southeastern United States in the sixteenth century, they came across large communities of Mississippians living in loosely knit confederacies headed by powerful chiefs. But the Mississippian civilization did not last long after that brief contact. Smallpox, measles, tuberculosis, and the common cold followed in the conquistadors' train. Within a few decades, alien diseases had depopulated much of the Southeast, and the economic and political structure of Mississippian life collapsed forever. By the time French explorers visited Louisiana in the early eighteenth century, little remained of the great estates of the past.

Nevertheless when the Spanish, French, and Eng- lish began to colonize the southeast in the seventeenth century, they came up against a powerful confederation of some fifty large settlements in the area of present Alabama and Georgia. This "Creek" Indian confederacy, as it was soon named, was made up of many different peoples and several languages. To the south and west of the Creek lived the Chickasaw and Choctaw, bitter enemies to one another, the latter cultivating the rich bottom soils of southern Mississippi. The Cherokee lived to the north of the Creek, an important group of more than 60,000 people living in at least 100 major settlements. The missionaries who first recorded Cherokee oral traditions heard them claim that their ancestors had built Grave Creek tumulus in West Virginia and other large mounds in Tennessee. These traditions were ignored by early antiquarians looking for ancient and exotic mound-builder civilizations.

The European colonists found the lower Mississippi from the Yazoo River to the delta ruled by a series of small, riverside states. Some of these states,

This 2,000-year-old, eight-inch-tall ceremonial pipe in the shape of a dwarfed man with a thick neck—probably from goiters—reflects the esteem in which the Adena seem to have held deformed people. The mysterious stone head at right was carved by the "Cole" people, little-known descendants of the Hopewell in Ohio.

notably that of the Natchez, perpetuated Mississippian culture, including the tradition of mound building, into the eighteenth century. The Natchez lived in seven villages clustered around the earthen mounds to the east of the present city named after them. They may have numbered 4,000 souls in the late seventeenth century.

A French trading post was opened at the Great Village of the Natchez in 1713, as a preliminary to systematic exploitation of the Louisiana colony. The Natchez area became the focal point of trading activity and of French plantations. Many Frenchmen left accounts of the Natchez and their remarkable society, with the result that they are the best known of all the lower Mississippi states of 300 years ago.

The Natchez were ruled by a chief, the Great Sun, whose powers were absolute and despotic. From his house on a flat-topped mound, he controlled land, lives, and property. Nearby, on a second mound, rose a temple where the bones of previous chiefs were buried. The Great Sun's relatives were known as Little Suns and stood a step above a class of Nobles. The Nobles in turn were a rank above Honored Men, a class open to anyone who distinguished himself in war or religious devotion. Commoners, sometimes called Stinkards, were the lowest of the low, treated with contempt by their superiors. The clan structure, though sharply defined, made provision for change in each generation. Every noble and every sun—even the Great Sun himself—had to marry a Stinkard. Everyone knew where they stood in rank, even slaves taken in war, who could on occasion be adopted into Natchez society and themselves achieve status.

One French chronicler, Le Page du Pratz, struck up a close friendship with the Natchez war chief, Tattooed Serpent. The chief spent many hours recounting details of Natchez society to the young traveler. Tattooed Serpent died in 1725, when Le Page was still among the Natchez. Le Page records how a terrible cry echoed from the villages at news that the chief's hearth was extinguished forever. A deep despair gripped his subjects. Funeral preparations were set in train, while the chief's body lay in state for several days. Eight sacrificial victims were selected to accompany the chief on his final journey. The French were astonished by the victims' sang-froid, until they realized that society considered it a great honor to be selected to go on such a journey. On the day of the funeral, the chief's body was carried to his temple in great state. Eight executioners quickly strangled the victims as they knelt on funeral mats. As the body of the chief and those of his companions were placed in a huge trench by his house, the dwelling was burnt to the ground.

Le Page's account is the only eyewitness description of a Mississippian funeral, and of a type of society that was responsible for one of the most remarkable of all native American cultures. It was only nine years later that the Natchez rose in bloody revolt against the French. Within a few years, almost no Natchez remained alive. Their mounds and villages were overgrown and silent forever. By this time Cahokia, Etowah, Moundville, and other great ceremonial centers were long abandoned. The banks of the Mississippi were largely depopulated, the earthworks at the river's edge merged into the levees and ridges and became virtually indistinguishable from the natural landscape. Complete oblivion had overtaken the last of the mound builders.

WHY WERE THE EASTER ISLAND STATUES CARVED?

Late on Easter Sunday, 1722, a Dutch navigator, Jakob Roggeveen, discovered and named Easter Island, an irregular triangle of grass-covered rock thirteen miles long set all alone in the Pacific 2,200 miles west of South America and 1,200 miles east of tiny Pitcairn Island. Next morning, one of Roggeveen's men observed the island's inhabitants had "prostrated themselves toward the rising sun and kindled . . . fires, which probably betokened a morning oblation to their gods." These "gods" were "certain remarkably tall figures . . . all hewn out of stone, in the form of a man, with long ears, adorned on the head with a crown. . . ."

Since then, few visitors to that remote speck of land have failed to marvel, as those first European visitors did, at these strange, brooding monoliths, carved out of the yellow-gray tuff of the volcano Rano Raraku. In Roggeveen's time, 261 of them stood facing inland on ceremonial platforms of packed earth and stones—singly, in pairs, or in rows of up to fifteen—their heads topped by cylindrical crowns of red scoria quarried from the volcano Puna Pau. Today, except for a few set back in place by archaeologists, every one of the enshrined *moai* lies toppled. And on the slopes below Rano Raraku (opposite page), half buried in the detritus of centuries, 276 more of them, uncrowned, stare skyward or out to sea.

Mysterious in themselves, these giant statues conjure up a cloud of questions. Who made them? When? And why were the standing ones overturned? The answers—some still only guesses—must be sought in the island's history.

It is generally believed that Easter Island was settled by Polynesians around the twelfth century.

The islanders' legends tell of their ancestors' arriving in canoes from the Marquesas, 2,000 miles northwest. But they also tell of the island being shared by two distinct peoples: the Long-ears, who extended their ear lobes by inserting heavy disks in them, and the Short-ears, who did not. Scholars believe that the first immigrants, the Long-ears, began raising the *moai* to honor their dead between 600 and 800 years ago, and, when the Short-ears arrived, got the newcomers to help them at it.

After two or three centuries of peaceful, if unequal, coexistence, the Short-ears apparently rose against the Long-ears. According to tradition the latter retreated to the plateau of Poike at the island's eastern end behind a wide ditch two miles long; they filled the ditch with logs and brush and set them ablaze. But some Short-ears crept around the ditch and onto the plateau by way of the cliff face; taking the Long-ears by surprise, they drove them back into their own defensive wall of flame, allowing only one to survive. From the number of generations said to have elapsed since then, scholars have long put the epochal battle at around 1680; carbon dating of charred material in the ditch has pinpointed a conflagration therein in 1676.

With the virtual elimination of the Long-ears, peace was restored. The Short-ears divided the land and the *moai* among themselves. But some time after Roggeveen's visit the social order broke down; there followed a protracted period of civil war—the *huri-moai* or statue-overturning time—which only ended definitively in the 1860s, when the islanders, their ranks thinned by intertribal fighting and a disastrous raid by Peruvian slavers, were converted to Christianity.

Is this the whole story? Thor Heyerdahl, the Norwegian scientist-adventurer, thinks not. There is, he says, persuasive evidence on Easter Island of non-Polynesian influence—notably hardwood tablets covered with ideograms. Since Polynesia had no writing of any kind, Heyerdahl is convinced that the islanders must have had some contact with South America. For him, the Long-ears were not Polynesians but pre-Inca Peruvians, skilled stonecutters and sculptors, who arrived on Easter before A.D. 300 in reed boats. (As he points out, reeds that grow in the island's crater lakes—and nowhere else in Polynesia—are the same species still used to make boats on Lake Titicaca.) After digging the Poike ditch (carbon dated to the late fourth century) and fashioning sophisticated statues, examples of which are still being unearthed, the Long-ears around A.D. 1100 began, says Heyerdahl, to build the *moai,* and about four centuries later initiated the newly arrived Marquesan Short-ears into the cult.

But the riddle remains: whether they were Polynesians or Peruvians, why did the original *moai* builders undertake this immense labor and persist so long at it? One motive, psychologists suggest, may simply have been to relieve the tedium of living in such extreme isolation. Perhaps it was because they lacked all diversion from the outside that they evolved a fanatical, ingrown religion which required them to create more and still more idols on an ever more gigantic scale. And perhaps it was for want of wild animals to hunt and enemy neighbors to fight that, once that religion lost hold over them, the Short-ears turned on each other and on the Long-ears' mighty statues.

WHY DID THE ANCIENTS NOT DEVELOP MACHINERY?

Energy is the basis of modern civilization; it dominates the headlines, makes and breaks the economy of nations, determines their foreign policy. Yet it is relatively a newcomer to history. It began to occupy men's minds only during the Middle Ages, not before. Egypt, Assyria, Persia, all fashioned their empires without it, Greece achieved her glory and Rome her splendor without it. Very possibly the glory and the splendor would have been still greater, had Greeks and Romans turned their attention to utilizing sources of power other than the muscles of man or beast. For some reason they did not.

They did not, even though they were fully acquainted with a number of easily exploitable forms of energy. As far back as 3000 B.C. the Egyptians had learned to harness the force of the wind to drive their craft up and down the Nile. But neither they nor anyone else ever went further than boats: as we shall see shortly, the earliest windmills date from the seventh century A.D. or even later. By the first century B.C. the Greeks and Romans had learned to use the flow of water to turn mills, but all over the world grain continued to be ground slowly and laboriously by hand or animal. They were even aware of more sophisticated sources of power, such as compressed air, hot air, steam. A Greek engineer named Ctesibius, who lived during the third century B.C. in the city of Alexandria—the center at the time of scholarly and scientific research—produced a hydraulic organ whose power was furnished by a column of water supported on a cushion of air. He designed a clock driven by water: flowing into a bowl at a fixed rate, it steadily raised a float topped by a figure whose hand pointed to lines representing hours engraved on a cylinder; the cylinder itself was made to rotate by the upward movement of the float.

Another Greek engineer named Hero, who also worked at Alexandria though at a later time than Ctesibius, perhaps the first century A.D., describes certain inventions for use in temples which, by exploiting the expansive property of hot air, were able to arouse wonderment and awe among the congregations. One consisted of a pipe and some figures

◄OVERLEAF (pages 138-139): Aqueducts were regarded by Roman engineers as their supreme achievements. They were carried over rivers and valleys on masonry arches like this one in Turkey. Superimposed in white is a design of a Roman catapult.
KAY LAWSON

mounted on a disk; when the altar fire was lit, the hot air from it, passing through the pipe, caused the disk to revolve and the figures to appear to dance. In a second device, hot air made the doors of a shrine open and shut. In a third, an altar flanked by two figures holding wine vessels and surmounted by a bronze serpent, the hot air produced a flow of wine from the vessels and a hiss from the serpent. Yet another is the earliest example on record of a steam engine: a hollow ball was mounted between two brackets made fast to the lid of a pot filled with boiling water; one of the brackets was also hollow, and the steam passing through it into the ball was vented in such a way that the ball was made to rotate. Hero even describes a windmill, a miniature version for providing the current of air required to power a small and simple type of organ. He includes any number of gadgets worked by means of levers and weights, among them the first known coin-operated machine: when a five-drachma piece was dropped through a slot in the cover of a sacrificial vessel filled with holy water, it triggered by means of a Rube Goldberg contraption a spurt from a spout on the side. But these and others like them were all that Alexandria's scientific savants turned out; their imaginative exploiting of water, wind, hot air, and steam went into toys and gadgetry, never into machines for replacing men's labor.

The ancients' failure in this regard stands in stark contrast with the accomplishments of their heirs, the men of the Middle Ages. By A.D. 983 there probably was a mill for fulling cloth on the banks of the Serchio in Tuscany. By 1008 there were water-driven grain as well as fulling mills around Milan. The windmill for grinding grain makes its debut in Persia, perhaps in the seventh A.D., certainly a century or two later. In the twelfth century it appears in Yorkshire—an independent invention, though possibly inspired by news of such machines in the east—and "spread over Europe almost explosively," to quote Lynn White, our ranking historian of technology, who has pioneered in bringing attention to the spectacular advances that took place in medieval times.

By the fourteenth century water- and windpower had replaced muscle not only for fulling cloth and grinding grain but for sawing wood, lifting water, operating the bellows of blast furnaces, driving triphammers, turning grindstones, and crushing anything from ore to olives. So wide and effective was the

technological surge that, as White puts it, "by 1492 ... Europe had developed an agricultural base, an industrial capacity, a superiority in arms, and a skill in voyaging the ocean which enabled it to explore, conquer, loot and colonize the rest of the globe during the next four centuries." Mighty Rome, restrained by its technological sloth, had been able to explore, conquer, loot, and colonize no farther than the Mediterranean and the western end of Europe.

Necessity, we say, is the mother of invention. We neglect to add that the necessity must be one that people are aware of. Greeks and Romans did not think it at all necessary to spare men the drudgery and time it took to grind grain into flour, even after the water mill had become known; the people of twelfth-century Yorkshire, it is clear, did. In the lands of medieval Islam the climate was so arid that streams with the flow to drive mills were few; on the other hand, since sparseness of vegetation generates air currents, there was plenty of wind. Here, if anywhere, a "need" existed for the windmill—and the Arabs did not even have to invent it but merely borrow it from Persia where, as mentioned above, it had been in use for centuries. They could not have been less interested. In 1206, by which time windmills were to be seen from Scotland to Syria, the leading Arab engineer of the day observed to his readers that the notion of driving mills by the wind was nonsense.

It was no one from the ancient world but a western European of the Middle Ages, Hugh of St. Victor, who said, *"Propter necessitatem inventa est mechanica,"* necessity is the mother of technology. By his time technology had become integrated into men's thinking habits. They had learned to turn to it automatically as the way of solving certain problems; they had, in short, invented invention. The phrase would never have come to the lips of a Greek or Roman. They totally lacked a tradition of carrying on sustained effort to produce a technological solution to a felt need. Invention, as they saw it, was the result of happy accident. Among their heroes are no James Watts, no Thomas Edisons, no men who devoted a lifetime to studying, experimenting, perfecting a device. Their classic story is of Archimedes' discovery of the principle of specific gravity while in his bath pondering how to test the honesty of a goldsmith.

What was it, then, that made people from the tenth century A.D. on aware of a need for labor-saving machinery and made them turn to technology for the solution? What was it that prevented the ancients from doing this? Let us take the second question first.

It is said that the Greeks never exploited steam, that they never converted Hero's toy into a useful engine, because they did not have the materials or technology for steamfitting, for fashioning and joining tubing to take the pressures. True enough—but beside the point: they simply did not think in terms of using steam power for utilitarian purposes. It is said that they never exploited the water mill because the Mediterranean does not have the rivers that would provide the flow required. This is not only beside the point but not even true. The rivers were perfectly adequate for driving the mills that were there during the Middle Ages. Moreover, the Romans—and the Etruscans long before them—were expert at providing a flow where there was none. What mills the Romans eventually did construct, as often as not were run by water from aqueducts.

These and other similar specific explanations that have been offered do not get us very far. What about the broad generalizations?

There is a school of thought, whose ranks have been swelled by the unswerving adherence of most Marxist historians, which holds that slavery was the culprit: the economy of the ancients was based on slavery and, the argument runs, with slaves to do the work there was no incentive to develop technology. "Their slaves were their machines," asserts Benjamin Farrington, author of a series of widely used handbooks on ancient science and technology, "and so long as they were cheap there was no need to try to supersede them. The supply of slave labor seems to have outlasted the heyday of ancient science." There is no denying that the Greek and Roman economy was based on slave labor, although the most important segment, agriculture, depended upon it only at certain times and in certain places. But one can emphatically deny that slave labor was always plentiful and cheap; there were long periods when it was nothing of the sort. And, if the ancients' technological backwardness is to be attributed to the availability of slaves, how can one explain the date of introduction of what labor-saving devices the Romans did use? It was in the second century B.C. that they replaced their hand-operated mills for grinding grain with the donkey-powered rotary mill—precisely when, thanks to Rome's conquest of the east and the consequent arrival on the block of hordes of prisoners, there was a glut of slaves. And, in the very next century, when there were still plenty of them around, Rome's bakeries began using horse-drawn machines for kneading dough.

Another school of thought holds that it was the abundance of labor in general, whether slave or free, which did the damage. "Labour was too cheap for much thought to be given to machinery," declares W. W. Tarn, one of the foremost historians of ancient Greece. "Labour . . . was plentiful and cheap until the end of the third century [A.D.], precisely the period when the donkey-mills or slave-driven mills of Rome were gradually ousted by the water mill," declares R. Forbes in the standard work in English on ancient technology. This explanation no more fits the facts than slavery. The water mill—to which we will come in a few moments—did precious little ousting of man- and animal-power in the third century; a few more mills were built than before, but it is perfectly clear that most grinding was still being done in the time-honored, time-consuming way.

There is an anecdote that the adherents of this school often cite. Rome's Emperor Vespasian, who ruled from A.D. 69 to 79, was once approached, we are told, by an engineer who offered to haul big stone columns to the top of the Capitoline Hill for a very small charge; Vespasian gave him a handsome reward but refused his services on the grounds that he wanted "to be allowed to feed the mob." They assume that the story indicates an excess on the Roman labor market, a mass of unemployed whom the government supported by work projects. But "unemployment" and "work projects" are twentieth-century concepts; antiquity knew nothing of them. Ancient governments did not go about creating work to provide jobs. Certainly the Roman emperors did not, even though they were faced with the chronic problem of maintaining "the mob," that is, the thousands of poor Roman citizens who centuries earlier had drifted to the city and whose descendants had led an idle existence ever since. The emperors took care of them by means of the proverbial "bread and circuses," feeding them through public handouts of grain and keeping them content by entertaining them with free gladiatorial combats and horse racing. In any case, these people were in no way part of the labor force. Besides, manual labor, such as the han-

dling of columns, was normally done by slaves, so the only ones who would have profited from Vespasian's rejection of the engineer's offer were not any theoretical unemployed but the owners of the teams of slaves who held the contracts for the hauling. Commentators on the story imagine that the engineer had in mind some power-driven lifting machinery, but this is pure fantasy. A more likely explanation is that he suggested to Vespasian something no emperor had ever thought of doing before—to entice some of the handout receivers to put in a few days or a few weeks of work for pay. This would no doubt have amounted to much less than the hire of teams of slaves, whose owners had to charge enough to cover the cost of maintaining them all year round, work or no work, and of writing off the loss whenever any died or were injured. Vespasian, however, said no; he wanted to "be allowed to feed the mob," that is, carry on the traditional policy of giving them handouts, not try any newfangled ideas of putting them to work.

Another argument against those who blame the technological laggardness on a surplus of labor is that what clues we can gather point just the other way. A number of treatises on farming in Italy, written between the second century B.C. and the first A.D., have survived. They make allusion to the difficulties farmers had because of the scarcity of hands. There were times when Egypt, one of the breadbaskets of the ancient world, suffered from country-wide shortages of labor. Indeed, it has been argued that a key factor inhibiting the internal growth of the empires that were established in the wake of Alexander the Great's conquests was the limited agricultural manpower available: it was never possible to increase the number of peasants beyond a certain figure, and, because of this, food production was never able to rise to levels that could support more or larger urban centers. Obviously the solution would have been the development of mechanical aids to relieve the peasants' backbreaking toil and increase his output. The Ptolemies, who ruled Egypt from 300 B.C. through the next few centuries, did their best to wring as much out of the land as they could. They reclaimed large tracts, improved the irrigation system, introduced new crops. At the same time, being openhanded patrons of the arts and sciences, they supported research of all kinds, including the experiments of Ctesibius and other scientists in the use of water and hot air as a force. Yet it evidently never

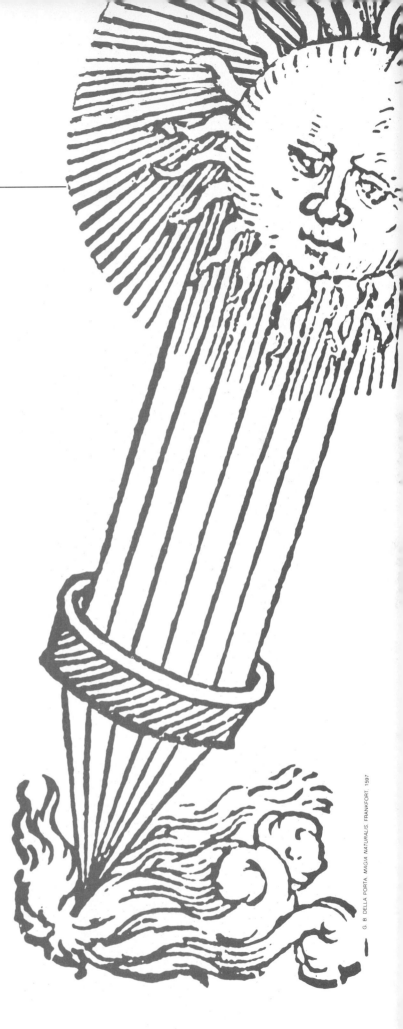

A giant burning glass (shown here in a fanciful six-teenth-century woodcut) was devised by Archimedes, the ancient Greek mathematician, to concentrate the sun's rays in order to set fire to enemy ships. Archimedes considered himself a geometrician and, except for his military inventions, disdained practical applications of his physical theories.

crossed their minds to suggest to these scientists that they give up playing around with toys and gadgets and get to work on a power-driven mill. Whether the effort would have succeeded is irrelevant; the point is that it was never made.

What is even more mystifying is that labor-saving devices actually came into existence and yet were not exploited. In the first century A.D. a mechanical harvester was developed. We know what it was like not only from descriptions of ancient writers but from a number of carved reliefs that picture it: it was, in effect, an oversize comb mounted on wheels and pushed by a donkey or mule; as it went along it took off the heads of grain, leaving the stalks standing. Admittedly, it could operate efficiently only on level ground and appeal only to farmers willing to forego the straw. So far as we can tell, the device was used in a certain section of Gaul, roughly between Reims and Trier, and nowhere else, though there surely were other areas in the ancient world where the machine's advantages outweighed its limitations. Moreover, no effort was made to adapt it for farms whose owners wanted the straw or where the terrain was not appropriately level, an adaptation that should not have been difficult. Ancient farmers, in short, were content to go on harvesting with sickles, even though this was a painfully slow way to do it and one of their complaints was a lack of hands.

Even more striking than the failure of the mechanical harvester to catch on is that of the water mill. We noted above that the Romans certainly knew the water mill by the first century B.C. A good argument can be made that the Etruscans knew it several centuries earlier. They were superb hydraulic engineers, particularly skilled in cutting long underground sewerlike channels through rock to control the direction and volume of the flow of water. In most cases these channels ran along the bottom of valleys to carry off rainwater and not let it erode the valley floors. At Veii, an Etruscan site some twelve miles north of Rome, the inhabitants cut one such channel, over one-third of a mile long and over eighty feet deep in one place, whose purpose could not have been to prevent erosion. It carried water from a larger stream to a point on a smaller, thereby increasing the velocity of the flow at that point. The only logical explanation for this elaborate piece of hydraulic engineering is that the Etruscans wanted to strengthen the flow at the point in question because

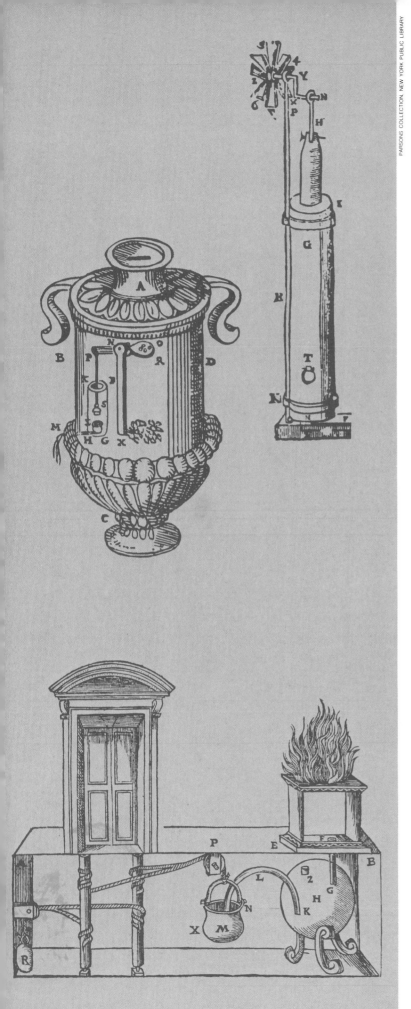

Hero, the Greek engineer who worked around the first century A.D., invented many ingenious devices. Though little more than toys or gadgets, they embodied principles that could have been used for labor-saving machines. At near left is a windmill that was used to make an organ play; the use of the windmill for grinding corn or raising water did not occur in the West until a thousand years later. To the left of the windmill is a water dispenser for a temple; when a coin was dropped through the slot it fell onto a disk that raised a stopper, thus dispensing lustral water through the spout. At left below is Hero's miraculous altar. When a fire was lit on the altar it heated the air in the base, which expanded into the sphere below; this in turn forced water from the sphere through a pipe into the center receptacle. As the receptacle sank under the weight, it pulled on the cords which then opened the temple door.

they maintained a mill there—and, indeed, a mill has stood in the area from the Middle Ages to very recent times.

In any event, when we come to the first century B.C. we do not have to depend on argument or inference: we know that water mills existed then because Vitruvius describes them in the famous book on architecture and building techniques that he wrote probably in the closing decades of the pre-Christian era. The very way in which he deals with them is significant. In a discussion of the devices in use for raising water, after treating various forms of treadmills, he describes a water-powered wheel that turns an endless chain of buckets; this, he goes on to inform us, differs from the water-powered mill in that the water-driven wheel in the latter case turns a millstone. When he comes to his summing up of the discussion, he does not even bother to mention the water mill. That is all he has to say about the piece of machinery that was destined to revolutionize agriculture and industry. Vitruvius' indifference was typical. A water mill can grind effortlessly in under three minutes what would take a man or beast an hour of hard work. Once discovered, it should have swept over the Mediterranean world as quickly as it was to sweep over Europe a millennium later. It did nothing of the sort. During the first three centuries A.D., the heyday of the Roman Empire, it saw scant use. The number of mills increased somewhat after that, but not importantly. In most places the age-old laborious methods of grinding grain still continued.

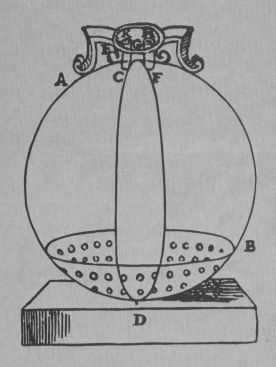

More of Hero's inventions are shown at right. The globe at top is a dispenser containing wine on one side of a diaphragm and water on the other. The ancients commonly mixed water with their wine. By placing a finger over one of the holes in the top of the decanter the host could pour wine alone or water alone or he could pour both in the desired proportion.

Hero's puppet theatre was an ingenious example of scientific showmanship. When the lead cylinder at the lower right corner of the automaton was released, its weight activated a mechanism of wheels and pulleys, hidden around the floor of a temple. Thereupon, the statue of Dionysus, which was located inside the temple, turned and poured a libation, while the Winged Victory located on the roof of the temple was made to revolve.

These modern drawings of Hero's inventions are based on descriptions in his Pneumatics.

Michael Rostovtzeff, author of the definitive studies on the social and economic history of the ancient world, was well aware of the shortcomings of slavery or cheap free labor as an explanation of the Greeks' "slow technical progress and . . . restricted range of output." He argues that "the causes of these limitations are chiefly to be found, on the one hand, in local production of manufactured goods and the arrest of the development of large industrial centers, and, on the other, in the low buying capacity and restricted number of customers." This explanation simply puts us in a circle. Industrial centers could not develop because they could not be fed without increasing the production of food, and, as we have just seen, the fixed or even declining number of peasants prevented this. And without such industrial centers, the number of potential customers would inevitably be restricted and buying power low. Men did not break out of the circle until the Middle Ages. Why did they not do it in ancient times?

We cannot call upon mountains of statistics to help us with the answer, for there are no such from the ancient world. All we can do is go through whatever writings have survived, from agricultural treatises to lyric poetry, in search of anything that will throw light, no matter how feeble, on the problem. There is an anecdote told by Lucian, a satirist and lecturer of the second century A.D., that is a good deal more to the point than the story about Vespasian and the engineer. In an essay that purports to be autobiographical Lucian recounts how he embarked

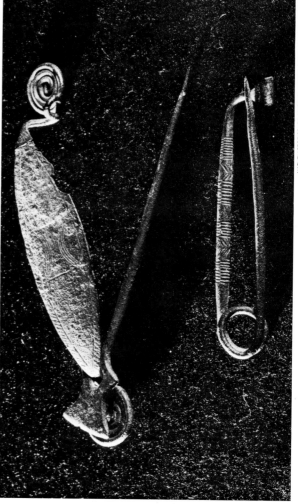

This Roman reaping machine was used in Gaul about two thousand years ago. A comb of steel blades, mounted on the front of a cart, cut off the grain stalks just below the heads and dropped them into the cart, which was pushed by oxen or horses. Though practical, at least on level ground, the machine was little used.

The safety pin was invented by some Bronze Age genius who took an ordinary pin, bent it double, and lodged the point in a protective slot or hook. These Roman pins, or fibulae (above, right), have the same design.

upon his career. He had a dream, he informs us, in which two women struggled for possession of him, one mannish and dirty and unkempt and covered with stone dust, the other lovely and poised and well dressed. The first sought to entice him to become a sculptor, to achieve the greatness of Phidias and Praxiteles, the other to turn to education and follow an intellectual career. If you become a sculptor, the lovely woman warned him, "hunched over your work, your eyes and mind on the ground, low as low can be, you will never lift your head to think the thoughts of a true man or a free spirit." Lucian did not hesitate: he joyously embraced the life of the mind.

The prejudice against the artisan that Lucian's words reveal can be traced throughout the fabric of

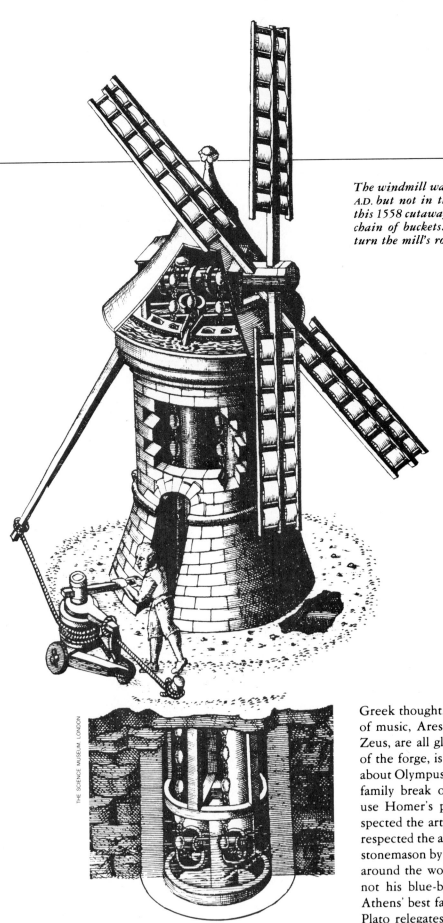

The windmill was used in Persia by the seventh century A.D. but not in the West until the twelfth. The mill in this 1558 cutaway drawing raised water in a continuous chain of buckets. The operator is using a windlass to turn the mill's rotating top to face the wind.

Greek thought. In the Greek pantheon, Apollo, god of music, Ares, god of war, Hermes, messenger of Zeus, are all gloriously handsome; Hephaestus, god of the forge, is ugly and lame and, when he hobbles about Olympus, the sight makes the rest of the divine family break out into "unquenchable laughter," to use Homer's phrase. The Greeks admired and respected the artisan's work; they neither admired nor respected the artisan. Socrates, who happened to be a stonemason by trade, was often to be found lounging around the workshops of his fellow craftsmen—but not his blue-blooded pupil Plato, scion of one of Athens' best families. In the utopias he conjures up, Plato relegates craftsmen to the lowest rung of the social ladder. Xenophon, a fellow aristocrat, points out that in those Greek cities that pride themselves

147

Even when Roman engineers had machines, they relied on muscle power to operate them. This crane, used to erect or repair public buildings, is powered by slaves treading inside a wheel.

on their military reputation, citizens are not allowed to practice a craft. Aristotle, tutor to Alexander the Great, sniffily remarks that "the finest type of city will not make an artisan a citizen."

One reason for the prejudice was that, from the very beginning, many artisans were slaves; one effect of the prejudice was to ensure that more and more of them would be. Throughout Greek history, the free and slave craftsman shared work, often laboring side by side. Records of the building of Greek temples and other structures have been preserved, and from them we can see that the stone blocks, the column drums, the sculptures, the scaffoldings, and all else, were fashioned by free and slave masons and carpenters working together and being paid exactly the same wage; the only difference was that the free man kept his while the slave turned his over to a master. Work of the hands, no matter of what quality, whether the rough hacking of stone in a quarry or the delicate carving of a sculpture, was something that could be done by slaves, and in the eyes of the upper class — the class to which without exception all ancient writers and intellectuals belonged — was not for them. Cicero, categorizing the pursuits that men follow, declares without qualification that "all craftsmen are engaged in a lowly art, for no workshop can have anything about it appropriate to a free man." They were all, as it were, sicklied o'er with the pale cast of slavery.

A passage in one of Plutarch's lives makes it crystal clear why Ctesibius, Hero, and the other scientists of antiquity stopped at toys and gadgets and never went on to machines — except in that one field which all through history has had a special claim on men's faculties, the art of war. In his *Life of Marcellus,* the famed general who led the Roman forces during much of the Second Punic War, he describes the trouble Marcellus had in besieging the strongly fortified town of Syracuse. Before the invention of cannon, laying siege to any walled city was no easy job, but Marcellus was having particularly rough going because the king of Syracuse had entrusted the defense to antiquity's most renowned engineer, Archimedes. Archimedes devised fiendish catapults which hurled monstrous stones upon attacking troops, fiendish cranes with huge claws that fastened upon attacking ships and lifted them right out of the water, even a Brobdingnagian burning glass that could set them on fire from a distance. After describing the formidable array, Plutarch remarks that Archimedes, though he had won universal acclaim for his military inventions "never wanted to leave behind a book on the subject but viewed the work of the engineer and every single art connected with everyday need as ignoble and fit only for an artisan. He devoted his ambition only to those studies in which beauty and subtlety are present uncontaminated by necessity." It was solely the intellectual challenge that led Archimedes to his discovery of the principle of specific gravity; its practical application, though it provided the occasion for his inspiration, was beneath his notice.

Thus the best brains of antiquity did not occupy themselves with technology except as a pastime or for war. Snobbishness played its part, but there were other causes as well. Science seeks to understand nature, and ancient thinkers welcomed this challenge. But technology seeks to tamper with it, and there was a feeling that this was forbidden territory. Herodotus tells a revealing story about the people of Cnidus. Their city was located on the tip of a peninsula, and once, fearing the attack of a powerful enemy, they began to cut through the neck to put a barrier of water between them and the mainland. As the work proceeded, they noted an inordinate number of injuries from rock splinters, especially about the eyes. It was serious enough for them to consult the Delphic Oracle; the response was that they were to quit work, that "Zeus would have made your peninsula an island had he so willed."

The split between science and technology was by no means limited to antiquity. When the ancient world died, its science lived on among the Arabs. For five hundred years the best scientists wrote in Arabic, yet this did nothing whatsoever to hasten the pace of technological development in Islam. The idea that science can advance technology was not clearly formulated until as late as A.D. 1450 and was not consistently acted upon until our own century.

Another key reason for the ancients' indifference to technology was their attitude toward profit, an attitude totally at variance with what we today unthinkingly accept as the natural order of things. The ancients were just as fond of money as we are. There were some philosophical sects whose members made a great show of scorning wealth—we all know the story of Diogenes, who preferred living in a barrel to

The Romans had a few water mills for grinding corn as early as the first century B.C. But this crucial labor-saving invention was not put to wide use until a thousand years later. The water wheel above is shown in a medieval Arab manuscript.

a house—but they were no more representative of society at large than hippies are today. Most men, upper-class or lower, were well aware that money was a good thing, that it was not possible to enjoy life without it. Where they differ from us is in their ideas about how it was to be made and what to do with it after making it. Throughout the whole of antiquity, men worked under the conviction that wealth should properly come from the land. All their great fortunes were landed fortunes: if they did not start out that way, they ended that way. Take the case of Trimalchio, the hero of the best-preserved scene in Petronius'

149

Satyricon, a brilliant and devastating satire about Rome's nouveaux riches in the first century A.D. Trimalchio, an ex-slave who became a multimillionaire, got his start by taking a flyer in the import of wine. When his ship came in, he made a killing—and promptly switched to real estate, the buying of farm properties. He acquired so much that though there were vast tracts of his holdings he had never even seen, he would not be content until he could buy up all Sicily, so that he could travel from Naples right to a port of departure for North Africa without once having to leave his own property. Trimalchio would have applauded enthusiastically Cicero's statement that "of all things from which income is derived, none is better than agriculture, none more fruitful, none sweeter, none more fitting for a free man." Cicero exaggerates: there were any number of pursuits more fruitful, but that was of secondary importance compared with agriculture's preeminent respectability, its fittingness for a free man.

Next to owning land came commerce, the sort of venture in which Trimalchio had gotten his start. But it was a good cut below. Hear Cicero on the subject: "Commerce, if it is on a small scale, is to be considered lowly; but if it is on a large scale and extensive, importing much from all over and distributing to many without misrepresentation, it is not to be too much disparaged"—in other words, at its very best, barely respectable.

Lower even than commerce was industry—industry, the form of endeavor in which results depend squarely upon productivity, which has most to gain from technology. Ancient industry, it is happens, never progressed beyond the large workshop stage. You will read in the writings of archaeologists descriptions of centers of ceramic production that sound like operations employing a labor force of thousands, but that is only because the archaeologist's stock in trade is potsherds and he tends to be overawed by the quantities he finds. The biggest pottery manufactories we know of were all owned by single individuals and never employed many more than fifty men. The very biggest privately owned (as against government-owned) industrial operation we know of was a shield-making establishment that employed something in the neighborhood of one hundred. Back in the eighteenth century David Hume wrote: "I do not remember a passage in any ancient author, where the growth of a city is ascribed to the establishment of a manufacture." Despite a century of archaeological discovery, his words need no qualification. There were no Manchesters or Birminghams in the ancient world, no equivalent of our New England mill towns.

Let us grant that Greeks and Romans did not exploit the potential of industry for making money and that we cannot therefore expect technological advance in that area. What about agriculture? We saw earlier that urban growth was restricted by the farmers' inability to feed more city mouths. Sometimes they could not even feed their own mouths; famines were not at all uncommon in ancient times. In the days of the Roman Empire there was plenty of land, with rich landowners holding the lion's share of it; why did they not seek to make better use of their resources? Pliny, Rome's savant whom we have several times quoted in earlier chapters, actually asserts that, for a landowner, "nothing pays less than cultivating your land to the fullest extent." Why?

The answer lies in another of the fundamental dif-

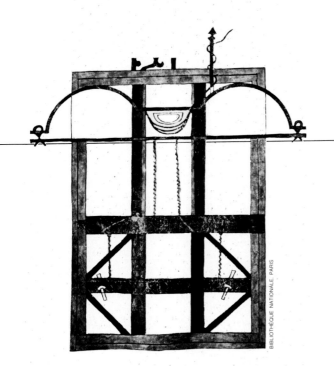

ferences in attitude between then and now: the ancients simply did not think in terms of maximum profits; the prevailing mentality of the age was acquisitive, not productive. One strove, like Trimalchio, to acquire as much land as possible, but not to wring it to produce as much profit as possible. Take, for example, old Cato, who lived in the second century B.C. and wrote one of the treatises on farming that have survived. He is the classic example of the shrewd, frugal, hardworking Roman landowner. He has endless advice to give on how to run a farm economically: precise prescriptions for the amount of rations of clothing and food to be issued to the help, how many hours to work them, what jobs to give them on rainy days; he cautions that they must be made to work on holidays, and that old and worn-out animals and slaves must be discarded just like worn-out tools. But if you had asked his advice on what crops sold the best or netted the most profit, about quickness of turnover, capital investment, and other standard bits of today's economic wisdom, he could not have known what you were talking about. Such matters were totally beyond the ken of the ancient farmer, peasant, or owner of vast estates. One of Cato's hard and fast rules was that a farmer "should be a seller, not a buyer." The same rule is expressed in different language by Columella, another expert on agriculture who wrote in the first century A.D. Some landowners, he tells us, "avoid annual expenses and consider it the best and most certain form of income not to make any investments." In other words, money not spent is money earned. If it costs more to install a watermill than a donkey-mill, then a donkey-mill it shall be.

As a matter of fact, profitability of operation was

Engines of warfare were almost the only machines that ancient inventors and engineers judged worthy of their talents. The two center drawings in the row above show Roman weapons: on the facing page, a siege tower which was pushed up to enemy walls; on this page, a catapult which used the same principle as that of the crossbow to hurl rocks at armies or fortifications.

Greek fire was an invention of the eastern Roman, or Byzantine, empire of the seventh century A.D. A flaming mixture of chemicals (probably naptha, sulfur, saltpeter and lime) was projected from a metal tube by pressure from a bellows. It could be used against an enemy boat, as shown at left on the opposite page, or against a tower, as shown above. This early flame thrower played a decisive role in turning back Moslem attackers for many centuries.

151

The rise in the status of the craftsman, from ancient to medieval times, is reflected in this illustration from a French illuminated manuscript of the thirteenth century. Here, God is portrayed with a carpenter's compass as the Architect of the Universe.

so far from the ancient farmer's mind that he did not even have the bookkeeping that would make it possible. We happen to have some of the records—they were a lucky find in an archaeological excavation—from a big Egyptian estate of the third century B.C. They reveal that the system of accounting in use was fine for the control of stock and staff but could not possibly yield the information required for efficient exploitation. The owner had not the slightest idea which of his numerous crops was the most profitable, what his cost per crop was, and so on.

We see, therefore, that it was not lack of knowledge which lay behind the poor technological record of the ancients but their lack of interest. The attitude of mind that made the artisan a human being of a lesser order, that glorified landowning as against land use, that left industry at a relatively primitive level, rendered technological advance of scant moment. And so we need not be surprised that the water mill and the windmill, though known, were, in the one case, far from fully exploited, and, in the other, not exploited at all. But what was it that changed matters so dramatically in the tenth century? Why was it that, from then on, men grasped eagerly at all ways to ease their labor, to increase their productivity?

Lewis Mumford thinks that the answer is to be found in that quintessentially medieval institution, the monastery. "The monastery," he writes, "through its very other-worldliness, had a special incentive to develop mechanization. The monks sought . . . to avoid unnecessary labor in order to have more time and energy for meditation and prayer; and possibly their willing immersion in ritual predisposed them to mechanical (repetitive and standardized) solutions. Though they themselves were disciplined to regular work, they readily turned over to machinery those operations that could be performed without benefit of mind. Rewarding work they kept for themselves: manuscript copying, illumination, carving. Unrewarding work they turned over to the machine: grinding, pounding, sawing."

It is an intriguing theory, but hard to prove. The earliest mills did arise in monasteries, but that could very well be nothing more than a reflection of the key position enjoyed by monasteries in the life of the times. At any rate, in short order, mills were saving labor everywhere, not merely in the monasteries. The earliest medieval mill we know of dates from 983, as we mentioned earlier; within a century there were at least 5,624 in England alone, serving some 3,000 communities.

Yet Mumford was on the right track in seeking an explanation in that feature which most of all divides the medieval world from the ancient: religion. Unlike the deities of paganism, the Christian god was a creator God, architect of the cosmos, the divine potter who shaped men from clay in his own image. In the Christian conception, all history moves toward a spiritual goal and there is no time to lose; thus work of all sorts is essential, becomes in a way a form of worship. Such ideas created a mental climate highly favorable for the growth of technology.

But this alone cannot explain what happened in medieval Europe. There were, after all, two forms of Christianity: that practiced in the Greek east as well as that of the Latin west, both equally ardent in embracing the fundamentals of Christian teaching; yet technology got no further in the east than it did in ancient Greece and Rome. Progress was limited to the Latin west. Why?

This is a problem that has particularly engaged the attention of Lynn White, whose work on medieval technology we had occasion to mention earlier. He looks for the explanation in a basic difference in spiritual direction between the two churches: the eastern generally held that sin is ignorance and that salvation comes by illumination, the western that sin is vice and that rebirth comes by disciplining the will to do good works. The Greek saint is normally a contemplative figure, the Latin an activist.

The effect of this theological difference was to restore respectability not only to the artisan but to manual labor, to remove the disrepute under which it had suffered during all of ancient times. And in this, monasticism played a significant role. From the beginning, the monks had been mindful of the Hebrew tradition that work was in accordance with God's commandment. Here, too, there was a division between east and west. The east had not suffered invasion and pillage as had the west; its level of culture had not descended as low, its intellectual and literary life continued much as before, and in this climate the Greek monks tended to concentrate on sacred studies. But in the west, civilization had fallen so devastatingly low that the monks had to assume responsibility for all aspects of culture, profane as well as sacred, the life of the body as well as that of the mind. Out of this grew an interest in practical affairs in general and, in particular, in the physical aspects of worship, a line of interest that led to the embellishment of the church and of the service through technology. Whereas eastern churches forbade music, holding that only the unaccompanied voice can worthily worship God, we find the cathedral at Winchester as early as the tenth century boasting a huge organ of 400 pipes fed by 28 bellows that required 70 men to pump them. By the middle of the twelfth century organs were given a part in the supreme moment of the service, the Mass itself. The east never permitted clocks in or on their churches; in the west, as soon as mechanical clocks were introduced they appear both on towers outside and walls inside.

The writings of western monks express their delight not only at the mechanical devices that embellished their religious life but at those that made their secular activities so much easier, the water-powered machines that did the milling, fulling, tanning, blacksmithing, and other such tasks. As one of them puts it: "How many horses' backs would have been broken, how many men's arms wearied, by the labor from which a river, with no labor, graciously frees us?" Technology was hailed as a Christian virtue. In a psalter that was illuminated near Reims about A.D. 830 an illustration of one of the psalms shows David leading a small body of the righteous against a formidable host of the ungodly. "In each camp," writes White, "a sword is being sharpened conspicuously. The Evildoers are content to use an old-fashioned whetstone. The Godly, however, are employing the first crank recorded outside China to rotate the first grindstone known anywhere. Obviously the artist is telling us that technological advance is God's will."

The western attitude toward work and toward technology, as an expression of Christian faith, thus stands in contrast equally to the ancient Greco-Roman attitudes and that of the medieval eastern church. It is dramatically symbolized in a manuscript of the Gospels produced at Winchester shortly after the year 1000. Here, God is portrayed as He would never be in the eastern church, as a master craftsman holding scales, a carpenter's square, and a pair of compasses. He is at the opposite pole from Homer's Zeus, who joined his fellow deities in laughing unquenchably at the gnarled, limping Hephaestus.

Medieval masons use ropes and pulleys to raise a stone column for a church. The illustration appears in a Byzantine psalter of the eleventh century.

Look upward from the floor of the nave at Amiens for this view of the soaring columns and arching roof of a perfect Gothic cathedral. One of the contributing factors to this sublime architecture was the dignity accorded to manual labor in the medieval world.

DID THE ANCIENT GREEKS MAKE A COMPUTER?

At the western entrance to the Aegean Sea, midway between the islands of Crete and Kythera, rises little Antikythera. It was off that island in 1900 that a sponge diver found, on the bottom, the wreck of an ancient ship loaded with statues, amphorae, and other objects.

This wreck was the first great underwater find of modern archaeology. It yielded not only a rich hoard of art treasures but an astonishingly sophisticated scientific instrument. But while the marble and bronze statues and the pottery were recognized at once as the work of Greek artisans around the time of Christ, the bronze instrument, encrusted with calcareous deposits, lay ignored. As it gradually dried, the ancient wood casing and internal parts cracked and split into four flat fragments, the inner sides of which revealed parts of geared wheels together with some barely legible inscriptions. Thereafter, as cleaning exposed more gears and inscriptions, scholars affirmed that the device was a navigational tool, an astrolabe, used to determine the altitude of the sun and other celestial bodies. This identification was remarkable enough, considering that only simple implements had previously turned up from the Hellenistic period; yet even so it was, more and more obviously inadequate for so complex an assembly.

What, then, could it be, this mysterious Antikythera mechanism?

In 1951, an American historian of science, Professor Derek de Solla Price of Yale, became intrigued by the riddle. While other scholars established that the wrecked ship, almost certainly bound for Italy with wares from Asia Minor and the Greek islands, had foundered in about 78 B.C., Price studied the device itself. At last, in 1959, he announced in print that the mechanism was, as he called it in the title of his article, "An Ancient Greek Computer"; one that indicated, by means of dials and pointers, the motions of the sun and moon past, present, and future, and, synchronously, the moon's phases.

A computer—in the first century B.C.? The claim excited much skepticism, and one retired professor insisted that the device had to be a modern orrery—of the kind he had seen as a child used to demonstrate the Copernican system—which had somehow intruded on the wreck. (He was, in fact, not far off on its function, but totally off on its date.) Certain popular writers, by contrast, eagerly accepted the identification of the device as a computer—but asserted it could only have been made by extraterrestrials from a technologically superior civilization.

Unfazed by any of this, Price continued to puzzle out the numerous small but critical problems the mechanism presented, attempting to complete computing the number of teeth on the gear wheels (none more than partially visible), and determining, as best he could, which gears meshed with which others. The work went slowly until 1971, when, learning that gamma-radiography could see through solid matter, Price persuaded the Greek authorities to let his collaborator, Dr. Karakalos, take gamma-radiographs and x-radiographs of the fragments. These revealed so much detail, so clearly, that after analyzing them the two men could confidently relate the gear ratios to known astronomical and calendrical data. And in 1974, Price submitted his definitive findings to the American Philosophical Society.

Activated by hand, the Antikythera mechanism consists of a train of more than thirty gears of greatly varied sizes meshing in parallel planes as shown in the overlay diagram (opposite). But its most spectacular feature is a differential gear permitting two shafts to rotate at different speeds, like the one that allows the rear wheels of a modern car to turn at different rates on a curve.

There is no mention of the Antikythera device in ancient literature. But a similar mechanism *was* described by Cicero, and later by Ovid and others: this was an ingenious planetarium, simulating the movements of the sun, the moon, and five planets, that had been devised in the third century B.C. by Archimedes. Cicero, incidentally, was on Rhodes between 79 and 77 B.C., just when the Antikythera mechanism was presumably lost at sea; while there he saw a geared planetarium that may have been built by Posidonios, a renowned geographer (among other things) who lectured in Rhodes.

The Antikythera device derives, then, from Archimedes, either by a gradual, unrecorded evolution or by the massive innovation of some unknown genius, perhaps of the school of Posidonios. If only for his use of the differential gear, "one of the greatest basic mechanical inventions of all time," its maker should, says Price, "be accorded the highest honors."

"Bringing of forty ships filled with cedar logs. Shipbuilding of cedarwood, one . . . ship, 100 cubits long. . . . Making the doors of the royal palace of cedarwood."

This entry, from the annals of Pharaoh Snefru, who ruled Egypt around 2650 or 2600 B.C., is our earliest written record of international maritime trade. It is also one of the least ambiguous. It tells us the object of trade (cedarwood), the country importing (Egypt), some indication of the amount (forty shiploads—in other words, no negligible quantity), even the purpose (shipbuilding and palace doors). The mention of palace doors, moreover, makes it clear that the shipment was ordered by and intended for the king. But even here one key piece of information is missing—the source. It is only a guess, a good one but still a guess, that the timber came from Lebanon, a land that we know had contacts with Egypt and was the home of fine stands of conifers, including, of course, its renowned cedars.

Imagine the reaction of an economist today if he were told to write a history of modern trade using no statistics, archives, newspaper files, or the like, but only a handful of random books, a few poems, some inscriptions on public buildings, a couple of hundred business letters grubbed up haphazardly from wastebaskets, and the contents of a town dump. Yet these are where we must go for our information in dealing with ancient trade, hunting for stray hints, for straws in the wind, which we then struggle to weave into some sort of pattern.

Our best straws are those in writing, like Snefru's entry. His left out one essential element: most are far short of even that mark. An inscription set up by Gudea of Lagash around 2200 B.C. reports that "Magan and Meluhha collected timber from their mountains, and—in order to build the temple of Ningirsu—Gudea brought [these materials] together in his town." Here we learn the purpose—beams, rafters, etc. for a temple—but, as we shall see, for wellnigh a century experts have been trying to figure out just where Magan and Meluhha were. A line of Homer informs us that in his day trade was in the

hands of "rascally Phoenicians with myriads of gewgaws in their black ship," but we are nowhere told what these gewgaws were or to what places they were brought for sale. From a passage in a Greek comedy of the fourth century B.C., copied out hundreds of years later by a collector of literary oddments, we happen to know of the amazing variety of imports that could be purchased in the markets of Athens at the time—but there is not the slightest indication of the quantities involved, of whether the items were rare luxuries occasionally shipped in or standard commodities always to be had.

These are all samples of the very best kind of information we possess, information from written sources, which, whether a remark dropped by a Mesopotamian monarch or a line of epic verse or a speech from a Greek play, whatever their shortcomings, make some sort of articulate statement. But written sources are totally lacking for the long and crucial centuries of prehistory and for many aspects of trade in historical times. There, all we have to go on are excavated objects that obviously came from somewhere else, Egyptian beads, say, found in Mesopotamian graves, or pieces of ivory in Cretan, or instruments of copper in Greek (Greece has no copper of its own), or—to come to the archaeologist's trade indicator par excellence—pottery of one country that turns up in another. All these reflect some sort of interchange— but was it commercial or casual? Regular or intermittent? On a small or large scale? And what were the sources involved? Ivory could have come to Crete from anywhere in India or Africa. Copper could have come to Greece from Asia Minor or Cyprus or central Europe or any number of other places. Pottery, though it necessarily tells its source, rarely says anything about the nature of the trade it was involved in. Excavators at Ras Shamra near the Syrian coast have uncovered the remains of thousands of unmistakably Mycenaean jars, proving that there was extensive trade between Mycenaean Greece and the Levant. But what did the Mycenaeans put in those jars that had such an attraction for the people who imported them? We do not have a clue.

Sometimes the objects of foreign exchange are so exotic that we are astonished at the interchange they attest. Trinkets of amber, for example, have been found at Mycenae in graves that go back to 1600 B.C. and at Troy and elsewhere in levels almost a thousand years older. There is only one possible place the

amber could have come from—the Baltic, not only a vast distance away but far beyond the boundaries of the civilization of the age. As late as the fifth century B.C. all Herodotus could tell his readers was that it came from the land of the Hyperboreans. Since the Hyperboreans were a semi-mythical people who lived "beyond the north wind," we can only conclude that Herodotus knew the source lay somewhere in the remote north and no more. However, the route from the frontiers of the civilized world onward he can give us with great precision: the material entered at Scythia—which would be the region around the Russian Crimea—was passed westward from one people to the next, until it reached the Adriatic, from there traveled south to northwest Greece, then across Greece to the eastern shore, then on to the islands of the Aegean. Herodotus, of course, had no notion of how it reached Scythia, nor do we. Those who argue for a route down the Russian rivers, or an alternate route from the Elbe to the Adriatic, and so on, are offering conjectures based on geographic feasibility, not information.

These, then, are some of the problems we face in trying to trace the commerce of ancient times. We hardly ever get any indication of volume, so we have to guess at whether we are dealing with an economically and politically significant traffic or a mere occasional one. Pottery will reveal the existence of trade from given places but rarely what the trade was in. Objects of foreign provenience, such as metals or stones, tell us what the trade was in but rarely where it originated. When geographical names happen to be mentioned, as like as not they are names that subsequently were lost to history and are either totally unidentifiable or identifiable only with a big question mark. Where was the land of Punt, where Egyptian vessels loaded up with ivory, myrrh, ostrich eggs, and baboons? Where was Ophir, whence King Solomon imported 420 talents of gold? Where was Tarshish, whose ships brought that gold, and where Tartessus, and were those places the same? Where, most tantalizing of all, was Thule—Ultima Thule?

For a long time it seemed to students of the earliest commerce as if they were going in nearly total darkness. But as archaeologists dug into the ruins of ancient cities and learned to read hieroglyphic and cuneiform writing, they began to see gleams of light here and there in the dark. We have been able to trace further and further back in time the paths people traveled and the goods they carried with them.

Indeed, the earliest trade route we have succeeded in identifying goes back to a time when men were still making their tools and weapons exclusively out of stone. Among the materials they found particularly useful for knives and other cutting instruments was the black volcanic glass called obsidian. It so happens that the island of Melos in the Aegean Sea is rich in a distinctive variety of it. Archaeologists have come upon tools of this Melian obsidian in excavations all over Greece and Crete that date as far back as 6000 B.C. In other words, even in those most ancient days men were sailing from various points over open water to the island to exploit its deposits; it had become the center of a web of trade routes.

Then there came the time when men learned to make tools and weapons not only of obsidian and flint and other stones but of metal, especially bronze. It was so crucial a step that we hail it as marking a new age. It certainly does in the history of commerce, for bronze is an alloy of copper and tin (the ancients also made bronze with arsenic, but that need not concern us), and there are only a limited number of places in the world where these most desirable minerals are available. In a word, the invention of bronze gave rise to one of the major forms of international trade in ancient times. And that has given rise to one of the major debates among those who write about ancient times: where did the makers of bronze in given areas get their supplies of copper and tin?

The smiths of Troy were among the first to learn the secret of toughening copper by alloying it with a small quantity of tin; the discovery probably goes back to 3000 B.C. A few centuries later the knowledge reached their fellow craftsmen in Mesopotamia and on Crete and the islands of the Aegean. The preferred ratio was six or seven to one, in other words, about 15 per cent tin, about the same as today's practice, which runs about 10 per cent and rarely more than 15 per cent.

Let us start with the question of where the copper came from, for that is the easier to answer. The precocious smiths of Troy had no problem, since Asia Minor has abundant deposits. They could have filled their needs from no farther away than the islands of Demonesi in the Sea of Marmara not far from Istanbul. The great mines of Ergani Marden in the southeast of Turkey today produce seventeen thousand tons of copper annually, and we can be pretty sure they were worked from very early times on. Another area that is well supplied is the island of Cyprus just below the southern coast of Turkey; the very name means "copper" in Greek. It seems logical to conclude that Cyprus supplied the Minoans on Crete and the peoples on the Aegean isles.

Today we have something more substantial than such inferences to go on. In 1958 divers discovered off the southern coast of Turkey the wreck of a ship that, about 1200 B.C., had gone to the bottom with its cargo of metal; they were able to salvage 34 ingots of copper weighing roughly between 35 to 60 pounds each, and 40 that were considerably smaller (from two to 12 pounds), two of which—the only ones tested—were certainly of bronze and almost certainly all the others were as well. There were also the disintegrated remains of at least one ingot of tin. Very likely the major part of the load, the copper, had been taken on at Cyprus, and the ship was heading westward to discharge at some Cretan or Greek port when it went down.

For Mesopotamia, fortunately, we never had to rely on inference alone. There, writing preceded the introduction of bronze, and since the Mesopotamians wrote in cuneiform characters on durable clay tablets, thousands of examples have survived, including quite a few that happen to furnish welcome information not only on where the local smiths got the materials for their bronze but how.

One tablet, for example, contains part of the paradise legend of the people of Sumer, who flourished in the third millennium B.C. Paradise, the story goes, is located in a land called Tilmun, and upon Tilmun the great god Enki poured forth blessings, including the wish that

- the land of Meluhha bring you . . . precious carnelian, *mes-shagan* wood, fine sea-wood, large ships;
- the land of Marhashi bring you precious stone, crystal;
- the land of Magan bring you mighty copper, the strength of . . . diorite.

All we have to do is work out where the "land of Magan" is, and we know where Mesopotamia got its copper. That, however, is not so easy.

Magan, as the lines quoted above reveal, produced

not only copper but diorite, the fine black stone which Mesopotamian kings favored for their statues. Naram-Sin, the ruler of Sumer, in reporting on one of his campaigns, mentions that he "smote the land of Magan, and Manium, the lord of Magan, he took prisoner. In their mountains he mined stones of diorite. He brought them to Agade his city." Other documents provide the further clue that the "*mes*-tree," which seems to be the mulberry, grew there.

The above gleanings are from legend and royal inscriptions. From some prosaic, everyday business documents we discover precisely how the trade in copper was handled. There is preserved a receipt, dated from 2000 B.C., from a shipper in the employ of the city of Ur's principal temple, in which he acknowledges that the temple gave him fifteen garments and a quantity of wool as "merchandise for buying copper from Magan." Other receipts reveal that the shippers themselves did not go to Magan but paid over their merchandise and picked up their copper at Tilmun, the place that, as we have just seen, the Sumerians once thought was the location of paradise.

We get some precious details about this traffic from a batch of letters found at Ur in the ruins of the house of a certain Ea-nasir. Ea-nasir, who lived about 1800 B.C., was in the Tilmun trade, one of a number of local businessmen making a very good living out of bringing copper from there into Ur. The amounts they handled are impressive: one document lists a shipment of over 13,000 *mnas* of copper ingots, no less than $18\frac{1}{2}$ tons; of this $427\frac{1}{2}$ *mnas* ($5\frac{3}{4}$ tons) was consigned to Ea-nasir alone. Ea-nasir has the distinction, if distinction it be, of being the recipient of the earliest-known letter of complaint from a dissatisfied customer. "You said," someone writes to him, " 'I will give good ingots to Gimil-Sin.' That is what you said, but you have not done so; you offered bad ingots to my messenger, saying, 'Take it or leave it.' Who am I that you should treat me so contemptuously? Are we not both gentlemen? . . . Who is there among the Tilmun traders who has acted against me in this way?"

The situation that emerges is clear: Tilmun was just a point of transfer; the copper was mined at Magan, brought to Tilmun, and there put aboard "Tilmun boats"—boats that plied from Mesopotamia to Tilmun and back. But where is Magan? And, for that matter, where is Tilmun? For good measure, let us throw in Meluhha as well, since it is usually coupled with these two: King Sargon I of Sumer tells

162

In the third millennium B.C. traders regularly channeled valued commodities into international commerce along routes shown on the map. Egyptian merchants imported spices, ivory, and other expensive goods from a mysterious land called Punt, on the east African coast. Far more ambitious voyages were Hanno's expedition along Africa's west bulge in 500 B.C. and the voyage of Pytheas to a far northern land he called Thule.

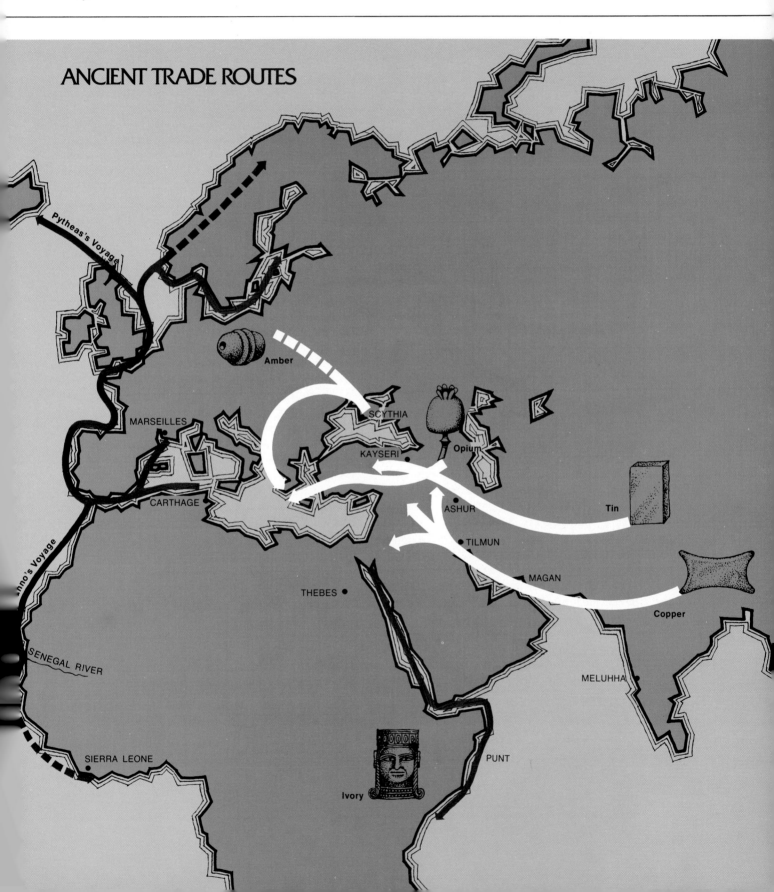

ANCIENT TRADE ROUTES

Pytheas's Voyage

Amber

SCYTHIA

Opium

KAYSERI

MARSEILLES

Tin

CARTHAGE

ASHUR

TILMUN

Hanno's Voyage

MAGAN

THEBES

Copper

SENEGAL RIVER

MELUHHA

SIERRA LEONE

PUNT

Ivory

in an inscription how "at the wharf of Agade he moored ships from Meluhha, ships from Magan, ships from Tilmun." If Magan provided Mesopotamia with copper and diorite, Meluhha was almost as important as a source of fine timber, to say nothing of such luxuries as ivory, gold, and carnelian.

Now, Magan and Meluhha reappear in Assyrian records of a much later age, the eighth and seventh centuries B.C. At that time, no question about it, Magan was Egypt and Meluhha Ethiopia. Some scholars insist that this was always the case, in the third millennium B.C. as well as the first. To be sure, Egypt has diorite, but on the other hand, not long before the time of Ea-nasir's letters, we find Egypt importing copper from Cyprus, rather than exporting it to others. And Ethiopia, while it can offer ivory, is not noted for timber and carnelian. Yet, more significant than all such considerations is the distinct impression one gets that all three places are along a single sea lane leading from Mesopotamia down the Persian Gulf and beyond. But how far beyond?

For over two decades Danish archaeological teams have been at work on the island of Faylakah, just off the delta where the Tigris and Euphrates flow into the Persian Gulf, on the island of Bahrain farther down the gulf, and at various points along the western, that is, the Arabian, shore. They have laid bare extensive remains that date from the end of the third millennium and the beginning of the second millennium B.C., all of which make it very probable that this area, what is today Kuwait, Qatar, and the coast of Saudi Arabia between them, was the ancient Tilmun. Their case is convincing enough to have produced agreement. But the agreement stops abruptly when we come to Magan. Some argue that it is Oman, on the Arabian shore just below the Strait of Hormuz, the gate to the gulf. Here there are splendid outcrops of diorite, and there is copper, though no overflowing amounts of it. Others argue that it is Makran, just across the Gulf of Oman on the Iranian shore. Here there is plenty of copper—though it is pretty far

inland, in the area about Kerman, and would have to be hauled to some port on the coast—but no diorite. On the other hand, there *are* mulberry trees. Some authorities cut the Gordian knot by arguing that ancient Magan included both sides.

Now for Meluhha. In 1921 and 1922 archaeologists working in northwest India (now Pakistan) uncovered the celebrated Indus Valley civilization, with its two great centers at Mohenjo-Daro and Harappa. Since then, objects that unmistakably originated there have turned up in Mesopotamian excavations, putting it beyond question that the two areas were in contact. A glance at the map will show that the natural means of communication between them was the sea. Cannot Meluhha then be northwest India? Meluhha, to repeat, supplied Mesopotamia with fine timber, ivory, gold, and carnelian—the timber could be Indian teak, the ivory from Indian elephants; India has gold, and Rajputana just east of the Indus is a bountiful source of carnelian. There is a serious problem, however: inscriptions of the kings of Agade, dating about 2300 B.C., tell how they conquered Anshan, which is the part of Iran just east of Shīrāz and Persepolis, and then went on to conquer Meluhha—which, if Meluhha is really the Indus Valley, would give them a long, long march and extend their conquests much farther than seems reasonable. One writer has adopted the desperate expedient of putting all three within the embrace of the Persian Gulf, making Magan just another name for Bahrain and identifying Meluhha with the opposite shore; it produces a tidy package, but, unfortunately, there is no copper or diorite in Bahrain and no ivory, timber, gold, or carnelian on the opposite shore.

So, there are the possibilities. The consensus is that Tilmun refers to the Arabian coast of the Persian Gulf from the head to Bahrain. A few die-hards still insist that Magan is Egypt and Meluhha Ethiopia, not only in the late Assyrian records but at all times, but most agree that Magan is a land just beyond the Strait of Hormuz, though they are divided as to whether it

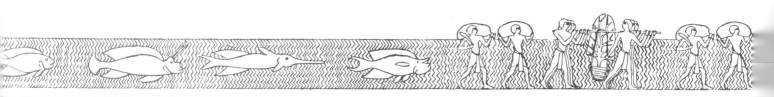

is on the Arabian or Iranian side. And, despite the problem raised by a Mesopotamian conquest of Anshan and Meluhha, most are willing to identify Meluhha with what is today Pakistan, the site of the Indus Valley civilization. Mesopotamia's copper, then, came from just beyond the Persian Gulf. As we saw earlier, Asia Minor had its own copper, and either it or Cyprus or both supplied Crete, the Aegean and the Levant.

This brings us to the next puzzle to solve, one that makes the question of the sources of copper simplicity itself: where did the ancient smiths get their tin? "In spite of much investigation and speculation the origins of the tin . . . used all over the ancient world by 1200 B.C. remain one of the great enigmas of Bronze Age history." So writes James Muhly, author of a recent profound study of the sources of metal in ancient times.

The problem in a nutshell is this: not long after 3000 B.C. smiths throughout the Aegean and Meso-

potamian world were turning out tin bronze; there was copper available nearby — but absolutely no tin. Where did it come from?

There were further complications. Smiths in the interior of Asia Minor and in Egypt and Italy were also turning out bronze objects. There are deposits of tin in all those places — but we have no proof whatsoever that they were used in ancient times. As we shall see in a moment, Asia Minor for a long while imported tin. For Egypt we have ample records, both written and pictorial, that go back to 3000 B.C., yet there is not the slightest indication in any of them that the Egyptians had recourse to their own tin. There is tin available, lots of it, in central Europe, and a number of authorities insist that this was the source tapped by the Mediterranean world. However, for one thing, the tin there has to be mined out of veins of granite, which was a feat beyond the capabilities of Bronze Age workers; until the first millennium B.C., the only tin exploited was alluvial, panned out of stream beds. For another, the people actually

living in the area for long used only copper, in other words, were unaware of the value of their tin.

Many centuries later the Greeks and the Romans got their supplies from the rich deposits in Portugal, Spain, and England, and there are those who argue that these same places were exploited almost from the very beginning. They conjure up voyages by intrepid Minoan and Mycenaean sailors out through the Strait of Gibraltar into the Atlantic to bring back the precious substance. After all, only one part of tin was needed to six or seven of copper, so even a modest cargo would assure a bold skipper of a fine return. As we noted in Chapter 2, archaeologists were long convinced that Aegean seamen had sailed west to the Mediterranean coast of Spain bringing the knowledge of megalithic construction to the primitives there; having gotten that far, could they not have made it the rest of the way to the tin lands? Then there was the presumed connection between the Mycenaeans and England during Stonehenge days, which we also discussed in Chapter 2. Today, the bringing of megalithic construction to Spain has become dead letter, the presumed commerce between Mycenae and England is fast losing ground, and people are coming round to the one view supported by the archaeological evidence, that British tin became important only after the seventh century B.C. and Spanish and Portuguese only during the days of the Roman Empire.

The tin, then, did not come from the west. Let us grant that Italian smiths were aware of sources in their own country and that the smiths of Troy drew on local supplies. This still leaves the Mycenaeans, Minoans, peoples of the Levant, of Mesopotamia, of the rest of Asia Minor to take care of. Aboard that ship which went down about 1200 B.C. off the coast of Asia Minor, presumably while en route to a market in Crete or Greece, there was a certain amount of tin; where had it been mined? Ingots of tin are pictured on Egyptian wall paintings and described as coming from Syria or Palestine. Since neither of these places has any tin deposits, they must have served merely as transshipment points; where, then, did the Syrian and Palestinian dealers get the supplies

Amber brooch
DEVIZES MUSEUM. EILEEN TWEEDY

EGYPTIAN MUSEUM CAIRO

Gold and carnelian earring from Egypt

Phoenician bowl with Mesopotamian motifs
MUSEO DI VILLA GIULA ROME

which they sent on to Egypt?

It so happens that, thanks to those long-lasting cuneiform tablets, we know even more about the shipping of tin than of copper. Archaeologists have discovered some of the correspondence of a group of merchants located in Ashur in Assyria who, between 1900 and 1800 B.C., were engaged in sending donkey caravans to customers in a town of Asia Minor not far from modern Kayseri. The donkeys carried bars of a metal called *anaku,* and while some experts hold that this means "lead," others, more plausibly, say "tin." What is more, certain cuneiform documents give good reason to believe that not all this tin went to Asia Minor, that some of it went on to ports in the Levant to be transshipped to Crete and Greece. Thus we have solved one part of the riddle: Minoans, Mycenaeans, peoples of the Levant and Asia Minor, all got at least some of the tin they needed from Assyrian middlemen. But the biggest part still remains: where did these middlemen get it?

There are a few clues. The land of Zabshali, we learn from a royal inscription, was once forced to pay a rich booty that included tin, and Zabshali is generally located in the mountains of Luristan in Iran some two hundred and fifty miles due east of Baghdad. Other inscriptions refer to massive amounts of tin from the Nairi lands, and these are generally located west of Lake Van, to the northwest of ancient Assyria. So, generally speaking, the tin should have come from northwest Iran or a little beyond and made its way via passes through the Zagros Mountains to Mesopotamia. There is only one trouble: despite all these pointed clues, as Muhly discouragedly wrote as late as 1976, "there is still no real geological evidence for tin in Iran." And there the matter must rest.

So much for the objects of trade and the obscurity that surrounds them. When we turn to the traders, we run into, if anything, even more obscurity. For they make but rare appearances, and these are invariably brief and shadowy. Take the tin traders of Ashur and the copper traders of Ur that we just mentioned. They step into the light of history — but it is

Mycenaean gold cup
THE BRITISH MUSEUM

Fancifully ornamented Minoan vase
THE ASHMOLEAN MUSEUM, OXFORD

Phoenician nude of African or Indian Ivory
ORIENTAL INSTITUTE, UNIVERSITY OF CHICAGO

Amber necklace
DEVIZES MUSEUM, EILEEN TWEEDY

only for a flickering second. Even Ea-nasir, the businessman of Ur who was accused of dealing in substandard merchandise, though he is mentioned in a sheaf of letters, is hardly more than a name.

There is, fortunately, one exception. A unique piece of writing was discovered in Egypt toward the end of the last century which gives us an intimate picture of an ancient trader, enables us to feel the quality of his mind and the strength of his spirit, to live with him through the day-to-day difficulties he was confronted with and witness the determination and resourcefulness with which he overcame them.

The man's name was Wenamon, and his home was Thebes on the Upper Nile, for long the seat of the pharaohs. As it happens, he was not a trader by profession but a priest of Amon. He became one only when, in the year 1130 B.C. or so, he was selected by his superior to go on a trip to Byblos in Lebanon to purchase a cargo of timber cut from the famous cedars: it was needed for the construction of the ceremonial barge to be used in the annual festival. The document that was found contains Wenamon's report, a bald and simple yet intensely personal and detailed narrative that turns on a brilliant light in the

darkness shrouding the commercial life of this age.

Wenamon made his way down the Nile to the delta, where passage was arranged for him on a vessel bound for Syria. On April 20 his ship shoved off, sailed to the river's mouth, and he "embarked on the great Syrian sea."

His first port of call was a town named Dor, a little to the south of Carmel, which had been established about a century earlier by a tribe of sea raiders called the Tjeker. Here Wenamon suffered catastrophe: as he tells it in his businessman's language, "A man of my ship ran away, having stolen one [vessel] of gold [amounting] to five *deben* [about 1.2 pounds], four vessels of silver amounting to twenty *deben*, a sack of silver—eleven *deben*. [Total of what] he [stole]: five *deben* of gold, thirty-one *deben* [about 7.5 pounds] of silver." The poor fellow had been robbed of every penny he had, his travel allowance as well as the cash he had been given to pay for the lumber.

Wenamon tried to bully the prince of Dor into making up the loss but got nowhere. The prince, however, promised to conduct an investigation and graciously offered Wenamon hospitality while he awaited the results. After nine fruitless days had gone by, Wenamon got impatient and left. At this point the papyrus is tattered, with mere scraps of sentences preserved—which brings us to the first of two mysteries surrounding Wenamon's doings. He did not give up the journey—but how to continue without money? If we interpret aright the battered traces of writing that are left, he solved his desperate situation with a desperate solution: he held up some Tjeker and took thirty *deben* of silver from them, "[I have seized] your silver," he explained to his victims, "and it will stay with me [until] you find [mine or the thief] who stole it! Even though you have not stolen, I shall take it." How could a priest of Amon, trained to handle nothing more dangerous than a reed pen, with no men accompanying him or, at best, a handful of domestics, overpower or hold at bay a parcel of professional pirates? We shall never know.

If Wenamon thought his troubles were now at an end, he could not have been more wrong. The moment he arrived at Byblos, the harbor master greeted him with a curt order from Zakar-Baal, the prince who ruled the place: "Get out [of] my harbor!" Very likely the Tjeker had sent ahead a wanted-for-burglary notice, and since they were Zakar-Baal's neighbors to the south and formidable sea raiders to boot, he doubtless was anxious to keep on good terms with them. But Wenamon was no easy man to discourage. For twenty-nine days he hung around the harbor even though every morning the harbor master dutifully brought the same message. Zakar-Baal apparently went no further than that. He wanted to stay on the right side of touchy neighbors but, at the same time, was reluctant to lose a sale. So he compromised by issuing an ultimatum and doing nothing to enforce it. However, when Wenamon showed unmistakable signs of giving up and returning to Egypt, Zakar-Baal abruptly changed his tactics and summoned the envoy for an interview. "I found him," Wenamon writes, "sitting [in] his upper room, with his back turned to a window, so that the waves of the great Syrian sea broke against the back of his head." Most unusual language for Wenamon, who elsewhere limits himself to an unvarnished tale; the scene must have burned itself into his memory. After much discussion, Zakar-Baal agreed to grant him an extension of time so that he could send to Egypt for goods to help defray the timber's cost; obviously the money he had stolen fell far short of what was needed.

Forty-eight days passed before the shipment arrived, a rich agglomeration of prized Egyptian exports: papyrus rolls, linen, hides, gold, silver, and other items. Zakar-Baal ordered the felling of the trees to start immediately, and finally, eight months after Wenamon had left Thebes, the timber lay on the beach cut and stacked, ready for loading. The prince could not resist a last bit of fun at Wenamon's expense. He proceeds to tell him about a group of envoys he kept waiting for seventeen years, until every one of them died—and then calls over his butler and says, "Take him and show him the tomb." "Don't show it to me!" replies Wenamon hurriedly. At this point, just when things looked brightest, eleven war galleys suddenly hove into the harbor bearing an ultimatum for the prince: "Arrest Wenamon! Don't let a ship of his [go] to the land of Egypt!" The galleys were manned by Tjeker warriors; they were demanding justice for the thirty *deben* of silver that had been robbed from them months and months ago. Wenamon did the only thing he could under the circumstances: "I sat down and wept," he reports. Zakar-Baal, either because he genuinely felt sorry or he did not want to let a profitable transaction slip through his fingers, tried to console the poor Egyptian. His method has a curious

modern ring: he sent him a ram, two jugs of wine, and a girl—no local talent, but an Egyptian entertainer who happened to be in Byblos.

Whatever surcease Wenamon derived from his food, drink, and girl must have swiftly evaporated when he heard Zakar-Baal's decision the next morning. It was another of the prince's cagey compromises. "I cannot arrest the messenger of Amon inside my land," he told the Tjeker, "but let me send him away, and you go after him to arrest him." He was going to discharge his obligation to Egypt—and at the same time save his sale—by not turning Wenamon over to the Tjeker; and he was going to avoid offending the Tjeker by sending Wenamon out of his jurisdiction where they could lay their hands on him.

The next portion of the narrative is tantalizingly bald. "So he loaded me in," Wenamon writes, "and he sent me away from there. . . . And the wind cast me on the land of Alashiya [Cyprus]. In other words, the wind took him in a direction almost opposite to that he wanted. Quite likely it was one of the southeasterly gales that are common off the coast of Syria. It very well may have been his salvation: a heavy cargo ship would have a chance of riding it out but not a light galley. This may explain why the Tjeker apparently never pursued him; possibly they figured the storm would save them the job.

But Wenamon had fled the frying pan only to fall into the fire. At Alashiya a group of natives descended upon him and hustled him off to kill him. Pirate incursions were chronic along all the coasts of that area at the time; these particular people had no doubt suffered their share, and Wenamon's appearance may have seemed a good chance to even the score. At this juncture, however, his luck at long last changed. He somehow forced his way to the palace of the local ruler, a princess, and "met her as she was going out of one house of hers and going into another. . . . I greeted her, and I said to the people who were standing near her, 'Isn't there one of you who understands Egyptian?' And one of them said, 'I understand [it].' So I said to him, 'Tell my lady—'," but the speech is unimportant and most probably represents what, later at his desk in Thebes, he reckoned what he ought to have said rather than what a wet, exhausted, and frightened wayfarer actually did say. The important point is that the princess listened. "She had the people summoned and they stood there," writes Wenamon, "and she said to me, 'Spend

Ritualistic protectors of ancient seafarers, these silent ranks of bronze figures once stood in a temple at the Phoenician commercial center of Byblos. Their purpose was to intercede with the gods to grant travelers a safe passage. Conical hats worn by the votive figures resemble those still worn in parts of Lebanon.

the night,'" and here the document abruptly breaks off. The rest has been lost. Since the chances of it ever being found are just about nil, what happened to Wenamon will forever remain a mystery. All we know is that he did get back to draw up this report, one of the most remarkable pieces of writing to survive from the ancient world.

Not long after Wenamon's time the sea lanes of the Mediterranean came under the domination of the Phoenicians, a seafaring people par excellence. They make several appearances in the Bible in connection with Solomon's overseas trading ventures. On one occasion they supplied him with the sailors for a merchant fleet to trade with Ophir, whence they "fetched . . . gold, four hundred and twenty talents, and brought it to King Solomon." The location of Ophir has sparked even more argument than Magan and Meluhha. Some claim that it lay to the east: the conservative-minded put it in India, bolder spirits as far away as Australia. Others think it lay to the west, on the coast of Africa: the conservative-minded of this school put it in Ethiopia, more or less the area that the ancient Egyptians called Punt, the bolder spirits as far south as Rhodesia.

Then there are the Phoenicians' "ships of Tarshish" mentioned in the Bible. Where is Tarshish? Ancient writers assumed it was the same as Tarsus, the native city of Saint Paul, on the coast of Asia Minor. Today most students hold that it was far to the west, possibly in Italy or Sardinia or Tunisia but most likely to be identified with Tartessus, site of a Phoenician settlement in Spain. However, recent studies make a strong case for not placing it in the west at all but along the Red Sea, a way point on the route to Ophir.

As early as the tenth century B.C. the Phoenicians had planted important colonies in the west, notably Carthage in Tunisia and Gadir (Cádiz) in Spain. These pioneered in sending merchant fleets out into the Atlantic. First they sailed north to pick up tin from the rich deposits in Brittany and Cornwall, a lucrative source of profit that they did their best to keep a trade secret. The story is told of a Phoenician skipper on this run who, finding himself tailed by a Roman ship, deliberately headed into shoal water, consigning his own vessel and his pursuer's to destruction; when he got back — he managed to survive, clutching a piece of wreckage — the state authorities, good businessmen that they were, reimbursed him

for the cost of the cargo he had lost.

Then, around 500 B.C., the city of Carthage decided to venture south into the Atlantic as well as north. So a full-fledged expedition was fitted out and dispatched to explore the waters along the west coast of Africa and found trading posts there. We know about the enterprise not through casual references in cuneiform inscriptions and letters or some vague verses from the Bible but through the very words of the expedition's commander, Hanno; he drew up a report which he had inscribed in bronze and set up in his home town; there, years later, an inquisitive Greek saw it and made a copy which has come down to us. It is sober, matter-of-fact, studded with detail — yet it has stirred up as much controversy as Tarshish and Ophir.

"The Carthaginians commissioned Hanno to sail past the Pillars of Hercules [the Strait of Gibraltar] and to found cities of the Libyphoenicians [Phoenicians residing in Africa as against the homeland in the Levant]. He set sail with sixty vessels of 50 oars and a multitude of men and women to the number of 30,000 and provisions and other equipment." So begins Hanno's account, and so begin the problems right at the outset: had the whole expedition been put aboard sixty 50-oared ships, they would have quietly settled down on the harbor bottom instead of leaving Carthage; such ships barely had room to carry provisions for the crew, to say nothing of passengers with all the equipment they needed to start life in a colony. One solution is to assume that these galleys were the escort of warships and scouting craft and that the colonists must have been put into a fleet of good-sized sailing craft. And very likely there were fewer heads than 30,000. The Greek manuscripts we have today are all the result of successive copyings over the centuries by scribe after scribe, and numerals, since they can rarely be checked by the context, are particularly liable to miscopying.

In following Hanno's narrative, as always we find the prime difficulty lies in identifying the places he records. Almost all names he mentions mean nothing to us today; there was no system available to him of identifying points by latitude and longitude (not used by geographers until more than two centuries later), and the physical details he records are rarely numerous and specific enough to make identification certain. He had clear sailing at the beginning, and so do we: there is no question that his first leg was

through the Strait of Gibraltar and southwest along the Moroccan shore, where he kept dropping off batches of colonists who founded half a dozen settlements. At the mouth of the Dra river he made friends with a local tribe of nomads, probably Berbers, and, since they were familiar with the coast farther south, took some aboard as guides and interpreters.

His very next step brings us to the knottiest point in the narrative. Some time after the interpreters joined him, Hanno led his fleet into a deep easterly gulf at the head of which he came upon "a small island with a circuit of five stades [about half a mile]. Here we founded a colony named Cerne. We estimated from the distance traversed that it lay in a line with Carthage; for the distance from Carthage to the Pillars and from there to Cerne was the same." Most authorities think that Hanno's Cerne is Herne Island, a little north of the Tropic of Cancer; the relative distances from Carthage to Gibraltar and from there to Herne Island are just about the same. But some argue that Hanno's estimate of the mileage he covered, being based solely on elapsed sailing time and his best guess as to his average speed, was off, and that Cerne is a good deal farther along, at the mouth

of the Senegal River. For, from Cerne Hanno "sailed through the delta of a big river, named the Chretes, and came to a lake containing three islands larger than Cerne. From there we accomplished one day's sail and arrived at the head of the lake. . . . Sailing on from that point we came to another deep and wide river, which was infested with crocodiles and hippopotami. Thence we turned back to Cerne."

Leaving Cerne a second time, the expedition resumed its voyage along the coast, passing Negro tribes who fled at their approach and whose speech the interpreters could not understand. They took two days to double a promontory marked by wooded mountains, probably Cape Verde, the westernmost point of Africa. Then, Hanno writes, they came to

a great gulf, which according to the interpreters was called the West Horn. In it lay a large island, and in the island a marine lake containing another island. Landing on the smaller island, we could see nothing but forest, and by night many fires being kindled, and we heard the noise of pipes and cymbals and a din of tom-toms and the shouts of a multitude. We were seized with fear, and our interpreters told us to leave the island.

172

We left in a hurry and coasted along a country with a fragrant smoke of blazing timber, from which streams of fire plunged into the sea. The land was unapproachable for heat.

So we sailed away in fear, and in four days' journey saw the land ablaze by night. In the center a leaping flame towered above the others and appeared to reach the stars. This was the highest mountain we saw: it was called the Chariot of the Gods.

Following the rivers of fire for three further days, we reached a gulf named the Southern Horn. In the gulf lay an island like the previous one, with a lake, and in it another island. The second island was full of wild people. By far the greater number were women with hairy bodies. Our interpreter called them Gorillas. We gave chase to the men but could not catch any, for they all scampered up steep rocks and pelted us with stones. We secured three women, who bit and scratched and resisted their captors. But we killed and flayed them, and brought the hides to Carthage. This was the end of our journey, owing to lack of provisions.

Hanno was the first to record the sorts of things that later became commonplace in explorers' re-ports from Africa: the jungle, the beating of tom-toms, the enormous grass fires that natives kindled to burn off stubble and help the following year's crops, the ubiquitous monkeys. Hanno's "Gorillas" cannot be what we know by that name; his men were tough, but they were not up to catching gorillas, even females, alive. Chimpanzees or baboons are the best guess. (It was an American missionary, Thomas Savage, who in 1847 applied Hanno's term to what we now call gorillas.)

Just how far did Hanno get? Most geographers hold that he stopped short of the calms and heat of the Gulf of Guinea and pushed no farther than Sierra Leone, that the West Horn is Bissagos Bay, that the Chariot of the Gods is Mount Kakulima in Guinea which, although relatively low (about 3,000 feet), stands out in the midst of low-lying ground, and that the Southern Horn is Sherbro Sound. Some take him as far as the Cameroons, arguing that the Chariot of the Gods is better identified with Mount Cameroon, the tallest peak in West Africa (13,370 feet) and a volcano to boot, which would explain the "leaping flame" from it. Others insist that he went still farther to Gabon. In any event, since the original purpose

173

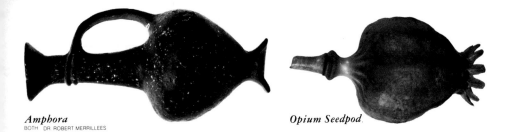

Amphora
BOTH DR. ROBERT MERRILLEES

Opium Seedpod

was the establishment of trading centers, the expedition was eminently successful, for the settlements Hanno planted survived nicely: according to an ancient version of a "coast pilot," almost a century and a half later Phoenician traders were still doing a thriving business at Cerne, his most distant outpost. Archaeologists have discovered the actual remains of a Phoenician colony at Essaouira (formerly Mogador) on the Atlantic coast of Spanish Morocco between Casablanca and Agadir. With any luck they may pick up the traces of others farther south.

There is yet one more to add to the list of place names that have stirred so much controversy, the most famous of all, the Thule of our phrase "Ultima Thule." It makes its appearance in what was probably another of the endless attempts to secure supplies of that scarce but essential metal, tin. Around 300 B.C. the Greek merchants of Marseilles organized a voyage of exploration into northern waters. Their choice to head the venture was inspired: Pytheas of Marseilles was not only a skilled navigator and leader of authority but a ranking astronomer. It was he who determined the true position of the polestar, calculated with just a slim margin of error the latitude of his home town, and, during his northern voyage, took solar observations that enabled later geographers to establish a number of parallels of latitude.

Pytheas slipped through whatever patrols the Phoenicians maintained at the Strait of Gibraltar, sailed around Spain and along the Breton coast, and then crossed the Channel to Cornwall; here he stopped to work up a careful report on the operation of the local tin mines. He then circumnavigated Britain, determining, correctly enough, that the island was roughly triangular but getting the length of the sides wrong, making them much longer than they actually are. Like Hanno, his only means for measuring was by converting the time spent sailing into distance covered, and he very likely overrated his speed. He established the location of Britain ("it extends obliquely along Europe") and Ireland and made several visits into the interior of Ireland.

So far it has been fairly easy to follow his track, but now the going gets rough. At some point, while voyaging in British waters, he heard of, and may even have sailed near to, an "island of Thule." It lay, he reports, six days' sail north of Britain and only one day south of the "frozen" sea. The sun there went down during the night for only two or three hours, no more, and enveloping the island was a mysterious substance which Pytheas actually saw but could only describe in an obscure and puzzling fashion: it was "neither sea nor air . . . but a mixture like jellyfish in which earth and air are suspended." Since scant crops could be raised in this bare and forbidding land, the natives lived off roots, wild berries, and what he calls "millet" but may well have been oats, which would be unfamiliar to anyone whose experience had been limited to the Mediterranean. They had plenty of honey, from which they prepared a kind of nourishing drink.

What, first, was this substance that was "neither sea nor air?" Modern geographers suggest it was concentrations of jellyfish or ice-sludge or the heavy seafog common in those regions of the North Atlantic, the ancient geographers said that it was a cock-and-bull story Pytheas made up. Next, where was Thule? Here again modern commentators offer us a triple range of choice: some say Iceland, some say the Shetlands, some say Norway. But Iceland, aside from the fact that it lies more than six days' sail from Britain (Pytheas, as we have seen, was not good at estimating distances), is too far north for bees; the Shetlands lie much too near for a six-day sail, and, anyway, the shortest nights there are five hours and not two or three; and Norway is neither an island nor north of Britain. Of course, there are ways out of the impasse. Norway at least has oats and bees, and one could always argue that Pytheas' informants, not knowing much about Thule, got its direction wrong and mistook it for an island; even Rome's paragon of learning, Pliny the Elder, calls Scandinavia an island.

After finishing with Britain, Pytheas crossed back to the French side of the Channel and followed the coast eastward, a voyage that took him, he reports, past an enormous estuary and to, or near, an island where amber was so plentiful the natives used it for fuel. Here, too, the experts cannot agree: some take him all the way into the Baltic, a source of amber, as we have seen, since prehistoric times; others take him no farther than the North Sea, identifying his estuary with the estuary of the Elbe and his amber island with Helgoland.

Pytheas' return was safe—but hardly happy. The merchants must have been disappointed, for he brought back only a report on Cornish tin, not a new way of shipping it to the Mediterranean. The cognoscenti decided he was a charlatan and the stories of his

174

Found in a sanctuary in Crete, the clay idol at right is bedecked with a tiara of three slit opium pods — suggesting the importance of the drug in the ancient world. The drug may have been packaged for export — mainly in Cyprus — in tiny clay amphorae such as the one at left, shaped like an opium pod.

discoveries a tissue of lies. Today, though we may not know exactly where he got to, we recognize him for what he was: the greatest explorer of ancient times, source of the first eyewitness report of the Arctic.

In tracing the trade routes by which metals and timber from the lands along the Persian Gulf came to Mesopotamia, or gold from Africa or India to King Solomon, or tin and other products to the Phoenicians, and so on, we have had the invaluable assistance of the written word. As we mentioned at the outset, for all of prehistory, and for many forms of trade in historical times, we have to rely on archaeology alone, on the inarticulate evidence of finds, particularly pottery, in alien contexts. One could read all the works of Greek authors that have survived, all the Greek inscriptions that have been found, without ever becoming aware that Athens of the fifth and fourth centuries B.C. was an active exporter of fine pottery. Because abundant remains of its distinctive, beautifully painted dishes, jugs, cups, bowls, etc. have been found from Italy to the south of Russia, we know that people throughout much of the ancient world prized Athenian ceramics the way we do English china. Indeed, the magnificent specimens that are the pride of the Classical collections in so many of our museums rarely are from Athens itself. More often than not they come from the Etruscan tombs in Italy, whose owners had so great a passion for the ware they arranged to go to the afterworld liberally supplied with it. Now, the presence of handsome pottery that obviously has been imported from elsewhere poses no problem. What poses the problems is the presence of cheap, undistinguished jars and flasks and the like that could not possibly have been brought in for their own sake. They must be containers — but of what?

These apparently worthless objects, the ugly ducklings of archaeology, interest the historian mightily for they are unmistakable signs of trade, and when found in great quantity, such as the Mycenaean jars we spoke of earlier, trade of importance. But trade in what? Empty ancient clay jars are as uncommunicative about their former contents as modern glass ones. In most cases all we can do is make an educated guess. Sometimes there seem to be clues — but one must be sure to read them aright. To take a recent and intriguing instance, was there an international trade in opium toward the end of the Bronze

In the murky light of 90-foot depths, underwater archaeologists use a plastic balloon to hoist large, fragile objects from a ship that foundered off Turkey's southwest coast in 1200 B.C. This trading vessel—the earliest shipwreck discovered—was bearing copper ingots from Cyprus to bronze-making centers in Asia Minor.

Age? It all depends on how you interpret a very special kind of little jug.

The ancients were well aware of opium and its narcotic property. When Odysseus' son Telemachus visited the court of Helen and Menelaus, and the conversation kept coming back to the casualties suffered in the Trojan War, and tears began to flow, Helen, who had learned pharmacology from a skilled Egyptian lady, brought everybody round by spiking the wine:

into the carafe from which they were drinking
she quickly put a drug which brings release
from passion and care, a forgetting of all life's ills.

We know from hieroglyphic records that Egyptian doctors used opium for alleviating the pain of wounds; they even recommended giving it to crying children. Hippocrates and other noted Greek doctors prescribed it for hysteria, stomach disorders, coughs, and other ailments, where its sedative effect was helpful.

Opium also served the cause of religion, perhaps even more than of medicine. Figures of goddesses have been found wearing ornaments made in the shape of the poppy-seed capsule, the part of the plant from which the juice that hardens into opium is extracted. A well-known statue of Demeter, found in the marketplace at Athens, shows her holding some of these capsules. The most striking evidence of all dates from the late Bronze Age, 1400 to 1200 B.C. At Gazi on Crete excavators have laid bare a building they call the sanctuary of "the goddess of the poppies," for in it they came upon five terra-cotta female heads, each bearing over her brow three terra-cotta replicas of the poppy capsule. The biggest head is rendered with the mouth open and the eyes closed, as if the goddess were on "a trip."

It so happens that at various sites the length and breadth of Egypt, in levels dating from about 1500 to 1300 B.C., excavators have come upon dozens and dozens of examples of a distinctive little jug, all of which, it can be demonstrated, were imported from Cyprus. They run about five to six inches in height and two to three in diameter, and have a most unusual shape, with a tall slender neck ending in a flare and a ring around the base. An Australian archaeologist, Robert Merrillees, has examined and analyzed the available specimens and has concluded that they

are an exact reproduction in clay of the poppy capsule: the tall slender neck repeats the tall slender stalk, the body the capsule itself, and the ring around the base the typical circular stigma at the top of a capsule. Very often the body is decorated with four to five parallel lines in white paint, and these Merrillees takes as reproducing the characteristic incisions made in a capsule to allow the juice to ooze out, the method of extracting opium that has been standard from ancient times to the present. The juglets, unlike most other forms of pottery, are not a type that gradually evolved; there is nothing like them from earlier times either in Cyprus or Egypt. They suddenly arrive on the scene in the sixteenth century B.C., last with little change for several hundred years, then equally suddenly vanish. Why the unusual shape, the abrupt appearance and disappearance? Because, says Merrillees, these jugs were a special design created for the opium trade: just as marketers of lemon juice today will put their product in a container shaped like a lemon and retain that shape with no change since it serves as an effective trademark, so the Cypriote opium handlers of the late Bronze Age thought up a jug in the form of a poppy capsule for their product and maintained it as long as they were in business. The purchasers in Egypt, he imagines, had medical purposes primarily in mind—he conceives of opium as the aspirin of the ancient world—but ritual use, of course, is not to be excluded.

It is an intriguing theory, but that is all it is, a theory. The opium poppy was to be found in many places in the Mediterranean (its original home seems to have been Asia Minor), and Merrillees has no explanation of why growing it became a specialty on Cyprus and precisely in the sixteenth century B.C. He suggests that the trade died out when the Egyptians decided to raise their own poppies, which is a reasonable hypothesis but cannot be proved. Since crude opium is a gum, for which a jug is hardly a suitable container, he has to assume that for shipping and sale it was thinned with honey or some other solvent. As it happens, a number of jugs were found with a residue of their contents still adhering. These have been subjected to chemical analyses, and though some early tests, admittedly unreliable, reported the presence of opium, all subsequent ones, done with proper care, have revealed neither opium nor a plausible solvent, only wax and fats. The Egyptians were by and large a frugal people, so it is quite possible, even

177

likely, that they did not throw away the attractive little vessels once the original contents had been exhausted but kept them for reuse—which would explain the wax and fats but does nothing to help Merrillees' case.

And this is the way the matter stands to date: the jugs certainly look as if they had been designed to hold opium, but so far none can be proved to have done so. Whether or not the drug trade goes back to the Bronze Age is still an open question.

In 1952 the renowned oceanographer Jacques Cousteau put his expertise at the service of archaeology. He had gotten word that off the tip of an islet called the Grand Congloué a few miles down the coast from Marseilles lay the remains of an ancient wreck. In cooperation with the director of antiquities for the region, he set a team of divers to work on it. After several painfully slow and difficult campaigns, they finally managed to bring up a good sampling of the cargo, enough to conclude that, when the vessel went down, it had aboard some 3,000 amphorae—clay shipping jars—containing about 15,000 to 20,000 gallons probably of wine, perhaps of oil.

That there were ancient wrecks to be exploited was known long before Cousteau turned his attention to the one off Grand Congloué. At the beginning of this century some Greek sponge divers had the incredible luck to blunder upon the remains of a ship that had been loaded with a cargo of works of art; some of the pieces they salvaged are now among the treasures of Athens' archaeological museum. A few years later yet another wreck containing works of art was found off Mahdia on the Tunisian coast. In both cases excavation had to be carried out with the only personnel and equipment available, professional divers dressed in suits and helmets and fed air by means of hoses and pumps. What revolutionized the nature of diving and brought into being the new discipline of underwater archaeology was Cousteau's development in 1943 of the simplified apparatus that today can be bought in practically any sporting goods shop, the aqualung or SCUBA (Self-Contained Underwater Breathing Apparatus) equipment, the set of tanks and mouthpiece that enables a diver to wander on the sea floor unencumbered by diving suit, helmet, pumps, hoses, and the like. More important, it converted diving from a métier open only to a narrow group of qualified professionals into a wide-open field that any healthy amateur could take up, even just as sport or diversion. The advent of the new technique suddenly made it possible to investigate wrecks at a fraction of the cost and time required hitherto; it was divers who excavated the wreck off of Grand Congloué. But it has brought evils as well as benefits: it has opened up ancient wrecks not only to archaeologists and those amateurs whose sole interest is the cause of archaeology but also to souvenir hunters and, worse, unscrupulous garnerers of merchandise to feed to the lucrative antiquities market. It is rare to find a wreck these days that has escaped plundering. For a long while those that lay in very deep waters where only the bold and well-trained dared to tread were safe, but now that more sophisticated apparatus is available and the prices of antiquities have reached irresistibly high levels, they too are being attacked. The one consolation is that even plundered remains are still able to supply a useful modicum of information. The divers, whether legitimate or clandestine, by finding wrecks from one end of the Mediterranean to the other, ranging in date from the Bronze Age to Byzantine times, have enabled us to sketch in the key lines followed by trading vessels of the ancient world.

The tell-tale sign of a wreck is usually a pile of amphorae on the sea floor. Amphorae were the ancient equivalent of our barrel or steel drum. Although there are quite small types, those used in overseas shipping were generally big, the commonest standing some three to four feet high and holding around five to ten gallons. They were made of clay so coarse and thick that even when empty they weigh a good fifty pounds. Since clay is well-nigh indestructible, long after the rest of the vessel's hull or cargo has been washed or eaten away, the amphorae will be left, forming a distinctive mound that quickly catches a diver's eye. To be sure, amphorae were no new discovery of underwater archaeology; for years numerous types and sizes have been turning up in land excavations. But underwater archaeology has uncovered not only a wealth of new varieties but unheard-of quantities. When loaded aboard a ship, amphorae were stacked in upright lines, one level upon another from the bottom of the hold to the deck, and sometimes upon the deck as well. Thus, even a freighter of ordinary size, running a hundred or so feet in length, could accommodate at least 3,000, and big carriers might hold up to 10,000. The museum at

Marseilles has 1,500 that Cousteau's men lifted from the wreck off Grand Congloué alone.

Amphorae are not as inarticulate as many other forms of pottery containers. The shape and certain features, such as the handles or lip or foot, differ according to where and when the jars were made, and today, after decades of intensive study, we have learned to recognize the source and date of the various types. Even an amateur can distinguish with ease jars that were made on the island of Rhodes or Chios or Cnidus, and, with some training, among those made in the fifth century B.C., the fourth century, the third, and so on. We can distinguish Italic jars, Spanish jars, African jars, etc., of various dates. Moreover,

amphorae often have identificatory marks stamped on them, generally on the handles. Jars from Rhodes bear a rose (*Rhodes* means "rose" in Greek), jars from Cnidus bear the legend *knidion* ("jar of Cnidus"), jars from Thasos bear the island's distinctive symbol of Heracles preparing to shoot an arrow, Italic jars frequently bear the name of the shipper.

Thus, an underwater archaeologist, from an examination of the amphorae he finds piled in a mound, can tell within general limits the date of the wreck they came from and where its cargo originated. Furthermore, since we know that among the key commodities traded back and forth across the Mediterranean were wine and oil, he can conclude that the jars very

179

Off the coast of Turkey, a scuba-diving archaeologist brings up a find from a Roman vessel that sank approximately 2,000 years ago. The sponge-encrusted amphora contained either wine or olive oil, and was probably destined for some Aegean port.

These two bronze pendants were found in a ship that sank off the coast of France in the sixth century B.C.

likely held one or the other. If the jars turn out to be Rhodian or Cnidian or Thasian, or the like, he can be even more specific, for all these islands specialized in the export of their local wine. If, on the other hand, they turn out to be, say, Spanish, then he is in a quandary, since Spain produced for export not only wine but olive oil and *garum,* the fish sauce that was so essential in ancient cooking, and all these products were shipped in the same sorts of amphorae.

The jars, then, though they give us indications of date and ports of call, are usually ambiguous about what was picked up at these ports of call, although the range of possibilities is, admittedly, fairly narrow. Some cases are practically cut and dried. In 1972 the wreck of a small coastal freighter was found in the harbor of Port-Vendres on France's Mediterranean coast just north of the Spanish border. The cargo included fourteen tin ingots, some amphorae from southern Spain, and some amphorae with the remains of fishbones. Obviously the vessel had loaded up in southern Spain, perhaps at Cádiz or Malaga, with a cargo of Spanish tin, Spanish fish sauce, and probably Spanish oil, followed the coast eastward to Port-Vendres, and came to grief there. The only point about which we are unsure is its final destination: Port-Vendres may have been only one of its ports of call, perhaps only a harbor of refuge.

But take, on the other hand, the wreck of a freighter of fair size, some eighty feet in length, that sank near the tip of an islet off the coast of France between Cannes and Juan-les-Pins. It had no less than ten types of amphorae aboard — some of Spanish origin, some of Italian origin, some from Rhodes, some from Chios. The Rhodian and Chian jars almost certainly had wine in them. In one of the others a test revealed the presence of sage, indicating it was probably filled with sage vinegar. The cargo also included a shipment of varied tableware, red pottery plates most probably of Italian manufacture, pottery goblets, and glass cups. Wine from the eastern Mediterranean; tableware, vinegar, and other unidentifiable products from Italy; either wine or oil or fish products from Spain; and all of it aboard a vessel that went down off the French coast — what route can we distill from such a miscellany? We cannot even figure out in which direction the ship was headed.

Next to amphora wrecks, those most commonly found are of ships that had been carrying building stone, and for the same reason: stone can last for cen-

A classically Greek, exquisite bronze Demeter was lost 2,300 years ago, but retrieved in 1953 by a sponge diver.

181

turies on the bottom, and a mass of huge blocks or column drums stand out there as clearly as any mound of amphorae. Of the two wrecks carrying works of art that were spotted in the early years of this century, one owes its discovery to a conspicuous stack of columns that had been loaded on deck. In 1951, in the infancy of underwater archaeology, a load of stone that was lying in shallow water just off the coast of St. Tropez on the French Riviera was plucked out with the help of a giant floating crane and deposited on a quay of the town's port. There were 13 pieces, consisting of massive column drums almost six feet in diameter and six feet high, column bases, a piece of an architrave — in all 200 tons of Carrara marble. Off the eastern shore of Sicily a whole series of such wrecks have been identified, three of them concentrated off the southeast tip of the island alone. One, like the wreck near St. Tropez, was carrying about 200 tons, 15 blocks of Athenian marble, including one that by itself weighs 40 tons. A second wreck was even bigger: it had aboard 39 blocks probably of Asia Minor marble, weighing close to 350 tons. The third is the most interesting: in addition to pieces of columns, columnettes, bases, and capitals, it had part of an ambon, a stone pulpit, of a type strikingly like those found in several churches of the eastern Mediterranean and almost the exact replica of one in the church of St. Mark's in Venice.

We did not need underwater archaeology to tell us about the ancient trade in building stone. Back in the third millennium B.C., as we have seen, Sumerian kings were importing diorite from Magan for their statues. The marble quarries on the Greek islands of Paros and Naxos served the ancient world from the seventh century B.C. to Byzantine times and beyond. The Roman emperors, during their heyday, the first to the third century A.D., having the wealth of a great state at their disposal, drew on all the resources of their vast realm for their ambitious building programs. From various sources of information, we know a good deal about the efficient way in which they organized the trade in the most important decorative stones, marble and granite and prophyry. They concentrated upon a limited number of state-owned quarries, introduced mass-production techniques which enabled them to build up stocks of rough-squared blocks or roughed-out columns, and arranged for cheap water transport to haul what was needed to the building sites. The buildings themselves tell clearly enough the story of the trade that lay behind them. The visitor to Rome's Pantheon enters through a portico supported by giant columns of granite that came from Egypt. Once inside, his eyes light upon columns and veneering of yellow marble from Tunisia, and he walks over a floor made up, among other stones, of slabs of pavonazzetto from Asia Minor and porphyry from Egypt. There it all is: where the stones were shipped from, where they were shipped to, what they were used for, even who paid for them (the imperial treasury).

And this reveals a paradox. We learn more from building stone found by traditional archaeology than by underwater archaeology. The cargo off St. Tropez vouchsafes far less information about trade than the stones from the Pantheon. The ship must have started from some Italian port, for it had aboard a load of Carrara marble; but of its destination we know only that it was sailing toward a port somewhere in the west. It has been suggested that the stone was intended for a temple at Narbonne — remains reveal that a colossal one existed there — but that is only a guess. We have not the slightest idea where the 350 tons of Asia Minor marble that went down off the southeast tip of Sicily was headed; and since no amphorae or other pottery were found round about, we do not even know the date. The vessel with works of art and a deckload of columns that was discovered in the early part of this century off Tunisia must have started from Athens, because part of its ballast consisted of discarded inscribed Athenian stones, but its destination is a mystery. It need not have been heading for North Africa at all, it may have fallen foul of the same kind of storm that drove Saint Paul to shipwreck off the coast of Malta.

Where was Magan? Ophir? Tarshish? Thule? How far down the west African coast did Hanno sail? Where did the Bronze Age smiths get their tin? Did Bronze Age merchants carry on a trade in opium? How is it that in what seems to be the cargo of a single vessel there can be shipping jars of widely separated provenience and date? For what buildings in what countries were the massive loads of stone that divers have found intended? We can trace the general lines of trade in ancient times and the products carried over them, but puzzles like these are nagging reminders that there are gaps in our knowledge which we very likely will never be able to fill.

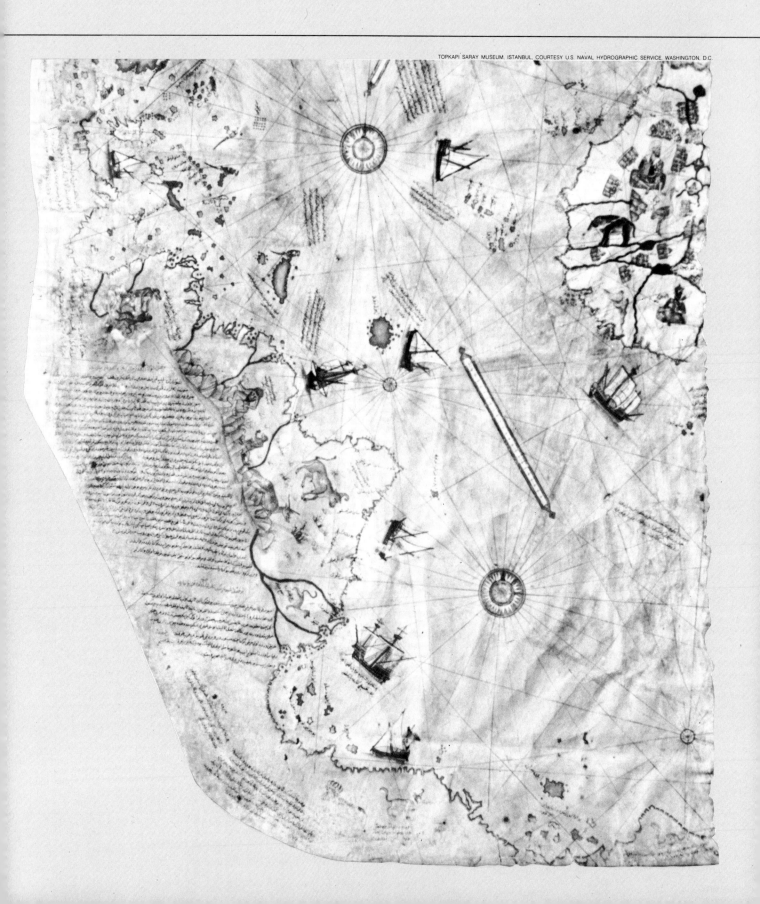

DID SEAFARERS MAP THE WORLD LONG BEFORE COLUMBUS?

On November 9, 1929, in the former Topkapi Palace in Istanbul, a museum official found a map dated 919 (A.D. 1513) painted on parchment by one Piri Re'is, a corsair who later served in the navy of Suleiman the Magnificent. The map, shown on the opposite page, was one of the first to show any part of the New World, and it positioned South America with remarkable accuracy in relation to Africa. In a marginal note Piri Re'is stated that he had consulted "about twenty" charts in compiling his map, including one by Columbus (a document scholars have sought in vain for centuries) and eight others "drawn in the days of Alexander, Lord of the Two Horns"—i.e., Alexander the Great.

For some time thereafter articles about the map appeared in Europe and America, but then interest abated; little more was heard of it until 1956, when a Turkish naval officer presented a facsimile to the U.S. Navy Hydrographic Office in Washington. After examining it, Captain Arlington H. Mallery, a student of old maps, declared that in his opinion the light-colored band at the bottom running east from South America represented bays and islands of Antarctica's Queen Maud Land that are now concealed under the Antarctic ice cap. The features shown corresponded strikingly, Mallery said, to a topographic profile of the area constructed in 1949 by a three-nation seismic survey.

Could men have mapped this coast in the remote past before it was covered with ice? And could their map or maps have been copied and recopied down the ages—most recently in Alexander the Great's time—to reach, ultimately, the eyes of Piri Re'is? The notion was too far-fetched for profes-

sional geographers. But when a New Hampshire college professor named Charles Hapgood heard about it he found it so fascinating that he decided to look into the matter for himself.

Throughout the late Middle Ages and Renaissance, Hapgood knew, geographers had posited the existence of a huge land mass at the Earth's southern extremity to "compensate" for the extensive distribution of land in the Northern Hemisphere. So far as anyone knew, however, Antarctica had never even been sighted before the nineteenth century, and its coasts not completely charted until the twentieth. Yet here, supposedly, was Piri Re'is's detailed map of part of it, drawn in 1513.

No less startling was a map of Antarctica drawn in 1531 by one Oronteus Finaeus: shown as if viewed from a point in space directly over the South Pole, the continent had a shape uncannily like the one it displays on modern maps. On some of its coasts, moreover, including that of Queen Maud Land, the map showed mountains and ranges where they actually do rise under the ice, and, incredibly, rivers flowing straight out to sea.

Rivers—even short, glacier-fed rivers—in Antarctica? Geologists maintain that during the last ice age, ending about 10,000 B.C., Antarctic ice extended north to cover Patagonia, and then contracted to its present continental dimensions. So Piri Re'is's ice-free coasts and islands and Oronteus Finaeus' rivers had to be imaginary. Yet as Hapgood was to learn, cores taken in 1949 from the bottom of the Ross Sea, across Antarctica from Queen Maud Land, consisted, at depths laid down over many millennia ending by about 4000 B.C., of the fine-grained sediment washed down by rivers in temperate lands.

In Renaissance maps of northern regions Hapgood found other puzzling features: an ice-free Greenland; the British Isles with glaciers covering

their centers; a partly glaciated Sweden; the Aegean Sea dotted with numerous extra islands that had since been drowned, presumably, by the melting of ice further north; and the precisely drawn Pacific Coast of North America still connected by a land bridge to Asia.

Analyzing the Piri Re'is map mathematically, Hapgood determined that it had been projected from a point on the meridian of Alexandria just south of that city. And when other notable old maps turned out to share the same projection center, he concluded that the early compilers of much earlier source maps had worked at the great university at Alexandria. Most of their handiwork, he conjectured, had been lost in the destruction of the Alexandrian libraries, but some maps had been taken to Byzantium—there, after many centuries, to become as Piri Re'is attested, sources for his map. Others, Hapgood said could have been taken west into Europe by the Venetians, who occupied Byzantium in 1204.

Is the analysis of Captain Mallery's theory—expounded in 1966 in Hapgood's book, *Maps of the Ancient Sea Kings*—tenable? Until he or someone else produces convincing proof that those supposed prehistoric mapmakers actually existed, most scientists will doubtless continue to remain highly skeptical—even while conceding that they have no ready answers to many of the tantalizing questions Hapgood has raised.

CHINA AND THE WEST: WHICH WAS FIRST?

Even in ancient times East was East and West was West—but the twain did keep meeting, at the edges. It was the lightest of contact, but enough to raise a hotly disputed point: what did each take from the other?

Actually the question involves the whole span of history, for the West went one way and China another, not only in prehistoric times and antiquity but also during the Middle Ages—indeed, right through the days of the industrial revolution, which came to China long after it had swept over Europe. In antiquity the West developed such political forms as democracy and republicanism, which China did not learn until yesterday, while China developed such administrative forms as a civil service, which the West did not learn until yesterday. Western thinkers turned mathematics into a handmaid of astronomy and physics: the Chinese never did. Through all its history China has clung to a system of writing whose likes most of the West gave up three thousand years ago. If the two great centers had arisen and grown in vacuums, sealed off from each other, their separate paths would be understandable. But they did not.

Let us limit ourselves to the first two historical periods, prehistory and antiquity. Each poses a different problem. What prehistorians puzzle over is this: did civilization, after arising in the Near East, spread from there to China as well as to Europe? Or did the Chinese civilization arise independently? What historians of antiquity puzzle over is this: we know that there was contact between the Greco-Roman world and China, at long distance to be sure, but contact nonetheless and over a considerable stretch of time; is it possible that there was hardly any technological interchange? Specifically, can it be true that the West showed little interest in numerous devices of manifest practical value that the Chinese, precocious inventors, were using?

The Chinese emerged from the Stone Age late, long after the people of Mesopotamia and Egypt. As we pointed out in an earlier chapter, until recently the diffusionists were riding high. And the delayed

development of China was grist for their mill: why presume that the Chinese independently discovered agriculture, stock-raising, metallurgy, and the other first steps in civilization? Is it not easier to imagine that the knowledge of these fundamental arts traveled from Mesopotamia east across the steppes, where nomads were in constant movement? The scholars who busied themselves with the subject, as it happens, were Westerners, and so their theorizing may well have been colored by geographical allegiance as well as commitment to diffusionism. During the past decades China's new regime has been vigorously promoting research into the country's ancient past, and Chinese archaeologists have been excavating, studying the finds, and drawing their own conclusions. It will come as no surprise to learn that, as they see it, their neolithic ancestors largely made their own way with scant assistance from outside.

China's first settled society arose in a relatively small basin of the Yellow River, the area where it makes its great angle to flow northeast to the Yellow Sea and where it is joined by important tributaries. This was an oasis amid discouraging terrain on all four sides: north lay a windswept plateau; west, semi-arid highlands; south, a mountain range; east, swampy lowlands. The rivers of the basin offered such good fishing that it was not until relatively late—some scholars say 5000 B.C., but others put it much after that—that men felt the need to supplement what they could catch by growing food.

Up until the very middle of this century, what excavation had been carried out seemed to show a definite break between the hunter-fisher's paleolithic way of life and the settled neolithic way. For the diffusion-minded Westerner this was proof positive of his case: the changeover was abrupt and tardy because it took place only when agriculture and domestication of beasts, so long known in the Near East, finally arrived in China. The intensive archaeological activity of the last decades has altered the picture considerably. Although it has confirmed that the paleolithic way of life continued for an unusually long time, it has also revealed that neolithic villages whose members raised cereals and grazed sheep go very far back. There is no break; rather, the two ways of life for a long time overlapped. Is it still possible that China's agriculture is indebted to the West?

"It is asking too much of coincidence to assume that such a fundamental revolution as had already oc-

◀OVERLEAF *(pages 186-187): A chariot appears with horses and riders in this Han dynasty bas-relief of the first century* B.C. *Western historians generally believe the chariot was a Western invention, as was writing (represented by the superimposed Chinese characters).*
LOUVRE

curred in the Fertile Crescent of the Near East should have happened a second time in China," declares William Watson, author of a shelfful of works on ancient China. But Kwang-chih Chang thinks differently: "It is all well and good to assume that the idea of food-production diffused from one region to another, but this assumption is as difficult to prove as it is to disprove.... For the present it is best, I think, to concentrate our efforts on learning more about the Neolithic culture in China itself before making any farfetched conclusions"; such is the view he expressed in a book published in 1968. And Chêng Tê-K'un, in an article that appeared in 1973, states flatly, "It was in the Central Plain that typical Chinese agriculture developed," with not the slightest allusion to possible influence from the Near East in farming or animal husbandry. This is how matters stand at the moment. Let us leave it at that and turn to the next debated aspect of Chinese civilization.

The Bronze Age makes a dramatic entrance in China, for it appears on the stage of history hand in hand with the first centralized government (the so-called Shang Dynasty), differentiated social classes, specialization of labor, slaves, writing, the chariot — in short, the trappings of a fully developed civilization.

Before 1950 its debut had seemed even more dramatic. Up to then the sole Bronze Age site that had been excavated was An-yang, lying on the northeastern edge of the heartland of neolithic China. Chinese historical accounts list An-yang as the last capital of the Shang Dynasty, dating to the fourteenth century B.C. As the excavation at An-yang proceeded, archaeologists were astounded by what their spades laid bare: a city with a planned quadrilateral shape crisscrossed by streets which were lined with houses, a cemetery with tombs in the form of elaborate chambers where kings had been laid to rest with their chariots amid the bodies of people slaughtered for the occasion, superbly crafted bronzework and jade and jewelry. The archaeologists had never expected such an advanced community, such riches. The Shang rulers and their retainers clearly were wealthy and powerful, men who rode to the hunt and into battle on horse-drawn chariots, who commanded the services of fluent scribes and skilled craftsmen as well as hosts of slaves.

How does one explain this sudden leap in material civilization? Again it was easy for diffusionist-minded

Western scholars, particularly since the Shang Dynasty seemed to date from about 1500 B.C., and they knew that, just about then, bronze-accoutered chariot-riding Aryans had moved into and overrun India. Either a portion of them had continued on and made their way into China, or if not that, their martial arts and equipment had.

However, the digging that has been carried out since 1950 makes it clear that An-yang had predecessors. According to Chinese records, the Shang court shifted the seat of its capital six times, and at least two other sites have been discovered. Both are earlier, but they reveal a high level of development consonant with that at An-yang. Furthermore, they also reveal that Shang beginnings predate 1500 B.C., possibly by as much as two or three centuries, and that Shang sites lie over earlier, more primitive sites and derive most of their basic characteristics from these. In short, China's progress could not possibly have been connected with the Aryan push into India.

But the new archaeological discoveries do not completely eliminate the problem, merely narrow it. Three elements appear in the Shang capitals which have no antecedents in the previous neolithic period: writing, the horse and chariot, and bronze metallurgy.

Let us take writing first. Here we find the by now customary division between Western and Eastern thinking. Some of the Chinese authorities insist that the art of writing is totally indigenous and can be traced right down from symbols found on early neolithic pottery; others feel that true writing does not appear before the Bronze Age and prefer to leave the question of its origin open. But the Westerners are well-nigh unanimous: since writing had been in use in Mesopotamia a millennium and a half before its appearance in China, the idea at least must surely have come from there. Even Joseph Needham, author of the monumental multivolume *Science and Civilization in China* and a passionate advocate of China and its contributions to the world, agrees that writing in China was the result of diffusion from the West.

Next, the horse and chariot. "The resemblance of the Shang chariot to chariots made in the Near East toward the end of the second millennium B.C. is too great to be dismissed as a coincidence"; so William Watson, the authority on ancient China whom we cited earlier. "The inference is irresistible: charioteers [from the steppes] must have overrun China also . . . and then proceeded to assimilate a large part

Chinese war chariots, buried with the horses that pulled them, were found in the tomb of Yuan T'u, a Chinese ruler of the seventh century B.C. *According to most archaeologists, the chariot originated in Mesopotamia in the third millennium* B.C.

of the culture of their subjects"; so William McNeill, in his magisterial *The Rise of the West.* But he adds in a footnote, "I have called the inference irresistible, but many Chinese experts do in fact resist it with considerable emotional energy." Kwang-chih Chang, whom we quoted earlier, sets forth with precision the relevant facts so far uncovered. Horse bones have definitely been found on sites inhabited by certain neolithic peoples. We may be pretty sure they did not use their horses for riding, since this particular art made its debut in human history much later, after the beginning of the first millennium B.C. We are certain they did not use them for food. That leaves only the pulling of carts or chariots—but of these, there is absolutely no trace until we come to the Shang period. Moreover, the horse bones that have been found are very very rare. "A great number of excavations and comparative studies of horse and chariot remains in China and in Mesopotamia must be made before we can be certain about the origin of the horse chariot in the Shang dynasty," Chang concludes. For the present, that seems the appropriate last word on this puzzle.

Finally, the question of metallurgy. For long it seemed that the art of working both bronze and iron had been developed in the West. The earliest known objects of bronze, dating about 3000 B.C., had been found in Mesopotamia; those of iron, dating about 1200 B.C., in Asia Minor. But spectacular new discoveries have changed all this. Recent excavations at Ban Chiang in the northeastern part of Thailand have brought to light finely fashioned bronze spear points which seem to have been made about 3500 B.C. and iron objects which seem to have been made about 1600 B.C. Clearly, if we are to see diffusion at work, the direction of travel was from east to west. And, if to the West, why not to China as well? After all, it is that much nearer. Perhaps not only the technology of

bronze but also the tin that went into it came to both China and the West from Southeast Asia. There is plenty of it there; Malaysia is today the world's greatest producer of tin.

One of the curious aspects of Chinese bronze metallurgy is that it started relatively late and then forged ahead with phenomenal speed. The early Chinese bronzes date from the sixteenth century B.C., perhaps a bit sooner but not much. However, by 1300, Chinese smiths were turning out exquisite cast-bronze ritual vessels which are far superior to contemporary work found elsewhere. The diffusionists for long bolstered their case for outside influence by pointing out the absence of any primitive stage in Chinese bronze casting; the earliest pieces discovered were just as fine as the later. Were we to conceive of it as coming into the world fully grown, like Athena from Zeus' head? It was easier to imagine that the Chinese had borrowed a developed technology.

But new finds have produced examples of bronze casting done in rougher, simpler fashion, which indicates that the art did indeed have an infancy. And the Chinese experts have worked out a plausible explanation for China's late start and precocious advance in it. Bronze is worked by casting in molds—and so are forms of ceramics. What the Chinese craftsman did was to adapt a technique he had long perfected in working with clay to the new material; the superb results were a measure of the skill he had acquired. Chêng Tê-K'un, the authority we had occasion to mention earlier, in a recent article offers an appealing reason for the rapid advance of such skill not only in bronze but in clay: the thirst of the Shang rulers. They were heavy drinkers, he reports, and adds darkly, "Many historians have seen this as the main cause of the downfall of the dynasty." Previously, pottery had been rather porous; for holding

Egyptian chariot, before 1300 B.C.

Chinese carriage, about A.D. 100.

wine the Shang potters were inspired to produce a finer, impervious ware, and did so thriving a business in it that, as excavation has revealed, they were able to afford workshops in many respects as elegant as any palace chamber. Since the majority of the bronze vessels found are also for wine, Chêng deduces that Shang tippling brought boom times to the smiths as well as the potters.

Thus one conclusion is now obvious—at least to Chinese scholars: their ancestors did not learn the technology of bronze from the West. Having settled this problem, if only negatively, we run right into another: why is it that the Chinese continued to make bronze weapons—arrowheads, halberds, daggers—for centuries after iron had come into use for agricultural instruments? A warrior of, say, the fourth century B.C. was still wielding a bronze halberd long after peasants had begun turning fields with an iron hoe. And this brings us to Chinese iron metallurgy, whose history presents even more puzzles than bronze.

The Shang Dynasty, which lasted until about 1000 B.C., knew only bronze. The Chou Dynasty, which dates from about 1000 B.C. until 221, saw the introduction of iron about 500 B.C., but, as we have just noted, for the longest while only for instruments of peace. Finally, in the third century B.C. iron weapons became common. They served the armies of the Ch'in Dynasty, which unified the land, and of the famed Han Dynasty, whose reign, from 206 B.C. to A.D. 220, parallels the rise and heyday of the Romans in the West. The Chinese, thus, were the last among the great culture-areas of the Old World to turn to the use of iron.

Did they turn to it because they finally became aware of its existence in other lands? Specifically, did the knowledge of reducing iron from ore and working it, both known, as we have just seen, in Southeast Asia from 1600 B.C., diffuse from there to China—for that matter, to the West as well? To the West, possibly, since the objects found there are of wrought iron, as they are in Thailand. To China, not possibly, for the Chinese smiths, when they finally did turn to iron, went their own special way: they produced objects of *cast* iron.

There are two basic methods for making iron. To make wrought iron the ore is heated in a furnace, which need be no hotter than that used for copper, whose melting point is 1083° Celsius: this results in a "bloom," a spongy mass of fused stone with pasty globules of iron embedded in it. By repeatedly heating this mass till it is red-hot and hammering it, the smith pounds away the slag and integrates the iron globules into a lump of wrought iron. The further processes of reheating, hammering, and quenching to produce iron of increasing strength as well as the various forms of steel need not concern us. Wrought iron was the sole kind known to the West not only during the whole of ancient times but right up to the fourteenth century A.D.

The second method results in cast iron. The ore is heated at a temperature generally of no less than 1400° Celsius, at which point it will liquefy, the slag is drawn off, and the molten iron can be poured into molds just like bronze. (It can also be allowed to cool and then hammered into wrought iron.) Now there are no words at all in Chinese that refer to the reduction of iron ore in a solid form: they all refer to a liquid form. Clearly, then, from the very beginning Chinese smiths knew only cast iron. It would appear that, just as they had transferred their skill in casting ceramics to bronze sometime before 1500 B.C., so, a thousand years later, they achieved a similar transfer from bronze to iron. The great difficulty in making cast iron is to create and maintain the heat. This necessity mothered a series of important inventions, which, like cast iron itself, do not appear in the West until after the Middle Ages. In the West the smiths were content to supply their furnaces with a natural draft by building them on hillsides. For artificial draft all they used were the leather bellows. But neither of these systems was suitable for the production of cast iron. The Chinese at the very outset must have devised a form of blast furnace, no doubt very small at first. By the fourth century B.C. they had invented the piston bellows, and, in the ensuing centuries, introduced even more efficient designs to produce a continuous blast. The water-power mill appears in China in the first century A.D.—not for grinding grain, as in the West, but for driving the bellows of the blast furnaces.

Iron, as Pliny the Elder, the Roman savant of the first century A.D., puts it, is "the best and worst instrument in human existence. We use it to split the soil, plant trees, cut vine props . . . build houses, dress stone. . . . But we also use it for war, murder, brigandage." Incredible as it may seem, the two great centers of ancient civilization through the whole course of their existence chose to go different ways in

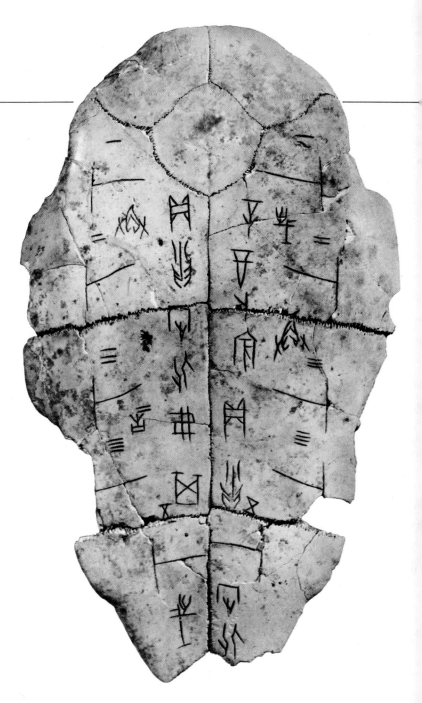

producing this all-important material. Chinese smiths did turn out objects of wrought iron and steel, but not by the process used in the West—rather, by transforming cast iron. Western smiths did occasionally turn out chunks of cast iron when the temperature in their furnaces accidentally went high enough, but they saw no value in them and tossed them away; archaeologists have found these discards in the remains about Roman ironworks.

This fundamental division in the iron technology of East and West brings us to the second question posed at the outset of this chapter: for long there was steady contact between these two greater centers of civilization—is it possible that the Chinese, as precocious in other phases of technology as they were in iron, invented numerous devices of obvious utility which Westerners cavalierly disregarded?

Of the contact there is no room for doubt. It can be traced, without a break, from the third century B.C. on. At that time Chinese silk, transported by caravan through central Asia, began to filter through to the Mediterranean, where its superiority to the only thing the Greeks had, produced from wild Asia Minor silkworms, was swiftly recognized. By the second half of the second century B.C. the Chinese were active in the trade. Each year they dispatched caravans which followed a route that started from Paochi, moved along the inside of the Great Wall to its western end, traversed Chinese Turkistan, by looping either north or south of the vast salt swamp in the Tarim basin, snaked through the Pamir mountains to Merv, and from there proceeded across the desert to link up with age-old trade routes across Persia and Mesopotamia to the Mediterranean. During the days of the Roman Empire, not only silk but camphor, cinnamon, jade, and other objects were included, though silk was always far and away the most important. It was exchanged for cash. A few Western objects have been found in the Far East—some Roman glass in Korea and perhaps in China, some gems and a Roman bronze lamp and a Greek bowl in Indochina —but these probably drifted there or were carried by travelers as souvenirs.

Neither the Chinese nor any other people involved in the trade went the whole distance. Somewhere in the Pamirs the Chinese caravaneers turned their merchandise over either to local traders or to Indian middlemen who had come up from the south.

The Bronze Age, it was long thought, made its first appearance about 3,000 B.C. in Mesopotamia, where the Sumerian lady above was made. But recent excavations in Thailand have brought to light bronze objects such as the dagger at right above, made as far back as 3600 B.C.

The Indians hauled their share back home to forward it to the West by ship, while the others plodded on to Persia, where they met up with Syrians and Greeks who took care of the final leg.

It was only on very rare occasions that East and West met face to face. We know of only two, mentioned in the Chinese records. In A.D. 97 an official Chinese envoy, K'ang Ying, was sent on an embassy to the West. He got only as far as Mesopotamia, for there he was told that to go farther involved a voyage on ship that might last two years, that people who did it fortified themselves with food for three years just to be on the safe side, that many lost their lives; it sounds very much like a cock-and-bull story concocted by the local business interests to discourage any attempts on China's part to cut them out of their position as middlemen, but K'ang swallowed it. The second occasion was in A.D. 166 when, according to a Chinese account, "the king of Ta-ts'in, An-tun, sent an embassy who, from the frontier of Jih-nan [Annam] offered ivory, rhinoceros horns, and tor-

toise shell. From that time dates the [direct] intercourse with this country." Ta-ts'in was the Chinese name for the Far West, and An-tun is Antoninus, the family name of the Roman emperor Marcus Aurelius. The account goes on to comment in raised-eyebrow fashion on the very commonplace gifts the embassy brought for the Chinese emperor; there were, for example, no jewels. No doubt it was not an official body at all but a group of shippers trying to get their Chinese silk without the intervention of middlemen. In any event, the direct intercourse could not have lasted very long since we hear of no further meetings.

Since the contact between East and West was indirect, the information that came back to either side was necessarily secondhand. Some of it was solid. Greek and Near Eastern traders were able to pick up from the middlemen with whom they worked place names and other points of geographical interest, which is why the geographers of the first and second centuries A.D., when the silk trade was at its height, are so much better informed about central Asia and Indonesia than their predecessors. But what filtered through to the man in the street was often fanciful hearsay. The Romans got the impression that the Chinese were all supremely righteous; the Chinese, that Westerners were all supremely honest. Apparently some information about iron came through. Pliny the Elder, in the discussion of iron in his encyclopedia, mentions *Sericum ferrum*, "Chinese iron"; of all the types of iron, he writes, "it is Chinese iron that takes the palm. The Chinese export it along with textiles and skins." There is something askew here, since what we would call Chinese iron (that is, cast iron) is hardly the finest type there is. Caravans from the East often brought in iron from India, which Pliny may have thought came from China. It was produced in Hyderabad and was a superb steel, the very same that in Islamic times served the smiths of Damascus for their celebrated blades.

Let us admit that the contact was indirect, that misunderstandings were common, that Westerners and Easterners rarely came face to face—yet the contact was there, and if there were few times when Greek and Chinese communicated directly with each other, there were plenty when their agents or employees did. There was enough contact, one would think, for each side to hear about each other's discoveries, especially for Westerners to hear about the immensely useful devices one saw in Chinese workshops,

The Chinese did not begin working with bronze until about 1500 B.C. but quickly raised it to a high art. (This wine jug in the shape of an elephant, with a smaller elephant on its lid, dates from the Shang dynasty about 1000 B.C.). Historians who thought China learned bronze metallurgy from the West now wonder if both China and the West got it from Thailand.

Precious goods from China reached the West by way of the ancient Silk Road. The journey across Asia was long and arduous, involved many middlemen, and was often made dangerous by brigands. At left is a fragment of embroidered silk that reached Palmyra in the first century A.D. The scene below from a seventh-century scroll shows envoys from Southeast Asia bearing elephant tusks and peacock feathers to the T'ang court.

houses, ports. For some mysterious reason, they paid them no heed whatsoever. Take so simple and practical a thing as the wheelbarrow. The Chinese were trundling around these humble but superbly efficient instruments by the third century A.D. and very likely before, but the Europeans did not adopt them until the Middle Ages. Westerners waited until the ninth century A.D. to use cranks or to mount in gimbals things which have to be kept level like shipboard lamps, until the twelfth to introduce treadles, until the eighteenth to cool themselves with rotating fans, all of which the Chinese had been using since the second century A.D. Not until after the Middle Ages did Westerners equip their forges with power-driven bellows or introduce the blast furnace, both of which, as we have seen, the Chinese had by the first century A.D. Not until after the eighteenth century did they build suspension bridges held up by chains, which the Chinese had been building since the sixth century A.D. Not until the sixteenth did they fly kites, a pas-

time the Chinese had been enjoying since 400 B.C.

Fans, gimbals, kites, and the like—these are only gadgets and toys. But, as we have seen in connection with the fashioning of iron, the indifference extended to far more than gadgets and toys. Perhaps the most striking case in point is naval technology. The various seamen—Greeks, Arabs, Persians, Indians, Malays, Chinese—who plied the sea lanes between the West and China passed each other on the water and rubbed shoulders in port; one would expect at least some interchange. Yet, with one exception, there was practically none of any significance.

We have already described the land route over which Chinese products came to the Mediterranean world. There was an equally important route by water. The first leg ran from the Red Sea or the Persian Gulf as far as India, and ever since the time of Eudoxus (see Chapter 1), this had been largely in the hands of Greek skippers, although Arabs and Indians

196

must have had some share. In the Indian ports the vessels loaded up not only with Indian goods, principally pepper and other spices, but also Chinese, principally silk. Some of these, as pointed out earlier, had come to India by way of Indian middlemen who had purchased them from caravaneers in central Asia. The rest were brought in by ship from farther east. Initially, this eastern leg of the route was totally in the hands of Indian and Malay seamen, but by the first century A.D. the Greeks who sailed to India began to cut in and by the second were actively involved, at least part of the way. At first they cautiously coasted around the shores of the Bay of Bengal, but eventually they learned to cut right across from southern India to the Malay Peninsula. On occasion they went farther, into the Tonkin Gulf beyond, for they clearly knew Sumatra, although they seem to have confused it with Java. Greek sailors who penetrated this far met up with the Chinese at a port which Ptolemy, the best-informed ancient geog-

rapher, calls Cattigara, and where Cattigara is has triggered the usual scholarly wrangling; the prime contenders are Hanoi, Canton, Hangchow, and Borneo, with the odds favoring Hanoi. Cattigara was as far as Westerners ever got. The third and last leg of the route, between Cattigara and China itself, was shared by Chinese, Malay, and Indian seamen. Thus, in a handbook of instructions drawn up in the first century A.D. for Greek skippers and merchants in the Far Eastern trade, all the author can tell of what lies beyond Maylaya is that "at the very north, on the outside the sea ends in a certain place, and here lies a huge inland city called Thina, from which originate raw silk, silk yarn, and silk cloth. . . . But it is not easy to go to this Thina; for rarely do people come from there, and not many." Three centuries later a Roman geographer candidly informs his readers that after "Cattigara, the leading port of the *Sinai*, [is] the end of the known and inhabited land in the regions of the south. . . . There are no witnesses to point out the

197

course beyond the port of the *Sinai* unless it be some god who knows." *Sinai* was the name the Greeks gave to the Chinese they encountered in these southern regions; it derives from the Ch'in Dynasty, the first to rule a united country, including the area of the Chinese ports, and from *Sinai* comes our "China." (The northern Chinese, whom the caravaneers along the land route dealt with, were called *Seres,* from the Chinese *ssu,* "silk.")

There was, thus, a mélange of Indian, Malay, and Greek ships plying the waters from the southern tip of India all around the Bay of Bengal to Malaya, and Indian, Malay, Chinese, and an occasional Greek ship beyond. In other words, some Greek crews had the chance to see Chinese junks with their own eyes, and many more to hear about them from Indian or Malay sailors, to whom the sight of a junk was not usual.

With the fall of the Roman Empire, the sea trade with China by no means came to an end. The Greeks made their exit, but their role was taken over by the Persians and also by the Chinese. Whereas up to, say, the third century A.D., junks rarely went west of Malaya, from the fifth century on they sailed regularly all the way to the head of the Persian Gulf, where they discharged cargoes for Babylon.

The contact, then, that might lead to exchange of ideas, new wrinkles, techniques, types of equipment, or what have you, existed for centuries. Yet the seamen involved—Greek, Arab, Indian, Persian, Malay, Chinese—sturdily resisted temptation. The Chinese took nothing from the others, and the others, with one exception, took practically nothing from the Chinese—and therein lies the puzzle, for the Chinese had a great deal to offer.

Chinese seagoing junks, observed Marco Polo, "have but one . . . deck, and on this deck there are commonly in all the greater number . . . quite sixty little rooms or cabins, and in some, more, and in some,

fewer, according as the ships are larger and smaller, where, in each, a merchant can stay comfortably. They have one . . . rudder and four masts. . . . Some ships, namely those which are larger, have besides quite thirteen holds, that is, divisions, on the inside, made with strong planks fitted together . . . if by accident the ship is staved in any place. . . . the water cannot pass from one hold to another, so strongly are they shut in." Staterooms, rudder, rig, watertight compartments—Polo's eye caught precisely the features in which a junk differed for the better from the ships he was familiar with. When a merchant booked passage on a Greek or Roman vessel, he got for his money nothing more than a spot on deck where at night he was entitled to spread bedding and put up a little shelter. The same rough-and-ready accommodations were all that were available on Arab, Persian, or Indian craft, a far cry from a private cabin where travelers could "stay comfortably." The single rudder, about which we will have more to say later, made its appearance on junks by the first or second century A.D., seven or eight hundred years before it turns up anywhere else. Junks had watertight compartments from the second A.D., sixteen hundred years before they are found anywhere else.

Most surprising of all is the total indifference of other seamen to the merits of the Chinese rig. The four masts Polo mentions were rigged with the distinctive type of sail that junks had been carrying since the third century A.D. and still carry today, the Chinese balance lug. The balance lug, to begin with, is one of the class of rigs called fore-and-aft—that is, with the sails set along the axis of the ship, running from fore to aft rather than crosswise—whose great advantage is that they enable a vessel to steer much closer to the wind than the squaresails favored by the Greeks and Romans and other maritime nations of the age. Arabs, Persians, and Indians, by the time the Chinese were sharing the Indian Ocean with them,

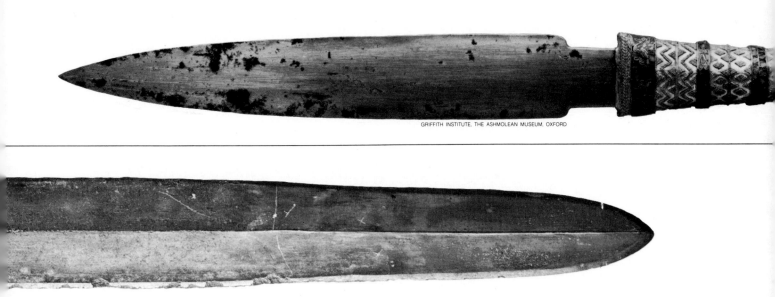

had adopted the lateen, itself a fore-and-aft sail but lacking many of the virtues of the Chinese version. The Chinese balance lug is stiffened by a series of parallel battens that reach from one side of the sail to the other, like so many horizontal stripes. From the after end of each batten a line — the sheet — runs down to the deck. By trimming this web of sheets, the sail can be set as well as the scientifically designed canvas of a modern racing yacht. The battens serve yet another all-important purpose, the shortening of sail, the reducing of the surface exposed to the wind when it gets too strong. This advantage would have been of minor interest to the Greeks and Romans, who had an equally efficient system, a web of vertical lines that rolled up the canvas much like a Venetian blind, but should have been of keen interest to the Arabs, Persians, and Indians. The lateen sail drives beautifully in both light and strong winds but is a hazard when the wind gets too strong, for there is no way to shorten it: all a crew can do is lower it and stow it away, and replace it with a smaller stormsail — a proceeding that is slow, cumbersome, and apt to be dangerous. But shortening sail on a junk is simplicity itself: the deckhands simply slack off the halyard (the line that holds the sail up), thereby allowing the sail to drop down, and, as that happens, the area between the lowest two battens folds up like an accordion; if they want to shorten sail further, they keep slacking off on the halyard and letting more battens pile up one upon the other. When the danger has passed, all they have to do to return to full sail is to haul the halyard tight again.

Though seamen of other nations turned up their noses at the junk's rig and other useful features, there was one Chinese contribution they may have adopted: the mariner's compass — if, as some say, the West borrowed it from China. A fiery argument rages over the point. E. G. R. Taylor, the ranking

The West was using iron weapons by 1350 B.C., when the sword on top (probably of Hittite manufacture) was deposited in the tomb of King Tutankhamen. The Chinese were making iron for tools and plows by 500 B.C. but for 200 years more kept on using bronze swords like the handsome one beneath, which is inlaid with turquoise.

British authority on the history of navigation, asserts, "As to the common story that it [the magnetic compass] had been brought in [to the West] from China by Arab sailors, there is no evidence whatsoever to support it." Needham, in his great history of Chinese technology, which we referred to earlier, stoutly affirms the opposite.

Needham presents lucidly and in detail precisely what China knew not only about the compass but about magnetism in general. The compass is one of the world's seminal inventions, Needham points out, for it is the earliest example of the dial with self-moving needle and, consequently, the direct ancestor of all the myriad types that today stud the spectrum of instruments from the housewife's stove to the atomic scientist's computer. The Greeks and Romans and other ancient peoples knew the sundial — but the sundial has no movable pointer. They had self-moving pointers such as weathervanes, but they never combined these with a dial. The wreck discussed in an earlier chapter that yielded a treasure of Greek sculpture yielded as well a spectacular example of ancient technological sophistication, a device for showing the position of heavenly bodies at any given moment; it had a series of dials which swiveled to indicate desired positions by means of most delicate and elaborate gearing, but the apparatus was not self-moving, it had to be activated by hand (see pages 200–201). Until a lucky archaeological strike changes the picture, the compass' claim to the lofty distinction Needham assigns it is unassailable.

CONTINUED ON PAGE 202

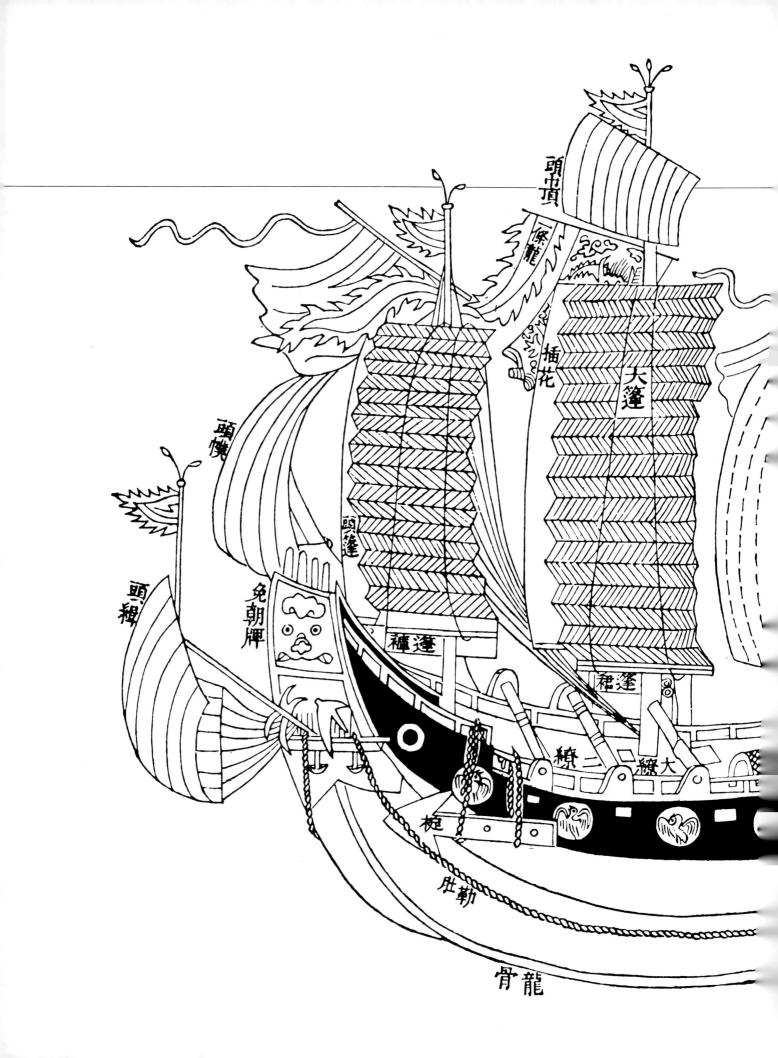

The principle of the compass was known in China from at least the first century A.D. and was probably used on Chinese ships long before it appeared in the West. The sixteenth-century instrument above consisted of a bronze disk with a central well in which a magnetic needle floated on water. Twenty-four compass points are marked on the outer circle.

Ancient Chinese ships had several features superior to those of Western ships, including stern-mounted rudders, watertight compartments, and passenger cabins. Shown at left is an ocean-going junk of a later period (about 1757) with sails set and flags flying. The sails on its foremast and mainmast have battens that allow them to be shortened easily, folding down like an accordion.

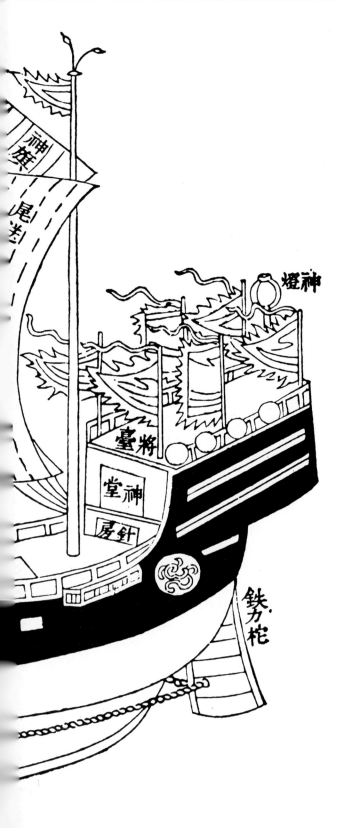

This machine, operated by a foot treadle, winds silk onto a reel at right. This may be the first application of the endless belt for transmitting power.

The "south-pointing carriage" had a system of gears that kept a figure of a man pointing south, no matter in which direction the carriage was turned.

The fishing reel (a form of the windlass pulley) was known in China at least by the twelfth century, some 500 years before the time of Izaak Walton.

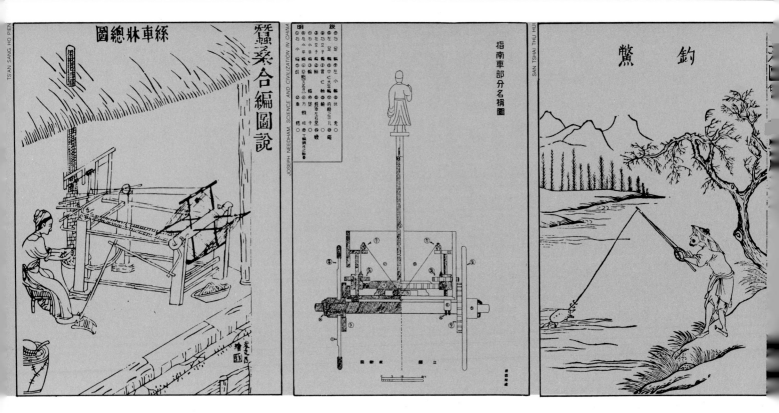

The first to note the attractive powers of a magnet was Thales, a Greek philosopher and scientist of the sixth century B.C., though we know about his achievement only through mention of it by Aristotle, who lived two centuries later. The earliest Chinese reference dates to the third century B.C. Clearly, then, the West was first off the mark.

But China very quickly caught up and shot ahead. What triggered this speed was not technological precocity but the flourishing art of geomancy. The geomancer, the "earth-diviner," was an all-important figure in China from about 400 B.C. on. He was called upon to predict, by the special supernatural means at his disposal, what was the divinely recommended spot for placing a city, a tomb, a building, or what have you. In practicing his art, he would take cognizance of the general nature of a terrain, of the various topographical features—of streams, woods, and so on—and, of course, in the process, establishing directions was of the essence. In a work written in A.D. 83, the author tells of a certain type of spoon, a "south-controlling spoon" or a "south-pointing spoon," which when "thrown upon the ground . . . comes to rest pointing at the south" (of course, the other end pointed north, but Chinese always favored orienting toward the south). If Chinese scholars are right in arguing that the spoon was one carved of lodestone, then China was aware of the magnet's uncanny gift for indicating direction as early as the first century A.D., a thousand years before the West. The geomancers of the age used an elaborate diviner's board for their work, and we know what it looked like both from descriptions and some actual fragments that have been found. It consisted of a square plate marked with 24 compass points and certain other directions, upon which was mounted a pivotal disk marked with the 24 points. In the center of the disk was engraved the Big Dipper, and as the disk was turned, the handle of the Dipper served as a pointer. However, to explain the "south-pointing spoon," Chinese scholars imagine that there was yet another kind of goemancer's board in which the disk was replaced by a spoon-shaped pointer carved from lodestone or magnetized steel; when the spoon was placed on the lower square plate, it duly turned till it came to rest facing south. The explanation is bolstered by a scene of A.D. 114, carved in relief, depicting various forms of magic and gadgetry and includes

By working treadles much like bicycle pedals, peasants ran a chain pump to lift water from a river to rice paddies, a device still used in the Far and Middle East.

This 17th-century Chinese warship was run by paddle wheels, turned by men on treadmills inside the hull. The painted demons were probably meant to frighten enemies.

Wheelbarrows reached the West a thousand years after their invention in China. The Chinese centered cargo over the wheel—a better design than the Western model.

an object that appears to answer this description.

There is a statement in another work dating from the Han period (ca. 200 B.C.–A.D. 200) which seems to show that these "spoons" were used for more practical purposes as well as geomantic hocus-pocus. It mentions that, in a certain area, when people "go out to collect jade, they carry a south-pointer with them so as not to lose their way." We have not the slightest idea what this "south-pointer" looked like, but it certainly sounds as if it were some magnetic device to show direction.

The first unmistakable description of a compass dates from A.D. 1044. A Chinese handbook on military technology completed in that year explains that *when troops encountered gloomy weather or dark nights, and the directions of space could not be distinguished, they . . . made use of . . . the south-pointing fish to identify the directions. . . . A thin leaf of iron is cut into the shape of a fish two inches long and half an inch broad, having a pointed head and tail. This is then [magnetized]. . . . To use it, a small bowl filled with water is set up in a windless place, and the fish is laid as flat as possible upon the water-surface so that it floats, whereupon its head will point south.*

This is the form the Chinese compass was to maintain until the sixteenth century—a pointer of lodestone or magnetized iron (later steel) floating in a bowl on the rim of which were inscribed the various directions. In this instance the device was used on land, but little more than half a century later we find it on the sea: in a text written in A.D. 1117 and perhaps referring to events that go back to A.D. 1086 we read that a ship's pilots "at night . . . steer by the stars, and in the daytime by the sun. In dark weather they look at the south-pointing needle." For a long time western scholars, fighting hard to keep credit for the invention in their part of the world, interpreted the passage to refer to non-Chinese craft, but this, it turns out, was based on a mistranslation; in any event, the context makes it perfectly clear that the author is talking about Chinese ships. Moreover, in an account of a diplomatic mission from China to Korea in 1123, the writer reports that

during the night it is often not possible to stop . . . so the pilot has to steer by the stars and the Great Bear. If the night is overcast then he uses the south-pointing floating needle to determine south and north.

203

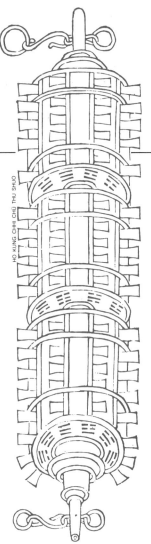

This rotating dredge was used in the eleventh century to deepen the channel of the Yellow River. Called a "bed-harrowing plough," it was towed behind a boat. Its purpose, according to the Imperial Censor in charge, was to "scrape the bottom . . . so that the sand has no peace to sink and settle."

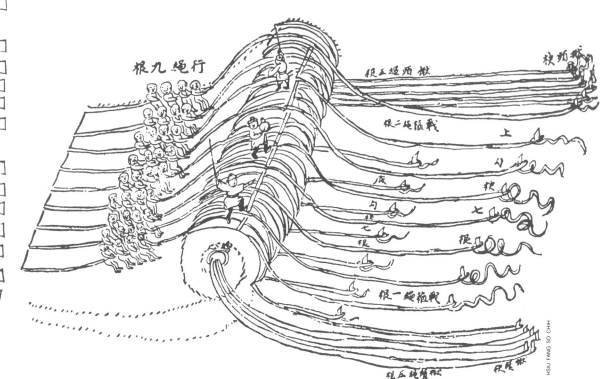

根九繩行   根五經兩枝   枝頭戟

So much for China. Now the West. In Europe there is no series of steps such as took place in China, from an embryonic form used for magical purposes through some sort of gadget for orienting oneself on a dark night to a needle floating in a bowl which served as a rough and ready direction-finder either on land or sea. The first preserved mention of a compass is at the same time our first indication that the West was aware of the magnet's capacity for indicating direction. An English monk, Alexander Neckam, writing in 1190 reports that

sailors . . . when in cloudy weather they can no longer profit by the light of the sun, or when the world is wrapped up in the darkness of the shades of night . . . touch the magnet with a needle. This then whirls round in a circle until, when its motion ceases, its point looks direct to the north.

Neckam, to be sure, does not say that the needle floated in a bowl of water. That it did is evident from the very next reference to a compass, in a poem by a French monk, Guyot de Provins, written in 1205. He had been on the Third Crusade (1189-92), so very

likely he reports what he saw in the course of his journeying to and from the Holy Land. There is an art sailors have, he explains,

which cannot deceive, through the special property of the magnet. An ugly brownish stone, to which iron willingly attaches itself . . . when a needle has touched it . . . they put it in water. . . . Then it turns its point right to the [pole]-star.

Next come two references from Arab sources. One, dating 1232, refers to voyaging on the Indian Ocean and mentions a mysterious iron fish which, when rotated in a bowl of water, settles to point south. The other tells of the use of a floating compass needle during a voyage in the eastern Mediterranean in 1242 and adds the remark that in the Indian Ocean sailors use iron fish, not needles.

So it seems beyond dispute that the earliest form of compass was a pointer floating in a bowl of water which marked north-south, and that this was in use among the Chinese around A.D. 1100 or a little earlier, in any event almost a hundred years before anywhere else. It made its way westward at least as far as

204

the Indian Ocean, for what is described in the Arab references, a fish-shaped pointer indicating south, is unmistakably Chinese. But did it travel from there to the Mediterranean? Or did the Mediterranean somehow come up with its own version, as claimed by E.G.R. Taylor—who points to the significant fact that the Arab word for the compass is neither an adaptation nor translation of the Chinese but a borrowing from Italian.

Moreover, there is another matter to consider. Exactly what do we mean by the word "compass"? If we mean the primitive device that enabled a sailor to orient himself in a general way during an emergency, then, yes, the Chinese were the inventors and the West possible borrowers, for the Chinese were the first to reach this goal. But if we mean what every ship has carried for the past five hundred years, the device set up in front of the helmsman by which he steers at all times, the device in whose terms a ship's navigator lays all courses, then the situation is just the reverse: the compass was a Western invention which the Chinese borrowed almost two centuries later.

In 1259 a brilliant medieval technological thinker, Pierre de Maricourt, wrote a treatise on possible uses for a magnetized pointer. All involved a "dry" pointer—that is, a pointer not floating in water but set horizontally on a vertical pivot. One of his designs included a dial marked off into 360° with not only a pivoted pointer but a needlelike wire sitting atop it which would enable the user to sight compass bearings very much in the manner we do today. To be sure, this was just something on paper; from a remark he drops it is perfectly evident that on shipboard, skippers were still managing to get along with a needle floating in water.

However, a Catalan savant, Ramon Lull, writing some twenty years later, talks of a ship's navigator establishing his position by using the needle together with charts and mathematical tables. This seems far

more than one could do with a compass whose function was merely to show where north or south lay. Again, we must recognize that such navigators must have been very rare, that most skippers went on steering by the sun and the stars, breaking out the needle and bowl only for an occasional peek.

Then, around 1300, the basic step toward the modern compass was taken. Tradition credits it to a certain Flavio Gioja of Amalfi, which at that time was a great port, precisely the sort of place to generate maritime inventiveness. Who Gioja was—or if there really was a Gioja—we have no idea. Obviously, he did not invent the compass from scratch. What he must have done was to take a pivoted dry pointer, such as Pierre de Maricourt had conceived of for his theoretical constructions, and attach it to a card on which compass bearings were marked—probably sixteen of them since this is the number on early wind roses figured on charts—so that, when it swiveled, the whole card swiveled with it. He may also have been the one who got the idea to package the pointer-cum-card neatly in a box. The Italian word for compass is *bussola,* which means literally "box," and there is even a reference in an Italian work dated

205

1315 to a portable compass mounted in a box covered by glass. The last essential step was to add the lubber line – that is, a line indicated on the box which, when the box was set up in front of the helm, coincided with the fore-and-aft axis of the vessel. Thus the steersman, when he looked at the compass and saw that the lubber line was aligned with, say, northwest, knew that his ship was heading in that direction. This last step must have been taken by the fifteenth century.

In its finished form the compass swiftly became essential equipment on all Western vessels, for it revolutionized the art of navigating and piloting a ship. Skippers no longer set courses by the stars or sun but by points of the compass, and their helmsmen steered with their eyes on the compass as well as on the stars, sun, direction of the waves and wind, or the like. Dutch and Portuguese ships brought the new device into Oriental waters, where the Japanese picked it up, and then the Chinese from them. This is incontrovertible, for, in a Chinese work of 1570, we read that

the needle floating on water and giving the north and south directions, is ordinarily called the Wet Compass. In the Chia-Ch'ing reign-period {1522-1566} there were attacks of Japanese pirates, so from that time onwards Japanese methods began to be used. Thus the needle was placed in the compass box, and a paper was stuck on it carrying all the directions. . . . This is called the Dry Compass.

At the present moment, that is where the matter stands. The Chinese invented the first compass, a primitive form of direction finder for emergencies. Westerners, probably the Italians, invented the modern compass, a device used at all times by helmsmen to keep a ship steadily on course. How and where the West got its version of the magnetized needle, which it converted into the modern compass, is still very much a mystery.

When Dutch and Portuguese vessels entered oriental waters, the Chinese, as we have just seen, were quick to borrow their style of compass, but they turned a blind eye to their style of rig – yet it was precisely this, square sails superimposed one over the other on lofty masts to produce towering pyramids of canvas, that gave the West control of the

oceans both economically and militarily until the coming of steam. The Japanese, who had borrowed the compass even before the Chinese, paid scant attention to both the Chinese and the western rig, preferring for the most part to lumber along under their traditional single huge square mainsail, a rig scarcely better than what the ancient Egyptians used 4500 years earlier. And they never bothered to introduce watertight compartments, nor did the West until as late as the end of the sixteenth century.

By at least the second century A.D., junks had given up the long steering oars on each quarter, which all craft had been carrying since time immemorial, in favor of the ancestor of the modern rudder, the flat blade hung vertically at the stern; this had no effect on the ships of other nations, which clung to the old system. Not until 1200 does the stern rudder appear in Europe – but then, for mysterious reasons, seamen, who for so long had turned their backs on the new device, rushed to adopt it, so that within a few hundred years it supplanted steering oars on seagoing vessels all over the globe.

The route that brought Chinese silk to the ports of the Mediterranean was long and arduous, whether by land or sea. Yet men continued to traverse it for over eight hundred years, until the day, around A.D. 550 when two Persian monks arrived from China with a few precious silkworms that they had smuggled out hidden in bamboo canes and therefore started the West on making its own silk. During all this time the thin but steady stream of merchants, porters, drivers, seamen, and so on that flowed back and forth never thought to bring back, along with the bales of silk, some of the many good things China had to offer. China, to adapt Emerson's words, had made not only one but several better mousetraps, yet people, far from beating a path to her door, did not even bother to knock when there. We have talked of the wheelbarrow, crank, kite, "south-pointing needle," Chinese lugsail, stern rudder; there were others, including that discovery so crucial for cultural history, the art of printing with type (done in China at least a millennium before Gutenberg). Eventually all were gratefully adopted, but only after a lapse of centuries, in some instances over a millennium. Why the delay? The answer surely involves deep-seated differences in attitudes, casts of mind, values, and the like, and we lack the information to lay these bare.

Only camels and strong men could withstand the rigors of travel on the Silk Road from the Middle East to China. This clay tomb sculpture, made during the Han dynasty, depicts a rider whose conical hat identifies him as a visitor from somewhere in the highlands of western Asia.

WHO WAS PRESTER JOHN?

How the letter had arrived, no one knew, but around A.D. 1165 copies of it began to circulate in Europe. Addressed to Manuel Comnenus, Emperor of Byzantium, it purported to be from a distant ruler who, though hardly modest, styled himself simply prester—that is, presbyter, or priest:

"If indeed you wish to know wherein consists our great power, then believe without doubting that I, Prester John . . . exceed in riches, virtue, and power all creatures who dwell under heaven. Seventy-two kings pay tribute to me. I am a devout Christian and everywhere protect the Christians of our empire.... We have made a vow to visit the sepulcher of our Lord with a very great army . . . to wage war against and chastise the enemies of the cross of Christ. . . .

"Our magnificence dominates the Three Indias, and extends to Farther India, where the body of St. Thomas the Apostle rests. It reaches through the desert toward the place of the rising sun, and continues through the valley of deserted Babylon close by the Tower of Babel. . . .

"In our territories are found elephants, dromedaries, and camels, and almost every kind of beast . . . Honey flows in our land, and milk everywhere abounds. . . .

"In one of the heathen provinces flows a river called the Physon, which, emerging from Paradise, winds and wanders through the entire province; and in it are found emeralds, sapphires, carbuncles, topazes, chrysolites, onyxes, beryls, sardonyxes, and many other precious stones. . . . During each month we are served at our table by seven kings, each in his turn, by sixty-two dukes, and by three hundred and sixty-five counts. . . . In our hall there dine daily, on our right hand, twelve archbishops, and on our left, twenty bishops. . . .

"If you can count the stars of the sky and the sands of the sea, you will be able to judge thereby the vastness of our realm and our power."

Readers of this document found much in it to cheer them. Concerned about the Saracens in the Holy Land, they rejoiced to learn that this mighty co-religionist stood poised to smite the common foe; dismayed by the bickering among Europe's monarchs, they were reassured by the example of this Asian potentate who imposed peace on his numerous and heterogeneous subjects while purging them of deceit and corruption, adultery, and drunkenness. The descriptions of his realm, more marvelous in each successive draft of the letter, excited wonder in all and cupidity in some; and the quest for Prester John would haunt the European imagination until, after some four hundred years, it would come to a sudden, dramatic end.

Where *was* Prester John? His reference to the Apostle Thomas's tomb pointed to India, but so muddled were medieval notions of geography that India was thought to be somewhere near the Nile; thus when, in 1177, the Pope wrote to Prester John, his letter was presumably carried into "Middle India," or Ethiopia. Many people, however, imagined "the prester" on the steppes east of Europe, where Christians adhering to the heretical Nestorian rite were known to live. Around 1220 he was rumored to be coming west to defend Christendom, but when, instead, Genghis Khan burst upon eastern Europe with mounted archers, killing, and pillaging, it was clear that someone had erred. In about 1250 the chronicler Joinville asserted that the Mongols had slain Prester John and in 1298 Marco Polo confirmed this, both reports reflecting, evidently, the fact that Genghis had killed his own godfather, a puissant clan-leader—and Nestorian Christian.

But Prester John would not stay dead: throughout the fourteenth and fifteenth centuries news of him kept cropping up. Some reports had him a descendant of the great prester, but in others he was that worthy himself, now hundreds of years old but preserved by miracle baths that periodically restored him to the age of thirty-two. By the beginning of the sixteenth century, geographers had narrowed the search to Africa: on the Diego Homem map of 1558 (opposite), the legendary ruler is enthroned south of the Red Sea. Finally, in 1520, the Portuguese decided to look for him in the remote mountain fastness of Ethiopia. They wanted his help in dislodging the Arabs from their Red Sea ports so as to open a direct route from India to Suez for Portuguese spice ships.

On October 20, 1520, after a grueling overland march of six months, the captain of the Portuguese expedition wrote that "We saw . . . to our great joy the tents and camps of the Prester John." At the center of this tent capitol, in a red pavilion guarded by warriors wearing lion skins and by live lions on leashes, the travelers beheld him: the negus, or emperor, of Ethiopia. That neither he nor any of his subjects had *heard* of Prester John fazed the Portuguese not at all, so elated were they to have found him at last.

Nothing much came of this first meeting. But some years later a successor "Prester John" was to smuggle out word that Moslems had overrun his domain; going to his aid, the Portuguese would help him rout the invaders. So in the end it was European Christians who saved Prester John, not vice versa.

And Prester John's letter? Scholars say it was concocted by some European monk whose name we will never know, for a purpose—if not merely for his own amusement—we can only guess at . It was one of the most successful hoaxes ever perpetrated.

Homo sapiens is the youngest of all primate species. We are also the most variable, the richest by far in variety. There are human populations so tall on the average that six-footers are common and populations so short that five-footers are rare. There are dark-skinned peoples and light-skinned peoples and every shade in between. There are peoples with long trunks and short legs and peoples with short trunks and long legs; fuzzy-haired peoples and straight-haired peoples, big-toothed peoples and small-toothed peoples. Modern-looking sapiens first appeared in the fossil record some 40,000 years ago, the blink of an eye in the 3.3 billion-year history of life on this planet. Yet today anthropologists are able to distinguish at least two dozen or more human populations sufficiently different from each other in certain hereditary traits to qualify as distinct local races of that upstart species, Homo sapiens.

How the living races of man came to be what they are and live where they live still remains shrouded in mystery. The history of the races is a vast, intricate jigsaw puzzle which no one has yet put together, at least not to the satisfaction of anyone else engaged in the enterprise of trying. As for that enterprise itself, it is at once a bold excursion into the uncharted past and a colossal mental exercise in detection with little to go on save a few theoretical principles and a miscellany of ambiguous clues, puzzling enough in themselves. Why, for example, are there two distinct dwarf-sized races of primitive hunters living six thousand miles apart, one in the Congo, the other in Southeast Asia? Why is it that in certain invisible hereditary aspects of human blood, Europeans and Africans resemble each other more closely than either resembles any other peoples of the world? Why do North American Plains Indians look so "European" in certain of their facial features and so little like the living Asian descendants of their own Asian forebears? What does the historian of race make of the Australian aborigines, isolated for several thousand years, who bear a closer resemblance in certain ways to pre-sapiens humans than any other living race does?

OVERLEAF *(pages 210-211): Two Bushmen stalk game in the Kalahari desert. These primitive people, with their short stature, yellowish skin, and bulbous foreheads, pose a mystery to anthropologists. Superimposed are human figures copied from prehistoric cave paintings.*
MARVIN E. NEWMAN, WOODFIN CAMP

When scientists first began classifying races in the eighteenth century, Charles Darwin had not yet upset all biology with his theory of evolution. The races of man, to eighteenth-century biologists, were simply *there*, fixed elements in an unchanging natural order, to be described, distinguished and labeled. Impressed by differences in skin color, the pioneer students of race confidently divided the human species into a convenient racial triad. There was a black-skinned or Negroid race; a yellow-skinned, or Mongoloid race, a white-skinned or Caucasoid race, so named by an eighteenth-century biologist because he believed they had entered Europe from the Caucasus mountains—a guess, as it turns out, not as wild as it might seem. Skin color being all important, a place had to be reserved for American Indians who were neither "black" nor "yellow" nor "white" but occasionally ruddy; hence a fourth or "red" race.

Sheer human variability, however, strained such simple classification to the breaking point. Following in the footsteps of European settlers, traders and colonial administrators, anthropologists discovered problems at every turn. In the islands of the southwest Pacific—Fiji, for example—they found a dark-skinned people with "woolly" hair and broad noses, who looked remarkably like the Negroes of Africa. Anthropologists dubbed them Melanesians ("black islanders") but it was not clear how they fitted into the racial picture. Were they Negroid or not? They looked too much like Negroes not to be Negroes and they lived too far from Africa to satisfy those who wondered how two populations could belong to the same race when they seemed to have had nothing to do with each other. In South Africa, anthropologists had to cope with a tiny yellowish-skinned hunting people, the Bushmen, who also defied classification. They looked considerably less like the neighboring Negroes than did the Melanesians who lived ten thousand miles away. In Australia, the aborigines seemed distinctive enough to qualify for a racial category all their own. In Hawaii and other islands of the eastern Pacific, anthropologists had to reckon with a tall, muscular, wavy-haired people who looked like members of no other race, but rather, in some respects, like members of all of them.

The spectacle of human variability not only taxed the classifiers, it challenged, more importantly, the traditional concept of race itself. Until recently, an-

thropologists classified races pretty much the way ornithologists classified species of birds. They decided that each race was represented by a "type specimen," an individual who represented, as it were, the quintessence of the race. The "typical" Mongoloid was deemed to be found in Mongolia; the "typical" Negro in the African forests. The members of a race consisted of all the people who conformed more or less to the racial "type." The conformity was not very close. Indeed, few individual members of any race actually resembled in every respect the "typical" member of his race.

A few generations ago anthropologists finally posed to themselves a question whose answer provides the historian of race with his most important theoretical tool—the modern concept of race itself, a concept without which it would be impossible even in theory to understand why there are races at all. Anthropologists simply asked themselves what in fact they actually saw when they tried to classify people into races. What they observed was not an individual "type" but a *population* which exhibited a greater incidence of certain hereditary traits than could be found in other populations. Some individuals exhibited all of the traits, others only some of them. Moreover the traits themselves were inherited separately. They did not go together in a racial package to create a hereditary racial type. Blue eyes and blond hair are commonly associated, for example, but not necessarily. There are numerous black-haired, blue-eyed people in Ireland. The incidence of occurrence of a given trait might be as high as 100 per cent, but most often the trait occurs less frequently. Some people in the population have it; others do not; still others have it to a lesser or greater degree. There is enormous variability between the individuals comprising any race. Nor are the traits which distinguish a race necessarily confined to that race. They rarely are. What distinguishes one population from another is usually not the presence or absence of particular traits but the difference in the frequency with which they occur in the two populations.

Nevertheless it is an observable fact of the human species (and not the human species alone) that groups whose members breed chiefly among themselves—form a "breeding population" in contemporary language—who share a common history and a common habitation will exhibit in due time distinctive frequencies in the occurrence of a number of hereditary traits which comprise their common genetic heritage. This is what modern anthropologists mean by the term "race." The term, often abused, does not refer to linguistic groups, to nations, or to so-called racial types. It refers to breeding populations whose "gene pool," the number and variety of genes which have combined and recombined among them over the ages, is distinctive from that of other populations.

Such reproductive isolation is the *sine qua non* of race. Unless the members of a population have bred among themselves far more frequently than they have with others they cannot develop in due time a distinctive genetic heritage. If two populations interbreed with each other the result will be the disappearances of their respective distinguishing traits.

In the history of the human species the chief deterrent to interbreeding has been the barriers imposed by geography. The mountain-desert barrier that stretches northeast from India to the Arctic Circle has reduced contact between East Asians and all humans to the west of it. Stretches of ocean have effectively isolated island populations from mainlanders. The disappearance of the land bridge joining Siberia to the New World isolated the New World's inhabitants for at least eight thousand years. It was precisely that isolation which enabled the Asian ancestors of American Indians to become—American Indians. The reproductive isolation of different human populations, chiefly through geographical barriers, is the key to the formation of race for it permits all the factors which tend to differentiate populations to exhibit their full effectiveness.

There are several of these differentiating factors. The first and the most important is the natural selection of favorable chance variations, the grand mechanism of evolution in general. It is—or at any rate it is supposed to be—familiar to every schoolchild. A hereditary trait may crop up in a given breeding population through mutation, or it may already be there in a very low frequency. If it gives its possessor a somewhat greater chance to survive and bear offspring (some of whom will inherit the trait), compared to members of the population who lack it, that trait in due time will inevitably increase its frequency of occurence in that population. It will, in Darwin's language, be favorably "selected." Over many hundreds of generations the entire population may be composed of individuals who have inherited the favorable

MARC AND EVELYNE BERNHEIM, WOODFIN CAMP   BUREAU OF AMERICAN ETHNOLOGY, SMITHSONIAN INSTITUTION   MARTIN WEAVER, WOODFIN CAMP

trait. What is true of one favorable trait will be true of all favorable traits in that population. Through the operation of natural selection the descendants of the original population will come to differ in many ways from their ancestors.

The advantage for survival and reproduction which a hereditary trait confers is often due to the particular environment in which a population lives. It is favorable in that environment though it may be unfavorable in a different one. Dark skin, for instance, is advantageous to individuals living in sun-scorched environments. In cloudy, dimly-lit environments it makes them prone to rickets in childhood. If favorable traits exist in a population, the net effect of natural selection is to increase the average ability of the individuals comprising it to survive in their environment. The population in that case is said to have become genetically adapted to its environment. Suppose, for example, that half the members of a given population move into a new environment and become isolated from the stay-at-homes—an event that has occurred innumerable times in the history of man. Their adaptation to the new environment through the natural selection of favorable traits will in time distinguish them from the parent population. Given sufficient time, the two populations will become distinct races though they share a common ancestry and may still resemble each other in many ways, too.

The second differentiating factor is the sheer act of migration itself. Populations do not usually migrate in a body. Usually a group of people will bid good-bye to the others and enter a new land. The population they left was distinguished by distinctive frequencies in the occurrences of a number of hereditary traits. The chances are small that the splinter group will be a perfect sample of the genetic make-up of the population. Most likely it will consist of a few closely related families who resemble each other genetically more closely than they resemble the original population as a whole. The descendants of the splinter group—the founders—will differ from the parent group simply because the founders differed from the parent group. Where a geographical bottleneck separates one region from another, say a sea barrier that has to be traversed with a raft, it is safe to assume that a small group did the traversing and consequently that "founder's effect," as it is known, played an important role in differentiating the inhabitants of that region from the parent population they left behind. Polynesians have lived in their island homes for only some two thousand years, yet they are distinguished today as the largest people in the world, taking height and weight together. Since their bulkiness cannot be explained by adaptation through natural selection it is safe to assume that founder's effect played *some* part in differentiating them.

Founder's effect itself is a special case of what geneticists call "sampling error." The same sort of error can occur without migration. If a breeding population is very small—and in the days before agriculture human breeding populations *were* very small—

214

there is a chance that the new generation of offspring will not exhibit the same frequency of occurrence of many hereditary traits that the parent generation showed. The smaller the population the more likely will this purely random-sampling error occur—just as in tossing a coin, the fewer times it is tossed the less likely will the result be the expected 50 per cent heads and 50 per cent tails. Using sophisticated mathematical and genetic principles, geneticists have demonstrated that in a very small population a trait which occurs in reduced frequency through sampling error is likely to be reduced in frequency still further by sampling error and in time disappear from the population entirely, a phenomenon known as "genetic drift." American Indians provide a striking example of this. A certain type of human blood—the B type—is fairly common in East Asia, yet it is almost totally absent from Indians, although their ancestors came from East Asia. The gene that determines the inheritance of that blood type has simply disappeared from the American Indian gene pool, and genetic drift is the likeliest explanation.

The last factor which differentiates populations is interbreeding and the consequent flow of new genes into that population's genetic make-up. If some members of a given population disperse into a new land they may be differentiated from the parent population not only through natural selection, founder's effect, and genetic drift, but through meeting and interbreeding with members of another population. There are peoples living in central Asia today who are indisputably of Caucasoid descent yet who exhibit a high incidence of certain Mongoloid traits. The differences between these people and other Caucasoids is simply the result of interbreeding with westward-moving Mongolian nomads during historical times. Unfortunately for the historian of race, however, such interbreeding has occurred innumerable times in the human past without a historian to record the event. That alone immensely complicates the task of reconstructing the history of living races.

In tracing origins, the historian of race must have in mind not only the factors that cause differences but those that cause resemblances. Common ancestry is one obvious cause of resemblances. If members of different races never interbreed, the resemblances between two populations might well be explained by inferring common ancestry. The two races, it could be assumed, had some trait in common because they evolved, probably in the not-too-distant past, from a single parent population. And thus an important part of their evolutionary history would have been reconstructed. But resemblances may equally be due to interbreeding in the past and not to common ancestry. Whenever it occurs, interbreeding produces resemblances between previously unrelated races, obscuring their separate evolutionary histories. Conversely it produces differences between races otherwise closely related, thus masking their common ancestry.

Interbreeding and common ancestry are not the only ways the historian of race may account for resemblances between races. The historian must also take into account natural selection, for natural selection produces resemblances as well as differences between populations. If two unrelated populations live long enough in similar environments they may come to resemble each other in many traits advantageous for survival in that environment. Modern anthropologists have accounted for a number of adaptive traits whose presence in more than one race were once falsely ascribed either to a presumed common ancestry or presumed interbreeding.

Nose form is one example of such an adaptive trait. It was thought by an earlier generation of anthropologists that high, narrow noses were an exclusively Caucasoid racial trait. Since American Plains Indians and Negroes in the East African highlands also showed a high incidence of beaky "European" noses, it was generally assumed that European genes had contributed to the genetic make-up of Sioux warriors and Kenyan cattle herders. But later students were more impressed by the fact that these and other peoples with beaky noses, belonging to four different major races, lived under a similar climatic condition. Plains Indians, East African highlanders, and Caucasoids in general all have lived for great lengths of time in environments characterized by cool dry air. While there are exceptions, the correlation is sufficient to suggest that narrow noses have a selective advantage under that atmospheric condition and in fact they do. In order for the lungs to function properly, inhaled air must be completely saturated with moisture. Since all that moisture cannot come from the air it must be supplied by the moisturizing action of the nose. The less moisture in the air (and cool air can hold less moisture than warm air) the greater the amount of moisture that must be supplied by the

The kinky hair of this Guinea woman has been teased, strung, and wrapped into a fantastic coiffure. Kinky hair is most common among the Africans, straight hair among the Mongoloids, and wavy hair among the Caucasoids, but many local races share all three types. Because hair form is considered a conservative trait, that is, little affected by changes of environment, it can be used to trace the movements of peoples.

nasal membranes. It has been shown that a high narrow nasal opening moisturizes air better than does a low, broad nasal opening, Given the selective advantage of a relatively high narrow nose, the trait over time becomes common in populations breathing air with low moisture content. The other side of the coin, namely that broad, flat noses are advantageous in hot environments, seems likely but as yet no explanation of the advantage exists.

Skin color is another environmentally adaptive trait once regarded as a major racial distinction. As with variations in nose form, variations in skin color show a fairly close correlation with a particular climatic condition. In general, the more intense the solar radiation the darker on the average will the skin color of a population be. The intensity of solar radiation is in part a function of latitude: the closer to the equator the greater the intensity. Dark-skinned peoples of the world are generally equatorial people: sub-Saharan Africans, Caucasoids of Southern Arabia and southern India, the aborigines of north-coastal Australia and the Melanesians of New Guinea and neighboring islands. The correlation between skin color and latitude appears even within a race. Mongoloid peoples of Southeast Asia are darker than Mongoloids in northern China; American Indians in Central America are darker than Indians farther north.

The correlation between skin color and latitude depends on the role played by melanin, a skin pigment, in maintaining an individual's health. It is the melanin granules in an individual's skin cells which absorb solar radiation; the more melanin the more light is absorbed and the darker the skin becomes. Most importantly, melanin filters out the powerful ultra-violet radiation which is stronger in equatorial latitudes than elsewhere. Since an excess of ultra-violet radiation can be harmful in many ways (it can produce skin cancers, for one thing), people whose skin cells are genetically disposed to produce large amounts of melanin have a selective advantage where solar radiation is intense.

Ultra-violet radiation, however, is beneficial as well as harmful. Humans need it in order to synthesize vitamin D, inadequate amounts of which cause crippling rickets in children. In cloudy, dimly lit northerly latitudes people with relatively small amounts of melanin enjoy a distinct selective advantage, for dark skin would filter out too much of the ultra-violet radiation available and so produce vitamin D deficiencies. Blond hair and blue eyes are also related to a hereditary paucity of melanin. That a high incidence of fair skin, blue eyes, and blond hair is found in northwestern Europe is readily explained, therefore, as a climatic adaptation by natural selection to a notably cloudy, dimly lit northerly environment.

Among the more striking effects of natural selection are adaptive variations in body build. In general, the colder the climate the heavier in proportion to their height are the people living there; the higher the mean annual temperature the more slender, on the average, they tend to be. The selective advantage of different body forms derives from the fact that the heat lost by an individual is proportional to the extent of his skin surface (from which heat is lost, through radiation and sweating) while the amount of heat his body produces is proportional to his body bulk. In cold climates the biological task is to reduce the amount of heat lost relative to the amount of heat produced. Stockily built people have a smaller ratio of body surface to body bulk than "skinny" people have. Consequently they lose less of the heat they produce than a thin person would. Stocky builds are therefore selectively favored in a cold climate. Since any reduction in skin surface areas will be favored under conditions of severe cold, peoples living long in cold climates also tend to have short arms and legs. The long, thick bodies and short legs of Mongoloid peoples probably attest to a long period of adaptation to a cold environment.

In hot, dry climates natural selection favors those who have a very high ratio of skin surface to body build, that is, with long limbs, relatively small trunks and generally linear proportions. The tall, pencil-thin

Africans of the eastern Sudan show this adaptation in the most marked degree. Where the climate is hot and humid, however, no selective advantage accrues to possession of a "skinny" linear build for it is too humid to cool off by sweating; the sweat will not evaporate. In hot, wet climates the increase in relative heat loss has been achieved by a radical reduction in overall body size and consequently in the amount of heat an individual produces. People living in the wet tropics tend to be short and slender. Mongoloids of Southeast Asia, for example, are shorter and more slender than Mongoloid peoples of northern China.

The selective advantage of small size in the wet tropics is greatly intensified among people who live and hunt in tropical forests. Dense forests are not rich in game; the smaller a person is, the less he need eat. Tropical forests are often difficult to traverse; the smaller a person is, the better able he is to move around and hunt successfully. Small stature in a rain forest is a matter of life and death, and the selective pressure is sharp. Rain-forest dwellers are generally extremely short; the Vedda of Ceylon and the Maya of Yucatán were little more than five feet on the average. Shorter than they by some three or four inches are the Negritos of Southeast Asia and the Pygmies of the Congo. The resemblances between these two dwarf populations can readily be ascribed to the similar dwarfing effects of natural selection on hunting populations living for a long time under similar tropical forest conditions.

Variations in nose form, skin color, and body shape are highly adaptive traits in the sense that resemblances in these traits among races dwelling in similar environments can reasonably be ascribed to natural selection. Few anthropologists today would attribute the resemblances between the Melanesians of the western Pacific and the people of Africa either to common ancestry or to an ancient migration of Africans to the Pacific. Conversely, knowing which traits are highly adaptive permits the historian of race to discount differences between races which are plainly due to adaptation to differing environments. Few anthropologists would regard the Pygmies of the Congo as a race unrelated to the populations around them, although adjacent to them live some of the tallest people in the world.

The historian of race must also know which traits are conservative, relatively nonadaptive traits, in the sense that their present-day distribution in the world shows no correlation with particular features of the natural environment. Traits that are nonadaptive and that are also found in high frequencies in a particular race are important historical tools, sometimes referred to as "race-markers." The incidence of such a trait in another, quite distinctive race, for example, would suggest interbreeding between the two races. If a number of such traits are common to two races, common ancestry might reasonably be inferred. Just what traits qualify as race-markers is a matter of much dispute among anthropologists. In general, many anthropologists would accept variations in hair form and details of tooth architecture as likely race-markers. An important, racially distinctive tooth feature is the incidence in a population of front teeth which are more or less concave or shovel-shaped on their inner sides. Shovel-shaped incisors occur with a frequency of 80 per cent or more among Mongoloids and American Indians. They occur with a frequency of only 12 per cent among Europeans and 9 per cent among Africans. The shovel shape is essentially a Mongoloid trait, its high incidence among American Indians being further proof of their common ancestry with living Mongoloid peoples.

Variations in hair form appear to be conservative, relatively nonadaptive traits. Coarse, straight hair, for example, occurs with remarkable uniformity among Mongoloid peoples (including American Indians) despite sojourns of ten or twenty thousand years in widely differing environments. The Mongoloid hair form is a striking race-marker. The straight hair of a Caucasoid, for example, can readily be distinguished from that of a Mongoloid by examining a cross section of the two hairs under a microscope. Mongoloid hair has a large diameter, Caucasoid hair a small one. The two kinds of straight hair, however, will resemble each other in having the same circular cross section, which is the reason the hair shafts are straight. The more a cross section of human hair deviates from a circle, the less straight it is. The tight, spirally — "woolly" — hair of Africans and Melanesians has a flattened cross section. Between the two extremes, individuals exhibit every possible degree of nonstraightness, from slightly wavy to curly to kinky, the last not uncommon among Caucasoids, who have the most variable hair forms of any race. Other aspects of human hair have also been proposed as race-markers — the amount of body hair found among members of a population, and the incidence of premature balding.

217

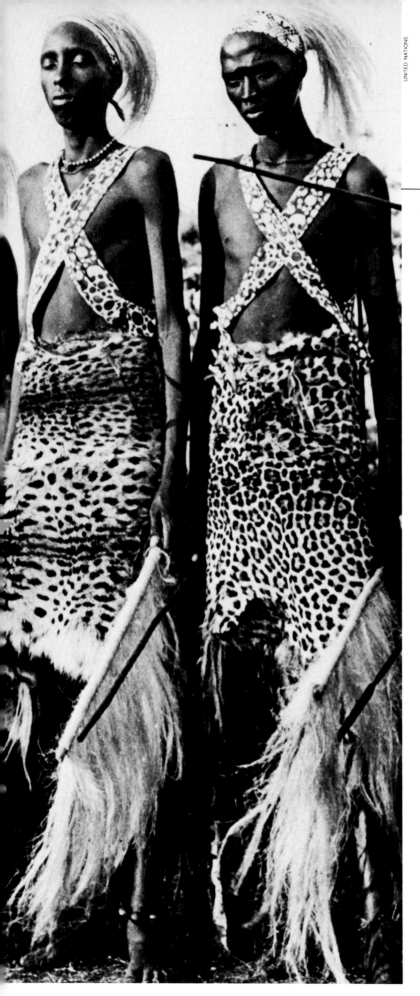

These pencil-thin Watusi tribesmen of the east central African highlands are thought to show the effect of climate on human stature. Tall slender builds give them greater body surface to be cooled by perspiration—an evolutionary advantage in a hot, dry environment.

With one exception—the Australian aborigines—hairy bodies and premature balding are virtual monopolies of Caucasoid peoples.

In recent years many anthropologists have proposed that all these physical traits, from skin color to tooth architecture, be shelved entirely in the study of race. They would replace them with genetically simple hereditary traits controlled by a single identifiable gene or its known alternatives. The most important of these genetically simple traits are certain hereditary attributes of human blood cells revealed when they are compelled to react to alien substances. In the course of giving blood transfusions it was discovered at the turn of the century that human blood fell into three distinct types—type A, type B and type O—and every human being had one or the other of them. Much later, researchers discovered additional blood groupings, quite distinct from the A, B, O series, such as the so-called Rh-series, the MN series, the Duffy series, and so on.

After World War II, anthropologists began using these hereditary blood-group traits in the study of race. Theoretically they have considerable advantages over the traditional visible traits measured by anthropologists, all of which are genetically complex. For one thing they are nonadaptive traits, in the sense that their incidence in a population shows no correlation with climate, latitude or possible race-markers.

More importantly, perhaps, they are all-or-nothing traits. An individual has one blood type or another and there are no shadings in between. The complex traits used by anthropologists in the traditional studies of race are never all-or-nothing traits, precisely because they are the cumulative effect of an unknown number of genes working at once. No single gene determines, say, the inheritance of a broad nose. As a result, human noses are not inherited as distinctive types. Broad noses are more or less broad, narrow noses are more or less narrow and every intermediate shade of difference will be found on people's faces. To say, for example, that a population is broad-nosed means that the average for the population is that of a broad-nosed person. Using the traditional visible traits—morphological traits they are called—anthropologists must deal in averages and in subjective judgments about matters of degree.

In contrast the all-or-nothing blood-group traits permit precise and unambiguous count of frequencies. An anthropologist can determine exactly how many people in a given population belong to one blood type or another, and directly compare such frequencies with those found in other races.

As a tool for classifying races and inferring historical origins, the blood group traits have a vast potential although the first results proved disappointing. The ABO blood-group series, for example, seemed to have no bearing on race history. The Blackfoot tribe in North America and the Mandjildjara of western Australia have the highest incidence of type A blood in the world but they are neither closely related nor in any genetic contact. Resemblances and differences in such frequencies seemed to be wholly fortuitous effects of genetic drift.

Nowadays, far more interesting results have been obtained by calculating the distribution of blood-group genes that are fairly uncommon in the human species as a whole. With these, clear-cut race-markers began to be obtained. The uncommon gene controlling the inheritance of Rh-negative blood, for example, turned out to be a virtual Caucasoid monopoly. It was found in slight incidence in Africa but nowhere else in the world. A rare variant of the "a" gene determining type A blood also turned out to be almost exclusively confined to Caucasoids. It, too, was found in slight incidence in Africa, but nowhere else in the world. On the other hand, a rare gene in the so-called Diego blood-group series is found almost exclusively among Asians and American Indians and is almost entirely absent among Europeans and Africans. In addition, a rare gene in the Rh-series was found only among mongoloids, American Indians, and Australian aborigines. In plotting the distribution of these and other rare blood-group genes, a striking picture has begun to emerge which has important bearings on the history of race. The deepest differences in blood-group traits lie not between races but between peoples living east and west of the great central Asian mountain-desert barrier. On these grounds alone, two students of race have suggested that the earliest division of Homo sapiens was a differentiation into Eastern and Western races.

We come now to the central mystery of where and when the existing races of Homo sapiens originated. As explored in Chapter 4, the fossil evidence suggests that modern man evolved out of Neanderthal man some time around 35,000 to 40,000 years ago. And the only place where fossil evidence of this transition has been found is in the Near East. Most anthropologists assume that over the course of many thousands of years, groups of the new breed—who might be called the Ur-race—spread out from their Near Eastern place of origin to populate the whole Eurasian land mass. In doing so they replaced and extinguished all humans of a lower evolutionary grade who still survived. Therefore, according to this theory, all living people are descended from one branch or another of the original Ur-race.

As the various groups of Homo sapiens settled down in different sections of the earth and became isolated from each other behind major geographical barriers, they became adapted to their separate environments, thereby producing the major geographical races found today. Those members of the parent stock who moved north into central Asia and Mongolia and northern China evolved into Mongoloids through adaptation to severe cold. Those who moved into tropical Africa became Negroids. The stay-at-homes became the Caucasoids, a major geo-

NATIONAL FILM BOARD OF CANADA

219

graphical race adapted to neither severe cold nor severe heat. Indeed it is a necessary consequence of this theory that since the Caucasoids had to undergo less adaptation, they are closer to the Ur-race than are other groups.

In the absence of a much more extensive fossil record than we have so far, this is only a theory — sometimes known as the "replacement hypothesis" because it supposes that members of the Ur-race replaced all other human types in their dispersal. Plausible though it sounds, the replacement theory is neither invincibly strong nor has it gone unchallenged. To see how it squares with what we know of the existing races of man we must examine the differences and resemblances among those races. For this we shall need some overall classification.

One of the stumbling blocks in making such a classification is this question: to what extent should we take into consideration the history, known or conjectured, of various people. American Indians, for example, share a common ancestry with Mongoloid peoples. Should they be classified as Mongoloid or not? To some anthropologists, the answer is no. Why introduce historic origins into a classification of present-day races when it is precisely the vexed question of historic origins that has yet to be settled? For these and other reasons, a distinguished student of race, Professor Stanley Garn, published in 1965 a two-tiered classification of living races which left out as far as possible historical presuppositions. Using both blood-group and traditional physical traits Garn distinguished nine "geographical races." They are, in his terminology:

1. African (all peoples living south of the Sahara)
2. European (the people of Europe, North Africa, and the Middle East)
3. Asiatic (peoples of East Asia, Southeast Asia, and Indonesia)
4. Amerindian (the aboriginal peoples of the New World)
5. Indian (peoples of the Indian subcontinent)
6. Australian (the aborigines of Australia)
7. Melanesian-Papuan (peoples of New Guinea, Fiji, and other Pacific islands)
8. Micronesian (peoples of Guam, the Marshalls, the Carolines, and other Pacific islands)
9. Polynesian (aboriginal peoples of New Zealand and other Pacific islands)

Garn's "geographical races" are each comprised of a number of "local races," distinctive localized breeding populations within the larger region — races, that is, in the strict definition of race. Geographical races, in Garn's words, are "geographically delimited collections of similar races" separated from other such "collections" by similar geographical barriers. Most local races within a geographical race probably share a common ancestry. They have been differentiated from each other by the known factors that tend to differentiate peoples who breed chiefly among themselves. One of Garn's five local races of the European race, for example, is labeled Northwestern Europeans. Their high incidence of blond hair, fair skin, and blue eyes are due, as noted earlier, to local adaptation to a dimly lit northerly environment. But some local races simply do not fit in with the others in their region, and with them the historical questions begin to arise. The Negritos of Southeast Asia are certainly not a locally variant "Asiatic." Are they then, relics of an ancient Southeast Asian race, a window on the ancient history of race in the region?

Before trying to sort out such problem cases as the Negritos, it will be best to deal with the main body of peoples included in Garn's third category, "Asiatic." These are the Mongoloids, the most numerous of all human groups and one of the most clearly differentiated. Today the Mongoloid race shows great uniformity from Siberia to Indonesia. Regional differences in facial features, skin color, and body build are readily accounted for by local adaptation to extreme cold on the one hand, to the hot, wet tropics on the other.

They seem to stand apart in many ways from the rest of humankind. One curious bit of evidence of this is that Mongoloid people alone secrete a dry, crumbly ear wax. Non-Mongoloid peoples produce sticky ear wax. In a general way the cause of Mongoloid distinctiveness is known. They are the only living geographical race whose ancestors were differentiated from other populations by selective adaptation to severe cold. According to some students of races, the epicanthic eye fold and the slitted eyes commonly found among Mongoloid peoples served to protect their eyes from the cold; the coarse Mongoloid hair, which contains large dead-air pockets within each hair shaft, served as an effective insulator for the head and brain. How rapidly natural selection worked to fix these traits in the ancestral Mongoloids cannot be determined, but it must have taken a con-

Passengers of many races sail forth upon the sea of eternity in this Persian miniature of the sixteenth century. Among them are an African, a Caucasian (wearing crown) and several Chinese (in the vessel at left). Under the canopy are the Prophet Mohammed and his son-in-law Ali, faces veiled to dim their blinding effulgence.

These Tahitian beauties belong to the Polynesian race, which has the largest physical stature of any people on earth. The ancestors of Polynesians who came by sea from Indonesia were of primarily Mongoloid descent, but the prevalence of wavy hair and bulky bodies points to interbreeding with some other racial stock.

siderable period of time. The distinctiveness of the Mongoloids points to prolonged isolation and a fairly independent evolutionary history. This is a weak spot, as will be seen, in the replacement hypothesis.

When the Mongoloids, in their great dispersal, moved down into Southeast Asia and eventually into the islands of the southwest Pacific they encountered people of different racial origin. Out of the resulting mixture has come a pattern of racial inheritance as complex as any in the world.

We may start with the Polynesians and Micronesians, who appear on Garn's chart as distinct geographical races. They are nevertheless of relatively recent origin. The earliest possible date for their appearance as island races is determined by a single historic fact—ocean-going crafts capable of long voyages are no more than 5,000 years old. Moreover, archaeological evidence suggests that the islands where they live were uninhabited until 2,000 years ago or a bit earlier. There is little doubt that the seafaring ancestors of modern Micronesians and Polynesians hailed from Southeast Asia and Indonesia in the recent past—at a time well after the Mongoloid agriculturists had moved into that area. Founder's effect certainly played a major role in differentiating these island peoples from each other and from mainlanders. And of course they have evolved independently since the original migrations. Making allowance for these factors, most anthropologists would agree that the predominant element in the genetic makeup of the two far-flung races is Mongoloid.

The two races, however, are by no means a geographically variant Mongoloid people. Mongoloids, for one thing, are almost uniformly straight-haired. The incidence of spirally hair among Micronesians and wavy hair among Polynesians would alone point to a significant non-Mongoloid contribution to their ancestral genetic make-up. In short, when the Mongoloids moved into Southeast Asia other non-Mongoloid peoples must have inhabited the region. With one or perhaps two exceptions these aboriginal peoples have ceased to exist in Southeast Asia.

The certain exception is the Negritos, who survive in a half-dozen widely dispersed forest enclaves in western New Guinea, Sumatra, Malaya, the Philippines and the remote Andaman Islands in the Bay of Bengal. There is no doubt that the Negritos were one of the aboriginal peoples whom the Mongoloids encountered. There is little reason to doubt, either, that the Negritos evolved through local adaptation to the tropical forests of Southeast Asia which were once far more extensive than they are today. Until 12,000 years ago, when the melting of the Ice Age ice caps raised the level of the world's oceans several hundred feet, Southeast Asia and Indonesia formed a single huge subcontinent known as the Sunda Shelf. A million square miles of land now under water were then largely covered by vast tropical rain forest almost as extensive as Amazonia. At the same time, a water gap of only some 75 miles separated the Sunda Shelf from Australia, which was linked by land bridges to New Guinea. The wide dispersal of the surviving Negritos indicates that they once peopled the entire forest of the Sunda Shelf.

To find the other likely aboriginal population of Southeast Asia we must look across the 75-mile water gap that once separated Australia from the Negrito homeland. According to the fossil evidence, that gap was crossed perhaps 30,000 years ago by full-statured people, some of whom must have trekked across land bridges from Australia to New Guinea and contributed to the makeup of the Melanesian-Papuan race. Living Australian aborigines appear so distinctive that their peculiar cranial traits—uniquely heavy brow ridges, broad noses with depressed nasal roots, long, narrow angular skulls, big teeth and sloping foreheads—appear to be indisputable markers of a unique, independently evolved racial stock. The incidence of some of these traits among living Australians and other populations nearby has usually been taken as proof of common ancestry. Dr. Carleton Coon of Harvard (whose theory of the origin of race differs drastically, as will be seen, from that of almost all other anthropologists) has concluded on the basis of these morphological traits that living aborigines, the stunted Negritos and the spirally-haired Melanesians, each evolved locally from a common Southeast Asian "Australoid" ancestor. Confirmation of Coon's reconstruction comes from anthropologists who use only blood-group traits in the study of race. They, too, agree that Melanesians and Australians differ little and probably share a common ancestor. If they are correct, then Southeast Asia some thirty thousand years ago was the homeland of a more or less uniform "Australoid" parent race.

Yet there are historically significant discrepancies

Facial traits offer only partial clues to the origin of races. From left to right: an Indian Sikh, an Australian aborigine, a Bavarian, a Laotian, an Ecuadorian Indian, a Melanesian from west New Guinea, a Negro from the Ivory Coast, an Arab from Jordan. Blood-type studies indicate that Caucasoids and Africans are closer to each other than either are to Mongoloids.

in the Australoid formulation, discrepancies which suggest that a non-Mongoloid people unrelated to the Negritos played an important part in the formation of the relic races in the region. One of these discrepancies is hair form. Negritos and Melanesians are spirally-haired people. Australians are wavy-haired. To ascribe wavy hair among living aborigines to the adaptation of a spirally-haired people to an Australian environment does not seem convincing. Hair form is a conservative trait, fairly impervious to selective environmental pressures over long periods of time. Australian aborigines are also moderately hairy-bodied and subject to premature balding. Their children are sometimes blond-haired until puberty, indicating the presence of "blondism" genes in their genetic make-up. These traits, too, cannot be ascribed to local adaptation in Australia. Still less can they be attributed to prolonged habitation of the tropical forests of the Sunda Shelf, the presumed homeland of the ancient Australoid stock. Such traits are found in no tropical environment. All of them, on the other hand, are the peculiar characteristics of Caucasoid peoples. On these grounds, Dr. J. B. Birdsell, who spent a lifetime studying the aborigines, has concluded that southern aborigines are, in part, the descendants of "primitive Caucasoid" migrants to Australia. He flatly denies that a homogeneous ancient Australoid stock ever existed.

Other evidence lends a degree of support to Birdsell's views. Southeast Asia is by no means cut off geographically from the west. The Burmese mountains separating the region from India have been crossed and recrossed countless times in the past. Moreover, India was certainly inhabited by Caucasoids many thousands of years ago. The possibility of a Caucasoid migration from India to Southeast Asia also fits in well with archaeological evidence. Ancient tools found in Java, for example, show the marked influence of Indian tool-making traditions. Whoever the remoter ancestors of the Negritos may have been, there is strong evidence that they coexisted, and probably interbred with, unrelated newcomers

from the west.

The meager existence of the fossil record also weakens the Australoid formulation. The earliest sapiens fossil found in Southeast Asia is a skull from a cave in northern Borneo which is around forty thousand years old. Unlike living aborigines, the Bornean fossil lacks a heavy brow ridge, lacks the distinctive Australian skull angularities, and lacks a sloping forehead. Its forehead is bulbous like that of living Negritos. It is actually a better candidate for an ancestral Negrito than an ancestral Australian. It supports the view that Negritos and Australians do not share a common ancestry but merely interbred. At any rate, normal-statured people, dwarfed people, wavy-haired people, spirally-haired people, people with bulbous brows, and people with sloping, beetle brows all seem to have lived in Southeast Asia a very long time ago. In short, we are probably dealing with a number of local races, some long adapted to the regional environment, others migrating into the area, and none of whom can be regarded as the sole parent population of the living races and relic peoples of the western Pacific.

The complicated racial picture in Southeast Asia underscores an important point about the history of race. It shows that if we push back the history of race in a major geographical area even twenty thousand years or more, we simply will not find homogeneous parent stocks. The complications of migration and interbreeding make it impossible to draw neat branching lines of descent on the model of a family tree in reconstructing the history of races.

If indeed there was an Australoid race or a collection of differing races living in Southeast Asia and Australia in the remote past, where did those people come from, and when? One possibility would be that they represented one of the original branches of the Ur-race, along with the Caucasoids, Mongoloids, and Negroids. Assuming that the original home of the Ur-race was in the Near East, the Australoid branch might have found its way to Southeast Asia some tens of thousands of years ago. There might also have been later migrations, perhaps through India, perhaps bringing the "Caucasoid" characteristics of baldness and blond hair to Australia, as well as other "Caucasoid" traits to people as far removed as the Ainu of Japan. In any event all these hypothetical migrants would be members of the race of Homo sapiens which, according to the replacement theory,

spread out from a single area of origin and replaced any existing pre-sapiens populations.

There is another possible explanation: that the Australoids are *not* the descendants of migrants to Southeast Asia from the supposed Near Eastern homeland of Homo sapiens; rather that they evolved independently to Homo sapiens status from some separate, indigenous branch of earlier human stock — an Asian equivalent of Neanderthal man. Most anthropologists believe in common descent from the single Ur-race. Carleton Coon, almost alone among ranking anthropologists, believes in the theory of separate descent.

We may test these conflicting theories of racial origins against the known facts in another theater of evolution, Africa. The resemblance and differences among people of that continent are easy to observe but their past is almost a complete mystery.

Garn and others distinguish a number of African local races, including East Africans, Sudanese, Forest Negroes, and Bantus. Differences among them are due in great part to local adaptation to the sharply differing local environments of tropical Africa. They are, in short, closely related local races. The Sudanese and East Africans are tall, extremely slender people well adapted to the hot dry climate of Africa's bush country. The Forest Negroes who practice agriculture in the humid forests of West and Central Africa are notably shorter and less linear in build. Exposed less to the glare of sunlight than Africans living in the open country, they are correspondingly lighter-skinned than the Sudanese, who number among them the darkest-skinned people in the world. Even the Pygmies, despite their distinctive appearance, are regarded by most anthropologists as a local race of the larger Negroid stock. Surviving now only along remote tributaries of the Congo River, they are categorized as a dwarfed local race, superbly well adapted for survival as hunters in the dense Congo forest. All these precise adaptations to local environment within tropical Africa strongly suggest prolonged habitation in the region and a considerable degree of isolated, independent evolution. That at least one blood-group gene (Rh°) is almost exclusively African lends further support to this view.

Yet the picture of a Negroid race evolving for tens of thousands of years in virtual isolation is belied by other facts and circumstances. For one thing, the Sahara Desert is neither an ancient nor an extremely formidable barrier to gene flow. During the so-called Climatic Optimum, lasting roughly from 7000 to 3000 B.C., the Sahara was bush country well stocked with game (see Chapter 10). Today there are a number of Saharan and Sudanese tribes which appear to be precisely intermediate between Caucasoids and African Negroes. The entire area from North Africa to the Sudan is one of the major zones of interbreeding in the world, comparable in extent to Central Asia. A massive interchange of genes between Caucasoids and Africans has clearly taken place in Africa in the past. That interchange probably accounts for the general resemblance in blood-group traits between Caucasoids and Africans, as well as for the occurrence in Africa of certain otherwise exclusively Caucasoid blood-group genes. Moreover, Africans and Caucasoids resemble each other in one conservative morphological trait — the general architecture and details of their teeth. According to one anthropologist, living Africans closely resemble in this respect Caucasoids whose fossil remains in Europe date back 25,000 years. One way or another, Caucasoids and their ancestors have played a major role in the genetic history of sub-Saharan Africa. Such being the case, the net result is a contradictory picture of racial history in the region, for it points simultaneously both to prolonged evolution in place and to massive gene flow from outside. The two factors plainly work at cross purposes. Caucasoids are not at all adapted to tropical environments. In consequence the influx of Caucasoid genes should, on the face of it, visibly distort the general picture of close environmental adaptation which living African local races present. Such gene flow would continually be working against natural selection, rapidly introducing traits which natural selection would be slowly working to eliminate.

What light might be shed on African racial origins ought to come from the Bushmen, whom few anthropologists consider to be merely locally adapted Negroes. The 50,000 surviving Bushmen hunters seem to stand apart from other African local races. They are as short as Pygmies. Adult male Bushmen range in height most commonly from 4'7" to 4'9", partly for nonhereditary reasons, namely an inadequate food supply. In contrast to Negroes, the Bushmen have small hands and feet and short legs relative to their trunks, as though infantile body proportions had somehow become preserved in the adults of the race,

225

who also have bulbous, "infantile" foreheads. Most anthropologists believe that the Bushman's ancestors were a full-statured people, but what relation they had to Negroes — if any — is a matter of conjecture.

The extremely sparse fossil record in Africa only brings more mystery to the question of African origins. At present time there is not a single African fossil even of fairly recent date which bears any resemblance to living Africans. Interestingly enough a few post-Ice Age fossils found in East Africa and southern Africa, homeland of the Bushmen, have variously been described as "Australoid" and "Primitive Caucasoid," labels which prove only that the various fossil craniums do not look at all like those of contemporary Africans. Do such fossils suggest further that the normal-sized ancestors of the Bushmen were literally Caucasoid peoples from North Africa and west Asia? The puzzle is at least as great as that of how the supposed "primitive Caucasoids" could have reached the southwest Pacific.

One recent theory, offered to solve the puzzle, proposes that the Pygmies and the Bushmen are both remnants of a separate branch of the original Ur-race — on a par with Caucasoids, Mongoloids, Negroids, and (perhaps) Australoids. Members of the original stock who dispersed into Africa from the Near East are deemed to have diverged into two "Proto-African" races, one adapted to the tropical forests — the Pygmies; the other to the tropical grasslands — the Bushmen. In this hypothetical reconstruction, Negroes did not exist as a race 10,000 years ago. They came into being only after the discovery of agriculture in west Asia and the expansion of west Asians into Africa. Gene flow between Caucasians and Pygmies living on the northern edge of the tropical forest produced the ancestors of modern Negroes. How then did they become so rapidly adapted to their tropical environments? The answer, presumably, is that dark-skinned, broad-nosed, spirally-haired Pygmies, already adapted to the tropical environment, contributed the adaptive genes and gave the new hybrid race a head start, so to speak. All Negroes are therefore partly Caucasoid by interbreeding, and also partly Caucasoid by common ancestry. When agriculture reached the Sudan around 3,000 years ago, members of this hybrid race acquired it and expanded in population. They began clearing the tropical forest, pushing the hunting Pygmies deeper and deeper into the remoter parts of the

Congo basin. They entered the East African bush country and began pushing the Bushmen farther and farther south. In this reconstruction, South African fossils labeled "Primitive Caucasoid' or "Australoid" may have belonged to members of the original Ur-race — those who pushed on south instead of staying and adapting to the tropical environment of equatorial Africa.

As in the case of the Australoids, we have an alternative theory from Carleton Coon. This theory states that the Bushmen are indeed relics of a separate race (called the Capoid by anthropologists with reference to the Cape of Good Hope) that evolved separately from different pre-sapiens stock. They were the aboriginal population of the African grasslands as far north as the Mediterranean.

It is now time to assess these two conflicting theories of the origin of races. To recapitulate, the "replacement theory" says that all modern men are descended from an original stock — the Ur-race — which arose out of Neanderthal man sometime about 40,000 years ago. Judging by the fossil evidence so far found, it originated in the Near East and spread throughout the world, replacing whatever early human populations it encountered.

This "replacement" model is clear, simple, and accords in a rough way with many known facts and reasonable conjectures about living races. Nevertheless it is open to some quite serious objections. For one thing it calls for extremely rapid differentiation through natural selection. Since the parent stock must be regarded as proto-Caucasoids — what else could they be? — the theory requires that such a population be altered by natural selection into, for example, the Pygmies, within scarcely more than 30,000 years, roughly 1,000 human generations. To many students of evolution that pace appears implausibly rapid. Moreover, if the date of the North Bornean fossil is correct, sapiens quite distinct from these early Caucasoids already inhabited Southeast Asia when their own hypothetical forebears first began dispersing from west Asia. That alone suggests that the theory's assumption of a single point of origin for modern sapiens is by no means strong. It is actually weak enough to be considered a second major objection to the theory.

The third serious objection to the theory is its basic premise — that modern Homo sapiens moved

226

out like a conquering army and extinguished every genetic trace of near-sapiens in the world. The premise does not seem very likely. It is based on the dogmatic insistence that modern sapiens, being members of a new species, were biologically incapable of successfully breeding with the few near-sapiens whom they encountered in their worldwide dispersion. Yet modern sapiens were simply not that radically different from their near-sapiens contemporaries to warrant that dogmatic assertion. If there was interbreeding, however, the whole replacement theory falls down. If members of the Ur-race interbred with near-sapiens they were exchanging genes with peoples long adapted to their natural environments. In that case what chiefly differentiated races was not the action of natural selection on the Ur-race, but genes from the already-adapted near-sapiens. Such genes would tend to be preserved in the new, somewhat hybrid populations precisely because they were advantageous for survival in that region. If such was the case, many existing racial differences among living populations must be regarded as predating the advent of modern Homo sapiens. Once admit the possibility of interbreeding and the replacement theory's picture of racial origins would have to be drastically altered.

Seizing on these objections, Coon proposed in 1962 his radically different theory of the origin of race. According to him, the races of man are hundreds of thousands of years old, immensely older than modern Homo sapiens. Coon's theory postulates the existence of five long-enduring human races: Mongoloids, Caucasoids, Australoids and two African stocks, Congoids, or Negroes, and Capoids. They are not geographically differentiated descendants of a single sapiens stock. On the contrary, each of these five "sub-species," in Coon's terms, is the direct lineal descendant of the ancient pre-sapiens humans who lived in the present-day homeland or "cradle" of each race hundreds of thousands of years ago. Known collectively as the fossil species Homo erectus, they include Pithecanthropus, a pre-sapiens living in Java and elsewhere several hundred thousand years ago. Pithecanthropus, in Coon's view, is the ancestor of all Australoids, from whom in his view Negritos, Australians, and Melanesians more recently evolved. Homo erectus includes Sinanthropus, whose fossil remains dating back three hundred thousand years were found near Peking. Sinanthro-

GEORGE HOLTON, PHOTO RESEARCHERS   MICHAL HERON, WOODFIN CAMP

pus, according to Coon, is the direct ancestor of all living Mongoloids. In this theory only the Caucasoids descended from west Asian fossil peoples (who, in the replacement theory, produced all of living mankind). Each of these races evolved more or less independently into modern Homo sapiens and today belong to that one species. If, in the replacement theory, one species diverged into a number of races, in Coon's theory, five races converged into one species.

Perhaps the largest objection to Coon's elaborate hypothesis is that there is no compelling reason to accept it. Coon's case is strongest when he deals with Mongoloid origins, He cites seventeen Mongoloid traits, including shovel-shaped incisors, found among the fossil remains of Sinanthropus. According to Coon this resemblance over time in the same area can be explained only as the result of the linear descent of Mongoloids from Sinanthropus. Although that is not the only way to explain them, the resemblances do exist, and they present a real problem for the replacement theory. The general distinctiveness of living Mongoloid peoples today also supports Coon's hypothesis of an independent evolution of the Mongoloid race. The view that the primordial racial division of Homo sapiens was that between Easterners and Westerners also lends plausibility to Coon's theory, at least as far as Mongoloid origins are concerned.

In other presumed racial cradles there are few if any such resemblances as those that Coon found in northern China. Pithecanthropus, according to Coon, reveals his ancestral ties to modern Australian aborigines by virtue of having a somewhat angular skull

227

Many of these aborigine children, playing at a mission station in Australia, have the Australian aborigines' characteristic light blond hair, which turns dark at puberty, and which is wavy rather than kinky. As adults, they have a tendency toward hairy bodies and premature balding. These typically Caucasoid features suggest that ancient Caucasoid migrants to Australia may have interbred with Mongoloids from Southeast Asia.

and large teeth, but these are traits found in fossils outside the presumed Southeast Asian cradle of the Australoid subspecies. In Africa Coon found no racial resemblances between the living and the long dead, but that can fairly be attributed to the paucity of fossils in Africa. In the Caucasoid cradle, however, where the fossil record is relatively rich, Coon's theory comes up against one of the major obstacles to accepting it—the fact of human variability in the past as well as the present. So far from looking like members of a single Caucasoid line, European fossils point to the existence of a great diversity of ancient peoples, including, of course, the Neanderthals. In Croatia, for example, there are skulls dating back some 100,000 years which have shovel-shaped incisors and flat "Mongoloid" faces. The Croatian finds alone shake Coon's theory. These ancient people also resemble Sinanthropus, but since they lived in the Caucasoid cradle cannot, according to Coon's theory, possibly have descended from the ancestor of Mongoloids. Why then conclude from similar resemblances that modern Mongoloid peoples descended from Sinanthropus? To account for the "Mongoloid" features of these Croatian fossils, Coon was forced to conclude that there was interbreeding between members of the Caucasoid lineage and members of the Mongoloid lineage some 100,000 years ago, and even that ancestral Caucasoids had entered the Mongoloid homeland at around that time.

The admission itself is damaging to Coon's theory for the theory requires that each of his five racial cradles be sharply isolated genetically from each other. Too much gene flow between the cradle regions would completely upset the independent evolution of his five racial lineages. Unfortunately for his theory, the evidence of local variability in the past compelled Coon to open gaping holes in his cradle lands for genes to flow through. The North Bornean fossil, for example, is quite divergent from either living Australians, their presumed Australoid ancestor, or their ancient Pithecanthropus sires. To account for these differences Coon had to invoke Mongoloid gene flow into Southeast Asia 40,000 years ago. If so, why call the Australoids a distinct subspecies evolving independently from Java man? Why not conclude that ancient peoples of Southeast Asia were hybrid people? Indeed, if "Caucasoids" interbred with "Mongoloids" 100,000 years ago and "Mongoloids" with "Australoids" 40,000 years ago, there is very little left of Coon's independent evolutionary lines. Gene flow destroyed them.

In effect, Coon's theory marshals much of the evidence for itself by a purely arbitrary process of racial labeling. The North Bornean fossil, Coon calls "definitely Australoid," although it bears little resemblance to that hypothetical ancient subspecies. The only reason he calls it "Australoid" is that it was found in the Australoid cradle and therefore could not be anything else. Fossils are given contemporary racial labels not on the basis of real resemblances but on the basis of where they were found. If they were discovered in the Australoid homeland they are Australoid by definition. By the same circular reasoning, Coon classifies Neanderthal people as Caucasoids because they inhabited Europe. Having thus given all the fossils in an area the same racial label it is not hard to conclude that all the fossils in a given area belong to the lineage of that presumed ancient race. With the possible significant exception of the Mongoloids there is no direct evidence to support Coon's theory of the origin of the races. That conclusion, however, is not as devastating as it sounds. The replacement theory does not have much direct evidence supporting it either.

Although Coon's theory met a generally hostile reception, some of his critics were nonetheless compelled to concede to the theory two important merits: first, its assumption of multiple origins for Homo sapiens is not only as likely as the assumption of a single origin, but, on purely theoretical grounds, probably more likely. Second, Coon demonstrated that there do exist resemblances between some living races and some pre-sapiens humans and to that extent, racial characteristics might well be said to predate the appearance of modern man. Having built his theory on the defects of the replacement theory, Coon has, in effect, laid down a gauntlet to its adherents. He has challenged them to explain why there should be *any* resemblances between living races of man and those ancient pre-sapiens peoples who, according to the replacement theory, have left no descendants. He has challenged them to justify their assumption of a single origin for modern man. He has challenged them to examine more skeptically the time frame of forty thousand years they have allotted for the formation of the human races. The challenge has not yet been met, and there, for the moment, the matter rests.

228

WHO ARE THE HAIRY AINU?

Some time after Commodore Matthew Perry, U.S.N., managed, in 1854, to induce Japan's rulers to abandon their centuries-old policy of near-total isolation, foreigners were at last able to travel around that mysterious country. Before long, their published accounts alerted readers in the United States and Europe to an intriguing fact: on Japan's northernmost main island, Hokkaido, and on Sakhalin and the Kuril Islands farther north, there lived a race of peasants and fisherfolk as light-skinned as themselves, whose eyelids lacked the epicanthic fold that makes Mongoloid people look slant-eyed.

These primitive "whites" called themselves Ainu (pronounced "Eye-noo"), meaning, in their language, "man," and were well aware of how they differed in appearance from the Japanese: to denote a member of their tribe they said he was "of the same eye socket."

The Ainus — or Hairy Ainus, as they came to be called for their thick and often wavy beards and abundant body hair — represent a major anthropological engima.Despite their Caucasoid appearance they are separated by thousands of miles from their nearest possible relatives, and surrounded by Mongoloid peoples. Who are they? Where did they originate? And how did they come to be where they are? Their language yields no clues, for it is unlike any other. Their legends are no more helpful, identifying their ancestors simply as beings that came out of the sky. And many of their customs are found nowhere else. Unique to their culture, or nearly so, are the men's use

of ceremonial mustache-lifters in drinking, the tattooing of women around their mouths, and the absence of rites marking important stages in a person's life, such as puberty.

But if the Ainus have continued to fascinate their supposed relatives in the West, they have mostly inspired contempt and impatience in their Mongoloid neighbors, the Japanese, much as the Mongoloid Indians of North and South America have been, until recently, looked down upon by their more numerous Caucasoid neighbors. For, like those Indians, the Ainus are a technologically backward people, resistant to modern ways.

That the Ainu have lived on the Japanese islands from very early times there could be no doubt, since both Hokkaido and Honshu contain many places bearing Ainu names, including even the sacred volcano Fujiyama, named for their fire goddess, Fuji. But the modern Japanese trace their own ancestry to a vanished Mongoloid race they call the Jomon people. According to traditional theory these Jomon people, originating on the Asian mainland, arrived long ago from the south — perhaps on a long-submerged land bridge to Korea — whereas the Ainus arrived from the north.

Emerging into nationhood, the Japanese pushed the "alien" Ainus farther and farther north, and finally off Honshu. Toward the end of the nineteenth century they began to displace them on Hokkaido. Today there remain only hundreds or at most a few thousand full-blooded Ainus, such as the man shown opposite with a bear. (Traditionally, the killing of a pet bear marks the climax of the Ainus' religious calendar.)

The Japanese belief that their ancestors have occupied the islands for millennia has been an important source of national pride. But that belief has lately been challenged by the findings of an American anthropologist, Dr. Christy G. Turner III. Turner is an expert on the shapes of human teeth, particularly of the cusps and grooves of their biting surfaces, which are genetically controlled and persist in consistent patterns within populations over numerous generations. In his investigation of Japanese prehistory he has compared the tooth shapes of the Japanese and the Ainu people and has compared both with the teeth of ancient skeletons found in Japan and China.

What Turner has found is that the teeth of modern Ainu are similar to those of prehistorical Japanese, whereas the teeth of modern Japanese are similar to those of ancient Chinese. Despite their Caucasoid appearance, the Ainu are definitely descended from Mongoloid stock. The modern Japanese, it would appear, immigrated from China in later times, very likely around 300–200 B.C., when such arts as writing, rice growing, and metalworking made their first appearance on the islands.

Whether or not the Ainu have Caucasoid genes remains a mystery. What seems certain is that they have a much older claim to the "Japanese" islands than the modern Japanese have. While this may do little to delay their likely extinction through assimilation, it may at least make the Japanese look upon them with new eyes — aslant, but no longer, perhaps, askance.

HOW HAS CLIMATE
AFFECTED HISTORY?

In the year 982 Eric the Red and his Viking comrades sailed across the far North Atlantic to found a settlement on Greenland. He gave the place its unlikely name, according to the Norse sagas, in hopes of attracting more settlers—a device not unknown to later real-estate promoters. But the truth is that parts of the Greenland coast in those days *were* green—greener than they had been in earlier times and greener than they are now. Annual temperatures averaged up to four degrees above the present range—enough to provide pasturage for sheep and cattle, and even to support the growth of a few trees, of which Greenland now has none. Therefore the Viking settlers could live in reasonable comfort on the products of their flocks and herds, supplemented by fish and marine mammals. Sealskins, furs, and walrus ivory could be traded to Norway for commodities such as grain and iron, which the island itself could not supply.

But the Viking settlements in Greenland did not last. The coming of a colder climate is recorded in the sagas which, from 1200 on, increasingly mention drift ice as a navigational hazard in the Denmark Strait between Greenland and Iceland. Trade with Iceland and Norway fell off; the last recorded voyage to Greenland was in 1410. The worsening climate must have reduced the productivity of the Greenlanders' livestock, both by shortening the grass-growing season and by increasing the area of permafrost. Evidence of the latter came from a 1921 excavation of a Norse graveyard in Greenland. The earliest graves were of normal depth, but later ones grew increasingly shallow as the permafrost moved upward.

We have no records of what this grim period was like in Greenland. Some notion of it can be gotten from documents describing a later and even colder period in Iceland, around the turn of the eighteenth century, when the island was almost depopulated. Thus the farm Breðamörk is described shortly after 1700 as "derelict . . . a little woodland, now surrounded by glacier." As late as 1698, say the documents, "there was some grass visible . . . but the glacier has since covered all except the hillhock on

which the farmhouse . . . stood, and that is surrounded by ice so that it is of no use even for sheep."

Faced with similar conditions in the thirteenth and subsequent centuries, the Greenland settlements dwindled and eventually died out. In the year 1540, a Dutch whaler, seeking shelter from a storm in one of the fjords of southwest Greenland, found "a dead man lying face down on the ground . . . clothed in frieze cloth and sealskin." Near him lay a sheath knife, "much worn and eaten away." The cloth garments and the "eaten away" (rusted iron) knife identify him as a Norseman rather than an Eskimo; to the best of our knowledge he was the last of the Norse Greenlanders.

The rise and fall of the Viking settlements in Greenland is a dramatic but minor example of how climate can affect history. No less striking, and far more significant, is the historical phenomenon of which the Viking thrust into the North Atlantic was merely a single fingertip: the Scandinavian expansion of the ninth and tenth centuries. This explosive process, of which we shall have more to say later on, kept much of Europe in a turmoil for nearly two hundred years, with less spectacular manifestations stretching from Spain in the west to Constantinople in the east. And there can be little doubt that it, like the Viking movement into Greenland, was made possible by an improvement in the climate of northern Europe, which by increasing agricultural production increased population.

If climatic change played so significant a role in ninth and tenth century Europe, one may ask whether it had an effect on other great historical events and movements. We know, for instance, that the Sahara was once a fertile grassland; that the Mediterranean basin grew cooler and rainier during the high periods of ancient Greece and Rome; that a time of dryness coincided with the fall of the Indus Valley civilization. Could climate have shaped events to which historians have long assigned other causes?

The tools to begin unraveling such mysteries have only lately come to hand, as scientists learn to reconstruct ancient climates. From the actual remains of plants preserved in peat bogs, and from the distinctive grains of plant pollen left in many other places such as lake bottoms, the specialist can reconstruct the type of vegetation that prevailed in a region at some past period. And since, as botanists know, the

<OVERLEAF *(pages 232-233): Snow covers Pueblo Indian ruins at Mesa Verde in Colorado. The agrarian Pueblos abandoned the site for lack of moisture around A.D. 1300. Though the climate later improved, they never returned. Superimposed is an ancient symbol of the sun.*
DAVID MUENCH

character of the vegetation anywhere largely reflects the climate there, a change in vegetation points to a change in climate. For example, if an archaeologist digging into a peat bog in northern Germany finds a layer containing pine needles, he concludes that the climate was much like the present. Oak, elm, and linden leaves point to warmer times, spruce needles to colder ones, while the tiny leaves of the dwarf willow indicate a tundra climate resembling that now found around the North Cape of Norway.

Other plant "records" reflecting past climates are found in tree rings, such as can be observed on any stump, or the butt end of a beam, or even, in some cases, a chunk of buried charcoal. In cold climates, such as those of Alaska or Lapland, wide rings mean warm summers: narrow rings, cold ones. In dry climates, like those of the U. S. Southwest, on the other hand, wide rings mean moist conditions, narrow rings, dry ones. Sequences of tree rings have been pieced together into climatic records covering thousands of years: the record for some parts of the southwest United States has been pushed back to around 6000 B.C.

One trouble with such plant records is that one must take them where one finds them—and where one finds them is not always where the historical action was occurring. Tree rings, for example, tell us that toward the end of the sixteenth century the climate of Lapland grew considerably colder, but while such information is interesting to the paleoclimatologist, the rest of us would prefer to know what was happening to the climate in Elizabethan England or the Italy of Michaelangelo. Unfortunately it is precisely in such more densely inhabited areas that natural climatic records are most likely to have been destroyed, or hopelessly scrambled, by agricultural and construction activities.

Where natural records are missing, the historian may still glean evidence from human records. A rise in the price of grain in, say, Catalonia suggests a period of drought in that region; similar inferences have been drawn from records showing how often the priests of Barcelona offered up public prayers for rain. Likewise, the abandonment of vineyards in northern France suggests a shift to cooler, rainier weather in which grapes would not ripen properly. However, such records must be interpreted with circumspection; as the well-known historian of climate Emmanuel LeRoy Ladurie has pointed out, they can

engender circular arguments. Thus the fourteenth-century abandonment of some French vineyards might be seen as evidence of worsening climate, ergo the change in climate caused the abandonment. In fact, more careful research has shown that the abandonment had little to do with any climatic change and a lot to do with the general rise in wages that occurred when the labor supply was reduced by the Black Death: it was not that the grapes didn't ripen but that it didn't pay to pick them.

These ambiguities, though they often blur the record of relatively recent, and smaller, climatic changes, are fortunately quite irrelevant to the last great climatic change. In that instance we know quite accurately what happened, and when, and where. Beginning about eighteen thousand years ago, the great ice sheets that had advanced to cover much of northern Europe and most of Canada, New England, and the upper Midwest began drawing back—at first slowly, but later at the rate of several miles a year. This retreat, though broken by many minor readvances, had, by about 7000 B.C. (in Europe) or a little later (in North America), obliterated the ice sheets outside of Greenland, Antarctica, and a few remnants in the mountains of Scandinavia and northeastern Canada. The result was warmer conditions almost everywhere, and in most places—for a number of meteorological reasons—moister ones as well.

Ironically, however, this shift toward "better" climates in much of the northern hemisphere may have disrupted and even destroyed some human societies—notably the rich Cro-Magnon cultures of southwestern France and northeastern Spain. During the Ice Age these Cro-Magnon peoples had enjoyed a plentiful life, living off the animals that roamed the plains and valleys south of the glaciers. Their societies were by some standards the first "high" human cultures, and were impressive enough by any standards. As we have seen in Chapter 4, they made many technological innovations, produced the first great flowering of art in the human record, and possessed, we can hardly doubt, a no less imaginative and elaborate ceremonial life.

But the prosperity of these cave-dwelling hunters depended on the rich resources of the land where they lived. South of the ice cap, that land was largely tundra—not the bleak tundra which exists today around the shores of the Arctic Ocean but a grassy

tundra supporting enormous herds of reindeer and wild horses, dozens or even hundreds of which could be killed by any reasonably skilled band of hunters. The animals were hunted not only one by one but sometimes in masses, as by being surrounded and driven over a cliff (a technique used by American Indians to hunt buffalo as late as 1800). At one site in France, the remains of some one hundred thousand horses have been found near a cliff base—doubtless slaughtered in many hunts over many generations.

As the ice sheets drew back, however, the tundra was replaced by forest, which is an environment far less attractive to the grazing animals on which the Cro-Magnons had feasted. Forest trees shade out most of the grass, and much of the low-growing herbage and shrubbery, on which grazers forage. The herds of reindeer were forced to find new pastures in the north, while the horses moved east into the grasslands of central Eurasia. Their replacements, such as deer and wild cattle, which can survive in woodland or forest-edge environments, were less numerous and much more scattered, living in groups of a dozen or less rather than herds of hundreds or thousands. The Mesolithic hunters who succeeded the Cro-Magnons were constrained to seek out and kill their game one or two at a time—with a consequent increase in time and energy expended per pound of meat. Where the Cro-Magnons had relied primarily on hunting the reindeer, horse and (in some places) mammoth, the Mesolithic peoples exploited a wide variety of game, including deer, elk (equivalent to the American moose), aurochs (wild cattle), and wild pig. To these they added wild fowl, fish, shellfish, and later sea mammals such as seal—plus, of course, roots, seeds, fruits, and nuts in season. As tools for these varied activities, they devised a great variety of fish spears, hooks, nets, and traps, as well as several types of arrows (though the bow and arrow had been invented earlier).

From a technological standpoint, the Mesolithic peoples were more advanced than the Cro-Magnons.

In their high-prowed boats, Vikings came to Greenland in about the year 982. In the warmer climate of that time they built settlements whose remains may still be seen (left). But around 1200 the climate turned colder and ice became a navigational hazard. The last voyage was made in 1410, and the colony soon disappeared.

Artistically, by contrast, they produced little of note: not only did they make no cave paintings, like the Cro-Magnon masterpieces—with a warmer climate they did not live in caves—but their everyday decorative art was sparse, simple, and, one is tempted to say, uninspired. Some prehistorians would go further, suggesting that the change in the economy accounts for the seeming retrogression in art: they argue in effect that the intensified struggle simply to stay alive left the Mesolithic peoples no time for cultural frills. Perhaps. Art has been produced in some remarkably meager environments, including the central Sahara and the coasts of the Bering Sea. A more likely explanation is that the Mesolithic cultures simply lacked artistic skills or interest.

Whatever the impact of the post-glacial climatic shift on art, its impact on population in southern and central Europe was pronounced and quite clear: as the climate "improved," the population shrank. According to the archaeological evidence, settlement was largely restricted to the shores of marshes, rivers, lakes, and the ocean. Such areas would have formed breaks in the forests, stimulating a denser growth of grass and underbrush which in turn would have attracted such animals as deer and aurochs. In addition, the open areas would have offered fish and waterfowl as valuable additions to the food supply. Elsewhere, population was far thinner: according to some prehistorians, parts of central Europe were virtually uninhabited. This depopulation, in turn, would have created ideal conditions for the subsequent immigration of peoples not dependent on hunting as a major source of food—primitive agriculturalists and herdsmen who, with stone axe and fire, could convert the forest into cropland and pasture. Some of these pioneers may have been representatives of the Indo-European peoples, whose remarkable expansion is described in Chapter 11.

By contrast with the ending of the Ice Age, and the radical ecologic changes it brought on in many regions, climatic changes during the last ten thousand years have been relatively minor: a few degrees' rise or fall in annual average temperatures, a few inches' increase or decrease in average annual precipitation. In many parts of the world such fluctuations were (and are) insufficient to affect human societies significantly, but in ecologically marginal areas a small climatic change could make a large differ-

Reindeer were a staple food of people who lived in southern Europe during the Ice Age. The animals appear, along with fish, on a piece of reindeer antler (of which this is a copy) found in southwest France. The retreat of the glaciers across Europe left warmer weather behind and caused the reindeer to move north too, reducing early man's food supply and, in consequence, his population.

ence in the land's productivity, and thus in human life.

Beginning perhaps as early as 7000 B.C., and for as much as four thousand years thereafter, much of the Northern Hemisphere experienced temperatures warmer than at present, while in some regions rainfall increased significantly. The causes of this shift to what is often called the Climatic Optimum are far from clear, and even its dates are less than certain; quite possibly its manifestations may have occurred at somewhat different times in different places, for instance Europe and northern Africa. What seems certain, however, is that for a substantial part of the period both Europe and the Sahara enjoyed climates rather different from those of today.

In Europe, this climatic episode was marked by prevailing westerly winds that carried mild, oceanic influences well into central Europe. The effects on human life, however, seem to have been small. The European cold-climate forests, dominated by pine and spruce, retreated toward the north, but these were replaced by broadleaf species such as oak, beech, elm, and linden—which is to say that the forest remained a forest, with both game and its hunters remaining sparse.

The Sahara, on the other hand, changed radically. Just how dry that region had been prior to the Cli-

239

matic Optimum is disputed, but at best it seems to have been a dry steppe resembling present-day Algeria just south of the Atlas Mountains. By 7000 B.C., however, large parts of the central Sahara had been converted into grassland interspersed with groves of such trees as Aleppo pine, and later also olive, cypress, juniper, and laurel. The vegetation was even richer in the mountainous areas which, for meteorological reasons, everywhere tend to be moister than the adjacent lowlands: a mixed oak-cedar forest, sometimes with the addition of elm, linden, and even maple. Across the grassland roamed herds of gazelle, ostrich, and antelope; moister areas were populated by giraffe, elephant, and even hippopotamus. Among these plentiful animals lived hunters who have long since vanished. On the walls of shallow caves cut into the rock by the rivers that once rushed through this land, they left a vivid pictorial record of their lives and, especially, the animals on which they lived.

While the Climatic Optimum clearly influenced directly the prehistory of the Sahara, the influence was only temporary. By 3000 B.C. or earlier, the region had become the almost totally uninhabitable waste that it is today. Ironically, however, this same shift to dryer conditions may have stimulated the emergence of civilization in Egypt.

When we say "Egypt," of course, we mean essentially the habitable parts of that land — the delta and long, narrow valley watered by the Nile and fertilized by silt deposited during the river's annual flood. (This was the case before the Aswan Dam was built; nowadays most of the silt is trapped in Lake Nasser above the dam.) It was this immensely fertile region that became the site of the Egyptian civilization whose mighty monuments still astonish the traveler. It is also a fact that civilization waxed as the Climatic Optimum waned.

There is good reason to believe that during the Climatic Optimum the Nile flowed more vigorously. In part, this was probably due to heavier rains in the Ethiopian and central African highlands, which now supply nearly all the river's water, but also in part to run-off from adjacent parts of the Sahara, which reached the Nile through *wadis* (arroyos) now dry for all, or nearly all, the year. The likely result is that the Nile Valley, and quite possibly the delta as well, were largely swamp, and therefore only marginally suitable for human habitation. Significantly, the earliest evi-

dence of agriculture in Egypt, dating from around 6000 B.C., is not along the Nile but in oases, or former oases, in the surrounding desert. The shift back to dryer climates, on the other hand, seems associated with the rather sudden appearance of agricultural settlements in the Nile Valley itself around 4000 B.C. Thus the end of the Climatic Optimum, by drying up the Nile swamps and opening up the perpetually rich soil along the rivers to agriculture, may well have made possible the subsequent — and rapid — development of Egyptian civilization, though it obviously did not *cause* that development.

Just as the waning of the Climatic Optimum may have helped open the way to civilization along the Nile, so a later climatic change may have helped close the door — temporarily — on civilization along the banks of another great river, the Indus. Perhaps the most interesting aspect of this episode in ancient history is that the climatic change in question may well have been partly man-made.

At its peak, the Indus Valley civilization rivaled, and in some respects surpassed, the contemporary civilizations of Mesopotamia and Egypt. Centered on its two great cities of Mohenjo-Daro and Harappa (the names are modern; no one knows what the Indus people called them), its territories extended from the mouth of the Indus a thousand miles northeast to the upper part of the Ganges river system, and from the Gulf of Cambay nearly five hundred miles west along the shores of the Arabian Sea. It dominated this immense area, larger than Egypt and Mesopotamia put together, for almost a thousand years, from before 2500 to around 1700 B.C. Our knowledge of it is limited by the fact that its people, though literate, employed a script that has never been deciphered; indeed its very language is unknown. Nor, in any case, has much written material survived the centuries; presumably most records were inscribed on perishable materials, perhaps the palm leaves used for some later Indian writings.

Despite the absence of written documents such as those that have so enhanced our understanding of ancient Egypt and Mesopotamia, the mute testimony of the spade has established that the Indus lands were no less rich and civilized. The people raised wheat, barley, peas, melons, and sesame, and were perhaps the first in the world to plant cotton; their domestic animals included cattle — both the humped, zebu type

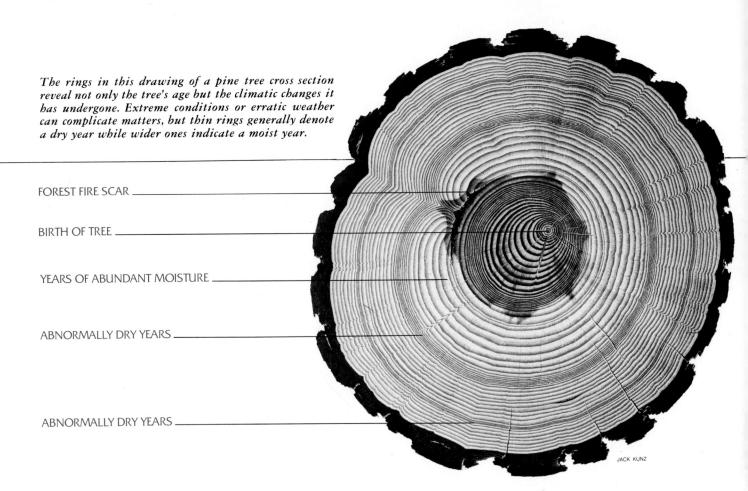

The rings in this drawing of a pine tree cross section reveal not only the tree's age but the climatic changes it has undergone. Extreme conditions or erratic weather can complicate matters, but thin rings generally denote a dry year while wider ones indicate a moist year.

FOREST FIRE SCAR _____

BIRTH OF TREE _____

YEARS OF ABUNDANT MOISTURE _____

ABNORMALLY DRY YEARS _____

ABNORMALLY DRY YEARS _____

JACK KUNZ

found in India today, and western-looking, straight-backed breeds — the buffalo, and, perhaps, the elephant, which in later times combined the functions of tractor, lifting-crane, and tank. The Indus people traded with Mesopotamia and other Persian Gulf lands, as well as with Afghanistan, Iran, and southern India. Their cities included enormous granaries of mud-brick (adobe) faced with baked brick, great "baths" resembling modern swimming pools — which, however, may have served religious rather than recreational purposes — and the world's first sewage systems. At Lothal, at the head of the Gulf of Cambay, they built another remarkable and unique structure: an artificial basin for shipping, some 710 feet long by 120 feet wide.

The origins of this mighty civilization are still mysterious; its fall, hardly less so. The simplest explanation is that it was destroyed by the invading Aryans, the Indo-European tribesmen whose descendants, linguistic and (in part) genetic, now populate Pakistan and northern and Central India. This theory is given color by some ancient Hindu (that is, Aryan) myths in which, for example, the leading god Indra is called the "fort destroyer" who "rends strongholds as age consumes a garment" — the "forts" in question presumably being the Indus cities. In the upper layers of Mohenjo-Daro, archaeologists have discovered several contorted groups of skeletons whose owners were apparently massacred.

More closely examined, however, this simple explanation seems a little too simple. That the Aryans conquered the Indus lands is clear, if only because they are there now; that they thereby destroyed the Indus civilization is considerably less clear, and in fact improbable. The Indus lands, after all, were not the only ancient civilization to undergo invasion by barbarian tribesmen; the same thing happened repeatedly in Egypt, Mesopotamia and, far to the east, in China. For that matter, they were not even the only ancient civilization to be invaded by Indo-European tribesmen. At just about the time the Aryans were moving into India, another Indo-European horde, the Kassites, was thrusting into Mesopotamia; later, Mesopotamia was again invaded by the Indo-Europeans we know as the Medes and Persians. Yet in every one of these cases, civilization — literate, urban societies — continued, and for good reason. First, the invaders were seldom numerous compared with the peoples they conquered; this was especially true of those moving in from inhospitable regions such as the dry plateaus of Iran and Afghanistan, as did both the Aryans and the Kassites. Second, the whole point of such invasions is not to destroy civilization but to enjoy its riches — which means, in effect, taking over the business, not liquidating it.

Sir Mortimer Wheeler, a leading expert on Indian prehistory, sees the liquidation of the Indus civilization as "rooted in deeper causes of decline." He

CONTINUED ON PAGE 247

Once the fertile domain of pastoral Stone Age peoples, the Tassili, a mountainous region in southern Algeria, is now part of the Sahara Desert. Thousands of rock paintings and engravings, like the graceful, stylized one at left showing a grain harvest, have survived the centuries to recall the long-vanished prosperity of the Tassili.

Tassili means "plateau of rivers," but the rivers dried up about 4,000 years ago, leaving this expanse of eroded rock formations that now receives under a millimeter of rain yearly. The elephants, giraffes, and antelopes disappeared, leaving behind a hardy band of descendants of the Stone Age peoples as virtually the only inhabitants.

OVERLEAF: Executed between 4000 and 1500 B.C., the rock paintings and engravings of the Tassili transform the area into an outdoor art gallery. Our picture is a copy of one such work, depicting a Stone Age cattle roundup. The white circles to the left are thought to be corrals; why the cattle are lined up in front of them is a mystery.

The Cliff Palace, covered with snow, is the single largest unit in the Pueblos' Mesa Verde complex. Thought to have served a religious purpose, it contains over 200 rooms and 23 ceremonial chambers. As rainfall diminished, however, more than 400 Pueblos moved in, freeing the nearby land they had lived on for farming.

notes, for example, a fall in the quality of artifacts during the civilization's last centuries: intricately painted, multicolor pottery is replaced by plain, unpainted ware; the delicately carved animal figures found on soapstone seals are discarded in favor of crude geometric designs, and so on. Seemingly, the Indus civilization had become gravely enfeebled before the Aryan invasion—presumably—gave it the coup de grâce.

If the decline of the Indus civilization was indeed due to "deeper causes" than invasion, what could these have been? The archaeologist George F. Dales, among others, has suggested repeated flooding. This, he believes, was caused by geological uplift around the mouth of the Indus, which periodically threw up dams of rock or mud, behind which lakes would temporarily submerge parts of the valley. Certainly there is plenty of evidence that Mohenjo-Daro and the lower valley generally did suffer from periodic floods, which may have been caused in part by earth movements. A probable alternative, or additional, cause is deforestation of the surrounding hills. The Indus Valley cities, unlike those of Mesopotamia, used great quantities of baked as well as unbaked brick, whose manufacture would by itself have consumed great quantities of wood for fuel. Forest destruction in hilly country inevitably speeds up runoff of rain, meaning that flooding becomes more likely; Italy has suffered from such floods for centuries.

But though the lower Indus Valley was periodically flooded, there is no evidence that any of these floods produced more than a temporary check on the activities of civilization. Floods, and severe ones, were no strangers to China and Mesopotamia—the latter was, indeed, the original source of the biblical deluge legend—yet civilization survived. Finally, on Dales' own showing, the floods would at worst have affected only the lower valley and Mohenjo-Daro, which accounted for only a fraction of the Indus territory, but not the upper valley, dominated by Harappa, nor yet the settlements in hilly country both northwest and southeast of the Indus.

With neither invasion nor flooding a wholly satisfactory explanation, then what *did* happen to the Indus civilization? One clue comes from examining the distribution of known Indus archaeological sites. Many of these settlements lie in areas where agriculture today is all but impossible: more than forty, for example, are found in the empty, lower valleys of

rivers—notably, the Ghaggar—which once flowed to the sea, or into the Indus, but today sink into the sands hundreds of miles away. The obvious inference is that in the time of the Indus civilization, the climate was moister and these rivers flowed more vigorously than they now do. Heavier rainfall would, incidently, explain why the Indus people went to the trouble of facing their buildings with baked brick: unbaked adobe would have slumped back into mud.

The inference of a moister climate is confirmed by pollen studies in the region. Today, it is a scrubby grassland or outright desert, but pollen counts indicate that at the beginning of the Indus period much of it was open woodland—in the lower, moister places, actual jungle. As the civilization grew, cultivation expanded, as shown by an increase in grain pollen in the records. Later, however, pollen from desert plants shows up—and the grain pollen drops off. There seems little doubt, then, that the drop-off was due to drought. This would have damaged agriculture even in the river valleys, by reducing water available for irrigation—as seems to have happened along the lower course of the Ghaggar: it would have wreaked havoc among the farmers and herdsmen of the uplands, where irrigation was impracticable and rainfall the only source of moisture.

If, as seems likely, a shift to dryer climates destroyed, or helped destroy, the Indus civilization, what caused the shift? An interesting—and, in the light of some present developments, rather ominous—explanation comes from Reid Bryson, a well-known climatologist at the University of Wisconsin. Bryson points out, first of all, that the present climate of the Indus Valley and adjacent regions is considered a "problem" climate, in the sense that there seems no very good reason, in terms of normal atmospheric processes, why it should be as dry as it is. In winter, to be sure, it is dry because, like most of the Indian peninsula, it is under the influence of the dry northeast monsoon winds. In summer, however, when the rest of India is being drenched, and in some places deluged, by the moist southwest monsoon, it typically receives only sparse and scattered showers.

To understand Bryson's explaination of this anomaly, we must first note that rain—in the Indus Valley or anywhere else—falls from moist air that is moving upward. As it moves upward, it expands, due to lower atmospheric pressure; as it expands, it cools. The cooling condenses water vapor into clouds, com-

247

Though the script remains a mystery on these tiny soap-stone seals, more than 2,000 of which have turned up in Indus Valley excavations, it probably identified the owners of the goods on which the seals were stamped. Animals that once roamed the Indus Valley are portrayed with remarkable realism on many of the seals.

NATIONAL MUSEUM OF INDIA, NEW DELHI

JANE POWELL NATIONAL MUSEUM OF KARACHI

Mud-brick ruins mark the sites of the Indus Valley civilization, possibly a victim of a man-made change in climate. At left below is the Great Bath at Mohenjo-Daro. It probably served as a religious complex for ritual bathing. Individual quarters bordering the main pool may have been used by priests for private ablutions.

Two sharply contrasting examples of Indus Valley artistic style are apparent in the figurines at left. The one at far left is a carefully molded steatite bust of a stern-visaged priest or diety. Extremely rare, it may have been used for ceremonial purposes. Much more common (left) is the crude terra-cotta bust of a woman.

FRANCES MORTIMER RAPHO/PHOTO RESEARCHERS

posed of droplets of liquid water; if the process goes far enough, the droplets coalesce into raindrops.

The feeble summer rains in the Indus region imply that the air there is, for much of the time, not moving upward, as it does elsewhere in India, but downward. It does not seem to be being *forced* downward by larger atmospheric movements, as occurs (for example) over the Sahara during most of the year. The only other explanation is that it is being cooled in its upper layers, since air that has been cooled sufficiently becomes dense enough to sink through the lighter, lower layers toward the surface.

Bryson sees the source of the cooling as atmospheric dust. This comes from the Indian desert, where it is whipped up by the fierce, dry winds to altitudes as high as thirty thousand feet, showing up clearly in space photographs of the area. The dust, he believes, cools the atmosphere, both by partially blocking the sun's heat and by accelerating the loss of heat back to space. The cooled air sinks—and the rain does not fall. In effect, the dust causes the desert—and the desert causes the dust.

But if, as seems clear from the pollen records, the desert was not always there, or at least was much smaller, where did it—and the dust—come from? Bryson's explanation, based on parallels from the recent history of India, centers on overpopulation. With increased population in modern times, he points out, "the forests have been destroyed for timber and fuel, so that large areas are almost completely cleared. . . ." As we have already noted, deforestation accelerates the runoff of rain, thereby decreasing moisture in the soil, and also lowers fertility, as a result of erosion and topsoil loss. In addition, when wood is not available, the population burns cow dung for fuel—instead of using it for manure. "The consequent loss of fertility," Bryson then notes, "can

249

promote overgrazing"; overgrazing, by partially stripping away the soil's plant cover, promotes the whipping up of dust, a reduction in rainfall, still less plant growth, still worse overgrazing, and so on around the vicious circle.

The process by which semiarid lands can be converted into man-made deserts by overgrazing and similar improvidences have been further elucidated by some recent computer studies by NASA and M.I.T. scientists; they find that in some situations reduced plant cover can reduce rainfall, quite independently of its effect on dust, simply by increasing the reflectivity or albedo of the surface. Higher albedo means that more of the sun's radiation is reflected back to space, with less of it available to heat the earth and its atmosphere. This type of atmospheric cooling, like Bryson's dust-induced cooling, would cause more atmospheric subsidence, less rain, still less vegetation, still higher albedo, and so on.

Thus it seems entirely possible that the Indus civilization may have perished from its own success— and its environmental excess: overpopulation, leading to overgrazing, leading to reduced rainfall caused either by dust or by increased albedo or both. Bryson himself believes that once this process was well underway it may have been catastrophically intensified by a general change toward dryer climates in the region shortly before 1500 B.C. "When man is pushing his environment to the limits," he points out, "he is especially vulnerable to natural changes." With so many societies now pushing *their* environments to the limits, and beyond, this is a sobering thought.

In somewhat later times there was a general, though slight, cooling over much of the northern hemisphere. For close to a thousand years—roughly from 700 B.C. to A.D. 300—most of Europe seems to have been somewhat cooler and moister than it is now. This climatic change manifested itself in a number of ways, all of which may have influenced history in one way or another.

First, the Mediterranean lands grew moister—notably the Greek and Italian peninsulas. According to the British paleoclimatologist H. H. Lamb, there was no really dry season in the Mediterranean even as late as A.D. 200—in contrast to the present when the climate, as he notes, "would be improved by some summer rain." Second, northern Europe grew cooler and moister—the latter probably due less to in-

creased rainfall than to decreased evaporation. As a result, forests in upland areas would have grown denser, while swamps and bogs would have expanded in the lowlands. Third, the same trend toward moister climates shifted the boundary between forest and grassland in eastern Europe. Around 2000 B.C., the grassy steppes of southern Russia stretched deep into what are now Romania and Hungary, much as they do today—or would, in the absence of cultivation. By around 500 B.C., however, wooded or partly wooded country extended nearly a thousand miles farther east, to the banks of the Don.

Moister weather around the Mediterranean probably favored the rise and expansion of civilizations in that area. More rainfall, more evenly distributed throughout the year, would have meant more abundant crops, meaning more of an economic surplus which could be applied to public works and the support of an expanding leisure, or part-time leisure class. Also, the increased agricultural prosperity would have brought a rise in population. Not surprisingly, then, we find this period marked by a wave of colonization. The Phoenicians of the Levant pressed along the coast of North Africa, founding cities and trading stations as far west as Gadir (Cádiz); the greatest was, of course, Carthage. The Greeks found outlets for their burgeoning population around the coasts of Asia Minor, along the northern coast of the Black Sea as far east as the Crimea, and in the northern Mediterranean as far west as Massilia (Marseilles) and Spain; so numerous were their settlements in southern Italy that the area became known as Magna Graecia—"Great Greece." Somewhat later, the Italians, under Roman rule, planted settlements in North Africa (whence they had driven the Phoenicians), in Spain, France, England, and large areas of the Balkans; their expansion is marked by the present range of the Romance languages, which stretch from Portugal to Romania.

Both Greece and Italy, however, remained heavily populated, and in both rising populations produced their expectable damage: overgrazing, deforestation, erosion, and a consequent decrease in the effective rainfall. An early description of the process is interesting enough to be worth quoting—not least because it typifies the "modern," rationalist view of the world which was perhaps the most precious legacy of the Mediterranean world. The account is by Plato, in his *Critias*, in which he describes how the soil of Greece "keeps continually sliding away and disappearing into the sea. . . . What now remains, compared with what once existed, is like the skeleton of a sick man, all the fat and soft earth having wasted away and only the bare framework of the land being left. . . . (Thus) the stony plains of the present day were once full of rich soil, the mountains were heavily wooded. . . . There are mountains in Attica which can now support nothing but bees [that is, are covered only with grass and scrub] but which were clothed, not so very long ago, with fine trees suitable for roofing the largest buildings—and roofs hewn from the timber are still in existence. . . . The country produced boundless pasturage for cattle."

Thus far the familiar deforestation erosion cycle. But the philospher sees even deeper: "The supply of rainfall," he points out, "was not lost, as it is at present, through being allowed to flow over the denuded surface into the sea, but was received by the country, in all its abundance, into her bosom, where she stored it . . . and so was able to discharge the drainage of the heights into the hollows, in the form of springs and rivers with an abundant volume and a wide territorial distribution. The shrines that survive to the present day on the sites of extinct water sources are evidence for the correctness of my present hypothesis."

A modern ecologist could hardly improve on this description for accuracy—and could probably not equal it for eloquence.

This inadvertent decrease in effective precipitation did not trigger the formation of a desert in Greece as it apparently did in the Indus Valley, mainly because the overall climate was moister. However, it does seem to have helped generate some significant changes in Greek society. The initial effect was to encourage replacement of grain fields, producing mainly for local consumption, with olive orchards and vineyards, both of which can survive in dryer and more impoverished soil. And much of the oil and wine thus produced was for export, notably to the northern shores of the Black Sea, where they could be exchanged for grain—the major crop in that region. The effect was to draw many more Greek farmers into market relationships—and therefore into closer contact with the cities where merchants and shippers were based. According to the historian W. H. McNeill, it was in this manner that "the rural population [became] vitally and actively concerned in the affairs of the state."

The general shift toward moister climates during the last millennium B.C. may also have influenced the outcome of the power struggle between the Greeks and the Persians through its effects on the nomadic tribes of the Russian steppes. These peoples, sometimes lumped together as the Scythians, had, with their herds of sheep, cattle, and horses, long roamed the grasslands—whence they periodically descended on the civilized lands to the south. Which of these lands they invaded at any given time would evidently depend on where they happened to be located—and this, in turn, would clearly be influenced by the position of the boundary between steppe, where the nomads thrived, and forest, where their herds could find little pasturage.

Greek legends indicate that in the earlier, dryer Mycenaean period, when the grasslands extended well into the Balkans, Greece was invaded at least once by these fierce warriors; indeed it has been suggested that the Greeks themselves may represent a still earlier wave of pastoral nomads (see Chapter 3). In the moister classic period, by contrast, with forest or open woodland covering the Balkans and much of southern Russia, the nomads would have sought pastures to the east—or shifted to a settled farming way of life, as some of them in fact did. In ei-

ther case, they would have ceased to threaten Greece. The eastward-shifting nomads, however, could and did attack Persian territories, to which they were a periodic military nuisance and sometimes a serious threat—serious enough, perhaps, to tip the military balance between Persians and Greeks. Centuries later the advent of warmer and dryer weather in Europe was accompanied by a new threat from the mounted nomads of the east. As the forests retreated westward, the advancing steppes gave the horsemen a highway into the heart of Europe. By the early part of the fifth century the hard-riding Huns had driven out or overrun the Germanic tribes and seized control of most of Europe between the Baltic and the fast-crumbling Roman frontiers.

The warming trend which probably aided the Hunnish advance into Europe reached its peak between about A.D. 700 and 1200, a period sometimes called the Little Climatic Optimum. It was this period, as noted earlier, that saw the great wave of Scandinavian expansion whose most conspicuous, and bloody, expression was the Viking incursions.

Seen from the safe distance of a thousand years, the Vikings are a rather romantic lot—virile warriors, skilled sailors, dauntless explorers and all that. The romance is given an extra fillip by their colorful nicknames: Thord Bellower, Hrafn Duel-fighter, Ulf Squinter and the like. A juster estimate of the contemporary impact of these worthies can be obtained by translating their colloquial Norse names into colloquial American: Loud-mouth Thord, Shoot-out Hrafn, Cockeye Ulf, not to mention Lowlife Steinholf, Dirty Eyolf, and that king of Norway known as Bloody-axe Eric. (Viking nicknames were not always without humor. Eric the Red's mother-in-law for example, was known as Ship-bosom Thorbjorg. Imagine the prow of a Viking ship. . . .) The Vikings' serious business in life was murder and pillage, with arson and rape for lighter amusements: when they were not massacring foreigners without distinction of age or sex, they kept in practice by knocking off one another—a fact which emerges clearly from even a quick reading of the early sagas, if one keeps a body count. The narrative of one voyage to Greenland, for instance, clocks off twelve murders in six paragraphs.

Some historians—many of them Scandinavians—aver that the Vikings were only a small minority of the Scandinavian population, most of whom were

253

peaceful farmers and fishermen. This is doubtless true, if only because the formidable Viking war machine could hardly have functioned for two centuries without a solid economic base at home. Other historians claim that the Vikings were some sort of ruling elite, separated by ancestry and ethos from the rest of their countrymen—who are thereby absolved from responsibility for Viking depredations. On this, the evidence is less convincing; it seems more likely that individual Scandinavians adopted warlike or pacific life-styles as opportunity afforded—as have many other peoples, before and since. Thus Eric the Red's father left Norway for Iceland in a hurry "because he had committed manslaughters"; Eric himself emigrated to Greenland for equally pressing reasons, after an affray in which Dirty Eyolf and Shoot-Out Hrafn bit the Icelandic dust. Yet Eric's son Leif, by contrast, emerges as a peaceful trader.

In the west, the various Norse peoples colonized—peacefully or otherwise—the Faeroe, Shetland, and Orkney islands, Iceland and a corner of Greenland, the east coast of Ireland, and eastern England, which became known as the Danelaw. Other Norsemen or Northmen made their home in Holland and along the north coast of France, where their domain, at first called "Pirate Land" by the French, ultimately became known as Normandy.

To the southeast, the Scandinavians were no less active. Having colonized the southeast Baltic, they rowed upriver, portaged to the headwaters of the Dnieper and Volga, and established a flourishing trade with Byzantium and the Moslem lands farther east, via the Black and Caspian seas: tens of thousands of Arab coins have been dug up in Sweden and Denmark. According to some accounts, it was these Scandinavians who laid the first foundations of the Russian state (*rus* is Norse for "oarsmen")—a theory however, that is violently disputed by Russian historians, both Soviet and anti-Soviet.

Meanwhile, the most predatory Scandinavian groups were robbing, raping, and murdering from the North Sea to the Mediterranean. The "Great Army." a fleet numbering up to seven hundred ships, dominated the North Sea and English Channel for two generations. In 885, a wing of it pushed up the Seine to attack Paris, discouraged a French counterattack by massacring a hundred prisoners, and departed only after extorting seven thousand pounds of silver from the French king. Other Viking fleets pillaged

Lisbon, Cádiz, and Seville and, having established a base of operations in the Rhone delta, went on to sack a whole series of towns in Provence and Italy. At the great battle which, in 1066, decided the future of England, both sides were led by Viking descendants: Harold, a nephew of Knut (Canute), who had ruled both Denmark and England, and William, a bastard great-great-great-grandson of the pirate Rolf who first seized Normandy.

Beginning about A.D. 800, in short, the Scandinavians, a hitherto obscure collection of barbaric tribes, suddenly leaped onto the stage of European history; their impact on it during the next three centuries approached that of the Romans a thousand years before. How did they do it?

One element was doubtless their mastery of shipbuilding and nautical skills. But these had been well developed as early as A.D. 600 when, says the historian Eric Oxenstierna, "sizeable sailing vessels were being built." A much more important factor emerges when one considers the logistics of the Viking era. It involved, to begin with, not merely sizable ships, but hundreds of them. These were built from hand-hewn timbers, planked with hand-sawn boards, and rigged with hand-twisted rope and hand-woven sails. They were then provisioned with sacks of meal and barrels of dried meat and fish, and finally manned by thousands of fighting men—some twenty thousand for the Great Army alone—*in addition to* the tens of thousands who must have remained at home to build the ships and produce the provisions. The various colonizing ventures would have taken thousands more, with other thousands accounted for as casualties of warfare, feuds, or simple Viking high spirits. What we are talking about, evidently, is something approaching a population explosion in Scandinavia.

The historian Johannes Brønsted, in fact, cites overpopulation in Scandinavia as a contributing cause to the Viking era—but ascribes it, curiously, to the sexual ethos of the Vikings, who, he says, "rather prided themselves on the number of sons they could beget; it was common for them to have wives, mistresses and underwives . . ." Viking machismo, however, hardly explains the Scandinavian population increase—unless one assumes that their mistresses and underwives would under other circumstances have remained virgins, which seems highly improbable. In Scandinavia or anywhere else, the amount of sexual intercourse has little to do with population

GÄVLE MUSEUM, SWEDEN

In the latter half of the ninth century, the Vikings roamed beyond Europe and into Russia and the Middle East as well, returning with objects like this bronze, Arab-made brazier, which was unearthed in Sweden.

growth; with children, as any parent knows, it's not the initial cost but the upkeep—which means, in the first place, food.

It can hardly be coincidence that food production in Scandinavia must have increased substantially shortly before the Viking era. We have no direct evidence of this—but the indirect evidence is overwhelming. The warmer temperatures of the Little Climatic Optimum are attested by tree rings from Alaska and Lapland, pollen studies from European peat bogs, and the existence in eleventh-century England of no less than thirty-eight vineyards. (These were listed in the Domesday Book, where William the Conqueror's clerks catalogued the riches of the land he had seized.) English wines, we are told, were almost as good as those of France—meaning that English summers must have been considerably warmer and sunnier than in later centuries. In Germany, vineyards extended north to the Baltic (their present limit is the Rhineland).

Scandinavia never became warm enough to produce wine, but its staple grain crops must have improved. It is known, for example, that in Norway cultivation was pushed up the mountain sides to an altitude as much as six hundred feet higher than at present. More food, in turn, meant healthier children, more of whom would have survived to maturity. And it would have been a taller and more vigorous maturity—no small matter when most fighting was done hand-to-hand. It was in this way that the Little Climatic Optimum, though it did not precisely *cause* the Viking explosion, certainly provided the essential precondition for that explosion: an expanding, vigorous population, capable of equipping, provisioning, and manning the Scandinavians' predatory and colonizing expeditions.

With the waning of the Little Climatic Optimum, the impact of climate on history becomes increasingly hard to assess, not least because of the competing claims of other, nonclimatic historical events. It is likely enough, for example, that worsening climate in northern Europe during the 1300s made for less abundance there—but any hardships that occurred were swamped by the horrors of the Black Death. Again, the cold period that began shortly before 1600—called, with some exaggeration,

255

the Little Ice Age—probably made life even more difficult for the German peasant, but its effects, whatever they were, would have been lost in the far worse ravages of the Thirty Year's War.

There is one rather limited area in which climatic change does not seem to have played a decisive role in human affairs: the southwestern United States. By around A.D. 1000, much of this area was sown with Indian villages, whose inhabitants raised corn, beans, and squash. Many of these settlements were built along the sides of the flat-topped mesas where the simple crops were planted, clinging to the steep slopes like swallows' nests under the eaves of a barn. In the latter part of the fourteenth century, however, nearly all these cliff dwellings, including those in the spectacular Canyon de Chelly, were abandoned—and for no obvious reason such as invasion. Significantly, however, tree-ring records show that between A.D. 1260 and 1300 rainfall in the area was almost everywhere below normal; faced with withering crops, the cliff dwellers evidently had no choice but to move to moister sites. During the succeeding forty years the rains returned—but the cliff dwellings, for some reason, were never reoccupied.

In marginal areas of human habitation today even minor and temporary climatic changes can have devastating effects. We had an example of this a few years ago in the African Sahel, that semiarid borderland between the Sahara and the moister regions to the south, where five years of drought had almost destroyed food production. People died by the tens of thousands from starvation and disease; livestock perished—or was slaughtered—by the hundreds of thousands for lack of fodder or water. The economic development of the entire region was set back twenty years or more.

Whether one classifies this drought as a change in climate or, perhaps more accurately, as merely a run of unfavorable weather, its effect on the communities of the Sahel was clearly disruptive, even catastrophic. No less clearly, had the drought continued not for five years but for fifty, the course of human development in the region would have been radically changed for the worse.

At this writing, then, climate again seems to be moving into a more central position on the historical stage. The expansion of world populations has increasingly pushed humanity into habitats such as the Sahel, where even a slight worsening of climate can

produce major effects on human existence. And we can be reasonably certain that the impact of worsening climate will be intensified by the familiar process of overgrazing, erosion, and destruction of soil and vegetation that we have already seen in operation in Greece and along the Indus. Whether or not these will themselves reduce actual rainfall, as Bryson and others believe can happen, they will certainly reduce *effective* rainfall—unless, indeed, their development is checked by far wiser economic planning than has yet been undertaken. If climate has changed history in the past, it threatens to work even more severe changes in the future.

By far the most ominous of these possible changes is one currently foreseen by a number of climatologists, including Bryson himself: the coming of another ice age. According to some accounts, the beginning of this process can be expected in the next few centuries; indeed, it may already be underway.

Most—though not all—climatologists ascribe the periodic advance and retreat of the glaciers to periodic alterations in the shape of the earth's orbit and the tilt of its axis, both of which change slightly over thousands of years. Since these variations are predictable, they provide—assuming the theory is correct—a forecast for the next twenty thousand years: colder to much colder. Unfortunately, however, even an accurate forecast for 20,000 years does not tell us much about what is going to happen during the next 20—or even the next 200. It is a fact that during the past quarter century temperatures in the northern hemisphere have dropped slightly (though they have risen in much of the southern hemisphere). This drop may indeed be the forerunner of another ice age—but it may, instead, be a minor, temporary fluctuation, such as has occurred scores of times during human history; at present, we have no way of knowing which.

In the long run then, we can expect the climatic catastrophe of a new glaciation—unless, indeed, science can devise ways of heading it off. In the short run, all we can be sure of is that the climate will continue to change in one way or another, and since our chances of preventing such changes are at present remote, we had best be prepared for them. The impact of climatic change on human history is, as we have seen, not always easy to ascertain, and perhaps, to some cosmic eye, not very important. But to mere mortals these same changes can be at best disruptive and, at worst, matters of life and death.

WHAT SET OFF THE BIGGEST BANG IN RECORDED HISTORY?

Shortly after 7 A.M. on June 30, 1908, early rising farmers, herdsmen, and trappers in the sparsely settled vastness of the central Siberia Plateau watched in awe as a cylindrical object, glowing with an intense bluish-white light and trailing a fiery tail, raced across a clear blue sky toward the northern horizon. At 7:17, over a desolate region of bogs and low, pine-covered hills traversed by the Stony Tunguska River, it disappeared; instantly, a "pillar of fire" leaped skyward, so high it was seen hundreds of miles away; the earth shuddered under the impact of a titanic explosion; the air was wracked by thunderous claps; and a superheated wind rushed outward, setting parts of the taiga on fire. At a trading post forty miles from the blast, a man sitting on the steps of his house saw the blinding flash and covered his eyes; he felt scorched, as if the shirt on his back were burning, and the next moment he was hurled from the steps by a shock wave and knocked unconscious. Four hundred miles to the south the ground heaved under the tracks of the recently completed Trans-Siberian Railway, threatening to derail an express. And above the Tunguska region a mass of black clouds, piling up to a height of twelve miles, dumped a shower of "black rain" on the countryside—dirt and debris sucked up by the explosion—while rumblings like heavy artillery fire reverberated throughout central Russia.

Since seismographs and barographs everywhere had recorded the event, the entire world knew that something extraordinary had occurred in the Siberian wilderness. But what? Scientists conjectured that a giant meteorite must have fallen, exploding from the intense heat its impact generated. On hitting the ground, such a body would, theoretically, have blown out a huge crater like the one in Arizona, three-quarters of a mile square, left by a meteorite that fell fifty thousand years ago, but the Siberian "impact site" turned out to be a dismal swamp, with no trace of a meteorite to be seen.

Nevertheless, for want of a better explanation, scientists continued to ascribe the cataclysm to a meteorite, and Leonid Kulik, a mineralogist who headed government-sponsored expeditions to the Tunguska in the early 1920s and again in 1938–39, searched for evidence to support this view.

Although this search proved fruitless, Kulik uncovered a wealth of information about the blast. Near the swamp into which the meteorite had supposedly plummeted, scorched trees, striped of branches, still stood, but around this weird "telegraph-pole" forest, except where intervening hills had shielded them, every tree within fifty miles had been blown flat, its trunk pointing away from the swamp. From this—and from his failure to find even a small impact crater—Kulik concluded that the meteorite had never reached the ground but had exploded two or three miles up in the air. The testimony of local herdsmen yielded other curious details: the blast's intense heat had melted the permafrost, causing water trapped underground for tens of thousands of years to gush forth in fountains, and those reindeer that had not been killed had developed mysterious blisters and scabs on their hides. Stranger still, examination of the trees that had been germinating in 1908 revealed that they had then grown at several times the normal rate.

During World War II Kulik was captured by the Germans and died a prisoner. The riddle he had worked to solve was forgotten. In August 1945, however, certain Russian scientists were abruptly reminded of it by the atom-bombings of Hiroshima and Nagasaki, events which seemed uncannily familiar in both their manifestations (the fireball, the searing thermal current, the towering "mushroom" cloud) and their effects (the instantaneous and near-total destruction, the radiation burns on living flesh, the accelerated growth of new plant life, even the "telegraph-pole" appearance of scorched and branchless trees standing below the point at which an atom

bomb was detonated).

Could the Siberian blast have been atomic? In 1958 a Russian engineer-turned-writer, Aleksander Kazantsev, published a story-article pinning that disaster on Martians killed on their way to Earth by cosmic rays or meteorite bombardment; their ship, with no one at the controls, hurtles into our atmosphere at unreduced speed and burns up from friction, triggering a chain reaction in its atomic fuel that sets off the explosion. Few informed readers by then still accepted the meteorite theory, and some, particularly younger men and women, found Kazantsev's hypothesis persuasive, but others rejected it in favor of an earlier alternate explanation, according to which the head of a comet had penetrated the atmosphere at such high velocity that the heat thus generated had caused the comet to blow up. (Skeptics pointed out, however, that a comet could hardly have approached Earth without being seen.)

Two further explanations involving natural causes have been advanced. The first is that a tiny "black hole"—a chunk of matter collapsed to minuscule dimensions and so dense that its gravity sucks up even light—hit Siberia and passed in an instant through Earth, emerging in the North Atlantic. The second asserts that an "anti-rock" of antimatter plunged into the atmosphere and exploded on contact with atoms of ordinary matter, producing a fireball of gamma rays. While this would account for the absence of residual material at the site, it is not, most experts say, compatible with observable physical effects of the blast. In the end, we do not know what caused the cataclysm in Siberia. We may never know. But today, fewer scientists than at any time in the past would be astounded to receive a message beamed from some corner of the universe inquiring into the fate of certain space voyagers who vanished on our planet in what we call the year 1908.

259

An American or Englishman who wants to indicate the numeral between two and four says "three." A Welshman says "tri," a Dutchman, "drie" — both with the same vowel sound as in English; a German says "drei." A Frenchman says "trois," an Italian, Swede, or Dane, "tre," a Spaniard or Latin American, "tres," a Romanian, "trei," and a Greek, "treis." A Lithuanian says "trys," a Russian or Yugoslav, "tri" — again with the English vowel sound. A Pakistani, a Bengali, or a Hindi-speaking Indian will all say "teen," while a Punjabi will say "tin." All these words are pretty clearly related: all begin with a "dental" consonant (one formed with the tongue against the teeth) — T, D, or TH — and nearly all follow it with an R. The vowels sounds are nearly all EE, EH, or AH, or a combination of them (thus "drei" blends AH and EE).

The similarities among all these terms for the same number reflect a fundamental relationship among the languages in question: they are linguistic cousins. Along with a number of other tongues, both modern and extinct, they are members of what is called the Indo-European language family. The modern representatives of this family are spoken by nearly all the inhabitants of Europe, the Americas, northern Asia and the northern and central parts of the Indian peninsula, plus Afghanistan, Iran, Sri Lanka (Ceylon), Australia and New Zealand, and several millions in South Africa. Collectively, they are the native tongues of about half the human race.

We owe our first awareness of this far-flung family of languages to the labors of a British jurist in India, Sir William Jones, who around 1780 set out to learn Sanskrit. Jones' original intention was simply to familiarize himself with the principles of native Indian law, many of whose basic documents were written in the ancient Sanskrit tongue — long since extinct as a spoken language. Like any educated Englishman of his day, however, Jones had studied Greek and Latin in school, and much to his surprise, he began encountering Sanskrit words showing clear similarities to words of the same or similar meaning to the classical tongues. The Sanskrit for "three" was *trayas*, comparable to the Latin *tres* and Classic Greek *trias*;

◀OVERLEAF *(pages 260-261): Speakers of the Indo-European tongue may have owed their expansion in part to their use of wheeled vehicles and draft animals. This relief shows Hittites in war chariots (with old Persian writing superimposed in white). The Hittite and Old Persian languages were descended from Indo-European.*

ISTANBUL MUSEUM. YAN PHOTO   ANKARA MUSEUM. PHOTO BY JOSEPHINE POWELL

Sanskrit *panca*, "five," resembled Greek *pente*, while the numbers from seven to nine, *sapta*, *ashta* and *nava* recalled the Latin *septem*, *octo* and *novem*. Sanskrit *sarpa*, "snake," was surely kin to Latin *serpens*; *rajan*, "king," was close to Latin *regem*; and *devas*, "god," resembled Latin *divus*, "divine."

These and innumerable other similarities, in both vocabulary and grammar, led Jones to a striking conclusion, which he presented in an address to the Asiatic Society in Calcutta on February 2, 1786. The Sanskrit language, he declared, bears to both Greek and Latin "a stronger affinity, both in the roots of verbs and in the forms of grammar, than could possibly have been produced by accident; so strong, indeed, that no philologer could examine them all three without believing them to have sprung from some common source, which, perhaps, no longer exists." There were similar, though less forceful reasons, he added, for linking Sanskrit to the Celtic and Teutonic tongues — the latter group, of course, including English.

Unwittingly, Jones had launched a revolution in linguistics — which in turn opened up a major archaeological mystery. His brilliant linguistic conjecture has been fully confirmed by nearly two centuries of research: we now know that not only the languages he mentioned but also the Slavic and two of the three Baltic tongues, the Iranian languages of Iran and Afghanistan, as well as a number of less prominent languages and dialects, must all have evolved from a single ancestor — in much the same way as all the Romance languages much later evolved from Latin. This "common source" — which, as Jones suggested, no longer exists — is now known as Proto-Indo-European, or simply Indo-European.

If an Indo-European language once existed, it must have been spoken by an Indo-European people. English, now spoken on every continent, descends from the Anglo-Saxon dialect of a few tribes living along the North Sea coasts of modern Germany and Denmark; Latin, parent of the Romance languages, was once merely the dialect of Latium (the district of Italy just south of the Tiber). Equally, Indo-European must once have been spoken by some tribe or group of tribes inhabiting an equally circumscribed area, whence their multiplying descendants carried the language, in dozens of variations, across the world.

And here is our mystery. We know, or can reasonably guess, a good deal about the Indo-Europeans —

in some respects, more than about some much more recent peoples such as the Etruscans. Though Indo-European was never recorded in writing, linguistic science has reconstructed much of its vocabulary—and through its vocabulary, the lives of those who spoke it. Knowing what the Indo-Europeans talked about, we are bound to know a good deal about what they did, and even what they thought—the nature of the gods they worshipped, fragments of the poetry their bards chanted. Yet with all this, we do not know with any certainty where they lived, or when. Scholars have placed them in Greece, Asia Minor, central Europe, eastern Germany, southern Russia, and the north Caucasus, and have dated them anywhere from 2500 to 8000 B.C. But there is still not a single potsherd, stone axe, or bone awl of which we can say, positively, "An Indo-European made this." Artifacts are mute, and though they can tell us many things about their makers, they cannot speak with their makers' tongues.

The search for the Indo-Europeans involves putting together fragmentary clues from a range of scholarly disciplines—linguistics, geography, ecology, and archaeology—and seeing if they can be maneuvered into any kind of plausible fit. Through linguistics, we can reconstruct words that reveal the natural environment they lived in; through geography and ecology we can then delimit areas corresponding to that type of environment; through archaeology, finally, we can—perhaps—identify some known human culture whose location, way of life, and subsequent spread matches what we have deduced about the Indo-Europeans. But even so we will emerge with no more than a balance of probabilities. The time and place where our remote linguistic forebears lived can be conjectured but not known for sure.

Before we embark on our search, however, one important point needs to be made: though "Indo-European" must once have meant a people and a culture as well as a language, it is today a purely linguistic concept. Some German scholars in the past made play with the notion of an "Indo-European race," and still refer to the Indo-European languages as "Indo-Germanic"—which gives rather short shrift to the Greeks, Latins, Slavs, and Celts. The Nazis, of course, carried this linguistic nationalism to its illogical conclusion, identifying the "German race" as the "Aryans"—a term which properly applies only to the branch of the Indo-Europeans that invaded India

around 1500 B.C. In fact we have no way of knowing whether even the original Indo-Europeans were a "pure race"—assuming the term means anything. What is absolutely certain is that as their descendants spread across the world, carrying their languages with them, they encountered and interbred with peoples of the most diverse hues and features. As proof, one need only contrast the appearance of an Irishman, a Scandinavian, a Russian, a Greek, an Armenian, an Afghan, a Bengali. All of them are Indo-Europeans in language, yet none of them are wholly Indo-European by heredity, and some, for all anyone knows, may be wholly non-Indo-European. Indo-European languages are a fact, and so—perhaps—are Indo-European cultural remains, but there are no Indo-European genes that anyone can identify.

We may start our detective work by examining the family tree of the Indo-European languages, living and dead. Like any tree, its structure divides into major limbs, and the latter into branches which in turn divide into individual twigs—i.e., actual languages or dialects. The full spread of these languages, from the Indo-Iranian limb in the east to the Germanic and Celtic limbs in the west, is shown in the chart on pages 270–271. The present state of health of the various limbs varies greatly. The Anatolian languages—their best-known representative is Hittite—are all extinct. The Celtic tongues survive only in a fringe along the Atlantic coast of Europe; they include Breton, Welsh, and the Gaelic of western Scotland and Ireland. Cornish, however, vanished from Cornwall some two hundred years ago, while the Manx dialect of Gaelic disappeared from the Isle of Man during this century. By contrast, the largest and most vigorous limb is the Germanic, which in turn splits into three major branches. The eastern branch, now extinct, included the various dialects of Gothic; the northern branch includes all the modern Scandinavian tongues and Icelandic, along with their common ancestor, Old Norse. Its western branch, finally, includes German, Yiddish, Dutch-Flemish, Afrikaans, and English—the last, of course, the world's most important language in terms of both its geographical spread and the number of its speakers.

During the past five centuries the Indo-European tongues have spread east and west far beyond their previous extent. For philologists seeking to reconstruct the ancestral tongue, however, this recent spread is irrelevant, and even the modern members of the family are of limited interest. Much more useful are the oldest recorded members of the various branches, which, being closest in time to the original common source, resemble it more than do any of their descendants. These Indo-European great-grandparents include Hittite, Sanskrit, Mycenaean Greek, and Old Persian. From a somewhat later period come Old Latin, dating from several centuries before our era, and (still later) Gothic, classical Armenian, and Old Church Slavonic—all recorded in early translations of the Bible.

By studying and comparing words of the same and similar meaning in descendant languages, linguistic scholars can reconstruct the original Indo-European "roots" of those words; by similar comparisons, they can deduce the grammatical rules by which the words were combined into sentences. They are certain, for example, that Indo-European was a highly inflected language, like classical Greek and Latin and modern Russian; that is, the function of a word within a sentence depended on which of various endings was added to a fundamental root. Thus the word *kerwos, "stag," (its English descendant is the archaic "hart") consists of the root *ker-, "horn," plus a noun suffix, -wo (that is, "the horned thing") plus an ending, -s, indicating that this particular stag was the subject of a sentence. (Forms preceded by an asterisk, such as *kerwos, are reconstructed—that is, they are not attested in writing.) We find relics of this system in English verbs—thus, "go," "go-es," "go-ing," and "go-ne." Other Indo-European syntactic changes were indicated by a change in the root vowel—as in English, "sing," "sang," "sung."

The Indo-Europeans also created new words by combining old ones, as have many of their linguistic descendants (thus, English "housewife," "strike-breaker," "blue-eyed," and so on). Such combinations, it appears, were specially common in Indo-European bardic poetry; philologists have reconstructed some of them, such as *klewos ngwzhitom, "imperishable fame," and *isarom menos, "strong-holy mind." Many similar epithets crop up in Homer— "rosy-fingered dawn," "wine-dark sea," "swift-footed Achilles" and the like. The poet himself was *wekwom teksos, "word-weaver." Similar compounds were often used for personal names, as can be seen in many historic names from Indo-European tongues: thus the Greek Sophocles meant "famed for wisdom," the

Slavic Wenceslaus, "having greater glory." The name of the Celtic chieftain Vercingetorix, who almost defeated Julius Caesar, appropriately meant "warrior king," while that of the Persian monarch Xerxes, equally appropriately, meant "ruling men." Similar examples are not uncommon in modern English (Shakespeare, Goldsmith, Wainwright) and Irish (Kennedy, meaning "hideous head").

More directly relevant to our search are Indo-European words that enable us to reconstruct—albeit cautiously—their way of life and their environment. The caution is necessary because words change their meanings as well as their sounds with time, and when the meanings have diverged widely it is sometimes impossible to be certain what the original significance was. Thus *teks- meant to "weave" (whence "textile"), but also to build house walls by weaving wattle (whence "architect") and even "to fabricate" in various other ways (whence "technology").

Nonetheless, when we find, for example, that the noun "plow" is arör in Icelandic, ëar in Old English, aratron in Greek, aratrum in Latin, arathar in Irish, arklas in Lithuanian and araur in Armenian, it seems safe to conclude that the Indo-Europeans possessed plows of some sort, which they called something like *arö-trom. The obvious conclusion—that they were farmers—is strengthened by such reconstructions as *grno- (whence both "grain" and "corn"), *mel- (whence "mill") and *yeug- ("yoke").

Yoking animals—presumably to pull the plow— points to domesticated cattle (*gwou-, whence "cow.") We also find words for "sheep" (*awi-, whence "ewe") and lamb, for swine (*su-) and piglet (*porko-). The horse (*ekwo-. whence "equestrian") was also known, but not necessarily domesticated. Perhaps significantly, the Indo-Europeans may not have had a specific word for "young horse"; (the English "foal" and "filly" come from a root—*pu-lo— which may originally have meant merely "young animal"). The dog (*kwon-, whence both "hound" and "canine") was present—domesticated, surely, since the wolf (*wklwo) was also known. Less useful domestic animals were the *mus and *lus.

The Indo-Europeans lived in houses (*domo-, whence "domestic"), probably with walls of wattle daubed with mud, and certainly with some sort of door (*dhwer-)—though this term may originally have meant the gateway to the compound where the family and its livestock lived. Gathered around the

This clay model of a four-wheeled cart, probably drawn by oxen, was made in the third millennium B.C. It was found in Hungary, along the route taken by peoples expanding outward from the Russian steppes. The existence of Indo-European word roots for vehicle, wheel, axle, and yoke suggests that the originators of the language were familiar with this method of travel.

domestic fire, (*pur-), they dined on cakes or porridge made from *grno- (probably both wheat and barley), and on meat from their animals—mainly, no doubt, their lambs, piglets and calves, the older animals being more useful for plowing, breeding and milk (*melg-). On occasion, the menu included fish (*pisk-), including the *laks- (usually interpreted as "salmon," whenc "lox"). For sweetening, wild bees (*bhei-) provided honey (*melit-, whence ultimately "molasses"), which was sometimes fermented into mead (*medhu-) for ceremonial or celebratory drinking. Clothing—or some of it—was made of wool (*wel-), spun (*spen-) into thread (*tretu-) which was then woven (*webh-) into cloth that was sewn (*syu-) into garments; other garments may have been made from the fibers of flax (*lino-, whence "linen"). The Indo-Europeans seem to have known copper (just possibly, bronze), but probably as a rather rare, imported material, since almost no other metallurgical terms have been reconstructed; most tools were presumably made of wood, bone, or stone (stoi-nō).

Lord of the household was the father (*pōter). His position is attested by several linguistic clues, among them the presence of more specific terms for the marital relationships of a woman (thus, "daughter-in-law") than for those of a man; evidently, when a woman married she moved to her husband's house, not vice versa. Moreover, in the mythology of all the Indo-European peoples who have left written records, the head god was invariably male. Sometimes he was known simply as *dyeu-, whence Jove, Zeus, the Norse Tyr and the Germanic Tiu (memorialized in "Tuesday"), but sometimes as *dyeu-pōter. "god-the-father"—whence Jupiter. Since *dyeu- also meant "shine," this god must have personified the sun or sky—as Jupiter, Zeus, and Tiu indeed did.

As the *pōter ruled the *mōter and their *sunu- and *dhugater-, so the chief (*reg-) ruled the clan or village (*weik-). Since *reg-, with a shortened vowel, also meant "move in a straight line," the *reg- doubtless led the people when concerted action was necessary, as in warfare or when the tribe shifted its village to a new site (as we shall see, this may have been often). But he seems also to have performed sacred functions, mediating between *dyeu- and *man-.

We come now to our central question: where and when did the Indo-Europeans live? They knew snow (*sneighw-), but had no words for "palm," "lion," "tiger," or "camel," and thus evidently did not live in the tropics. They also had no words for "vine," "olive," "laurel," "ass," "island," or—probably—for "sea" (the English word comes from a purely Germanic root), which would rule out the subtropical lands along the Mediterranean. On the other hand, the lack of terms for "spruce," "fir," "lemming," "grouse," and "ptarmigan" seems to rule out northern Europe or Asia.

So much for environmental words that are missing; what words were present? For animals, in addition to the domesticated species listed above, we have the (wild?) horse, wolf, bear, beaver (*bhibru-), and otter. For vegetation we have the birch (bherag-), ash (*as-), beech (*bhago-), oak, willow, maple, elm, and alder. Not all these names are known with equal certainty, but collectively they add up to the type of deciduous forest or open woodland found in a broad belt between the Mediterranean and Baltic lands, and stretching from the Atlantic to the Urals; a much smaller area of similar vegetation lies north of the Caucasus mountains.

Before winding up this environmental discussion, we had better take a quick look at a question which has bedeviled Indo-European studies for several generations: the "lox problem." If *laks- indeed meant the Atlantic salmon, as many scholars have claimed, this would place the Indo-European homeland in northern or western Europe, since the fish is found only in streams and rivers draining into the Atlantic and Baltic (rather than the Mediterranean and Black seas). However, modern studies of European fresh-water fish show plenty of salmon-*like* fish in these more southerly and easterly regions. One is the salmon-trout, whose many subspecies include the brown trout and the lake trout—both of which can reach salmon size under favorable conditions. Another likely candidate is the *huchen*, found throughout the Danube and adjacent Dniester basins, which, apart from its slender build, looks almost exactly like a salmon. Any of these fish could have been the original *laks-*, whose name was then transferred to the true salmon by such Indo-Europeans as came to know it, just as English settlers in America applied their word "robin" to a bird which, apart from its reddish breast, is not much like the European robin. Significantly, the Russians, who know the *huchen*, the salmon-trout, and salmon, refer to all of them as various kinds of *lososh*—a word which derives from *laks-*. So it now appears that we may forget about the salmon in trying to pin down the Indo-European homeland.

We have placed the Indo-European farmer-herdsmen somewhere in or near the deciduous forest belt of Europe; this immediately allows us to narrow down the time span in which they occupied their homeland. Farming cultures did not reach this environmental zone of the world much before 6000 B.C., when people and influences from the Aegean moved north into the Danube basin. Thereafter, farming spread north, west, and east from this center, reaching the north European plain around 5000 B.C., western Europe around 4500 B.C., and the Volga-Don region of Russia about the same time. (All of these regions except western Europe have been named as possible locations for the Indo-European homeland.) Clearly 6000 B.C. is the *earliest* possible date when the Indo-European culture, as reconstructed from its language, could have flourished.

Setting a latest possible date is more problematical, in part because we are not talking about some single, datable event. At one time, the initial Indo-European dispersion from their homeland was seen in terms of what later specialists sardonically nicknamed the "campfire theory." The Indo-Europeans, that is, were visualized as all seated around the tribal campfire and then, at some given moment, standing up, gathering their household goods, and setting off in all directions. In fact, the dispersion must surely have taken place gradually, over many, many genera-

tions. Thus what we are talking about is not the date of *the* Indo-European dispersion, but merely when that process began.

The only useful evidence on this—and it is far less precise than one would like—is the degree of difference among various ancient tongues that are descended from the original Indo-European. Since languages change with time, the degree to which they have changed reflects—very roughly—the amount of time they have been changing. Thus most of us can read *Hamlet* (c. A.D. 1600), albeit with some difficulty, while the *Canterbury Tales* (c. 1400), despite the many familiar words they contain, make little sense unless rendered into modern English. And when it comes to *Beowulf* (c. 900), we might as well be reading German or Dutch, so different is its Old English from the language we speak today.

Putting it another way, when two groups of people speaking the same language become geographically separated, their languages will take divergent courses of evolution—if the separation continues long enough, to the point where they are speaking two mutually unintelligible tongues. Consequently, the differences in grammar and vocabulary between two related languages measure—very roughly—how long ago their speakers became separated. We can see this process at work in the many differences in pronunciation and vocabulary between American and British English, though the two peoples separated physically only a few centuries ago and have remained in loose contact, via the printed and (later) broadcast word, ever since. The two tongues are still mutually intelligible, but not completely so: while educated Americans and Englishmen can converse quite freely, a London Cockney and an Alabama farmhand can exchange information only with some difficulty.

Another familiar example is the Romance languages. These, as we know, all derive from Latin, but became separated as Roman legionaries, officials, and merchants spread across Europe; the process must have begun at least seventeen hundred years ago. As one would expect, all these languages are mutually unintelligible—yet anyone who has studied two of them (say, French and Spanish) is aware they are much more like one another than either is like English.

The earliest documented Indo-European languages, as indicated above, are Hittite, Mycenaean Greek, and Sanskrit. The Hittite documents, written in the cuneiform script borrowed from Mesopotamia,

Over an area stretching from Iceland in the west to India in the east, the word for "mother" sounds similar in nearly every language, evidence to philologists of the range of the Indo-European tongue. Comparing this and other such cognates, they have isolated or reconstructed over 1,300 word roots that they say must have originated in a single language.

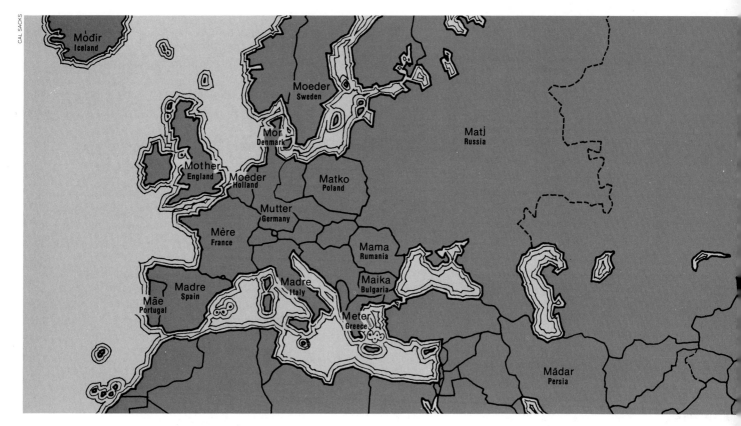

date from around 1500 B.C. or perhaps a little earlier. The Greek texts, in the Mycenaean Linear B script, date from around 1400 B.C. The Sanskrit documents, written in a native script, date from much later, but represent very accurately the language spoken in northern India shortly after 1400 B.C., which was preserved intact for cultural and religious reasons. Thus we have three Indo-European languages of roughly the same age—and they are already very different languages—far more different than the Romance languages. The obvious conclusion is that by 1400 B.C. these languages must already have been separated for considerably longer than the 1,700 years that the Romance languages have been evolving more or less independently. The smallest conceivable period would seem to be 2,000 years, and many Indo-Europeanists such as Calvert Watkins of Harvard feel that double the Romance period, or some 3,500 years, is none too long a span to account for the differences among these early Indo-European tongues. On this reasoning, the Indo-Europeans most likely existed as a single people some time between (in round figures) 6000 and 5000 B.C., and certainly no later than 3500 B.C.

There is one possible snag in locating the Indo-Europeans this early: the existence in several branches of related words for "wheel." These include the Greek *kyklos* (whence "bi-cycle"), the Old Church Slavonic *kolo*, the Sanskrit *cakra*, and the Germanic root of "wheel" itself. The wheel was invented, probably somewhere between the Caucasus and Mesopotamia, some time before 3500 B.C., but there is no evidence that it reached any part of the Indo-European "environmental zone" much before 3000 B.C.—too late for the time span we have bracketed. However, the conflict may be more apparent than real. The original meaning of the relevant Indo-European root, *kwel-* seems to have been simply "to turn" (derivatives in both the Germanic and Italic tongues concern the neck—"what the head turns on") and even "to dwell" in a locality (another Italic derivative is found in "colony"). It seems likely enough, then, that the first Indo-European group to encounter the wheel coined a name for it from this root—and passed on the name, along with the wheel itself, to some other Indo-European groups. History

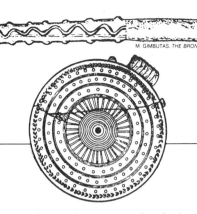

M. GIMBUTAS, *THE BRONZE AGE CULTURES OF CENTRAL AND EASTERN EUROPE*.

shows that new technologies carry their specialized vocabularies along with them more often than not: for example, "alcohol" and "alembic," both derived from the Arabic, testify that the technique of distillation originated in the Arabic world, whence it spread to Christian Europe.

Having roughly bracketed the period when the Indo-Europeans existed, we can now examine some archaeological theories of where they existed — that is, attempts to identify particular cultural remains as Indo-European. The two leading theories can be described as the Kurganian-Steppe theory and the Danubian theory.

The Kurganian-Steppe theory exists in a number of different versions. One of the better known — and the one most compatible with the time frame we have been talking about — is put forward by Marija Gimbutas of U.C.L.A. She, like most other partisans of this theory, identifies the ancentral Indo-Europeans with the so-called Kurgan culture of southern Russia and the Ukraine — so named from the "kurgans" or burial mounds that are prominent among their relics.

According to Gimbutas, the Kurgan people first become identifiable around 4500 B.C., in the area between the Don and Volga rivers. The region, now a flat grassland, with patches of woodland mainly along watercourses, was somewhat moister at that time, with rather more woodland. The Kurganians, as Gimbutas describes them, were "predominantly pastoral," herding cattle, sheep, and horses, and keeping pigs. Horses seem to have been by all odds the most important, with their bones accounting for 70 per cent to 80 per cent of the domesticated animal bones in early Kurgan settlements. Though agriculture was practiced, it was "not highly developed," and indeed the evidence she cites — a few sickles and grinding stones — does not point to extensive agriculture, or even necessarily to agriculture as all. (They could have been used for harvesting and grinding wild grass seeds, as such artifacts were in some other preagricultural cultures). From the apparent fact that the Kurganians herded horses, she deduces that they must have been able to ride, claiming that controlling a herd of horses on foot is "inconceivable." The

Kurganians made some pottery, and perhaps used copper — though there is no evidence that they had learned to smelt it.

Between 4500 and 4000 B.C., as Gimbutas tells it, the Kurganians expanded westward, eastward, and southward, "searching for pasture lands." Thus they typically settled "in flat grasslands," a landscape favorable to horse and cattle grazing. As they expanded westward, they overcame and absorbed several more settled agricultural societies such as the Tripolye and Cucuteni cultures of the southern Ukraine. The decisive elements in this successful expansion were the use of horses for riding — and, presumably, for mounting archers — and the acquisition of "fighting carts" — wagons with solid wooden wheels, drawn by oxen.

Beginning around 4000 B.C., according to Gimbutas, the growing "hordes of pastoralists" expanded into the Danube basin, and over the next thousand years took over most of the farming cultures of the Balkans and Central Europe and began moving vigorously north, northwest, and northeast from that area. A little later, beginning around 2500 B.C., the easternmost wing of the Kurganians moved from the steppes across the Caucasus, infiltrating southwest into Asia Minor, where they presumably became the ancestors of the Anatolian Indo-Europeans, and south into Iran, as the ancestors of the Indo-Iranians.

The chief thing that must be said about Gimbutas' version of the Kurganian-Steppe theory is that despite a brilliant job of marshaling archaeological facts in support of it, her arguments go far beyond the facts. She says, for example, that the Kurganians "must have been seafarers" on the Black Sea; there is no "must" about it. The only actual facts she cites in support of this claim are that the Indo-Europeans possessed a word for "boat" (*nau-*, whence "nautical") and probably one for "rowing"; to expand a rowboat into a seagoing ship takes either a lot more evidence — which does not exist — or a lot of imagination. We should not forget, moreover, that the Indo-Europeans probably did *not* have a word for "sea" — Black or otherwise.

Equally, there is no archaeological evidence for mounted archers — in "hordes" or otherwise — until much later, and the same is true for "fighting" or any other kind of carts. In any case, ox carts moving at two or three miles per hour could hardly have played any decisive role in warfare. Indo-European pig keeping does not fit the picture of a seminomadic grassland folk. Swine are forest animals (in ancient times, they were typically fattened on acorns and beechnuts), and moreover are virtually impossible to drive over any distance; European folklore is full of tales emphasizing the difficulty of moving the animals even the few miles from home to market. Finally, if the Kurganians were indeed "searching for pasture lands" in flat, grassy country, one wonders what they were searching for in the densely forested and often hilly terrain of central and western Europe.

There is general, if not universal, agreement among archaeologists that at some point in prehistory the Kurganians, or some related steppe people — very possibly speaking a language of Indo-European origin — did overrun much of Europe. But according to most archaeologists this movement began a good deal later — anywhere from 3500 to 3000 B.C. These dates would perhaps allow the Kurganians. carts, which though useless for fighting would have given them mobility both in following their herds and in migration. The same dates would, or at any rate could, have given them bronze weapons, which would have provided a much more decisive military advantage than putative mounted archers or fighting oxcarts. Various other experts have indeed cited these possibilities in identifying the Kurganian expansion — whether from the grasslands, or from the more wooded parts of the southern Ukraine — as the original Indo-European expansion. The trouble with these theories is that if one puts the Kurganians late enough in time to have either wheels or bronze weapons, they are also too late to fit the time frame we have already described. Thus Calvert Watkins, for example, believes that the Kurganians were indeed Indo-Europeans, but sees the date of their expansion as too late to allow for the radical differences in Indo-European languages as of around 1500 B.C.

These and many other aspects of the Kurganian expansion involve technical and disputed questions about the interpretation and dating of archaeological evidence. What is not disputed by any of the partisans of this theory, however, is that the Kurganian conquest, however and whenever it occurred, must have happened at a time when Europe had *already* been settled by farming peoples, a process which was essentially complete by around 4500 B.C. — which is to say that the population of Europe was already

beginning to be fairly numerous. The Kurganians, if they indeed were predominantly pastoral, must have been relatively less numerous, since pastureland yields considerably less food than agricultural cropland. Thus the Kurganian conquest must have been much as Gimbutas describes it: "an infiltration . . . by Indo-European warriors who subsequently formed a superstratum in conquered lands." This means that a large part, perhaps most, of the population in the conquered lands would have been non-Indo-European. And this, in turn raises the thorny question: what became of the language (or languages) that these people spoke?

History tells us that when a people speaking one language is conquered by one speaking another, only one of the two tongues will survive — but there is no telling which. Conquest brought Greek into Greece, Sanskrit into India, and Latin into western Europe. On the other hand, the Vikings who secured Normandy in A.D. 911 exchanged their Norse tongue for a dialect of French within a few generations — and when some of them conquered England in 1066, exchanged French for English within a couple of centuries. The only general rule seems to be that no matter which language disappears, it does not disappear without a trace: it will make its contribution, great or small, to the vocabulary (and sometimes also the grammar and phonetics) of its successor. To take a familiar example, the French that the Normans brought into England had all but vanished as a spo-

269

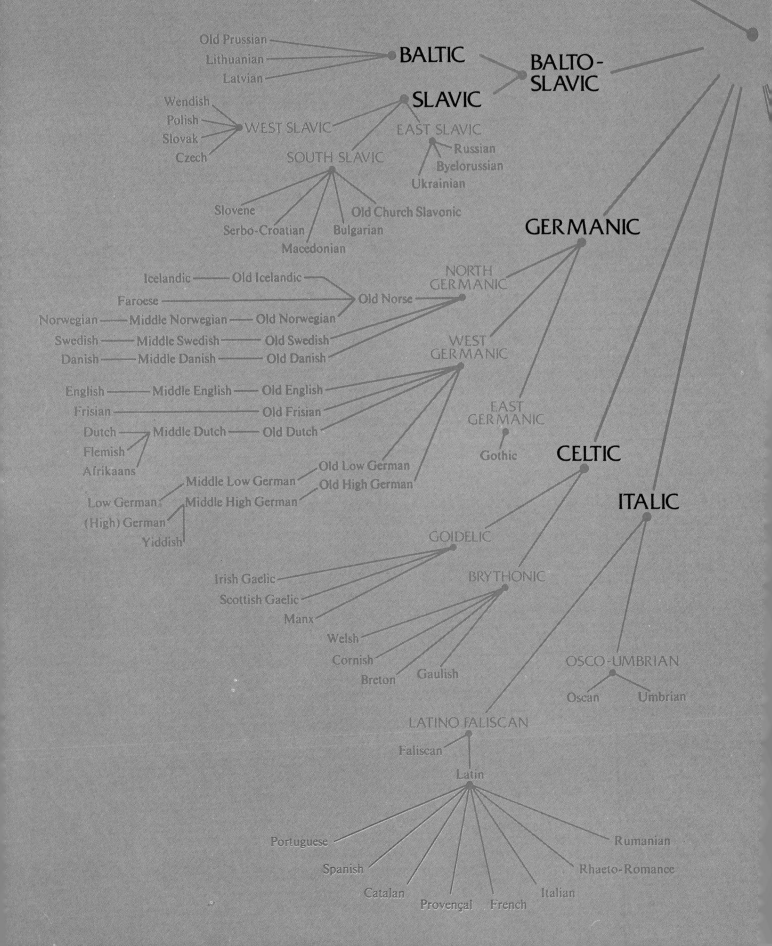

INDO-EUROPEAN

Old Prussian
Lithuanian
Latvian
BALTIC

BALTO-SLAVIC

Wendish
Polish
Slovak
Czech
WEST SLAVIC
SLAVIC
EAST SLAVIC
Russian
Byelorussian
Ukrainian
SOUTH SLAVIC

Slovene
Serbo-Croatian
Macedonian
Bulgarian
Old Church Slavonic

GERMANIC

Icelandic — Old Icelandic
Faroese — Old Norse
Norwegian — Middle Norwegian — Old Norwegian
NORTH GERMANIC
Swedish — Middle Swedish — Old Swedish
Danish — Middle Danish — Old Danish

WEST GERMANIC

English — Middle English — Old English
Frisian — Old Frisian
Dutch — Middle Dutch — Old Dutch
Flemish
Afrikaans

EAST GERMANIC
Gothic

Old Low German
Old High German

Middle Low German
Low German
(High) German
Middle High German
Yiddish

CELTIC

ITALIC

GOIDELIC

Irish Gaelic
Scottish Gaelic
Manx

BRYTHONIC

Welsh
Cornish
Breton
Gaulish

OSCO-UMBRIAN

Oscan
Umbrian

LATINO FALISCAN

Faliscan

Latin

Portuguese
Spanish
Catalan
Provençal
French
Italian
Rhaeto-Romance
Rumanian

WHAT IS THE SECRET OF BRITAIN'S CHALK GIANTS?

Stretching 360 feet across a green hillside of the Wessex Downs is a stark white horse, delineated by bold swaths cut deep into the sward to an underlying chalk surface. Left to nature, this peculiar artwork—known as the White Horse of Uffington (shown on the opposite page)—would rapidly disappear under encroaching weeds. But for nearly 2,000 years the countrymen of western England have fought back the vegetation and cleansed the gouges that comprise the equine figure. And not one of these faithful attendants has ever been able to explain the local compulsion to preserve the White Horse. Nor does history record who constructed it—or what it signifies.

The White Horse is only one of nearly a score of such chalk renderings in the west country. Most of the earth drawings of horses in neighboring counties, however, are far more recent—eighteenth- and nineteenth-century chronicles describe the carving of these figures by local artisans moved, possibly, by whimsy or by envy of neighboring representations. The White Horse of Uffington and one other chalk outline—the Giant Warrior (or God?) of Cerne (above, right) —are dated by antiquarians to around the first century B.C., on the eve of the Roman conquest of Britain.

Though their motives are unknown, the creators of the White Horse accomplished a mammoth piece of artwork. Placed well up the steep slopes of a 500-foot hill, the horse was constructed by carving deeply through the

sod to the solid chalk surface of the downs. The swaths in many areas are actually terraces—banked up in some places—and the horse's eye is a leveled platform raised above deeper trenches in the surrounding chalk. Slightly longer than the length of a football field from tail to forehead, the horse measures 130 feet at its maximum height. The Cerne Giant, on the other hand, is of simpler construction: ditches scratched into the sward. But the giant's proportions are nonetheless impressive, pacing out at 180 feet from head to toe, and 167 feet across from tip of the club to opposite hand.

Atop the hill where the White Horse is carved are the remains of a hill-fort called Uffington Castle, and between the castle and the figure is an oval mound where excavations in 1857 turned up 46 Roman burials. To the north is a flattened natural hillock, called Dragon's Hill, which is a prominent feature in local legend. One of the earliest recorded accounts of the White Horse is an entry in the Cartulary of Abbingdon abbey, and in thirteenth- and fourteenth-century documents, the Horse is mentioned several times in connection with accounts of nearby land tenures. The first attempt to explain its origin in more recent times was Dr. Francis Wise's published speculation in 1738 that the creature was carved to commemorate King Alfred's victory over the Danes at Ashdown in 871. Though at least one contemporary disagreed rather violently, due to the lack of any evidence, Wise's theory was generally accepted until fairly recently. Archaeologists now believe that both the White Horse and the Cerne Giant were created between 100 B.C. and A.D. 43. And in the case of the Horse, part of the proof is its un-

usual attenuated and disjointed shape, which closely resembles horses depicted upon Celtic coins minted towards the end of the early Iron Age.

The cleansing, or "scouring," of the chalk outlines appears to have been a lively event in the often dreary lives of the west country folk. Villagers turned out with hoe and scythe once every seven years—the normal date being Whitsuntide, which is celebrated the seventh Sunday after Easter. The scouring was accompanied by festivals and merrymaking, and the caretakers of the Cerne Giant danced around a maypole—raising a hearty hue and cry from local clergymen who decried the pagan rites and the real or imagined debauchery. Churchmen were especially scandalized by local lore that advised barren wives to sleep overnight upon the most appropriate part of the virile Giant to magically induce pregnancy. Rites such as these are among the evidence which suggest to modern archaeologists that the chalk horse and giant probably trace back to animistic religious practices of the ancient Celts. Stuart Piggott, the celebrated British archaeologist, is especially intrigued by the proximity of Dragon's Hill to the White Horse. Legend has it that St. George slew the Dragon upon this hill, and Piggott speculates that the Christian saint may be a replacement of an earlier Celtic demigod who was closely associated with horses. But no one knows why ancient Englishmen chose to etch upon the earth such mythic figures—or for what divine gaze they might have been offered as a sign of devotion.

WHAT CAUSED THE COLLAPSE OF THE MAYA?

A small toy deer from Veracruz proves that pre-Columbian Indians were familiar with the principle of the wheel; yet for some unexplained reason they did not put that knowledge to practical use. No evidence exists of any wheeled vehicles or draft animals in the Americas.
LEE BOLTIN

the remains of living and eating areas, the distribution of tools and objects and the like, archaeologists have been able to reconstruct some aspects of the villagers' life. The staple of their diet was maize, supplemented with some game and vegetables. A few families made stone knives or shell ornaments which they exchanged with their neighbors or with other villages that lay nearby. The various families in each village were linked one with another by hereditary lines of descent, each lineage claiming a mythical ancestor like the were-jaguar or the fire serpent. The same lineages also linked one village to another in organizations whose leaders played the chief roles in village religious rituals.

Every village was also a link in an elaborate network of trade that extended over hundreds of miles, from one valley to the next, from the highlands of the interior down to the Gulf and Pacific coasts. Villages far apart exchanged cakes of salt for maize, obsidian (a volcanic rock used for making fine knives) for many essential foodstuffs and other necessities. People of the highlands were eager to obtain oyster shells which they used for their own adornment. They also imported quantities of stingray spines, sharks' teeth, conch shells, and turtle shells—all of which were necessities for religious ceremonies. Such shells have been found buried at highland settlements far from either the Atlantic or Pacific coast. So we know that even as early as 1200 B.C. the trade networks were in operation.

The mythical spirits that controlled the destinies of the villages were worshiped through human intermediaries—men of high rank who maintained shrines and used the conch shells and the turtle-shell drums in their rituals. There were personal rites as well, in which marine fish spines were used to draw blood. The practice of self-mutilation, as a form of penance to assure divine favor, continued until the time of the Spanish conquests. Sixteenth century chroniclers have described how Aztec priests used stingray spines to draw blood from their tongues, lips, ear lobes, and sexual organs. The more eminent one's rank, the more torture was necessary.

Those who conducted village rites were also closely engaged in the importation of the special and exotic shells they needed. The objects of commercial and religious significance found in these buildings suggest that as they gained control over the trade, they also assumed administrative power over

public religion and, to some extent, economic life. The stage was in this way set for the emergence of a priestly ruling class, with potentially great economic and sacred powers.

By three thousand years ago village life was on the threshold of major social and economic change. The settlement pattern in both highlands and lowlands had changed, as some villages grew larger and wealthier than others. The religious leaders in these communities began to live in their own special enclaves, close to large buildings erected on stone or earth platforms. Since stingray spines and conch shells have been found in these buildings, they were presumably public temples. The more elaborate communities were spaced out at regular intervals, as if each held sway over a specific region. The smaller villages not only supported themselves but also sent produce to the larger ones, perhaps as taxation for the support of those who now controlled the trade and religious life of the countryside. The most telling signs of social change during this period are the burials. For the first time in the history of this area the archaeological record shows more elaborate grave furniture deposited in some burials than in others.

The direction that society was now taking can be seen most vividly in one of Mesoamerica's most ancient civilizations—that of the Olmec in the Gulf Coast lowlands of southern Veracruz and western Tabasco. "Olmec" means "rubber people," for their homeland has long been famous for rubber production. The region is humid and low-lying, as well as densely forested; communication is difficult and any agriculture requires extensive forest clearance. But by 1250 B.C. the Olmec people had developed this land in a pattern of settlement unique to Meso-

287

america. As their numbers increased, they did not congregate in cities, as people did at a similar stage of development in Mesopotamia or other centers of early civilization. They continued to live in villages, scattered through the forest. But at more or less regular intervals they built impressive centers for ceremonial, civic, and perhaps also commercial use. Each of these centers was the focal point for the life and culture of some ten thousand people.

The Olmec ceremonial precincts were overlooked by carved stone idols of peculiarly menacing aspect. Some of them were eight feet tall or more, with sneering features and drooping lips, silent heads that gazed contemptuously into the distance. Olmec art depicts the legendary figures of Mesoamerican mythology—the were-jaguar, half human and half cat, and the fire serpent, figures revered to the very threshold of modern times. The were-jaguar occurs again and again, depicted with curiously infantile face, drooping lips, and large swollen eyes. Human figures display the same features, a convention that gives them a vicious and savage look.

More than mere decoration, Olmec art was rather a reflection of a pervasive religious ideology that spread far and wide through long-distance trade routes. But just as Olmec culture was becoming dominant in Mesoamerica, it suddenly collapsed. The breakdown can be observed at La Venta, one of its ceremonial centers. Many of its sculptures were deliberately mutilated, and the site abandoned forever. What happened? Was it warfare, starvation, or some other catastrophe? No one really knows. But there are some signs that the major ceremonial centers were making unbearable demands on the labor and production resources of their subject villages.

Despite the sudden collapse of the Olmecs' society, the religious and artistic revolution that they had begun continued unabated. Within 300 years a new Mesoamerican center had arisen at Teotihuacán in the Mexican highlands. This was not simply a ceremonial center, like those of the Olmecs or the later Maya, but a full-fledged city, covering an area of eight square miles. At its center rose the huge, truncated Pyramid of the Sun, 210 feet high and 650 feet square. A wooden temple on its summit looked down upon a great plaza and the long Avenue of the Dead. The Avenue was lined with public and religious buildings and led to another complex of plazas and pyramids to the north. To the south of the Pyramid of the Sun, near a well-organized, highly diversified marketplace, stood the temple of Quetzalcoatl, the Feathered Serpent, the greatest of ancient Mexico's gods. In its heyday Teotihuacán had a population of 120,000, living mostly in dense huddles of small houses, with courtyards separated by winding alleyways. A network of villages also surrounded the city —all ruled by the central authority at Teotihuacán.

Just as the city was entering a period of great artistic and architectural creativity, its political, economic, and religious fabric began to collapse. The first strains appear about A.D. 650. A century later the once proud ceremonial center had shrunk to little more than a series of hamlets extending over an area of about a square kilometer. Teotihuacán's collapse had been fully as sudden as that of the Olmec, but with one important difference: a highly structured and sophisticated state with an elaborate political, economic, and social organization had collapsed just as suddenly as the much simpler Olmec society of the lowlands.

For a long time archaeologists believed that it had been overrun and destroyed by warriors from northern Mexico. Indeed there are signs that the city was destroyed about A.D. 700. But this explanation is undoubtedly too simple. Even if there were invaders, why did the population decline so rapidly? If there had been a war, where are the defenses that one would expect a city with the resources of Teotihuacán to erect? Where did the invaders come from —was there an equally powerful city somewhere else? Or was there some unexpected economic stress on the government and the people at large that caused this huge state to crumble within a century? If so, no record of it has been found in the many excavations at Teotihuacán. But whatever the reasons, the demise of the city had important repercussions all over Mesoamerica, not least on the Maya of the lowlands.

In the first century B.C., when Teotihuacán was just getting underway, the Maya were still villagers living in thatched houses in the dense rain forest. This homeland was an area known as the Petén in the southern part of the Yucatán peninsula. They were farmers, subsisting on a diet of corn, beans, and squash, and they cleared their land by the slash-and-burn system; that is, they cut down the vegetation

The homeland of the Maya (between the straight black lines) comprised the Yucatán peninsula and adjoining areas of southern Mexico, Guatamala, and Belize. Their culture evolved first in the Petén jungle around A.D. 300 and, over the course of the next six centuries, spread south to Copán, west along the Usumacinta River and north to the hilly Puuc region.

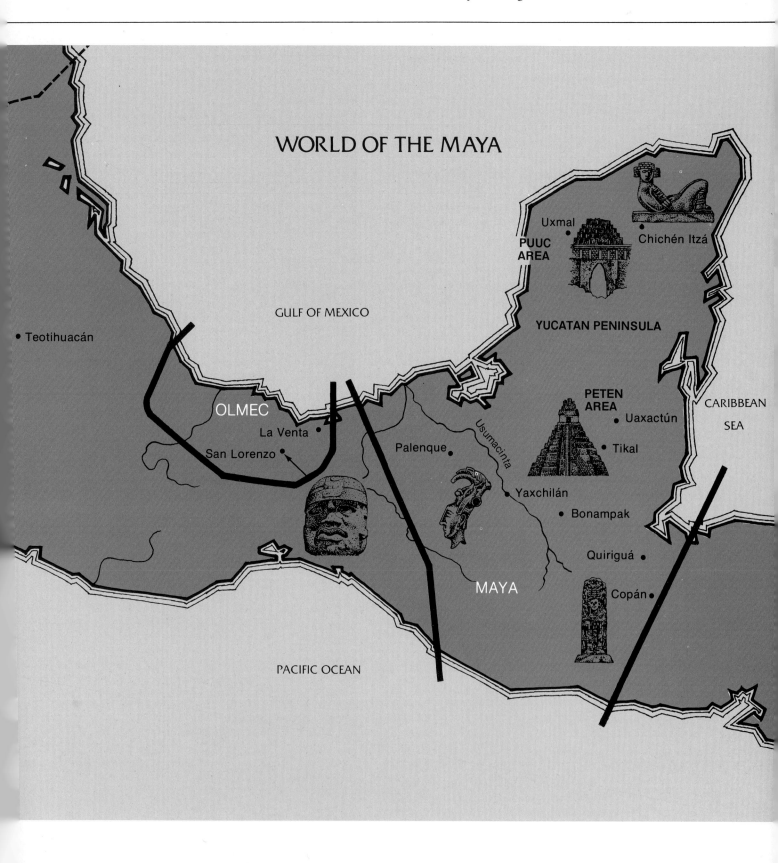

WORLD OF THE MAYA

GULF OF MEXICO

• Teotihuacán

OLMEC

La Venta •

San Lorenzo •

PACIFIC OCEAN

Palenque •

Usumacinta

MAYA

PUUC
AREA

Uxmal •

Chichén Itzá •

YUCATAN PENINSULA

PETEN
AREA

Uaxactún •

Tikal •

Yaxchilán •

Bonampak •

Quiriguá •

Copán •

CARIBBEAN

SEA

Sixteen jade, granite, and serpentine figures with feline eyes and jaguarlike snarls—participants in some secret ceremony—are clustered in front of upright blades of engraved jade. Arranged just as it is here, the group had been deliberately buried in sand three feet under a court of the great Olmec ceremonial center at La Venta.

with machetes and set fire to it. Land thus cleared, if planted and replanted, is often exhausted within a few years and can be drastically eroded by the heavy tropical rains. But the Maya seem to have understood the problems, for by carefully combining different crops, they got a high per-acre yield. Their tall maize protected the precious soil from the force of the rain, and under the corn they planted beans and squash as a ground cover. Surprisingly enough, the Maya managed not only to survive in their inhospitable environment but to produce an abundance. They must, in fact, have produced sizable surpluses, for around A.D. 300 their way of life began to change.

Suddenly, at about that time, the old pattern of roughly equal settlements gave way to a distinctive hierarchy in the rain forest, involving dozens of villages which now found themselves under the control of some large ceremonial and administrative center. Smaller centers were set up throughout each territory, providing services for the outlying villages. The largest centers were far enough apart that their authority did not overlap. Each of these competed with the others, yet each was self-contained. This was the beginning of the great era of Maya civilization. It had taken its basic form from its Mexican predecessors, and it was destined to flourish even more brilliantly than they and to fail just as abruptly.

The earliest Maya ceremonial centers appear in the northeastern Petén—at Tikal by at least A.D. 292. Within a short time Maya civilization with all its institutions had spread westward to the Usumacinta valley, northwards to the tip of the Yucatán peninsula, and far southwards into Honduras and onto the edge of the Guatemalan highlands. In these areas all the great Maya centers were established: Palenque, Copán, Uxmal, Yaxchilán, and Quiriguá. Maya society shared common beliefs that unified thousands of scattered villages into a well-organized state.

The new Maya religious symbolism and the strong old bonds of kinship and myth were the base on which the new society was founded, but religion was not the only reason that the Maya were better organized than their Olmec predecessors. The Maya heartland is a landlocked and isolated region, almost totally devoid of minerals, and the villages were short of basic commodities. There was no local source of salt—vital in an essentially vegetarian diet. Nor were there any natural outcrops of rock hard enough for making corn grinders, the *metates* that every house-

CONTINUED ON PAGE 294

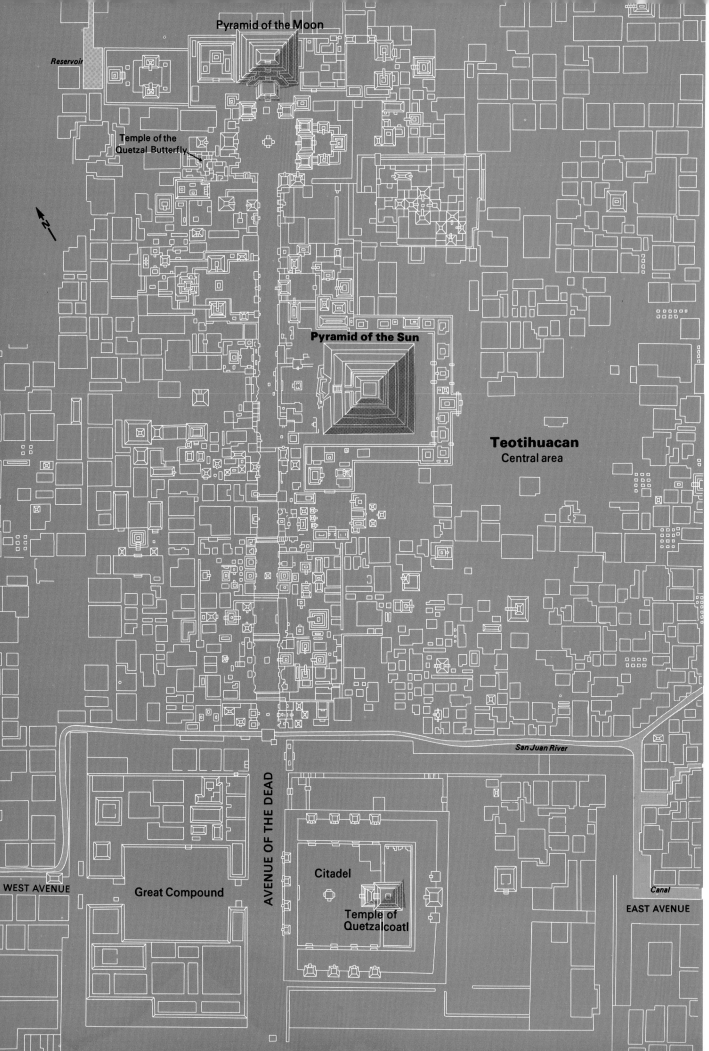

Pyramid of the Moon

Reservoir

Temple of the
Quetzal Butterfly

Pyramid of the Sun

Teotihuacan
Central area

San Juan River

AVENUE OF THE DEAD

WEST AVENUE

Great Compound

Citadel

Temple of
Quetzalcoatl

Canal

EAST AVENUE

This carved stone head of the plumed serpent god, Quetzalcoatl, emerging with bared fangs from a crown of feathers, is one of many that cover the temple in Teotihuacán bearing his name. In the bottom picture, snake heads also border the temple's precipitous staircase, running alongside the elaborately carved panels of the stepped wall.

◀*Dotted with pyramids and palaces, the ceremonial quarter of the great Mesoamerican metropolis, Teotihuacán (left), was bisected by the broad Avenue of the Dead. Lined with official buildings, it ran south from the Pyramid of the Moon, past the huge Pyramid of the Sun, to the citadel containing the Temple of Quetzalcoatl. Unlike Maya ceremonial sites, Teotihuacán was a true city, with about 20,000 one-story houses and over 500 craft workshops.*

293

Graceful ceramic figurines shed light on the everyday life of the Maya. At left, a bejeweled lady balances a tall hat on her head. At right, magnificently frozen in action, a ball player is protected by leggings, gauntlets, and body padding secured with an ornamental belt.

BRADLEY SMITH. PHOTO RESEARCHERS

JERRY COOKE. PHOTO RESEARCHERS

hold required. Therefore the Maya were forced to trade with foreigners. They imported salt all the way from the Guatemalan highlands or northern Yucatán, as well as obsidian for making knives and hard rock for *metates*. The importance of the trade can be gauged by looking at the hundreds of *metates* unearthed at Tikal. More than 85 per cent of them were made from imported rock. Many other minerals were also imported — hematite, pyrite, and jade — in addition to numerous seashells required in the temples.

Once the Maya had opened up the trade lines to the north, they naturally sought to maintain and control them, and had to devise a relatively sophisticated political organization to keep the trade going. Craftsmen, accountants, commercial diplomats, and experts of all kinds would have been needed to run the network. The Maya trade, which rested on the importation of essentials, was quite different from that of

Teotihuacán, whose huge marketplace drew a wide variety of goods from all over the area. Teotihuacán had no need to organize and standardize their trading connections as the Maya did.

For Maya civilization was held together by two complicated networks that affected every household, great and small. Every village, every shrine, every temple, every Maya, owed allegiance to some large ceremonial center, to which they were tied by faith and by the bonds of kinship. At the same time, each community depended on the ceremonial center as a commodity exchange where they could get the necessities of life. Yet in spite of this quite monolithic pattern in Maya life, each ceremonial center retained its own identity, and artistic and architectural styles varied from one to another. However uniformly the Maya may have believed in their gods, there was no single political authority in the Petén — no nation.

294

A 12-foot stele, incised so deeply that the figure stands almost free from the soft, volcanic rock, is one of a series dominating the great court at the ceremonial center of Copán. A profusion of glyphs and decorative motifs cascades from the ornate animal headdress to the figure's massive feet.

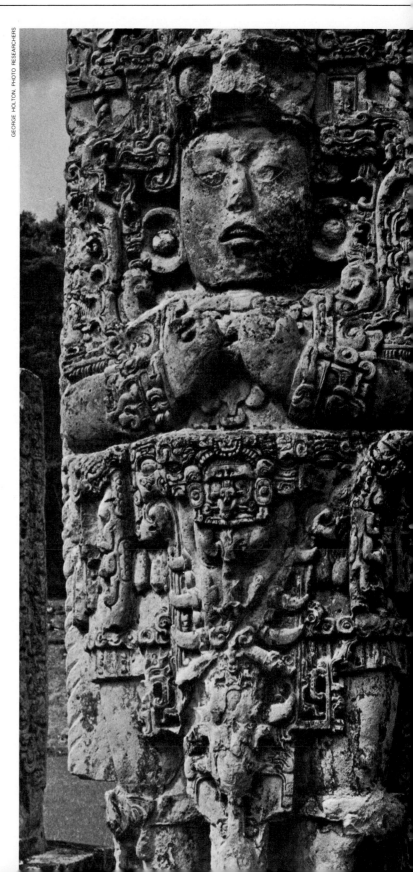

Their religion worked as Islam does, uniting people of divergent cultures through a common and fervently held belief.

The Maya, or at least the priestly and educated classes, were as profoundly intellectual in their approach to life as any people who ever lived. Their great genius was astronomy, their obsession was time. They devised a concept of universal time, and a method of keeping track of it, that is (so far as we understand it) as grandiose as any achievement in Western philosophy. They believed, as we do, that time had an infinite span: their calendar reached millions of years into the past, encompassing more than one creation. As astronomers they accurately calculated the length of the solar year (365.2420 days was their figure, as compared with our slightly more precise count of 365.2422), and in the sixth century A.D., at Copán, they recorded their correction for the 365-day year—a thousand years before Europe caught up to its calendrical inaccuracies and adopted the present Gregorian calendar with leap year. The Maya understood the movements of the moon, the sun, Venus, and possibly the other planets. Their mathematics included the concept of zero—a notion not adopted in Europe until the fifteenth century.

Like the Olmec before them, the Maya believed that their universe passed through long cycles of creation and destruction. These eras, each about 5200 years long—13 *baktuns*—ended with terrible earthquakes. The modern era had started in the equivalent of 3113 B.C., the first year of the Maya calendar, set down in the so-called Long Count; it would end with vast cataclysms on December 24, A.D. 2011. Within the *baktun,* the Maya calendar ran in cycles of 52 years, but there were two permutating timetables. The religious calendar, often called the *tzolkin,* lasted 260 days, with a sequence of 13 numbered days intermeshing with 20 named days. Each day, designated by a combined number and name, has its distinctive omens and religious associations, and this calendar served as a kind of perpetual fortune-telling device for the Maya. In addition, a secular year of 365 days meshed with the religious year of 260. It consisted of 18 named months of 20 days each, followed at the end of each year by five dreaded unlucky and unnamed days. The secular and religious calendars came round once every 52 years, when their New Year's days coincided, and then began again.

The Maya had refined the counting of years to a

CONTINUED ON PAGE 298

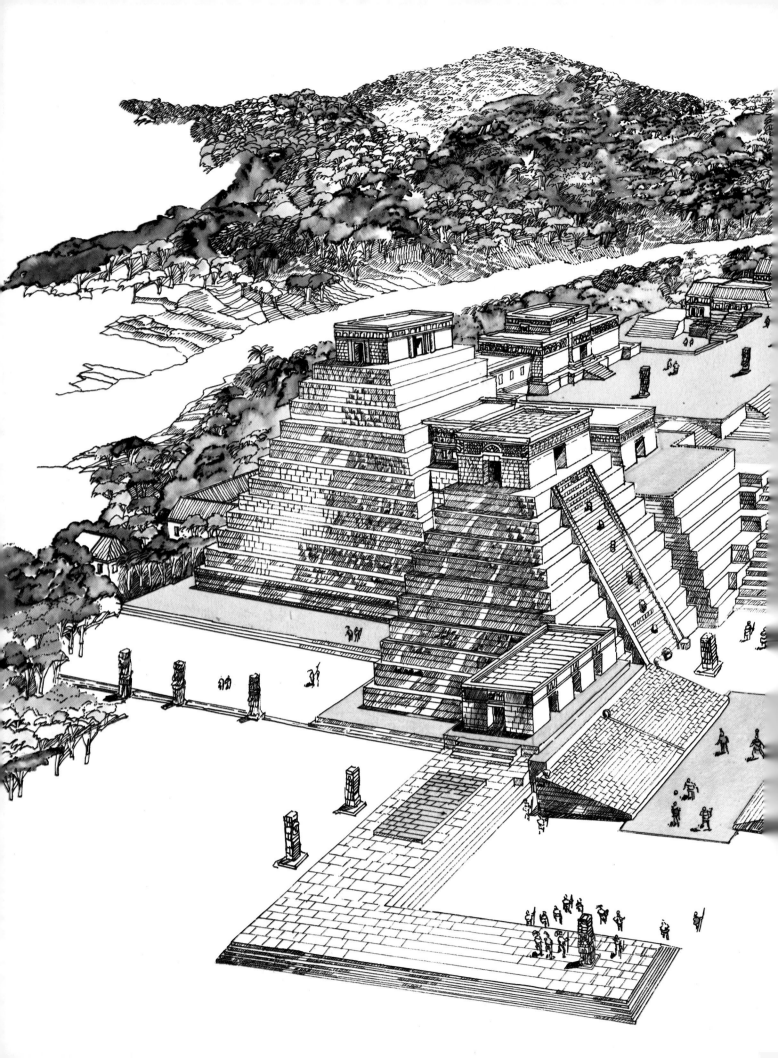

CEREMONIAL CENTER AT COPAN

Although lying at the border of Maya territory, on the Copán River in modern Honduras, the ceremonial center of Copán was unfortified. The complex of plazas, ball court, and pyramids topped with temples, is a classic example of the climactic period in Maya architecture.

The great plaza in the foreground, dotted with stone stelae like the one on page 295, is dominated by the ball court with its sloping walls. Beyond, a broad flight of steps leads to an upper level and the tallest of the structures. The pyramid to the immediate left of the ball court has a stairway that is unique in Maya architecture. Each stone in the 63 steps leading to the temple on top is carved with a glyph; together they make up the longest Maya inscription ever discovered.

VICTOR LAZZARO

fine art. Their Long Count calendar with its huge cycles of creation and extinction was an ancient institution in Mesoamerica (probably originating with the Olmec) when the Maya took it over and refined it. The Long Count itself was divided into five cycles, ranging from the *kin,* which was a day, to the *baktun* of 144,000 days. The Maya wrote their dates on their stelae simply by listing the number of the *baktun* and then the lesser cycles in descending order. The earliest recorded Long Count date found is about 36 B.C.

The Maya thought of the earth as flat and four-cornered, with many layers of the sky supported at the corners by trees and special gods. There were nine layers of the underworld, thirteen of the sky, each with its own deities and their consorts. The Maya had dozens of gods, of whom the most important was Itzamná (Lizard Horse), depicted in the codices as an old man with a Roman nose. He was the patron of learning and the sciences and the inventor of writing. Ix Chel (Rainbow Lady), his wife, was the goddess of weaving, medicine, and childbirth. All the other gods, including the sun god Ah Kinchil, the moon goddess, Ix Ch'up, various rain gods and patrons of different classes and crafts, were descended from Itzamná and Ix Chel.

The Maya priesthood was responsible not only for the regular public rituals but for the maintenance of the calendar and the astronomical observations associated with it. They were, in fact, the guardians and keepers of all Maya erudition and history. Their duties included not only daily and annual rituals, and the many sacrifices that went with them, but the heavy responsibility of maintaining official records and genealogies.

The Maya calendar was based on observation of the heavens, so the priests developed elaborate tables to predict celestial movements and such events as solar eclipses. This obviously required a system of record-keeping, so the priests devised a written language based on at least two hundred eighty-seven hieroglyphic signs. No one has so far succeeded in deciphering all these hieroglyphs.

Unfortunately the depredations of Landa and his colleagues have deprived us of most Maya learning. We are left with the surviving codices, and the inscriptions that were carved on door lintels or on the huge stelae erected at Copán and other major ceremonial centers. One study made of twenty-five dated stelae at Piedras Negras showed that each one

was a biographical record of an aristocrat, his wives, and family. The stelae bore symbols that told of births, accessions to power, military victories, even personal names. A series of stelae at the Yaxchilán center was even more informative. They set forth the history of the militaristic Jaguar dynasty which ruled the site in the eighth century A.D. The deeds of the Jaguar leaders—their victories, battles, and heroic acts—were faithfully recorded on the door lintels of their dwellings. Each dynasty had its characteristic hieroglyphs; so did each major ceremonial center. But the primary use for the Maya script was in the recording and perpetuating of the state calendar, for every public ceremony, indeed every day, was regulated by calendrical omens.

The Maya built their ceremonial centers of earth and limestone, which abounds in the Petén. Limestone rubble and clay provided the cores of pyramids, while blocks of the same stone were used on the sides. The stonemasons produced fine white plaster, too, by burning limestone fragments and mixing the resulting powder with water. All the building materials needed for complex public works were at hand.

The minor Maya ceremonial centers consist of little more than a small pyramid and a few more elaborate public buildings that served a small network of surrounding villages. But the major ceremonial centers like Palenque, Tikal, and Uaxactún were the focus of Maya architectural and artistic genius. Tikal is, perhaps, the most impressive of all. Its sprawling pyramids, temples, and house mounds cover an area of about 38 square miles in the dense rain forest of northeastern Petén. At least 45,000 people lived at or around Tikal at the height of its power.

The Great Plaza lies at the core of Tikal and covers more than two acres, bounded by the Temple of the Great Jaguar and the Temple of the Great Mask, both built in about A.D. 700. The crenelated roof of each temple rises from a steep-sided, earth-filled, and stone-encased pyramid. A cluster of courts and ceremonial plazas lead from this central area. The northern side of the Great Plaza is occupied by Tikal's most elaborate structure, the so-called Northern Acropolis, which covers two and a half acres, conceals approximately 100 buildings, and at one time supported 16 temples.

The Acropolis went through many changes. The earliest buildings at Tikal were located here, about

200 B.C. Succeeding generations set their temples on the same site, so that the present structure consists of an elaborate palimpsest of Maya architecture. To the south of the Great Plaza lay the residences of the aristocracy. In the thousands of small thatched houses clustered around the ceremonial precincts lived the craftsmen, artisans, and peasants whose labors made the lavish displays of the nobility possible.

Palenque, one of the most finely decorated Maya centers, is dominated by a pyramid on which stands a stucco structure called the Temple of Inscriptions. In 1952 the Mexican archaeologist Alberto Ruz noticed a perforated flagstone on the floor of the temple. Beneath it a vaulted stairway led down through the pyramid to a passage blocked by a great slab of stone. At the face of the slab were six unadorned skeletons—evidently sacrificial victims. When the slab was removed Ruz found himself in a burial crypt whose walls were carved with ancestor figures. At the center was a stone sarcophagus containing a skeleton which must have been that of a priest-ruler. The face had been covered with a jade mask (see above), the body by a veritable cascade of jade ornaments. It was the Maya equivalent of King Tutankhamen's tomb, its treasures less numerous but just as breathtaking.

The Temple of Inscriptions had been built during the priest-king's lifetime, perhaps in anticipation of his death. The discovery of the burial suggests that other Maya temples, such as that of the Great Jaguar at Tikal, may also have been built as monuments to dead rulers. If so, they betoken a cult of the dead which rivals that of ancient Egypt.

Each Maya ceremonial center has its special features—Tikal and Palenque their high pyramids, Copán its monumental sculptures and stelae—but every center has its plaza and also its ball court, for ball games were an important part of Mayan life.

The ball game the Maya played was not a gentle sport. Its traditions go back a long way, to at least A.D. 300. The game was still being played by the Indians when the Spanish arrived, and there are some eyewitness accounts of the play. On the appointed day, thousands of spectators flocked to the stands wearing their gaily colored ceremonial clothes. An anticipatory hush fell on the crowd as the two opposing teams took their places in the court. After a brief prayer the game began. A solid rubber ball weighing several pounds was thrown into the arena. The teams pounced on it, keeping it in constant motion with

shrewd body blows. Hands and feet were not allowed, so the players lunged and leapt at the hard ball, even butting it with their heads to keep it going.

As the game went on, the pace grew more furious, and the play rougher. Two opposing players might collide and knock each other out. Another might be carried out with a fractured skull, and a cry would go up as he went into convulsions and died. But the game would go on until suddenly a star player managed to knock the ball through one of the rings at the side of the court. Then there would be a vast shout, for his team had won. They would set off in pursuit of the vanquished, and any laggards they could catch would quickly be stripped naked, their jewels and clothing seized as part of the spoils.

Amazingly, for a people so advanced in astronomy and mathematics, and so well organized in their social life, the Maya brought a relatively primitive technology to their architecture. They were expert potters,

CONTINUED ON PAGE 303

OVERLEAF: *Built a century after the Toltecs invaded the homeland of the Maya, the Temple of Warriors at Chichén Itzá, while predominantly Toltec, includes elements of both cultures. At left is a Toltec reclining figure called a Chac-mool. Each of the columns is a stylized representation of the Toltec feathered serpent god Quetzalcoatl, with opened jaws at the foot and tail in the air. The projections at the far corner of the building are noses of the Maya rain god.*
CARL FRANK, PHOTO RESEARCHERS

M. COVARRUBIAS, *INDIAN ART OF MEXICO AND CENTRAL AMERICA.* ALFRED A. KNOPF, 1957

In their persistent quest for an accurate measurement of time, Maya priests scanned the heavens through slits in the domed roofs of observatories like this one at Chichén Itzá. Their obsession with calendrical calculations also led them into sophisticated mathematics; their numbers, which included a zero, were written both as glyphs and a system of dots and bars (above).

weavers, leather workers, toolmakers, and carvers, but they never developed wheeled vehicles, nor did they have domestic draft animals. All the limestone blocks for their temples and pyramids had to be dragged through dense forest. Given their architectural propensities for grouping large structures around an open space, they could certainly have profited from improved technologies. The sheer scale of their ceremonial centers is prodigious, and the labor needed to erect even one pyramid must have been appalling. Ironically, the temples were small and dark inside, for their builders did not know of the arch. Instead they roofed their temples and burial chambers with corbeled vaults, slanting the slabs to form peaked roofs.

Wandering through Palenque or Tikal one is immediately struck by the conventions that seem to have dominated Maya ceremonial life. Temples, architecture, art, pottery, all testify to a rigidly organized society that would have seemed alien to an Olmec visitor from earlier times. By A.D. 700 Maya society had at least four main social classes. At the highest rank, and regarded as semidivine, were the warriors, administrators, and religious functionaries whose activities were surrounded by elaborate ceremonies and carefully regulated convention. Below them were skilled artists and lesser administrators who carried out public projects. A large artisan class —potters, painters, weavers, and other craftspeople —was a step above the great masses of the people, the peasants and slaves who provided food for the whole community and did the menial labor for public works. These four classes were apparently relatively inflexible, for the aristocratic elite had supreme authority over all aspects of Maya life—an authority that they jealously guarded.

Why did the Maya develop such a hierarchy? The key element in Maya society was a complicated marriage of the secular and the religious, a marriage that deployed the society's wealth mainly to enhance religious authority and to embellish the public rituals that were so much a part of Maya life. There is plen-

tiful archaeological evidence that this is so. During the early centuries of Maya dominance, richly adorned burials of course turned up in the temple precincts but there were still rich burials—usually of young adults—in rural villages as well. But as time went on, the wealthy Maya began to live exclusively in the palaces and houses at the ceremonial centers, and to be buried there when they died. Only the poor were buried in the country. Had Maya society undergone a gradual transformation, with the rich living in urban comfort while the poor subsisted in villages in the countryside? Was there no longer any means for redistributing wealth? If so, how had this transformation occured?

A clue may be found in a study carried out some years ago by Harvard anthropologist E. Z. Vogt at the modern town of Zinacantán in the Mexican state of Chiapas. Zinacantán could be loosely described as a ceremonial center bearing some resemblance to the classical Maya centers. Vogt found that it was supported by the people living around it in small villages of between 50 and 1,000 people. Only some 6 per cent of the population actually lived in Zinacantán itself. There was, however, an elaborate network of office rotation among the wealthy farmers of the country side. Each farmer held office in the religious hierarchy for a year, during which time he enjoyed special prestige in local society. Then he returned to his farm—much poorer for the experience—to rebuild his resources so that he could rise still further in the hierarchy when his next turn at office holding came around. Here is a mechanism for the redistribution of wealth and for social mobility that may well date back to Maya times and that could have acted as a strong integrative force in Maya society. Wealthy farmers might regularly have come into the ceremonial center to participate for a time in religious and economic life. As office holders came and went, the country people would continually be involved in the affairs of the center and the wider concerns of a whole region.

On the other hand, it would be relatively easy for such an informal system to turn into something quite different. As the class structures hardened and the Maya leaders grew wealthier they would be less concerned with the needs of the small communities they had orginally come from. Offices might become almost hereditary, and office holders would never leave the centers. The aspiring villager would find it pro-

ABOVE: *Eerily evoking ancient rites, an archaeologist taking floodlit pictures stands silhouetted in the tiny Temple of the Jaguar, perched atop a steep, 145-foot pyramid at Tikal, in modern Guatemala. Five such pyramids dominated this ceremonial center composed of nearly 3,000 buildings covering some seven square miles.*

LEFT: *The last flowering of Classic Maya architecture evolved in the inhospitable uplands of western Yucatán, at sites like Labna. Typical of this Puuc or hill style are massive corbeled archways, columnar façades, and a lavish use of decoration at the upper levels.*

gressively harder to break into the new hierarchies of ceremonial-center society. Perhaps it is no coincidence that the wealthy Maya of later times never went home to die, and were buried almost exclusively in ceremonial centers.

The later centuries of Maya civilization were remarkable both for warfare and for elaborate public ceremonies. We can catch a glimpse of Maya life at its height in about A.D. 800 in a set of murals found at Bonampak, in Mexico, which tell the story of a minor skirmish between Maya warriors. The battle is joined as musicians play war trumpets in the background. Then the scene shifts. The magnificently clothed victors have herded their prisoners to their temple, where they are stripped and tortured. We see their fingernails being torn off as the victorious warriors surround their leader. The great lord himself is dressed in a jaguar skin, and among the spectators is a white-robed woman with a fan in her hand. One of the captives is pleading for mercy, while the severed head of one of his companions lies on a pile of leaves. The closing scenes show noblemen and their consorts watching the dance of the water gods, accompanied by an orchestra with rattles, trumpets, and turtle-shell drums. Some of the women are drawing blood from their tongues, in the rite of self-mutilation that their ancestors had practiced for centuries.

By the time the Bonampak murals were painted, Maya society had become deeply militaristic. The nobles who ruled the great ceremonial centers now vied with one another for prestige in religious affairs and in warfare. They embarked on an orgy of temple building, and Maya civilization might have seemed poised for new heights of cultural achievement. But, suddenly, like that of Teotihuacán and the Olmec before it, the civilization of the lowland Maya collapsed. In the century from A.D. 800 to 900, the major ceremonial centers of the Petén were abandoned one by one, their stelae mutilated and the calendar discontinued. The last stelae carved with the classic Long Count dates were made in A.D. 889. The great centers were nearly all empty by then, except for Tikal, which was at some point occupied by squatters who allowed garbage to pile up in the courtyards and stairways and who finally disappeared themselves. The very fabric of Maya society had collapsed like a house of cards. History had repeated itself in a remarkable way: yet another Mesoamerican civilization had disintegrated for no apparent reason

just as it was reaching the zenith of its powers.

Few archaeological mysteries have generated as much controversy as the Maya collapse. Many pioneer scholars believed that an earthquake, a hurricane, or possibly an epidemic had so devastated the Maya that they were unable to rebuild their society. Other scholars disagreed and suggested that the Maya outgrew their agricultural capacities and exhausted the soil—a process that caused disastrous erosion. But the trouble was that in the archaeological record there were no signs of great natural upheavals or of mass starvation. Nor did the skeletons of Maya who had died at about the time of the collapse show any signs of catastrophic disease. One anatomist, Frank Saul, who examined the few available Maya skeletons, found that those from a ceremonial center named Altar de Sacrificios displayed a high incidence of malnutrition and parasitic diseases. Unfortunately these skeletons came from all periods —not just the final one. Could it be, however, that the later Maya suffered more often from malnutrition than their predecessors? Unfortunately Maya skeletal remains are too scarce to provide an answer.

Another explanation for the Maya collapse might lie in the rigid social structure of their society, and in the large peasant population ruled by a militaristic and blood-thirsty nobility. Did the oppressed peasants rise in revolt against their masters and lay waste the palaces and the vast temple organizations that oversaw their every deed? Or were the Maya conquered by invaders from the highlands? The trouble with each of these theories is first of all that the archaeological evidence that might support them is still highly incomplete, and secondly, as archaeologists working in the Petén have come to realize, peasant revolts and invasions would hardly be sufficient to put an elaborate and highly organized civilization to a sudden end. Even if the peasants had somehow been able to stage a successful coup, why would they have abandoned the centers?

Furthermore, the Maya were not the first Mesoamerican civilization to die in this way, nor the last. The Olmec centers and Teotihuacán had collapsed in a short period of time, and the Aztec followed the same pattern after the Maya were gone. Was there a common explanation for all this?

Whatever the explanation, it is probably not simple. The whole of Maya society in all its complexity was an elaborate, interlocking system of checks and

CONTINUED ON PAGE 310

Newly returned from a raiding party, Maya warriors in fantastic animal headpieces stand in judgment with priests and two women over their terrified captives. Some of the victims bleed from their fingers in a ritual mutilation; another begs for mercy while a companion lies dead or in a swoon at his feet. This vivid depiction of the sacrificial rites of the Maya is a water-color copy of one of many murals covering the walls of a Bonampak building.

balances—economic, social, political, and religious. At the pinnacle of society were the nobles and great priests; at the base, most of the population. The ceremonial centers and their burgeoning numbers of inhabitants depended upon the produce harvested by the peasants, who also built and maintained the temples and palaces that reflected the power and prestige of each center. Religion and its public and private rituals were the main unifying force in Maya society, as well as the elaborate trade routes that provided not only luxury goods but precious raw materials and essential household needs as well. A change in, say, agricultural productivity would trigger reactions in all segments of Maya society—malnutrition and loss of energy, lower food surpluses to feed craftsmen, unfinished temples. Normal stresses and strains, such as a series of poor harvests could probably be accommodated by the system. But if, added to those, had come external and internal problems, which the rigid Maya social structure was not equipped to adjust to, the results could well be catastrophic. The Maya house of cards would then collapse in a series of interlocking reactions.

In 1970, a group of Maya scholars, gathered at the School of American Research in Santa Fe, agreed that the Maya collapse was due to such an interlocking set of factors, and developed hypothetical scenario for the event. It went something like this: the collapse of Teotihuacán about A.D. 600 put the Maya in a position to enlarge their entrepreneurial role in Middle American trade. Their leaders got increasingly involved in trading and grew rich from it. The ceremonial centers began to compete for power and prestige —notably in elaborate building projects. And this rivalry led to a series of costly wars. Both public works and the military placed ever-increasing demands on the Maya labor force. Urban populations grew as more and more people left the country and moved into hovels on the outskirts of Tikal and other great centers. Fewer and fewer peasants were left to supply the centers with food. Soon agricultural production declined. The malnutrition and disease added to the peasants' burden. The priests and nobles living in their palaces failed to realize what was happening or to analyze the intense pressures that were building within their society. Even if they had been aware of them, the only redress would have been a major and deliberate social reorganization—not easy to achieve even under favorable conditions. The priestly Maya

had built on the Olmec success by tightening their stranglehold on society. But now, tighter controls were not the answer, for suddenly, in addition to the troubles at home, the Maya leaders had external problems. Alien peoples from the surrounding highlands were beginning to encroach more heavily on the western lowlands. The profitable long-distance trade networks to the highlands began to break down, along with the Maya nobles' monopolies. The cutting off of these trade routes and the costly raids and campaigns undertaken to prevent their being cut off placed critical new strains on a society that was already under tremendous pressure. And, sometime after A.D. 800, the Maya socio-cultural system simply broke down over much of the lowlands.

This version of the Maya collapse leaves many questions unanswered and the mystery of the chronic instability of Mesoamerican civilization unsolved. When did the breakdown begin? Why did the nobles fail to see what was happening? Did a blind passion for religious and social prestige close their minds to reality? Which ceremonial center collapsed first? Did foreign invaders sack Tikal and other centers? We still do not know.

The collapse of Maya civilization was catastrophic but not complete. Some Maya families continued to flourish in northern Yucatán, where they preserved their religious beliefs and economic patterns until the arrival of the Spaniards and Christianity. The highlands saw the rise of the Toltec and Aztec empires— new, militaristic states that did, however, perpetuate many of the age-old religious beliefs and rituals as well as political and social institutions of the Maya. But, like the Maya, the Aztec had a curious lack of resistance to external pressure. In 1519, in only a few short months, Hernán Cortés and his conquistadors destroyed Tenochtitlán and the entire fabric of Aztec civilization.

Neither the institutions of the Aztec nor those of the Maya of northern Yucatán survived the massive onslaught of Spanish domination and single-minded Christianity. A historical oblivion set in that was broken only by the artist's brush of Frederick Catherwood, the dramatic pen of John Lloyd Stephens, and the excavations of archaeologists eager to unravel the mysteries of one of the world's great prehistoric civilizations. But so far these excavations have failed to provide more than tentative solutions to the mystery of the Maya collapse.

A corbeled arch (below) soars to the roof of the Governor's Palace at Uxmal, one of the last and most beautiful cities of the Classic Maya. Two of these arrow-shaped arches, set in recesses, pierce the long, graceful lines of the building's façade.

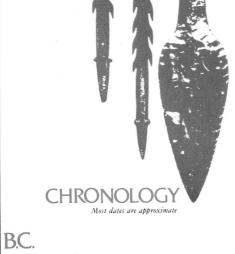

CHRONOLOGY
Most dates are approximate

B.C.

PALEOLITHIC AGE

45,000–40,000	Modern man (Homo sapiens) appears in the Middle East
35,000–30,000	Disappearance of Neanderthal man
30,000 or later	Asians cross Bering Land Bridge to New World
18,000	Glacial ice sheets covering much of North America and northern Europe begin to recede (completed by 7000 B.C.)
15,000	Lascaux cave paintings

MESOLITHIC AGE

8000	Beginnings of agriculture in Middle East
7000–4000	Climatic Optimum. Temperatures warmer in Europe. Sahara a grassland occupied by hunters
6000	Settlement of Lepenski Vir in Danube Valley
6000	Beginnings of trade in the Aegean

COPPER AGE

4500	Beginnings of megalith building in northern Europe (Brittany)
4500	First evidence of Kurgan culture in southern Russia and the Ukraine
4500	Europe settled by farming peoples
3500	Beginning of writing in Mesopotamia
3500	Invention of the wheel somewhere between the Caucasus and Mesopotamia

BRONZE AGE

3500	Bronze objects made in Thailand
3000	Beginnings of Bronze Age in Greece, Anatolia, Mesopotamia
2800	Beginning of Minoan civilization (peaked at 1700, declined by 1400)
2600–2500	Building of great Egyptian pyramids
2600	Stage I of Stonehenge
2500–1700	Indus Valley civilization
1800	Polynesian and Micronesian islands settled
1600–1200	Flowering of Mycenaean civilization
1600	Destruction of Thera
1600	Beginnings of Bronze Age in China

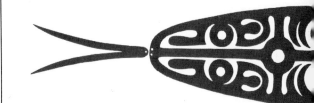

A.D.

50	Nazca markings laid out in the Andes
50	Tollund man buried in Danish bog
300–900	Maya civilization
600–1400	Mississippian culture in America South and Midwest
600	Earliest windmill — Iran
700–1200	Little Climatic Optimum in Europe
800	Viking expansion begins
1000	Viking settlement at L'Anse aux Meadows, Newfoundland
1200	Easter Island statues erected
1492	Columbus' first voyage

IRON AGE

1600	First iron making in Thailand
1250–400	Olmec culture
1200	First iron making in Asia Minor
1000–200 A.D.	Adena culture in Ohio
700–250	Etruscan civilization
700–300 A.D.	Cooling trend in Europe
500	Iron making begins in China
492–330	Classical Age of Greece
200–550 A.D.	Silk trade between China and Mediterranean
200–550 A.D.	Hopewell culture in midwest United States
27–476 A.D.	Roman Empire
100	Greeks and Romans use water mills to grind grain
100–700 A.D.	Teotihuacan civilization
50	Construction of Antikythera machine

AMERICAN HERITAGE BOOKS

Editor-In-Chief   Ezra Bowen

STAFF FOR MYSTERIES OF THE PAST

Editor   Joseph J. Thorndike, Jr.
Art Director   Elena M. Bloomfield
Picture Editor   Olivia Buehl
Assistant Text Editor   Peter Ainslie
Copy Editor   Kaari Ward
Editorial Assistant   Carol Caldwell

AMERICAN HERITAGE PUBLISHING CO., INC.

Chairman of the Board   Samuel P. Reed
President and Publisher   Rhett Austell
Editorial Art Director   Murray Belsky

Library of Congress Cataloging in Publication
Data
Main Entry under title:
Mysteries of the Past.
  Includes index.
  1. Civilization, Ancient—Addresses, essays,
lectures. 2. Man, Prehistoric—Addresses, essays,
lectures. 3. Curiosities and wonders—Addresses,
essays, lectures. I. Casson, Lionel. 1914–
II. Thorndike, Joseph J., 1913–
CB311.M9 3930 77-22838. ISBN 0-8281-0206-6
ISBN 0-8281-0207-4 deluxe bdg.

INDEX

Page numbers in boldface type refer to picture captions.